T0134497

Built-in Fault-Tolerant Computing Paradigm for Resilient Large-Scale Chip Design

Xiaowei Li • Guihai Yan • Cheng Liu

Built-in Fault-Tolerant Computing Paradigm for Resilient Large-Scale Chip Design

A Self-Test, Self-Diagnosis,
and Self-Repair-Based Approach

 Springer

Xiaowei Li 🆔
State Key Lab of Processors
Institute of Computing Technology, Chinese
Academy of Sciences
Beijing, China

Guihai Yan 🆔
State Key Lab of Processors
Institute of Computing Technology, Chinese
Academy of Sciences
Beijing, China

Cheng Liu 🆔
State Key Lab of Processors
Institute of Computing Technology, Chinese
Academy of Sciences
Beijing, China

ISBN 978-981-19-8553-9   ISBN 978-981-19-8551-5   (eBook)
https://doi.org/10.1007/978-981-19-8551-5

This Springer imprint is published by the registered company Springer Nature Singapore Pte Ltd.
The registered company address is: 152 Beach Road, #21-01/04 Gateway East, Singapore 189721,
Singapore

To all the students and colleagues in Integrated Circuit Design Group in the State Key Lab of Computer Architecture.

Preface

If your computer crashes, you can revive it by a reboot, an empirical solution that usually turns out to be effective. The rationale behind this solution is that transient faults, either in hardware or software, can be fixed by refreshing the machine state. Such a "silver bullet," however, could be futile in the future because the faults, especially those existing in the hardware such as Integrated Circuit (IC) chips, cannot be eliminated by refreshing. What we need is a more sophisticated mechanism to steer the system back on the right track. The "magic cure" is the on-chip fault-tolerant mechanism, which relies on a suite of built-in design-for-reliability logic, including fault detection, fault diagnosis, and fault recovery, working in a unified manner.

With the shrinking semiconductor feature sizes and continuous scaling of the IC designs, silicon defects caused by manufacture defects, radiation particles, or progressively aging are almost inevitable and pose critical influence on both the yield and quality of IC products. Under this context, we have successfully applied on-chip fault-tolerant computing mechanism onto a set of different chip designs including generic circuits, general-purpose processors, network-on-chips, and deep learning processors in the past decade, and gradually formulate a systematic built-in fault-tolerant computing paradigm, which can be utilized to guide IC designs against these typical silicon defects. In addition to the basic fault detection, fault diagnosis, and fault recovery, the proposed built-in fault-tolerant computing paradigm also provides additional benefits, such as facilitating graceful performance degradation, mitigating the impact of verification blind spots, and improving the chip yield.

In this book, we mainly illustrate the built-in fault-tolerant computing paradigm with practical demonstrations on genetic circuits, general-purpose processors, network-on-chips, and deep learning processors. The entire book consists of six chapters. Chapter 1 presents the background of fault-tolerant chip designs and overview of the built-in fault-tolerant computing paradigm. Chapter 2 presents on-line fault detection, on-chip path delay, and lifetime fault-tolerant pipeline design for genetic circuits. Chapter 3 investigates the vulnerability of general-purpose processors under silicon defects and presents a core salvaging approach, particularly for multi-core processor architecture. Chapter 4 focuses on fault-tolerant network-on-chip designs from distinct angles including topology reconfiguration, routing design, and architecture design. Chapter 5 focuses on built-in fault-tolerant deep learning processors fabricated with both conventional CMOS-based technology and emerging ReRAM-based technology. Chapter 6 concludes this book with a brief summary of the proposed built-in fault-tolerant computing paradigm and a discussion of future fault-tolerant computing directions on large-scale VLSI designs.

The majority of the content involved in this book is collected from peer-reviewed papers of Guihai Yan, Cheng Liu, Lei Zhang, Wen Li, Songwei Pei, Songjun Pan, Bingzhang Fu, Ying Wang, and Hang Lu supervised by both Prof. Xiaowei Li and Prof. Huawei Li who lead the Integrated Circuit Design Group in State Key Lab of Computer Architecture, and has already been published in the journals of TVLSI, TCAD, TC, JCST, and Journal of China Science. Prof. Xiaowei Li organized this book in general, Prof. Guihai Yan mainly worked on Chaps. 2 and 3. Prof. Cheng Liu worked on Chaps. 1, 4, 5, and 6. Dr. Jingya Wu also helped a lot to edit this book. Prof. Huawei Li and Prof. Guojie Luo reviewed this book. Prof. Tim Cheng wrote foreword for this book. All the efforts are indispenable for this book and greatly appreciated.

The techniques presented in this book are partly selected from research founded by the National Key Research and Development Program of China under grant 2020YFB1600201, and the National Natural Science Foundation of China (NSFC) under grant No. (62174162, 62090024, 61902375, U20A20202, 61876173).

Beijing, China   Xiaowei Li
May 2022

Foreword

Hardware systems must have sufficient robustness to cope with failures resulting from various variability and reliability concerns. This requirement not only applies to safety-critical advanced systems in avionics and automotive applications but also becomes a necessity for consumer electronics where cost has been a serious constraint. For integrated circuits, device geometry shrinkage, very low power supply levels, and ultra-high operating speeds have significantly reduced noise margins and increased variations in process, device, and design parameters. These continuing trends in technology scaling have resulted in lower reliability and higher design uncertainty for highly integrated chips. Not just technology, the environment, energy, thermal resources, and even applications have also contributed to greater variations and more diverse sources of errors. Thus, high variability and low reliability have become the predominant challenges for chip design and manufacturing.

While verification, test, and fault tolerance technologies have been foundational disciplines for multiple decades for which the readers can find good textbooks for their respective basic knowledge, principles, techniques, and solutions, these fields all continue to evolve and advance, some of which have even reinvented themselves, in order tackle the enormous variability and reliability challenges. As a result, new and more effective and efficient solutions continue to emerge, replacing classical approaches for designing and manufacturing robust and reliable hardware.

For fault tolerance, a suite of techniques, ranging from built-in redundancy and online reconfiguration capability to tolerate errors, to built-in self-test/-diagnosis/-repair to recover from errors, to post-fabrication tuning/adaptation capability (either off-line or online) to bypass errors, to automatic compensation to alleviate the negative effect caused by variations, or to dynamic adaptation to mask environmental noise and transient errors, have been developed; some of which have even been advanced from the proof-of-concept and prototyping stages to actual deployment.

Researchers at the Institute of Computing Technology of Chinese Academy of Sciences have been among the most productive and impactful research groups in addressing the technical challenges and contributing new solutions in this area. Over the past decade, they have developed and employed a number of built-in and/or online fault-tolerant solutions. Their solutions are either generic, broadly applicable to digital designs and general-purpose processors, or specific to special-purpose designs including network-on-chips and deep learning processors. This book gives in-depth and coherent explanations of these very interesting results. Particularly, the solutions are introduced in a unified "3S" framework supporting a *built-in fault-tolerant computing paradigm*, where "3S" stands for self-test, self-diagnosis, and self-repair (or self-recovery). The description of each technique also includes clarification of the key differences from the conventional counterparts which I am sure the readers will find informative and insightful. It is commendable that the authors have done an outstanding job in producing this self-contained book covering multiple aspects of built-in fault-tolerant design for resilient chips. Publishing this book also serves very well for motivating research graduate students and researchers to gain the latest results and insight into this subject of significant importance.

Hong Kong University   Kwang-Ting (Tim) Cheng (郑 光 廷)
of Science and Technology
December 12, 2022

Contents

Acronyms

3S	Self-test, self-diagnosis, self-repair
ACE	Architecturally correct execution
AET	Adversarial example testing
AGU	Address generation unit
ALU	Arithmetic logic unit
AMAA	As many as available
AMAD	As many as demand
AR	Accumulated results
ARSC	Aging resistant stability checker
AT	Active time
ATE	Automatic testing equipment
AVF	Architecture vulnerability factor
BAFF	Backward adaptable flip-flop
BAR	Base accumulated results
BER	Bit error rate
BIST	Built-in self-test
BL	Burst length
BP	Backward propagation
BTA	Backward timing adaptation
BTI	Bias temperature instability
BW	Bandwidth
CCFF	Calibration capture flip-flop
CDG	Channel dependence graph
CF	Congestion factor
CiM	Computing-in-memory
CLB	Checking list buffer
CLFF	Calibration launch flip-flop
CLR	Core-level redundancy
CLT	Central limit theorem
CMOS	Complementary metal Oxide Semiconductor
CNN	Convolutional neural network

CONV	Convolutional layers
CPI	Cycle per instruction
CR	Column redundancy
CRC	Cyclic redundancy check
CUT	Circuit under test
DBP	Default backup paths
DEC	Detection error codes
DF	Distance factor
DLA	Deep learning accelerator
DLL	Delay-locked loop
DMR	Dual module redundancy
DNN	Deep neural networks
DPPU	Dot-production processing unit
DR	Diagonal redundancy
DVFS	Dynamic voltage and frequency scaling
ECC	Error correcting code
ELR	Execution-level redundancy
EM	Electromigration
FAFF	Forward adaptable flip-flop
FC	Full connected layers
FD	Fault diagnosis
FGSM	Fast gradient sign method
FIT	Failures in time
FPT	Fault PE table
FPU	Floating-point unit
FSM	Finite state machine
FTA	Forward timing adaptation
GFF	Generous flip-flop
gSA	RRCS-guided simulated annealing
H-AVF	Hard-fault architectural vulnerability factor
HCI	Hot-carrier injection
HVF	Hardware vulnerability factor
HyCA	Hybrid computing architecture
IAT	Inactive time
IC	Integrated circuit
IFM	Input feature maps
IKTR	Intermediate knowledge transfer retraining
IPC	Instruction per cycle
IRF	Input register file
ISA	Instruction set architecture
ITRS	International technology roadmap for semiconductors
IVF	Intermittent vulnerability factor
IVV	Initial value violation
KD	Knowledge distillation
LDU	Lower delay unit

LUT	Look-up table
LSB	Least significant bit
MAC	Multiply-accumulate operation
MBISR	Memory built-in-self-repair
MIPS	Million instructions per second
MLC	Multi-level cell
MLP	Multilayer perceptron
MSB	Most significant bit
MSE	Mean square error
MTTF	Mean time to failure
NAS	Network architecture search
NBTI	Negative bias temperature instability
NoC	Network-on-chip
NUCA	Non-uniform cache
OCDM	On-chip path delay measurement
OFM	Output feature map
ORF	Output register file
OS	Operating system
P&T	Pause-and-Test
PBTI	Positive bias temperature instability
PDP	Propagation detectable period
PE	Processing element
PER	PE error rate
PMOS	Positive channel metal oxide semiconductor
PR	Partial computing result
PUM	Path under measurement
PVF	Program vulnerability factor
PVT variation	Process, voltage, temperature variation
QAP	Quadratic assignment problem
ReRAM	Resistive random access memory
RMT	Redundant multithreading
RR	Row redundancy
RRCS	Row rippling and column stealing
RTL	Register transfer level
SA	Simulated annealing
SC	Stochastic computing
SDD	Small delay defect
SER	Soft error rate
SET	Single event transient
SEU	Single event upset
SLC	Single-level cell
SNR	Signal-to-noise ratio
SoC	System on chip
SSTA	Statistical static timing analysis
STA	Static timing analysis

STC	Signal transition conversion
SV	Stability violation
SVFD	Stability violation-based fault detection
TDDB	Time-dependent dielectric breakdown
TDM	Time division multiplexer
TDS	Throughput-driven scheduling
TLR	Thread-level redundancy
TMR	Triple modular redundancy
TRP	Topology reconfiguration problem
TVV	Terminal value violation
UDU	Upper delay unit
UFF	Unadaptable flip-flop
VCD	Value change dump
VDL	Vernier delay line
VLSI	Very large-scale integration
VPAQ	Vectorial quadratic assignment problem
WL	Word-line
WRF	Weight register file
YAT	Yield-adjusted throughput

Chapter 1
Introduction

Abstract Although the probability of a single transistor error can be low, the error rate of a large-scale VLSI design that involves up to billions of transistors because of the continuously increasing transistor density can be non-trivial. While silicon faults can be caused by various factors such as process variation, progressive aging, and manufacturing defects, it remains challenging despite the advancements of semiconductor technology. Conventional automated test equipment (ATE) can be utilized to identify the faulty designs from mass production, but it is typically expensive and cannot salvage the failed designs. In this context, built-in fault-tolerant computing paradigm that takes various silicon faults into consideration by design can greatly alleviate the above problems with much less overhead and are gaining increasing attentions of researchers from both industry and academia recently. Usually, it integrates techniques such as fault detection, fault diagnosis, and fault recovery in chip design such that it can work independently without additional offline testing equipments. In this chapter, we will introduce the background of various silicon faults first and then elaborate the general idea of built-in fault-tolerant computing paradigm.

1.1 Typical On-Chip Faults

Although the advancement of semiconductor technology contributes greatly to the smaller feature sizes and higher transistor density, it makes the large-scale VLSI designs more vulnerable to various silicon defects induced by process variation, manufacturing defects, progressive aging, and soft errors when exposed to high-energy particles, and poses dramatic challenges to the circuit design reliability. Before diving into the fault-tolerant design techniques, we will illustrate the major silicon defects in this section.

1.1.1 Process Variation

Process variation becomes one of the major sources of silicon defects recently and exacerbates greatly when the transistor feature size scales down to nanometre era and it gets more difficult to control all the complex VLSI manufacturing processes precisely [52]. For instance, lithographic process becomes extremely challenging when the wavelength of the utilized light is close to the transistor feature size. As a result, the fabricated transistors that are supposed to be identical can vary on many device parameters such as gate width, channel length, threshold voltage, and oxide thickness. Accordingly, the transistors with process variation will lead to different circuit latency, and can result in delay violation or lower the maximum operation frequency especially on critical paths of a circuit. Other than delay violation, process variation also has many other high-level negative influence on large-scale VLSI designs such as yield, performance, and energy consumption [3, 12]. Worse still, process variation is usually sensitive to the working environments such as voltage and temperature variation. The combination of these different variation further exacerbates the negative influence on VLSI designs and varies at runtime, which makes the process variation aware or process variation tolerant design more complex.

Despite the complexity, process variation can be divided from different angles. From the perspective of variation distribution, it can be roughly split into systematic variation and random variation [43, 58]. Systematic variation is mostly caused by imprecise control of manufacturing and is the major driver of yield improvement [42]. For instance, phase deviation in lithography process can induce similar device parameter variation of chips fabricated in the same batch. It indicates that the process variation of a batch of chips follows certain specific patterns. The management of systematic variation is critical to achieve competitive yield for semiconductor manufacturers. It can be addressed with either manufacturing improvement or process variation aware design when the variation pattern is known. Random variation refers to the process variation without particular patterns such as threshold voltage variation [52, 69]. It can be caused by factors like inconsistent doping and continuously lowering operation voltage, and is particular difficult to predict in practice.

From the perspective of process variation analysis granularity, it can also be divided into wafer-to-wafer (W2W), die-to-die (D2D), and within-die (WID) variations [25]. Basically, process variation consists of parameter fluctuations across dies and wafers, whereas within-die variation refers to variations of design parameters within a single die. As technology scales, WID has become a more significant threat to future processor design. Particularly in multi-core processors, WID variation is also considered as core-to-core (C2C) variation and attracts intensive architectural design efforts [52, 55].

If the process variation is left unaddressed, it can offset the benefits of a new generation of semiconductor process technology substantially [52]. For example, dramatic yield drop is observed when the semiconductor technology scales from 350 to 45 nm [2, 17, 19, 54]. Chip frequency loss will be as high as 30% with advanced process technology [11]. A 20× increase in leakage power has also been reported [10]. Many prior study also showed that process variation even becomes one of the barriers that hinder the adoption of new semiconductor technologies such as carbon nanotube FETs [72–74] and memristor based devices [45].

1.1.2 Manufacturing Defects

VLSI design is getting extremely complex at the nanometre technology era and includes up to 10,000 fabrication process steps. Many of the fabrication steps such as lithography, etching, deposition, chemical mechanical polishing, oxidation, ion implantation, and diffusion are not fully digital and cannot be perfect, which will inevitably result in electrically malfunctioning circuitry in certain area of the fabricated chips. The malfunctioning circuitry can be considered as manufacturing defects. It poses significant influence on the VLSI yield and determines the economic profits of semiconductor manufactures directly [44]. Hence, defect density even becomes one of the most critical metrics that exhibit the semiconductor technology quality and maturity.

Manufacturing defects are usually sensitive to the transistor feature sizes because the size of manufacturing defects remains similar under different semiconductor technologies and will affect more transistors under smaller semiconductor feature size given even the same design accordingly [41, 63]. Particularly, some of the small defects may not even cause any design failure under 180 nm technology node but can probably lead to multiple transistor faults under 14 nm technology node, which are more likely to cause design failure.

When the design is small, the probability of manufacturing defects induced design failure is much lower. In this context, we may pick out the failed chips with offline test and discard them directly [66]. Basically, the overhead of test and discarded chips can cover the fault-tolerant design induced chip area overhead. The test based fault-tolerant approach is utilized in early VLSI designs. However, the computing requirements grow much faster than the transistor density driven by the semiconductor technology nodes and the scale of the VLSI designs increases along with the transistor density. More and more larger VLSI designs appear in the past decades. Take AMD processors as an example, AMD K8 in 2003 includes 105 million transistors and the chip area is 193 mm^2 under 130 nm technology. In contrast, AMD Epyc 7773X (Milan-X) in 2022 has more than 26 billion transistors and the chip area is 1352 mm^2 under hybrid 7 and 12 nm technology. The chip area of AMD Epyc in 2022 is almost 7× larger than that of Intel K8 in 2003 even when the semiconductor technology advances by more than 10 generations [1]. The cost of a single large chip is expensive and discarding the entire chip whenever there are manufacturing defects can no longer be afforded, which demands a new fault-tolerant design paradigm to protect against manufacturing defects effectively.

1.1.3 Chip Aging

According to International Technology Roadmap For Semiconductors (ITRS) projection, silicon aging tops the impending (above 22 nm) reliability challenges. The industry and academic communities have performed significant work to understand the failure mechanisms of semiconductor devices, such as electromigration (EM), bias temperature instability (BTI) including negative and positive BTI (also known as NBTI and PBTI, respectively), time dependent dielectric breakdown (TDDB), hot carrier injection, and temperature cycling, etc. Both NBTI and TDDB draw the most attention concerning several transistor aging mechanisms. Both of them can gradually degrade performance over time. The researchers have evidence that circuit path delay can increase by 10% during the five-year lifetime [68]. Even worse, with technology scaling to the nano-scale, the transistors tend to become more vulnerable and more prone to aging impacts [68].

The integrity of the wires is also degraded. The shrinking size leads to increased current density. Increased current density causes aggravated EM effects, which also contribute to the in-filed performance and reliability degradation. The effects of EM produce increased resistance of the wires and thereby result in increased RC delay. The increasing delay will eventually outgrow the timing margin and, even worse, the wires will eventually breakdown, causing break faults, bridge faults, or stuck-at faults in the chips.

Since the whole chip is exposed to these aging mechanisms, some parts of the chip suffer faster aging than the others. The main reason can be attributed the following two aspects.

First, the "weak" chips, which are more sensitive to aging, mainly results from process variations [10]. As the feature size relentlessly shrinks generation-by-generation, the impacts of process variations become increasingly evident. Because of the wafer-to-wafer, die-to-die, and within-die variations, the proportion of the circuits with serious mismatches to the golden reference in the design print should be marked as weak silicon and removed from the production batch as yield loss. For example, the typical threshold voltage V_{th} of transistors may exhibit obvious deviations from the standard settings because of width/length fluctuations caused by an unstable lithographic process. Those transistors with the elevated V_{th} have smaller tolerances to withstand the aging induced V_{th} increasing and are therefore prone to be more sensitive to it than those with larger tolerances.

Second, the aging rate of silicon devices (including the metal wires) depends not only on the intrinsic constitution of the devices themselves, but also on the stressing duty cycles [12]. From a microscopic perspective, the data patterns, which determine the BTI aging degree, are intrinsically non-uniform across the all bits. Consequently, some transistors are always positively or negatively-biased and therefore degrade much faster than those that are evenly-biased. The heavily-biased BTI aging has a slight chance to enjoy the recovery effect, which exacerbates the aging degree. From a microarchitectural perspective, for another example, the usage of some cores in a multi-core processor could be always higher than the others because an oracle round-robin scheduling algorithm is not an option in modern operating system (OS) design. The jobs assigned to different cores can show very distinct stressing degrees. The computationally intensive jobs are usually more power-hungry and therefore generate more heat which can speed up the aging, while those computationally non-intensive jobs are the opposite.

1.1.4 Soft Errors

Soft errors in memory that will change the value of the stored data temporally have been a well-known problem [60]. Typically, the error lasts until a new write, and it will not damage the physical structure of the memory. In contrast, registers may update in each cycle, so soft errors last for only a short time, which usually induces a short signal pulse and has less influence on the design working at lower clock frequency under older semiconductor technology. Hence, soft errors in memory attract more attentions in early fault-tolerant VLSI designs [59]. Nevertheless, VLSI designs fabricated with nanoscale semiconductor technologies become increasingly vulnerable to soft errors because of the reduced node capacity, supply voltage, and higher transistor density. The influence of soft errors in CMOS logic can no longer be ignored and even exceed that in memory blocks in high-end processors working at more than 2.2 GHz according to the study in [22].

Soft errors can be roughly classified as single event upset (SEU), single event transient (SET), and multiple bit upset (MBU) [59]. When high-energy particles hit on an memory cell, the stored value in the cell may flip and keep until the next write. This is called SEU. Since memory arrays typically have very high density, the rate of SEU is usually high. When the memory cell gets smaller along with the advancements of semiconductor technology, high-energy particles may cause multiple bit flips in neighboring memory cells. This is called MBU and gains increasing attentions of researchers in the past decade. When high-energy particles hit on combinational logic, a short pulse signal ranging from 0.35 to 1.3 ns will be produced and propagate along with the circuit. When the circuit such as a high-end processor operates at higher clock, the pulse signal can be captured by the downstream registers and incur computing errors. This is known as SET.

Similar to manufacturing defects, soft errors also pose more significant influence on the performance and functionality of the VLSI designs with growing transistor density and circuit scale [20, 22]. Particularly, soft error rate of the entire design, as known as system error rate, increases continuously despite the utilization of fault-resilient semiconductor technologies like FinFET [18]. In order to compensate the transistor variability induced errors, Intel proposed to explore hardware-based self-monitoring and self-management mechanisms and estimated that at least 5–10% of a processor's 10 billion-plus transistors will be dedicated to ensure reliability according to the report in [9].

1.1.5   Intermittent Faults

Intermittent hardware faults occur frequently and irregularly for a period of time, commonly due to manufacturing residuals, oxide degradation, process variations, and in-progress wear-out. Although intermittent faults and soft errors may manifest similar effects, there are several differences between them. First, from the spatial aspect, an intermittent fault occurs repeatedly at the same location, while a soft error rarely occurs in the same place. Second, from the temporal aspect, an intermittent fault will occur at burst, while a soft error is usually a single event upset or a single event transient. Third, if an affected structure has been replaced, intermittent faults will be eliminated; soft errors, however, can not be reduced by repair. There are also some differences between intermittent faults and hard faults. A hard fault exists during the lifetime of a chip and continually generates errors if the failing device is exercised, while an intermittent fault may be periodically activated and deactivated due to process and environmental variations. Intermittent faults also may turn to hard faults finally [61].

An intermittent fault has three key parameters: burst length (BL), active time (AT), and inactive time (IAT) [30]. Burst length is the lifetime of an intermittent fault; active time is the positive pulse width of one activation, while inactive time is the time between two consecutive activations. The relationship among the three parameters can be expressed as $BL = N \times AT + (N - 1) \times IAT$ where represents the number of activations in an intermittent fault. These three parameters determine the characteristics of an intermittent fault, and their values can be dissimilar for different intermittent fault configurations. Figure 1.1 shows the temporal feature of intermittent faults within a period of time. Intermittent faults have adverse impact on program execution only during their active time. The time interval between two consecutive bursts is called safe time which means no intermittent fault occurs during that time, and the safe time could be varied because the occurrence of an intermittent fault is uncertain.

In order to characterize the vulnerability of circuit designs to intermittent faults, it is important to establish appropriate logic fault models for them. The established logic fault models should represent physical intermittent abnormal phenomena. Based on the root causes and behaviors, intermittent faults can be classified into the following fault models [27, 30].

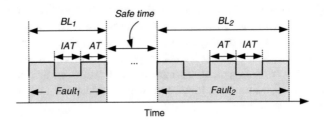

Fig. 1.1 Key parameters of intermittent faults

- *Intermittent stuck-at faults (including intermittent stuck-at-1 and stuck-at-0 faults):* Intermittent stuck-at faults are caused by residues in storage cells or solder joints during manufacturing. Unlike a soft error to upset a bit, an intermittent stuck-at fault transforms the correct value on the faulty signal line intermittently to be stuck at a constant value, either a logic value "1" or a logic value "0". Structures most vulnerable to intermittent stuck-at faults are storage structures, such as memory and register file. In this work, we assume an intermittent stuck-at fault only causes one-bit of corruption.
- *Intermittent open and short faults:* Intermittent open and short faults are usually caused by electro-migration, stress migration, or intermittent contacts. Intermittent open faults are breaks or imperfections in circuit interconnections such as wires, contacts, transistors and so forth. Intermittent short faults are shorts in wires or shorts in transistors. If an element being intermittently shorted to power or ground, it is equivalent to an intermittent stuck-at fault. If two signal wires are shorted together, an intermittent bridging fault occurs [66]. Figure 1.2 illustrates several examples of intermittent open and short faults. As shown in the circuit that consists of a two-input NOR gate and an NOT gate, I1 is an intermittent open fault in transistor N2 and I2 is an intermittent open fault in wire C between the two gates. I3 is an intermittent short fault to wire D and I4 is an intermittent bridging fault. Intermittent open and short faults may turn to hard faults if existing for a long time. Elements most vulnerable to these faults are signal buses and I/O connections.
- *Intermittent timing faults:* Intermittent timing faults are mainly caused by inductive noises, aging, crosstalk, or process, voltage, temperature (PVT) variations. Intermittent timing faults will result in timing violations and affect data propagation when they occur. They usually lead to write wrong data to storage cells (i.e., flip-flops miss to latch the newly computed value due to path-delay) and finally become reliability problems. Intermittent timing faults can be broadly classified into intermittent path-delay faults and intermittent transition faults.

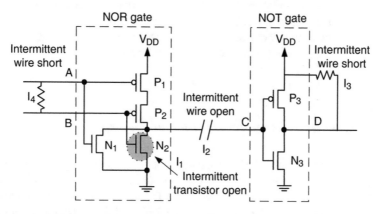

Fig. 1.2 Examples of different intermittent open and short faults

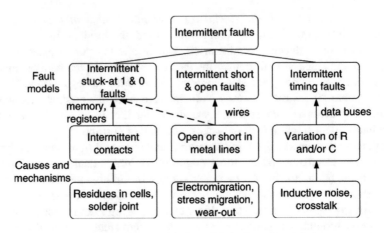

Fig. 1.3 Physical causes, mechanisms, and fault models for intermittent faults

In this work, we mainly focus on intermittent path-delay faults. Besides, an intermittent timing fault may affect multiple bits of the data captured by storage structures or just a single bit in a structure. For example, a crosstalk induced delay fault may either affect multiple data lines or only one data line. We only consider the former situation that an intermittent timing fault affects multiple data lines.

Figure 1.3 summarizes the main physical causes, mechanisms, and fault models for intermittent faults. Each kind of fault model has different causes, behaviors, and its own representative analysis method. Although the causes of these fault models may be different, they may have some physical causes in common. For example, an open or short in metal lines can also lead to intermittent stuck-at faults as presented in Fig. 1.2.

It is also necessary to know the probability distribution of intermittent faults after establishing fault models. Srinivasan et al. [62] show intermittent open and short faults obey log-normal distributions during the lifetime of microprocessors, which means the failure rate is low at the beginning of a microprocessor's lifetime and it will grow as the microprocessor ages. Intermittent stuck-at faults and intermittent timing faults mainly obey uniform distribution and are highly dependent on the applications.

1.1.6 Emerging Technologies Induced Defects

As the feature size of the CMOS-based semiconductor technology is getting close to the physical limit, many researchers from both industry and academia resort to new semiconductor technologies such as 3D fabrication, resistive random-access memory (ReRAM), and Carbon Nano Tube FET (CNFET) which enable more effective implementations in terms of performance, power, and energy efficiency

[15, 32, 33, 48, 73]. For instance, 3D VLSI that enables much higher transistor density fabrication and shorter interconnection promises higher performance and energy efficiency [48, 75]. ReRAM works by changing the resistance across a dielectric solid-state material and covers a broad range of memory and storage types of semiconductor devices. It is usually non-volatile but typically much faster than existing non-volatile storage such as flash and hard disk. At the same time, the structures are usually simple and can be adapted for energy-efficient computing in memory [14, 32]. In addition, many of the ReRAM technologies can reuse conventional CMOS-based manufacturing processes and are cost-effective in terms of fabrication. CNFET that has much lower leakage current and enables high-speed operations has been demonstrated to be an order of magnitude faster and energy-efficient compared to the CMOS-based design at similar technology node [33, 73].

Despite the overwhelming advantages of these emerging technologies, they generally suffer various manufacturing defects and process variation because of both the imperfect control of the manufacturing and immature device designs, which hinders the adoption of these technologies for mass production. In this context, built-in fault-tolerant design methods at device level, circuit level, architectural level, and even application level can greatly alleviate the shortcomings of these emerging technologies and promote the advancements of these emerging technologies [47, 72, 73]. There have been many successful demonstrations in the past decade [32]. Gage Hill et al. proposed a set of fault-tolerant design approaches ranging from device design, EDA design, and architectural design to address the unique process variations in CNFET and developed a CNFET-based RISC-V processor [33]. Li et al. took advantage of the inherent fault tolerance of neural network models and developed a unified design framework to detect and mitigate faults in ReRAM-based deep learning accelerators [45]. Liu et al. proposed a Through Silicon Via (TSV) reuse strategy for 3D network-on-chip architecture to reduce the use of expensive and vulnerable TSVs without performance penalty [48, 70]. In summary, built-in fault-tolerant computing paradigm can also be utilized to mitigate the various faults caused by immature emerging semiconductor technologies and lower the manufacturing requirements in terms of precision and overhead.

1.2 Conventional Fault-Tolerant Chip Design Wisdom

Fault-tolerant design originated in early chip designs when silicon faults were common due to the immature semiconductor technologies. Although semiconductor technology advances rapidly over the years and the probability of a single transistor fault decreases, the probability of faults in a chip increases continuously because of the growing chip scale and transistor density. A series of fault-tolerant design methodologies including design for test, design for diagnosis, and design for reliability have been explored systematically. Although they are not sufficient for existing fault-tolerant chip designs, these conventional wisdom has been demonstrated to be successful in practice and can still be widely utilized nowadays. They will be illustrated briefly in this subsection.

1.2.1 Design for Test

In both chip prototyping stage and early chip mass production stage, test is critical to identify the failures in chips caused by manufacturing such that the reasons to the failures can be found through yield learning and physical failure analysis [66, 71], which helps to improve the manufacturing as well as chip design and ensures high yield during mass production. However, it is rather challenging to test a circuit comprehensively with limited time and overhead constraints especially for large-scale circuits. Particularly, sequential logic with Flip-Flop usually cannot be controlled or observed directly and results in low testability and fault coverage. To this end, design for test becomes indispensable for general IC designs in practice [39].

Scan chain that mainly revisits the structure of basic Flip-Flop to improve its testability and controllability becomes a major approach for IC test [37]. Figure 1.4a

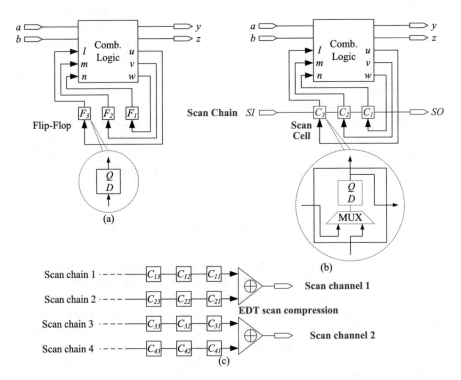

Fig. 1.4 An example of scan chain based design for test

presents a basic sequential circuit without scan chain. port a and b represents the primary input of the circuit, port y and z are the primary output of the circuit, and F_1, F_2, and F_3 are the flip-flops while clock for the flip-flop is removed for simplicity. When the flip-flop structures are modified as shown in Fig. 1.4b, scan cells denoted as C_1, C_2, and C_3 can connect to the same scan chain which has an input port SI and an output port SO.

In scan cells, the 2-to-1 MUX essentially decides the status of the circuit which can either be normal functional state or test state. When the circuit is at functional state, the functionality of the circuit in Fig. 1.4b and that in Fig. 1.4a is the same. When the circuit is at test state, it includes three consecutive processing stages i.e. scan-shift-in stage, capture stage, and scan-shift-out stage. In scan-shift-in stage, the flip flops in the three scan cells are sequentially connected and the test vector will be loaded to the flip flops sequentially with three-cycle shifting. The value of the signals including l, m, and n connected with the flip flops are determined accordingly. In capture stage, the value of signals including u, v, and w can be calculated with the combinational logic immediately and captured by the flip flops. Finally, in scan-shift-out stage, the three flip flops are connected sequentially again such that the value of signals including u, v, and w can be read through the scan chain and observed at output port SO. According to the small test example, we notice that scan-chain based design makes the signals including l, m, and n controllable and the signals including u, v, and w observable. Thereby, scan-chain improves the controllability, observability, and testability of the circuit.

With the growing circuit scale, the number of scan cells in circuits increases substantially over the years. In a typical multi-core processor fabricated with TSMC (Taiwan Semiconductor Manufacturing Company), a single core includes 18,796 scan cells [80]. The number of scan channels in an automatic test equipment (ATE) is usually limited. Suppose 8 scan chains are utilized to the connect these scan cells, 2350 cells will be allocated to each scan chain and it takes 2350 cycles to load a single test vector, which is time-consuming and includes considerable data transmission. To address the problem, scan compaction becomes widely utilized and needs to considered along with the test coverage [66]. Usually, we try to explore the redundant data in multiple scan cells and reduce the scan cells in each scan chain for shorter test time. The top 3 EDA vendors including Mentor Graphics, Cadence, and Synopsys proposed their own test compaction methods. For instance, Mentor Graphics proposed embedded deterministic test (EDT) and utilized XOR gate for efficient test compaction [35]. As shown in Fig. 1.4c, every two scan chains output via a single XOR such that the four scan chains can be compressed and handled by two scan channels. When this approach is applied in the same example, 18,796 scan cells can be connected with 160 scan chains and each scan chain has 118 scan cells. With EDT, 20 scan chains can be compressed to a single scan channel. Given 8 scan channels, it takes only 118 cycles to scan in a test vector and scan out the output data, which greatly reduces the test overhead.

1.2.2 Design for Diagnosis

Fault diagnosis mainly identifies the fault sites and fault behavior by analyzing the failing response obtained in chip test. It is typically much more efficient than physical failure analysis because it narrows down the scale of the fault sites considerably and helps to accelerate the fault analysis process [29, 79]. In addition, prior work demonstrated that many systematic chip failures can be found through statistical analysis of a batch of chips without physical failure analysis [7, 34, 49]. With the detected systematic failures, we may improve the corresponding manufacturing processes to avoid the same failures, which accelerates the yield learning significantly. With the increasing transistor density and design scale, many failures are caused by multiple faults rather than single fault. As a result, the fault diagnosis approaches based on single fault model can be futile in many cases. According to the study in [38], 41% of the failed chips cannot be diagnosed correctly. Hence, multiple-fault diagnosis becomes a critical problem for fast yield improvement in mass production.

For more effective fault diagnosis, additional design efforts are required to distinguish the behavior of the circuits among different fault configurations, which is also known as design for diagnosis [57]. Diagnosiability can be improved by revisiting the circuit structures or adding some auxiliary logic, which essentially improves the observability or controllability of the circuits and is similar to design for test from this perspective. However, design for test and design for diagnosis are still different in terms of the design goals. Specifically, design for test aims to distinguish the circuits with faults and without faults while design for diagnosis seeks to differ the circuits with different faults.

Based on the target fault locations in circuits, fault diagnosis approaches can be roughly divided into scan-chain fault diagnosis and combinational logic fault diagnosis. For the scan chain fault diagnosis, it can be further split into two categories. One of them is based on fault simulation. Basically, it repeats the processes including fault injection, fault simulation, and fault analysis until a similar fault response is captured. The other one is to load determined diagnosis vector to an ATE and determine the faults based on the response. For the combinational logic fault diagnosis, cause-effect analysis and effect-cause analysis are the major solutions. Cause-effect analysis approach is also known as dictionary-based analysis. The basic idea is to build a fault model and record all the possible fault response in a dictionary. Then, the dictionary will be utilized as a reference for fault diagnosis. The major problem for this approach is that it is sensitive to the fault models used for the dictionary building and the dictionary can be large and expensive. Effect-cause analysis is more complex and consists of three components including structural pruning, fault simulation, and evaluation strategy. With structural pruning, we can find the circuit that will not be affected and reduce the circuit that needs further diagnosis. Then, fault simulation is applied to the reduced circuit. Based on the evaluation of simulated fault response, we can determine the fault sites [36].

1.2.3   Design for Reliability

As the semiconductor technology steps into nanometer scale, the increasing transistor density together with the continuously growing computing requirements trigger the design of large-scale integrated circuits such as multi-core processors, GPUs, and high-capacity memory, which consists of dozens of billions of transistors. Unlike early small-scale and medium-scale IC designs of which reliability issues can be mostly screened with testing and handled at device level through manufacturing process improvement, large-scale IC designs are more likely affected by various faults and it is usually not an economic choice to discard a large chip with small or minor faults [16, 50, 78]. Reliability becomes vital to not only the functionality of the design but also yield and cost [51]. In addition, many reliability issues are closely related with the time-dependent aging and eventually cause failure of an entire chip, which is prohibitively expensive to test before entering the market. In this context, reliability becomes a critical metric especially for safety-critical scenarios like avionics, automotive electronics, and medical electronics, and must be considered by design, which is also known as design for reliability (DFR) in IC industry.

DFR covers a variety of fault-tolerant techniques that allow a chip to perform its intended function in presence of faults [51]. It includes both generic fault-tolerant techniques such as computing redundancy that can be adapted to various circuits and specific fault-tolerant techniques such as error correction code (ECC) that are mainly utilized for memory blocks and data transfer logic.

For the generic fault-tolerant techniques, we take hardware redundancy as an example and illustrate it in detail. Hardware redundancy techniques can further be divided into two categories: passive redundancy and active redundancy. Passive redundancy assumes that faults always happen or happen frequently, and fault recovery is conducted without any external acknowledgement. Triple modular redundancy (TMR) and N modular redundancy (NMR) are typical passive redundancy practice. The same processing are duplicated multiple times and checked with an additional voting mechanism [53, 65]. The duplicated processing is always enabled no matter whether faults occur. They are widely utilized in mission critical scenarios and can protect the chip against both soft errors and persistent faults. To alleviate the considerable redundancy overhead, active redundancy has a lightweight fault detection module or mechanism implemented and it conducts the fault recovery only when faults are detected. It avoids expensive passive redundancy processing and can be beneficial especially when the probability of the faults are relatively lower. However, the fault detection may be slow and faults may already corrupt the design when the faults are detected. Usually, the active redundancy approach may need more complex fault recovery mechanism to address the problem.

For the specific fault-tolerant techniques, we will take the fault-tolerant encoding as an example and illustrate it in this section. Unlike the hardware redundancy that usually requires hardware duplication and can be utilized to resolve faults in any specific component of the design, fault-tolerant encoding typically has redundant information embedded in the data and the corrupted data can be detected and recovered with the redundant information [6, 23]. Basically, it ensures reliable data transfer from one component to the other and cannot protect the components that generates or modifies the data. There have been many different fault-tolerant encoding methods such as parity codes, hamming codes, cyclic redundancy check, and Reed-Solomon, which mainly differ in terms of encoding/decoding overhead and fault-tolerant capability. For instance, parity code is friendly to hardware implementation and consumes very little chip area, but it can only detect errors and cannot correct them. In contrast, hamming code that needs more chip area to implement can detect and correct errors simultaneously [26].

1.3   Built-In Fault-Tolerant Computing Paradigm

Reliability is one of the mainstay merits of virtually any computing system. Beyond conventional fault tolerance computing [8], built-in on-chip fault tolerance faces several unique challenges: (1) Resource limited. On-chip fault tolerance is engaged during the duty time so that any dedicated automatic testing equipment (ATE) are unavailable. Therefore, the only viable strategy is to build all required test supports on the chip, which makes the on-chip fault tolerance mechanism operate in a self-supporting manner. (2) Overhead-sensitive. Even though silicon has become increasingly cheap thanks to the Moore's law, it is still unwise to extravagantly use the silicon for non-performance goals. For ordinary users, it is probably highly risky for the chip makers tout for customers with the probability of a system crash rather than the more appreciable performance.

Over the past decade, we have exploited the on-chip fault tolerance to build a holistic solution ranging from on-chip fault detection to error recovery mechanisms [24, 31, 46, 76–78, 81]. We applied them to generic circuits, processing cores, Network-On-Chip (NoC), deep learning processors. The on-chip fault tolerance framework usually consists of three key components: self-test, self-diagnosis, self-repair, or '3S framework' for short. Some prototypes have been built to demonstrate how on-chip fault tolerance responds to the in-filed silicon degradation. More interestingly, we find that the 3S framework is not only a powerful backbone guiding various on-chip fault tolerance designs and implementations, but also has more far-reaching implications such as maintaining graceful performance degradation, mitigating the impact of verification blind spots, and improving the chip yield. We believe that these design principles will be critical for the chip makers to maintain a competitive edge in the future.

As a fault tolerance mechanism, on-chip fault tolerance has the ingredients of generic fault tolerance mechanisms: fault detection, fault diagnosis, and fault recovery. Fault detection is used to judge whether the system suffers from erroneous executions, then fault diagnosis digs deeper to determine where and how such errors happen, which is followed by a recovery routine to correct the error to the expected outcomes. For the on-chip fault tolerance, the generic framework evolves with several new attributes which provide the essences of the self-supportive 3S approach.

1.3.1 Self-test

The fault detection, which is virtually realized with dual-module redundancy either in spatial or temporal dimensions, is not viable due to its notoriously high overhead in terms of hardware or performance. For example, there are many fault detection schemes based on thread-level redundancy (TLR), core-level redundancy (CLR), and execution-level redundancy (ELR). Both TLR and CLR detect faults at the expense of computing throughput, a typical spatial dimension overhead. Furthermore, ELR virtually needs re-execution of the code and thereby dictates a large temporal overhead, even though such strict redundancy schemes promise perfect detection coverage.

To enable on-chip fault tolerance, we must resort to more thrift detection approaches. To achieve this, what we can compromise is the perfect detection coverage, given that the principal objective of on-chip fault tolerance is to isolate the Sick Silicon, rather than protect every instruction from fault contamination at all times. We design a highly cost-efficient self-test with respect to a probabilistic principle, rather than a deterministic principle. The detection routine should not take a significant number of processor cycles, and should be as transparent as possible to the kernel and user threads. Symptom-based fault detection which is built upon low-level circuit timing monitoring can fulfill this purpose [67, 77].

In symptom-based fault prediction, a symptom is defined as a signal stability violation. Basically, the stability violation of a signal is defined as at least one transition happens in the time interval during which the signal should be kept stable. A setup time violation, ascribed to progressive silicon aging for example, is a type of typical stability violation. As Fig. 1.5c shows, in a clock cycle, we should reserve a timing span, that is a safeguard band, to meet the minimal setup time requirement. For the degradation-free case, there should be no single transition during the safeguard band; By contrast, if the transistors involved on the relevant timing paths suffer sufficient aging, the transition-free condition can no longer hold. By detecting the transitions in the safeguard band, the impending faults can be detected. Of course, whether an aged circuit can result in a stability violation is determined not only by the "sickness" of the silicon, but also by the data patterns which can sensitize the corresponding timing paths. However, the timing paths of Sick Silicon will show a much higher probability than healthy silicon to trigger the stability violations. By detecting the distribution of the stability violation, we can discriminate the sick parts from the healthy parts.

The key instruments to detect the stability violation is timing sensors, which are commonly based on dynamic circuits satisfying sub-nanosecond to even tens of picoseconds detection resolution. Figure 1.5 shows a sensor design. The basic stability checker (Fig. 1.5a) can be derived from a sensing circuit for on-line delay

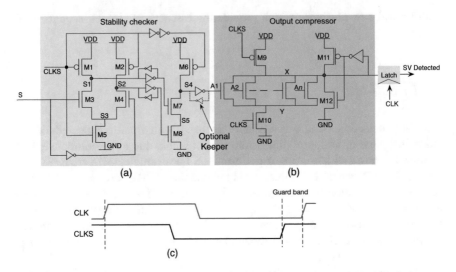

Fig. 1.5 Timing sensor design. (**a**) stability checker; (**b**) output compressor; (**c**) clock timing

fault detection, in which the integrity of the signal (S) is verified by a pair of exclusive nodes (S1 and S2), a stability violation will discharge the charged node and thereby cause both nodes to be at the "0" state, which signifies a timing violation. The outputs are compacted with a dynamic NOR for reducing the number of output latches (Fig. 1.5b), where the M11 and M12 serve as a level restorer for node X. Multiple timing sensors are embedded in the host chip during fabrication. These sensors collectively form a monitoring system with fine-grained spatial detection resolution. The problematic component, such as an arithmetic logic unit (ALU), or a L1 cache bank, can be pinpointed. These faulty components can be masked from the other healthy parts, simply like a patient undergoes a surgery. These circuit-level adaptations can be automatically executed transparently on the host operation systems.

1.3.2 Self-diagnosis

In on-chip fault tolerance, the diagnosis has two objectives: (1) pinpointing which components have been suffered permanent faults, and (2) estimating the level of performance degradation will be taxed due to the faults. Before delving into the details, we would like to first clarify the key differences between the built-in on-chip fault diagnosis and conventional chip diagnosis routines. The built-in on-chip fault diagnosis routine, called self-diagnosis, is very different from conventional diagnosis used in the yield learning phase, in terms of objective, techniques used, target granularity, and fault models.

- First, self-diagnosis is used to identify and locate the malfunctioning components, while the diagnosis in the production phase is mainly to help locate the defective physical or electrical contexts [4]. The designers refine the physical designs to avoid these cases to ramp up the yield learning rate.
- Second, the self-diagnosis intrinsically relies on built-in logic to locate the defective component, while the conventional diagnosis heavily relies on the silicon scan test and is conducted off-line by using sophisticated logical diagnosis tools.
- Third, the granularity of self-diagnosis uses relatively coarse-grained components, such as core-level granularity, which have independent functionality and are usually loosely coupled with other parts, while the conventional diagnosis works at much finer-grained granularity at the logic gates or standard cells. In other words, self-diagnosis is based on functional testing and conventional diagnosis is based on structural testing.
- Accordingly, the fault models of self-diagnosis describe the malfunction of components and therefore are more ad hoc, such as parity mismatch in the ALU components, while that of conventional diagnosis targets more silicon-level imperfections, such as bridge, open, abnormal leakage.

For on-chip fault tolerance, determining which parts of a chip get sick usually is trivial with the fine-grained self detection facility. If the corresponding timing sensors keep alerting stability violations, the faulty components can be switched off to avoid erroneous computations. In this case, the diagnosis and associated repairs are trivial. From Fig. 1.6, for example, there are four homogeneous ALUs in the processor core, the diagnosis agent logs the number of alarms reported by the self-test procedure. Each logging period can be as long as days or weeks to improve the diagnosis confidence level. By analyzing the alarm distribution, the self-diagnosis agent can discriminate the faulty ALU. In this example, the alarm density ascribed to ALU2 is significantly higher than the others, so the diagnosis agent marks that

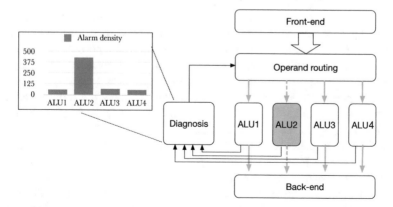

Fig. 1.6 An self-diagnosis logic example for a 4-ALU processor

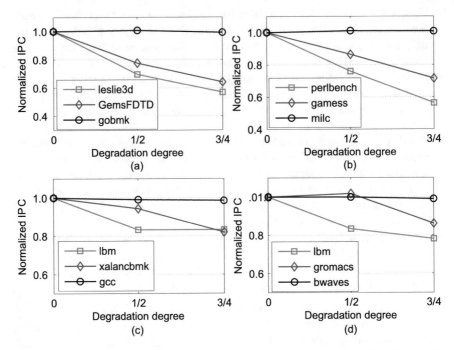

Fig. 1.7 Performance degradation vs. defect degrees of (**a**) instruction window, (**b**) L1 instruction cache, (**c**) L1 data cache, (**d**) L2 cache, where the following SPEC CPU2006 benchmarks are used: leslie3d, GemsFDTD, gobmk, perlbench, gamess, milc, lbm, xalancbmk, gcc, gromacs, and bwaves

ALU2 should no longer be available anymore. The computation is thereby offloaded to the remaining three health ALUs. Consequently, this core will continue to work at the degraded performance level. The similar diagnosis logic can be also applied in the core-level, especially for many-core processors.

It is more challenging to determine the performance impact given the faults detected, because the performance degradation depends on both the applications and the extent of the defects. For example, Fig. 1.7 shows the performance responses of the cores under various types of degradation. The cores are salvaged from instruction window defects, or L1 instruction/data cache defects, or L2 cache defects, respectively [56]. For simplicity, we do not show the more complicated compound defects. The degradation degree of "0" indicates defect-free, and 1/2 indicates half of the resource is unavailable, and so on. The results show that the performance response not only depends on the degree of degradation, but also exhibits to be highly application-specific. For example, the gobmk (a SPEC CPU2006 benchmark) in Fig. 1.7a shows to be very resilient to the instruction window degradation; however, by contrast, the leslie3d and GemsFDTD are very sensitive to it. Such complexity is never unique for the instruction window only, but also to other resources, as exemplified in the other three sub-figures. Hence, even though the defect and associated defect level are accessible to the OS, we still have no ways to determine the level of performance impact such a degradation causes the running applications.

Yan et al. [78] proposed the CoreRank approach to address this challenge. The CoreRank quantifies the core-level performance degradation towards more meta-program representations, called snippets, which are dynamic micro-operation streams and are oblivious to all the software level interference. The snippet can be readily characterized by built-in performance counters, without any instrumentation into the running workloads. The performance of core C_i on the snippet S_m is denoted as $P(C_i|S_m)$, which can be obtained by reading the corresponding performance counters [21]. If $P(C_j|S_m)$ differs from $P(C_i|S_m)$, the relative degradation can be easily extrapolated as the ratio of $P(C_j|S_m)$ to $P(C_i|S_m)$. Given any running program is composed of a sequence of various meta-programs (snippets), the program-level performance degradation can be estimated by aggregating the degradation on each individual snippet. Please refer to [78] for more details.

For on-chip fault tolerance, the diagnosis is triggered only when the test procedure prompts the alarms. To minimize the overhead, one diagnosis agent can be shared by multiple timing sensors in a round-robin manner [76] controlled by a finite state machine. To minimize the penalty of power and performance in the fault-free scenarios, the diagnosis procedure is not always on, but is periodically invoked by abnormal states such as a machine crash.

1.3.3 Self-repair

Generally there are two types of core-salvaging approaches: (1) Fault isolation. Decoupling the faulty components [4] can avoid execution contamination and maintain a graceful degradation of performance. (2) Adaptive voltage-frequency setting and timing recycling [64]. For example, if the critical path delay increases due to aging, the functionality is maintained provided the working frequency is slowed down to accommodate the extra delay. The self-repair can be implemented at three abstract levels: circuit level, microarchitectural level, and architectural level. But we should note that such a classifying scheme is never strict, but only provides a roughly categorical image for easier understanding.

1.3.3.1 Rejuvenation at the Circuit Level

Figure 1.8 illustrates a circuit-level pipeline with a rejuvenation facility. Each stage is monitored by a set of periodically-invoked aging sensors used to detect the signal transitions in the safeguard band. The aging sensors are deployed to monitor the critical paths. In the fault-free scenarios, no transitions could happen in the safeguard band, but after suffering from aging, some transitions could be delayed into the safeguard band, represented as a stability violation [77], a type of faulty

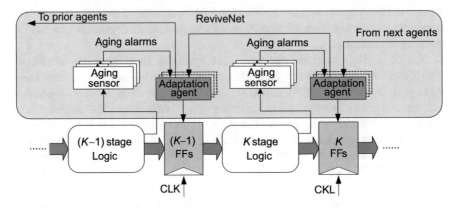

Fig. 1.8 Circuit-level rejuvenation with timing adaptation

symptom. With the awareness of aging, we can accommodate the impending aging failures by adapting localized timings. The adaptation to each stage is implemented with a set of time-borrowing agents which are fed by not only the local stages aging sensors but also the next stages agents, thereby enabling bidirectional adaptation, namely backward timing adaptation (BTA) and forward timing adaptation (FTA). The BTA uses the $(K + 1)$st stages timing slack to accommodate the aging emergencies in the Kth stage, while the FTA uses the $(K 1)$st stages slack to accommodate the emergencies in the Kth stage. When an aging sensor detects an alarm, the BTA, FTA, or BTA and FTA can be simultaneously enabled to tolerate this aging delay.

1.3.3.2 Rejuvenation at the Microarchitectural Level

The microarchitectural rejuvenation largely relies on decoupling the faulty components from the remaining healthy parts, or reconfiguring the microarchitectures [56]. The components which can be readily modified to be reconfigurable include the ALU arrays, cache banks, and register files. They share the common feature of regularity with intrinsic spares. The repaired procedure is also similar: marking the faulty component as unavailable so it will never be allocated to dynamic instructions. With some more sophisticated circuit techniques, these components can even be totally decoupled from the power grid, thereby preventing them from leakage.

For example, as shown in Fig. 1.9, Core A and Core B suffer a pipeline defect and an L1 I-cache defect, respectively. The defect-affected partitions, marked as dark parts, are decoupled from the rest to make each core functionally correct, but in a degraded manner.

In fact, such microarchitectural approaches are more common in on-chip memory subsystems. A cache or scratchpad memory, always occupies a significant

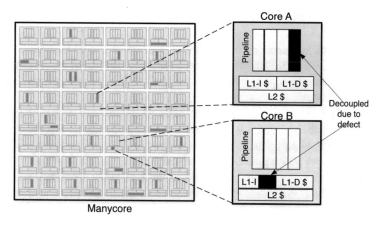

Fig. 1.9 Microarchitectural rejuvenation

proportion of silicon real-estate. Using the last level cache for example as the
failure mechanism in the SRAM cells, it suffers from different fault models, such
as permanent read/write failures due to the SNR issue, retention fault or single-
event upset (SEU). Regarding the granularity of the cache failures, it includes
conventional bit failures and array or bank failures that occur in large-scale
cache structures like distributed NUCA architectures. Fine-grained cache failures
can be cured with conventional error correction or bit/row/column replacement.
However, in modern large scale chip multi-processors, bank-level failures due to
interconnection issue or isolation requirements are less discussed. For example,
when a NoC-node is isolated from a resilient chip multiprocessor, it also creates
inaccessible NUCA cache banks because of the connectivity issue, which should
be tolerated to enable a degradable cache system. We propose a bank remapping
method to cure the coarse-grained NUCA cache failure within the framework of
self-test, self-diagnosis, self-fault-isolation. It utilizes the routing logic in NoC to
transparently remapping the physical space associated to failed banks to healthy
cache banks, so that the system will not see the cache failure and maintain a
wholesome physical memory space on-chip.

Furthermore, to reduce the negative impacts imposed by the bank failures, our
work uses a utility-driven remapping policy to match the failed cache banks to
an under-utilized cache bank, so that the system receives the least performance
penalties caused by the bank failures. The remapping method relies on a dynamic
stack-distance analyzer to measure the space utility of different address spaces and
keeps on remapping the failed banks to their favored compatible healthy banks.
In this way, the bank sharing induced block conflict will be reduced and the
conflict-induced eviction cache miss rate will be minimized. The whole framework
guarantees that the bank failure will be tolerated with a very small performance cost.
When future systems are built with unstable devices or an unstable environment,
such an inexpensive fault tolerant mechanism is very useful.

1.3.3.3 Rejuvenation at Architectural Level

The architectural rejuvenation is usually conducted at the core-level. There are two major rejuvenation styles: topology-invariant and topology-reconfigurable approaches, where the topology refers to the NoC topology connection of tens even hundreds of cores.

Using core level DVFS to tolerate a cores degradation is a typical topology-invariant approach. The cores initially have the same maximum frequency, Fmax, but with the in-field aging degradation, the Fmax of the cores can differ from each other. If a core ages with a prolonged critical path delay, we can scale down the cores frequency to maintain safe timing, at the expense of more sophisticated per-core DVFS. Meanwhile, the topology, that is the cores location related to other cores, remains intact.

The topology-invariance can simplify the NoC implementation and traffic management. However, if a core suffers an irreparable failure, we must either map it out of the healthy region, or find a substitute. In either case, the topology must be changed and topology-reconfigurable approaches must be employed [24, 81]. One typical solution is called N + M paradigm, i.e., there are N normal cores, which are visible to the OS, and M spare cores, which only serve as substitutes for failed cores and are invisible to OS. The similar solution is adopted in the "Cell" processor (N = 7, M = 1), where an N-core processor is provided with M redundant cores and we always provide customers with N operational cores. The spare cores are viewed as overhead. However, as the number of on-chip cores increases, the overhead of leaving a few redundant cores on-chip unused is acceptable because a single core is inexpensive compared to the entire chip.

In fact, the industry has started to employ core-level redundancy in their products. Even though the objective is mainly for yield or performance, a similar rationale should be also applied to enhance the lifetime reliability. In such a case, rejuvenation is about substituting the faulty cores with the spares. The topology determines the ideal performance whereas the routing algorithm and the flow control mechanism determine how much of this potential is realized. However, when the failure cores are replaced by spare cores, the topology of the target design can be different. For example, suppose we want to provide 9-core processors with a 3 × 3 2D-mesh topology, as shown in Fig. 1.10a. Also, suppose three redundant cores (1 column) are provided, as shown in Fig. 1.10b. If some cores (no more than three) are defective, we could still get 9-core processors. However, from Fig. 1.10c, if the faulty cores are replaced by the spare cores, not only are the topologies different from what we expect, but also the topologies of different chips can be very distinct. Consequently, there is a mismatch between the logical topology, 2D-mesh in this example, and the physical topology, namely the topology with the disabled cores. Clearly, there could be many ways to map the logical topology to the physical topology. So, the challenge in the N + M paradigm is to determine which topology is optimal. The problem has been proven to be NP-complete and can only be solved with a heuristic algorithm [81].

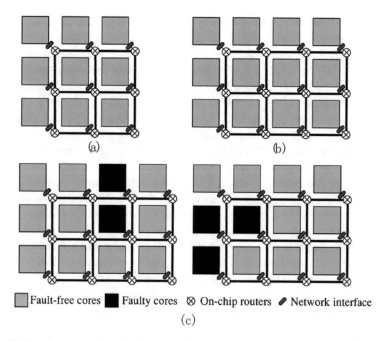

Fault-free cores ■ Faulty cores ⊗ On-chip routers ✎ Network interface
(c)

Fig. 1.10 Topology reconfiguration-based architectural level rejuvenation for a manycore. (**a**) The topology demand; (**b**) the topology with spare cores; (**c**) the topology with faulty cores

1.3.4   General Benefits

The on-chip fault tolerance computing paradigm has great potential to critically complement the state-of-the-art IC designs. However, we should note that the specific techniques mentioned above should not be supposed to be comprehensive, but the concept of the 3S-based on-chip fault-tolerant design framework can be tailored for more purposes. We summarize three perspectives in the following section.

1.3.4.1   Maintaining Graceful Degradation

Faults could happen during the lifetime of a system. If the faults are transient, the system may be recovered by rebooting. However, if the faults are permanent, some resources of the system, such as cores in multi-core processor or interconnections of NoC will no longer be functionally correct. Without isolating the faults, the whole system may even turn off completely. However, by detecting, diagnosing, and isolating the faulty components, the system may still be able to work correctly using the remaining good components, though at a lower performance degree, i.e., Graceful Degradation. No redundant components are assumed, which means the components of the system have already satisfied the capability of reconfiguration for correct function. It is not surprising that these two design philosophies converge since they share the same objective. There are two key questions required to be answered for the on-chip fault tolerance computing paradigm based graceful degradation: (1) what is the granularity? (2) how to implement it? The on-chip fault tolerance computing paradigm sheds light on the answers.

The processor core and the NoC interconnection are two typical reconfigurable components used in graceful degradation. In multi-core processors, when one core is faulty, other cores can still function. In the NoC, when one interconnection node is faulty, other nodes may substitute its routing function. With on-chip fault tolerance, there are more redundant resources to keep the whole system working properly. More fine-grained components can also be considered. For example, a redundant arithmetic logic unit (ALU) can be added to a core, so when one ALU fails, the core can still work correctly.

Using more fine-grained components for fault tolerance and performance degradation can improve the lifetime of the system, but its disadvantage is the hardware cost, not only including the hardware for isolating the faulty components, but also including the hardware of detecting such fine-grained components. However, FPGA is an exception, since it is programmable. Hence detecting the faulty Look-Up Tables (LUTs), interconnection boxes, or other fine-grained components of FPGA can be realized by specific circuits, and isolating the faulty resources can be achieved using placement and routing constraints while designing FPGA circuits. Hence, it is possible for FPGA to perform fine-grained analysis without any hardware overhead, but with a performance penalty.

Furthermore, on-chip fault tolerance computing paradigm provides more possibilities and opportunities for effective graceful degradation. The implementation of graceful degradation requires accurate diagnosis of the faulty components. For example, in NoC, it is necessary to diagnose the switch, the router, the link, and so on [40]. With the knowledge of locating the faulty components, the routing for graceful degradation is an optimization process with the constraint that the faulty interconnections should not be used. With more faulty components, more constraints exist in the optimization problem, so its solution, i.e., the performance, will become progressively worse, until it reaches a limit that no available routing can be found, and then the whole system will fail. Moreover, on-chip fault tolerance computing paradigm can make the graceful degradation more simplified and effective. If an interconnection node has two routers, one of which is redundant, then when the working router fails, the node can simply switch to the redundant one. In this case, the routing delay remains similar, so the performance is maintained.

1.3.4.2 Helping Fix Some Verification Blind Spots

Modern designs have become more complicated, which poses serious challenges for verification. The verification techniques cannot scale to the complexity of the modern designs, so some bugs could escape from verification and remain in the silicon. If the bugs really exist, they are like permanent faults. If these faults are not detected during testing, the products with bugs will enter the market. If the bugs are encountered by customers, it will be a large financial loss to recall the chips. In this situation, On-chip fault tolerance computing paradigm is an alternative method to fix the problem. On-chip fault tolerance computing paradigm has at least two benefits for verification: (1) locate the verification blind spots; and (2) fix the escaped bugs.

From the perspective of behavior, the escaped bugs are like permanent faults. Both cause the system to work incorrectly. In on-chip fault tolerance computing paradigm, the preliminary step for isolating faults is to detect and diagnose the faults. The same function is suitable for finding the escaped bugs. Learning how and why the bugs escaped from the adopted verification techniques is important for improving the verification process and avoiding the similar bugs remaining in silicon. A more fine-grained fault detection can provide more precise information about the escaped bugs. For example, it is easy for the designers to learn the escaped bugs by informing them just the ALU is faulty than informing them the whole processor core is faulty.

Therefore, the detection circuit for escaped bugs should be designed properly. For example, the detection circuits can be inserted in some critical points in the control flow [28]. Within the on-chip fault tolerance computing paradigm, the faults are isolated to allow the whole system to work correctly. Some bugs can also be isolated. However, since the bugs may be repeated, isolating the bugs may not be effective. For example, in the multi-core processor, if all the cores have the same design, they will contain the same bugs as well, so it is meaningless to isolate faulty cores.

Under this scenario, there are three ways to correct the bugs. First, heterogeneous cores can be designed so that even if one type of core contains bugs, other types of cores may still function correctly by isolating the faulty cores. But this method may result in a large performance losses, since a portion of the cores are unavailable. Second, during the design, combined with fine-grained bug detection circuits, some configurable components can be inserted into the critical locations [5]. If bugs are detected, specific configuration bits can be downloaded to the configurable components to correct the circuit behavior. Furthermore, in the CPU+FPGA SoC, if some bugs exist in the computing components, it is also possible to use the FPGA as a fault-tolerant component to perform the correct function. Third, for some bugs, it is also possible to use software-hardware cooperation to bypass the bugs [13]. For example, if there is a bug in the subtraction computation hardware component, the OS can compile a subtraction operation into an add operation. In this way, the same function is performed by detouring the bugs. Therefore, using the above methods, with properly inserted bug detection and recovery design, some escaped bugs from the verification phase can still be fixed after the chips are manufactured and sold to the customers, though with some performance degradation.

1.3.4.3   Improving Gross Yield

Bugs may escape from verification, and defects may happen during manufacturing. There are mainly two types of defects: the permanent defect and the transient defect. The permanent defects such as stuck-at faults will permanently affect the behavior of the chip. More specifically, they destroy the Boolean relation within the chip. In certain situations, the chip or the corresponding component will definitely fail. The transient defects, such as small delay defects, are types of timing faults. The chip only fails under a certain condition. Different from bugs which may be repeated, e.g., in multi-core processors, the cores with the same design have the same bugs, the defects do not have such characteristics. Hence the on-chip fault tolerance computing paradigm can also tolerate some defects. The chips with defects are considered as faulty chips, but if the defects can be tolerated, then the chips can still work correctly and be considered as good chips. Hence, the yield can be improved, but the promised performance may be degraded.

1.4   Summary

In this section, we introduce the background of fault-tolerant computing for VLSI designs including various fault types in VLSI chips and classical fault-tolerant wisdom that has been intensively explored. At the same time, we notice that conventional fault tolerant computing approaches become insufficient for the continuously increasing VLSI designs fabricated with nanoscale semiconductor technology and reliability design becomes a critical design metric that must be fulfilled by not only mission-critical designs but also chips in consumer electronics like desktop CPUs and GPUs. In this context, we present a built-in fault-tolerant computing paradigm, which is an incorporative framework to build synergy among many advanced fault tolerance oriented techniques. Basically, we place self-test, self-diagnosis, and self-repair (self-recovery) into a unified framework, namely the "3S" framework, and clarified the difference from their conventional counterparts whenever possible. We use the manycore undergoing various degrees of aging faults as the baseline to show the efficacy of on-chip fault tolerance, and discuss three far-reaching implications in terms of graceful degradation, verification, and yield. Although we have made some initial attempts to solidify this framework, the potential has never been fully exploited. We believe on-chip fault tolerance can help deliver more reliable SoC systems suffering in-field degradation in the future.

References

1. Transistor count in electronic devices, May 2022. https://en.wikipedia.org/wiki/Transistor_count.
2. Amit Agarwal, Bipul Chandra Paul, Hamid Mahmoodi, Animesh Datta, and Kaushik Roy. A process-tolerant cache architecture for improved yield in nanoscale technologies. *IEEE Transactions on Very Large Scale Integration (VLSI) Systems*, 13(1):27–38, 2005.
3. Aditya Agrawal, Amin Ansari, and Josep Torrellas. Mosaic: Exploiting the spatial locality of process variation to reduce refresh energy in on-chip eDRAM modules. In *2014 IEEE 20th International Symposium on High Performance Computer Architecture (HPCA)*, pages 84–95. IEEE, 2014.
4. Rob Aitken. Yield Learning Perspectives. *IEEE Design & Test of Computers*, 29(1):59–62, 2012.
5. Bijan Alizadeh and Masahiro Fujita. A debugging method for repairing post-silicon bugs of high performance processors in the fields. In *2010 International Conference on Field-Programmable Technology*, pages 328–331, 2010.
6. Wendy Bartlett and Lisa Spainhower. Commercial fault tolerance: A tale of two systems. *IEEE Transactions on dependable and secure computing*, 1(1):87–96, 2004.
7. R. D. (Shawn) Blanton, Wing Chiu Tam, Xiaochun Yu, Jeffrey E. Nelson, and Osei Poku. Yield learning through physically aware diagnosis of ic-failure populations. *IEEE Des. Test Comput.*, 29(1):36–47, 2012.
8. S. Borkar. Designing reliable systems from unreliable components: the challenges of transistor variability and degradation. *IEEE MICRO*, 25(6):10–16, 2005.
9. Shekhar Borkar, Pradeep Dubey, Kevin Kahn, David Kuck, Hans Mulder, Steve Pawlowski, and Justin Rattner. Platform 2015: Intel processor and platform evolution for the next decade. *Technology*, 1:30–6, 2005.
10. Shekhar Borkar, Tanay Karnik, Siva Narendra, Jim Tschanz, Ali Keshavarzi, and Vivek De. Parameter variations and impact on circuits and microarchitecture. In *Proceedings of the 40th annual Design Automation Conference*, pages 338–342, 2003.
11. Keith A Bowman, Steven G Duvall, and James D Meindl. Impact of die-to-die and within-die parameter fluctuations on the maximum clock frequency distribution for gigascale integration. *IEEE Journal of solid-state circuits*, 37(2):183–190, 2002.
12. Karthik Chandrasekar, Sven Goossens, Christian Weis, Martijn Koedam, Benny Akesson, Norbert Wehn, and Kees Goossens. Exploiting expendable process-margins in drams for run-time performance optimization. In *2014 Design, Automation & Test in Europe Conference & Exhibition (DATE)*, pages 1–6. IEEE, 2014.
13. Chia-Wei Chang, Hong-Zu Chou, Kai-Hui Chang, Jie-Hong Roland Jiang, Chien-Nan Jimmy Liu, Chiu-Han Hsiao, and Sy-Yen Kuo. Constraint generation for software-based post-silicon bug masking with scalable resynthesis technique for constraint optimization. In *2011 12th International Symposium on Quality Electronic Design*, pages 1–8, 2011.
14. Yangyin Chen. Reram: History, status, and future. *IEEE Transactions on Electron Devices*, 67(4):1420–1433, 2020.
15. Benjamin Chen Ming Choong, Tao Luo, Cheng Liu, Bingsheng He, Wei Zhang, and Joey Tianyi Zhou. Hardware-software co-exploration with racetrack memory based in-memory computing for CNN inference in embedded systems. *Journal of Systems Architecture*, page 102507, 2022.
16. Ayse K Coskun, Tajana Simunic Rosing, Yusuf Leblebici, and Giovanni De Micheli. A simulation methodology for reliability analysis in multi-core SoCs. In *Proceedings of the 16th ACM Great Lakes symposium on VLSI*, pages 95–99, 2006.
17. Abhishek Das, Serkan Ozdemir, Gokhan Memik, and Alok Choudhary. Evaluating voltage islands in CMPs under process variations. In *2007 25th International Conference on Computer Design*, pages 129–136. IEEE, 2007.

18. YQ de Aguiar, Laurent Artola, Guillaume Hubert, Cristina Meinhardt, Fernanda Lima Kastensmidt, and RAL Reis. Evaluation of radiation-induced soft error in majority voters designed in 7 nm FinFET technology. *Microelectronics Reliability*, 76:660–664, 2017.
19. Saurabh Dighe, Sriram R Vangal, Paolo Aseron, Shasi Kumar, Tiju Jacob, Keith A Bowman, Jason Howard, James Tschanz, Vasantha Erraguntla, Nitin Borkar, et al. Within-die variation-aware dynamic-voltage-frequency-scaling with optimal core allocation and thread hopping for the 80-core teraflops processor. *IEEE Journal of Solid-State Circuits*, 46(1):184–193, 2010.
20. Paul E Dodd and Lloyd W Massengill. Basic mechanisms and modeling of single-event upset in digital microelectronics. *IEEE Transactions on nuclear Science*, 50(3):583–602, 2003.
21. Stijn Eyerman, Lieven Eeckhout, Tejas Karkhanis, and James E Smith. A top-down approach to architecting CPI component performance counters. *IEEE micro*, 27(1):84–93, 2007.
22. Veronique Ferlet-Cavrois, Lloyd W Massengill, and Pascale Gouker. Single event transients in digital CMOS—a review. *IEEE Transactions on Nuclear Science*, 60(3):1767–1790, 2013.
23. JA Fifield and CH Stapper. High-speed on-chip ECC for synergistic fault-tolerance memory chips. *IEEE Journal of Solid-State Circuits*, 26(10):1449–1452, 1991.
24. Binzhang Fu, Yinhe Han, Jun Ma, Huawei Li, and Xiaowei Li. An abacus turn model for time/space-efficient reconfigurable routing. In *Proceedings of the 38th annual international symposium on Computer architecture*, pages 259–270, 2011.
25. Xin Fu, Tao Li, and José AB Fortes. Soft error vulnerability aware process variation mitigation. In *2009 IEEE 15th International Symposium on High Performance Computer Architecture*, pages 93–104. IEEE, 2009.
26. Kiyohiro Furutani, Kazutami Arimoto, Hiroshi Miyamoto, Toshifumi Kobayashi, K Yasuda, and K Mashiko. A built-in hamming code ECC circuit for DRAMs. *IEEE Journal of Solid-State Circuits*, 24(1):50–56, 1989.
27. Daniel Gil, Joaquin Gracia, Juan Carlos Baraza, and Pedro J Gil. Study, comparison and application of different VHDL-based fault injection techniques for the experimental validation of a fault-tolerant system. *Microelectronics Journal*, 34(1):41–51, 2003.
28. Dimitris Gizopoulos, Mihalis Psarakis, Sarita V Adve, Pradeep Ramachandran, Siva Kumar Sastry Hari, Daniel Sorin, Albert Meixner, Arijit Biswas, and Xavier Vera. Architectures for online error detection and recovery in multicore processors. In *2011 Design, Automation & Test in Europe*, pages 1–6, 2011.
29. S Gorlich, H Harbeck, P Kebler, E Wolfgang, and K Zibert. Integration of cad cat and electron-beam testing for ic-internal logic verification. In *Proc. of 1987 International Test Conference*, pages 566–574, 1987.
30. Joaquin Gracia, Luis J Saiz, Juan Carlos Baraza, Daniel Gil, and Pedro J Gil. Analysis of the influence of intermittent faults in a microcontroller. In *2008 11th IEEE Workshop on Design and Diagnostics of Electronic Circuits and Systems*, pages 1–6, 2008.
31. Yin-He Han, Cheng Liu, Hang Lu, Wen-Bo Li, Lei Zhang, and Xiao-Wei Li. RevivePath: Resilient network-on-chip design through data path salvaging of router. *Journal of Computer Science and Technology*, 28(6):1045–1053, 2013.
32. Yintao He, Ying Wang, Cheng Liu, Huawei Li, and Xiaowei Li. Tare: Task-adaptive in-situ ReRAM computing for graph learning. In *2021 58th ACM/IEEE Design Automation Conference (DAC)*, pages 577–582. IEEE, 2021.
33. Gage Hills, Christian Lau, Andrew Wright, Samuel Fuller, Mindy D Bishop, Tathagata Srimani, Pritpal Kanhaiya, Rebecca Ho, Aya Amer, Yosi Stein, et al. Modern microprocessor built from complementary carbon nanotube transistors. *Nature*, 572(7771):595–602, 2019.
34. Pei-Ying Hsueh, Shuo-Fen Kuo, Chao-Wen Tzeng, Jih-Nung Lee, and Chi-Feng Wu. Case study of yield learning through in-house flow of volume diagnosis. In *2013 International Symposium on VLSI Design, Automation, and Test, VLSI-DAT 2013, Hsinchu, Taiwan, April 22–24, 2013*, pages 1–4. IEEE, 2013.
35. Yu Huang, Wu-Tung Cheng, and Janusz Rajski. Compressed pattern diagnosis for scan chain failures. In *IEEE International Conference on Test, 2005*, pages 8–pp. IEEE, 2005.
36. Yu Huang, Wu-Tung Cheng, Kun-Han Tsai, Greg Crowell, and Chris Mcmahon. Diagnosing DACS (defects that affect scan chain and system logic). In *ISTFA 2004*, pages 191–196. ASM International, 2004.

37. Yu Huang, Ruifeng Guo, Wu-Tung Cheng, and James Chien-Mo Li. Survey of scan chain diagnosis. *IEEE Design & Test of Computers*, 25(3):240–248, 2008.
38. Leendert M. Huisman. Diagnosing arbitrary defects in logic designs using single location at a time (SLAT). *IEEE Trans. Comput. Aided Des. Integr. Circuits Syst.*, 23(1):91–101, 2004.
39. Aurangzeb Khan. Recent developments in high-performance system-on-chip ic design. In *2004 International Conference on Integrated Circuit Design and Technology (IEEE Cat. No. 04EX866)*, pages 151–158. IEEE, 2004.
40. Adán Kohler, Gert Schley, and Martin Radetzki. Fault tolerant network on chip switching with graceful performance degradation. *IEEE Transactions on Computer-Aided Design of Integrated Circuits and Systems*, 29(6):883–896, 2010.
41. Israel Koren and Zahava Koren. Defect tolerance in vlsi circuits: techniques and yield analysis. *Proceedings of the IEEE*, 86(9):1819–1838, 1998.
42. Kelin J Kuhn. Moore's law past 32nm: Future challenges in device scaling. In *2009 13th International Workshop on Computational Electronics*, pages 1–6. IEEE, 2009.
43. Kelin J Kuhn, Martin D Giles, David Becher, Pramod Kolar, Avner Kornfeld, Roza Kotlyar, Sean T Ma, Atul Maheshwari, and Sivakumar Mudanai. Process technology variation. *IEEE Transactions on Electron Devices*, 58(8):2197–2208, 2011.
44. Way Kuo and Taeho Kim. An overview of manufacturing yield and reliability modeling for semiconductor products. *Proceedings of the IEEE*, 87(8):1329–1344, 1999.
45. Wen Li, Ying Wang, Cheng Liu, Yintao He, Lian Liu, Huawei Li, and Xiaowei Li. On-line fault protection for ReRAM-based neural networks. *IEEE Transactions on Computers*, 2022.
46. Cheng Liu, Cheng Chu, Dawen Xu, Ying Wang, Qianlong Wang, Huawei Li, Xiaowei Li, and Kwang-Ting Cheng. Hyca: A hybrid computing architecture for fault tolerant deep learning. *IEEE Transactions on Computer-Aided Design of Integrated Circuits and Systems*, pages 1–1, 2021.
47. Cheng Liu, Zhen Gao, Siting Liu, Xuefei Ning, Huawei Li, and Xiaowei Li. Fault-tolerant deep learning: A hierarchical perspective. *arXiv preprint arXiv:2204.01942*, 2022.
48. Cheng Liu, Lei Zhang, Yinhe Han, and Xiaowei Li. Vertical interconnects squeezing in symmetric 3d mesh network-on-chip. In *16th Asia and South Pacific Design Automation Conference (ASP-DAC 2011)*, pages 357–362. IEEE, 2011.
49. Renee Liu, Aaron Chin, Seah Pei Hong, and Lee Wenfeng. Successful failure analysis using fault diagnosis tool and product characterization board in BiCMOS technology low yield investigation. In *Proceedings of the 20th IEEE International Symposium on the Physical and Failure Analysis of Integrated Circuits (IPFA)*, pages 624–627. IEEE, 2013.
50. Andreas Löfwenmark and Simin Nadjm-Tehrani. Fault and timing analysis in critical multi-core systems: A survey with an avionics perspective. *Journal of Systems Architecture*, 87:1–11, 2018.
51. Atul Maheshwari, Wayne Burleson, and Russell Tessier. Trading off transient fault tolerance and power consumption in deep submicron (DSM) VLSI circuits. *IEEE transactions on very large scale integration (VLSI) systems*, 12(3):299–311, 2004.
52. Sparsh Mittal. A survey of architectural techniques for managing process variation. *ACM Computing Surveys (CSUR)*, 48(4):1–29, 2016.
53. Keith S Morgan, Daniel L McMurtrey, Brian H Pratt, and Michael J Wirthlin. A comparison of TMR with alternative fault-tolerant design techniques for FPGAs. *IEEE transactions on nuclear science*, 54(6):2065–2072, 2007.
54. Serkan Ozdemir, Debjit Sinha, Gokhan Memik, Jonathan Adams, and Hai Zhou. Yield-aware cache architectures. In *2006 39th Annual IEEE/ACM International Symposium on Microarchitecture (MICRO'06)*, pages 15–25. IEEE, 2006.
55. Abu Saad Papa and Madhu Mutyam. Power management of variation aware chip multiprocessors. In *Proceedings of the 18th ACM Great Lakes symposium on VLSI*, pages 423–428, 2008.
56. Michael D. Powell, Arijit Biswas, Shantanu Gupta, and Shubhendu S. Mukherjee. Architectural core salvaging in a multi-core processor for hard-error tolerance. In *Proceedings of the 36th Annual International Symposium on Computer Architecture*, pages 93–104, 2009.

57. SJ Sangwine. Deductive fault diagnosis in digital circuits: a survey. *IEE Proceedings E (Computers and Digital Techniques)*, 136(6):496–504, 1989.
58. Smruti R Sarangi, Brian Greskamp, Radu Teodorescu, Jun Nakano, Abhishek Tiwari, and Josep Torrellas. Varius: A model of process variation and resulting timing errors for microarchitects. *IEEE Transactions on Semiconductor Manufacturing*, 21(1):3–13, 2008.
59. Selahattin Sayil. A survey of circuit-level soft error mitigation methodologies. *Analog Integrated Circuits and Signal Processing*, 99(1):63–70, 2019.
60. Ronald D Schrimpf and Daniel M Fleetwood. *Radiation effects and soft errors in integrated circuits and electronic devices*, volume 34. World Scientific, 2004.
61. Jared C Smolens, Brian T Gold, James C Hoe, Babak Falsafi, and Ken Mai. Detecting emerging wearout faults. In *Proceedings of the IEEE Workshop on Silicon Errors in Logic - System Effects*, pages 1–6, 2007.
62. Jayanth Srinivasan, Sarita V Adve, Pradip Bose, and Jude A Rivers. Exploiting structural duplication for lifetime reliability enhancement.   In *32nd International Symposium on Computer Architecture (ISCA'05)*, pages 520–531, 2005.
63. Charles H Stapper, Frederick M Armstrong, and Kiyotaka Saji. Integrated Circuit Yield Statistics. *Proceedings of the IEEE*, 71(4):453–470, 1983.
64. James Tschanz, Keith Bowman, Shih-Lien Lu, Paolo Aseron, Muhammad Khellah, Arijit Raychowdhury, Bibiche Geuskens, Carlos Tokunaga, Chris Wilkerson, Tanay Karnik, et al. A 45nm resilient and adaptive microprocessor core for dynamic variation tolerance. In *2010 IEEE International Solid-State Circuits Conference-(ISSCC)*, pages 282–283, 2010.
65. Julien Vial, Alberto Bosio, Patrick Girard, Christian Landrault, Serge Pravossoudovitch, and Arnaud Virazel. Using TMR architectures for yield improvement. In *2008 IEEE International Symposium on Defect and Fault Tolerance of VLSI Systems*, pages 7–15. IEEE, 2008.
66. Laung-Terng Wang, Cheng-Wen Wu, and Xiaoqing Wen. *VLSI test principles and architectures: design for testability*. Elsevier, 2006.
67. Nicholas J Wang and Sanjay J Patel. ReStore: Symptom-based soft error detection in microprocessors. *IEEE Transactions on Dependable and Secure Computing*, 3(3):188–201, 2006.
68. Wenping Wang, Shengqi Yang, Sarvesh Bhardwaj, Rakesh Vattikonda, Sarma Vrudhula, Frank Liu, and Yu Cao. The impact of NBTI on the performance of combinational and sequential circuits. In *Proceedings of the 44th annual Design Automation Conference*, pages 364–369, 2007.
69. Yih Wang, Uddalak Bhattacharya, Fatih Hamzaoglu, Pramod Kolar, Y Ng, Liqiong Wei, Ying Zhang, Kevin Zhang, and Mark Bohr. A 4.0 GHz 291Mb voltage-scalable SRAM design in 32nm high-κ metal-gate CMOS with integrated power management. In *2009 IEEE International Solid-State Circuits Conference-Digest of Technical Papers*, pages 456–457. IEEE, 2009.
70. Ying Wang, Yin-He Han, Lei Zhang, Bin-Zhang Fu, Cheng Liu, Hua-Wei Li, and Xiaowei Li. Economizing TSV resources in 3-d network-on-chip design. *IEEE Transactions on Very Large Scale Integration (VLSI) Systems*, 23(3):493–506, 2014.
71. Xiaoqing Wen, Tokiharu Miyoshi, Seiji Kajihara, Laung-Terng Wang, Kewal K Saluja, and Kozo Kinoshita.   On per-test fault diagnosis using the x-fault model.   In *IEEE/ACM International Conference on Computer Aided Design, 2004. ICCAD-2004*, pages 633–640. IEEE, 2004.
72. Dawen Xu, Kexin Chu, Cheng Liu, Ying Wang, Lei Zhang, and Huawei Li. CNT-cache: an energy-efficient carbon nanotube cache with adaptive encoding. In *2020 Design, Automation & Test in Europe Conference & Exhibition (DATE)*, pages 963–966. IEEE, 2020.
73. Dawen Xu, Zhuangyu Feng, Cheng Liu, Li Li, Ying Wang, Huawei Li, and Xiaowei Li. Taming process variations in CNFET for efficient last-level cache design. *IEEE Transactions on Very Large Scale Integration (VLSI) Systems*, 2021.
74. Dawen Xu, Li Li, Ying Wang, Cheng Liu, and Huawei Li. Exploring emerging CNFET for efficient last level cache design. In *Proceedings of the 24th Asia and South Pacific Design Automation Conference*, pages 426–431, 2019.

75. Qiang Xu, Li Jiang, Huiyun Li, and Bill Eklow. Yield enhancement for 3D-stacked ICs: Recent advances and challenges. In *17th Asia and South Pacific Design Automation Conference*, pages 731–737. IEEE, 2012.
76. Guihai Yan, Yinhe Han, and Xaiowei Li. Revivenet: A self-adaptive architecture for improving lifetime reliability via localized timing adaptation. *IEEE Transactions on Computers*, 60(9):1219–1232, 2011.
77. Guihai Yan, Yinhe Han, and Xiaowei Li. SVFD: A versatile online fault detection scheme via checking of stability violation. *IEEE transactions on very large scale integration (VLSI) systems*, 19(9):1627–1640, 2010.
78. Guihai Yan, Faqiang Sun, Huawei Li, and Xiaowei Li. CoreRank: redeeming yan2015corerank"Sick Silicon" by dynamically quantifying core-level healthy condition. *IEEE Transactions on Computers*, 65(3):716–729, 2015.
79. T Yano. Fast fault diagnostic method using fault dictionary for electron beam tester. In *Proc. IEEE Int. Test Conf.*, pages 561–565, 1987.
80. Jing Ye, Yu Huang, Yu Hu, Wu-Tung Cheng, Ruifeng Guo, Liyang Lai, Ting-Pu Tai, Xiaowei Li, Weipin Changchien, Daw-Ming Lee, et al. Diagnosis and layout aware (DLA) scan chain stitching. *IEEE Transactions on Very Large Scale Integration (VLSI) Systems*, 23(3):466–479, 2014.
81. Lei Zhang, Yinhe Han, Qiang Xu, Xiao wei Li, and Huawei Li. On topology reconfiguration for defect-tolerant NoC-based homogeneous manycore systems. *IEEE Transactions on Very Large Scale Integration (VLSI) Systems*, 17(9):1173–1186, 2009.

Chapter 2
Fault-Tolerant Circuits

Abstract With the scaling of semiconductor process technology, the performance of modern VLSI chips improves significantly. However, the aggressive technology scaling poses serious challenges to lifetime reliability. Two of the paramount challenges are soft errors and aging-driven lifetime reliability. Although many studies have been done to tackle the two challenges, most take them separately so far, thereby failing to reach better performance-cost trade-offs. To achieve an optimum performance-cost trade-off, we propose a unified fault detection scheme—stability violation-based fault detection (SVFD). Besides, since the performance of modern VLSI chips improves significant, the on-chip path delay measurement techniques have been gained many attentions for researchers in recent years, for it can provide a cost-effective alternative way to perform delay defect detection and silicon debug in modern VLSI chips. Furthermore, to help to reduce hardware overheads and delay measurement time for on-chip path delay measurement, we propose a novel on-chip path delay measurement architecture, OCDM, for path delay testing and silicon debug. Since paramount challenges come from a variety of aging mechanisms that can cause gradual performance degradation of circuits. Prior work shows that such progressive degradation can be reliably detected by dedicated aging sensors, which provides a good foundation for proposing a new scheme to improve lifetime reliability. Based on our previous researches, we further propose ReviveNet, a hardware-implemented aging-aware and self-adaptive architecture. Aging awareness is realized by deploying dedicated aging sensors, and self-adaptation is achieved by employing a group of synergistic agents. Each agent implements a localized timing adaptation mechanism to tolerate aging-induced delay on critical paths.

2.1 On-Line Fault Detection

In ultra-deep submicrometer technology, soft errors and device aging are two of the paramount reliability concerns. Although many studies have been done to tackle the two challenges, most take them separately so far, thereby failing to reach better performance-cost trade-offs. To support a more efficient design trade-off, we propose a unified fault detection scheme—stability violation-based fault detection (SVFD), by which the soft errors (both single event upset and single event transient), aging delay, and delay faults can be uniformly dealt with. SVFD grounds on a new fault model, stability violation, derived from analysis of signal behavior. SVFD has been validated by conducting a set of intensive Hspice simulations targeting the next-generation 32-nm CMOS technology. An application of SVFD to a floating-point unit (FPU) is also evaluated. Experimental results show that SVFD has more versatile fault detection capability for fault detection than several schemes recently proposed at comparable overhead in terms of area, power, and performance.

2.1.1   Challenges for On-Line Fault Detection

The advancement of the semiconductor technology in the following decade will bring a broad set of reliability challenges at a dramatic fast pace [33]. Two of the paramount challenges are soft errors and aging-driven lifetime reliability. Many researchers focused on soft error modeling and mitigation within a wide design spectrum: device level, circuit level [38, 53, 72], microarchitecture level [84], and software level [60]. In addition, the industry and academic communities have done much work on understanding the semiconductor device reliability failure mechanisms and models, such as Electromigration [2], negative bias temperature instability (NBTI) [13, 87, 91], time dependent dielectric breakdown (TDDB), hot carrier injection (HCI), temperature cycling [69] etc.

Aging failure prediction [8, 51] is a promising approach to cope with aging effects. Unlike soft errors, device aging is a gradual process, which makes the prediction of aging degree achievable. Before the devices totally breakdown and thereby lose their functionalities, they always tend to exhibit performance degradation, e.g. increased threshold voltage instability, soaring leakage power, worse heat characteristics etc. Most of these negative effects can result in the degradation of switch performance of the transistors[15], and eventually excessive path delay. In other words, most of the aging failures can be predicted by sensing the gradually increased aging delay. Agarwal et al. designed an aging sensor for this purpose [8].

On the other hand, semiconductor devices are becoming increasingly prone to soft errors (SEUs and SETs) as feature size decreases [75]. Abundant redundancy design solutions have been proposed to combat the soaring soft error rate, such as spatial redundancy by duplicating the flip-flops [55, 72], or temporal redundancy by multiple-sampling [62]. Even if the overhead imposed by these redundancy can be kept in check, these "redundancy" resources, however, help little in mitigating aging effects, and in contrast even speed up the aging process due to the extra heat generated by those redundancy resources. This dilemma makes the goal of providing a not only aging-resistant but also soft error-tolerant scheme hard to achieve, unless a cumbersome combination of the previous aging-sensor and redundancy-based approaches is conducted.

Rather than attempting to exploit such a cumbersome combination, we propose a unified mechanism to face the two challenges. Based on signal behavior analysis, we find that the soft errors and aging delay can converge into the same signal behavior: *Stability Violation* to the target circuits. Even the conventional delay faults, which could result from such as transition hazard, crosstalk, can be represented as stability violations. Hence, it is promising to propose a unified fault model and associated detection mechanism, thereby creating the chance of reaching a more optimum trade-off between detection capability, design complexity, and implementation overhead. To our knowledge, this is the first work to handle the soft errors, aging delay, and delay faults under a unified fault detection mechanism.

2.1.2 Stability Violation Based Fault Detection

The stability violation of a signal is defined as at least one transition happens in the time interval during which the signal should be kept stable. Setup time violation, which the progressive aging delay tends to contribute to, is a typical example of stability violation. Apparently, only coping with setup time violation is far from sufficient to handle soft errors and delay faults. In the rest of this Section, we will present how to comprehensively describe the rationale behind stability violation, and meanwhile how to generalize it to propose a unified fault model.

First, we specify the target fault types, and then move to the unified stability violation model and associated SVFD mechanism.

2.1.2.1 Target Fault Types

Soft Error *Single Event Upset* (SEU) and *Single Event Transient* (SET) [52]. If some high energy radioactive particles induce a storage cell to be flipped, this unintentional bit-flip is called SEU. If the particles cause a node of combinational logic to collect enough charge, a transient current pulse could be generated. This pulse can transform into a voltage pulse and propagate along logic paths [75]. This type of soft error is called SET. A soft error might not be captured by flip-flops due to three masking effects [75]: Logic Masking, Electrical Masking, and Latching-window Masking.

Aging Delay The aging effects, such as NBTI, can cause aging delay which can be used for aging-failure prediction[8]. Usually, the aging delay increasing is a gradual process over time, though the abrupt delay increasing is possible when the devices suffer from breakdown induced by mechanical stresses. This type of "abrupt" aging delay will not be covered in this chapter.

Delay Fault This type of faults refers to the conventional delay faults [25] which is caused by device defect, signal crosstalk, etc. We handles the delay faults with size less than the width of the Detection Slack.

2.1.2.2   Modeling Faulty Signals

Mathematically, a signal S can be expressed as a function of time t, expressed as $S = f(t)$. Given the time interval of (t_i, t_t) in which S gets into a stable state before t_t, this interval can be divided into two periods: *variable period* denoted by $T_{vp}^S = (t_i, t_s)$, and *stable period* by $T_{sp}^S = (t_s, t_t)$, where t_s is the complete time of the last transition of S within the specified interval. In addition, the initial value and the terminal value of the signal are expressed as $F_i^S = f(t_i)$ and $F_t^S = f(t_t)$, respectively.

According to the above definition, we define a faulty signal, S_f, that commits at least one of the three violations:

- Initial Value Violation (IVV): The obtained value of $F_i^{S_f}$ at time t_i differs with $f(t_i)$.
- Terminal Value Violation (TVV): The obtained value of $F_t^{S_f}$ at time t_t differs with $f(t_t)$.
- Stability Violation (SV): One or multiple transitions happen in the stable period.

The above violation behaviors, strictly speaking, can not precisely capture all details of signal mismatch between a fault-free signal and its faulty counterpart; However, the above violation definitions are actually robust enough to guide high efficient on-line fault detection, as the following presents. In fact, given the target fault types including soft errors, aging delay, and delay faults, only the stability violation of a signal is needed to be verified. The following explains how to use this model in a practical way.

First, the variable period T_{vp} and stable period T_{sp} for a specified signal need to be established. Figure 2.1 models a general logic circuit. The input signal S_i comes from the upstream flip-flop, and the output S_o is captured by the downstream flip-flop. Both flip-flops are synchronized by the same clock *clk* with cycle period of T. Several timing parameters are summarized below:

- t_{pd}: the propagation delay of the combinational logic;
- t_{cd}: the contamination delay (a.k.a. short-path delay) of the combinational logic;
- t_{cq}: the flip-flop's clock-to-q time.

Fig. 2.1 Generic logic circuit

The S_i gets updated only at every effective clock transition and is held for the whole cycle period, which means almost no variable period exists. Thus the variable period, and the stable period of S_i in the nth clock cycle $((n - 1)T, nT)$ can be expressed as:

Fig. 2.2 Variable period vs. stable period

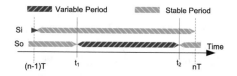

$$T_{vp}^{S_i} = ((n-1)T, \ (n-1)T + t_{cq}), \tag{2.1}$$

$$T_{sp}^{S_i} = ((n-1)T + t_{cq}, \ nT). \tag{2.2}$$

The variable period of S_o, unlike that of S_i, is much more prominent; the S_o's variable period and stable period in the nth clock cycle can be expressed as:

$$T_{vp}^{S_o} = ((n-1)T + t_{cq} + t_{cd}, \ (n-1)T + t_{cq} + t_{pd}) \tag{2.3}$$

$$T_{sp}^{S_o} = ((n-1)T + t_{cq} + t_{pd}, \ nT + t_{cq} + t_{cd}) \tag{2.4}$$

Figure 2.2 illustrates the time periods of both S_i and S_o in the nth cycle, where $t_1 = (n-1)T + t_{cq} + t_{cd}$, $t_2 = (n-1)T + t_{cq} + t_{pd}$.

With the defined time periods, we can explain how the target faults commit the above violations and, what's more, how these IVV and TVV converge to SV.

1. Suppose that a delay fault occurs, the delayed S_o will cause SV in Detection Slack (T_{DS}) during which the S_o should keep stable. Equivalently, the delay fault will result in S_o's TVV since at the end of the cycle, S_o can not reach the expected value. This TVV then causes the IVV of the signal in the next stage of logic. Hence, SV, TVV, and IVV are equivalent to each other for the delay fault.

2. Suppose that an aging delay occurs, the delayed S_o will cause SV in Guard Band (T_{GB}). Unlike the delay fault, the progressive aging delay will not cause TVV and IVV; therefore, an aging delay just represents as SV. Here the aging induced SV actually is quite similar to setup time violation.

3. Suppose that an unmasked SEU strikes the upstream flip-flop. Clearly, the S_i's SV is committed because, after transient clock-to-q time, S_i is supposed to keep stable during the whole cycle period. This SV could also potentially cause the downstream flip-flop to capture faulty data, and thereby results in S_o's TVV, then IVV of input signals in the next stage logic. So, the SEU will represent as SV, and possible IVV and TVV.

4. Suppose that an unmasked SET happens in the combinational logic. If the duration of the SET is less than $T_{DS} + T_{GB}$, the behavior of the SET fault is similar with the commonly referred delay faults: unexpected signal transitions within the S_o's stable period. Therefore, the analysis result for the delay faults also holds for SET faults. That is SV, TVV, and IVV are equivalently to each other for the SET.

From the above analysis we conclude that, from the signal behavior perspective, the target faults either induce equivalent SV, IVV, and TVV (for delay fault and

SET), or only represent as SV (for aging delay), or SV and possible equivalent IVV and TVV (for SEU). In other words, the target faults can be uniformly modeled as SV. The implication is that we can employ a unified stability checker to handle the detection for all of the target faults. This unification can potentially support a more efficient implementation of the online fault detection scheme than the traditional redundancy-based approaches such as [38, 72]. In addition, the capability for aging failure prediction [8, 51] can be exploited in place with the same scheme; thereby greatly facilitating the aging-aware designs.

2.1.3   Timing Constrains Exploration

The object of SVFD in essence is to distinguish those transitions violating the signals' stability specification from normal signal transitions, thereby achieving the goal of fault detection. The detection of SV can be accomplished with some kind of stability checkers.

2.1.3.1   Propagation of Stability Violation

The stability checkers are usually implemented with dynamic circuit style. So, the first concern is how to schedule the precharge period. Neither the traditional cycle-begin precharge (using the first half cycle period to precharge) nor cycle-end precharge (using the second half cycle period to precharge) styles are applicable in our detection mechanism. The checker should be on duty during the *Guard Band* in aging delay detection and the *Detection Slack* in traditional delay fault detection according to [8] instead of staying in precharge state. Given S_o with prominent variable period, the precharge can be scheduled in the variable period. However, the same schedule strategy is unallowable for S_i because there is almost no any variable period can be exploited for precharge. If we "brutally" borrow some time from S_i's stable period for precharging the checker, the fault coverage has to be sacrificed.

To address this problem, we find if the precharge stage is scheduled according to some specific timing requirements, the fault coverage will not be compromised. The discussion about timing manipulations can be started with describing a key observation, called **Propagation of Stability Violation**.

Suppose that an unmasked SEU occurs in an upstream flip-flop at time t in the nth cycle, then the effects of the SV of S_i should be propagated to S_o within the time interval of $(t + t_{cd}, \ t + t_{pd})$. If the effects of S_i's SV can propagate into S_o's stable period, that is

$$(t + t_{cd}, \ t + t_{pd}) \subset (nT - T_{GB}, nT + T_{DS}), \tag{2.5}$$

Then the SEU induced S_i's SV can be represented as S_o's SV since the S_o should keep stable during the *Guard Band* and *Detection Slack*. Hence, the checker deployed to detect S_o's SV can indirectly handle a part of S_i's SV within a particular time interval, referred to **Propagation Detectable Period (PDP)**. From (2.5), we have

$$\begin{cases} t + t_{cd} > nT - T_{GB}, \\ t + t_{pd} < nT + T_{DS}. \end{cases}$$

Then, the PDP can be expressed as

$$\{t \mid nT - T_{GB} - t_{cd} < t < nT + T_{DS} - t_{pd}\}. \tag{2.6}$$

2.1.3.2   XOR Protection

Not all unmasked SEUs occurring in the upstream flip-flop can translate into the S_o's SV; for example, if a S_i's SV happened during the $((n-1)T, \ t_1)$ (Fig. 2.2), then it could not be detected by S_o's checker because (2.5) dose not hold in such case.

To cover this period, one way is to set another stability checker for S_i, at the expense of almost doubled area and power overhead. In contrast, we propose a simple but far more efficient way to cover this period, referred to *XOR Protection*, as Fig. 2.3 shows. The effectiveness of this scheme is based on the observation: the $S_o^{(K-1)}$ is consistent with the S_i^K within the period of $((n-1)T, \ (n-1)T+t_{cq}+t_{cd})$; therefore, one XOR (or NXOR) gate is capable of capturing any S_i^K stability violation during this span of time. The overhead imposed by an XOR gate is much less than that imposed by another stability checker or other traditional redundant

Fig. 2.3 XOR protection

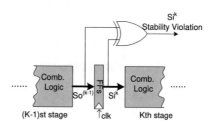

flip-flop based schemes [72]. How to efficiently handle the output of XOR will be presented in next section.

2.1.3.3 SEU Detection "Blind Zone"

The above timing constrains are still not comprehensive without taking another time interval called "blind zone" into account. Considering the propagation delay of a SEU, we can claim that the SEU must be benign if

$$t > nT - t_{cd}. \tag{2.7}$$

To protect S_i (from SEUs), besides the XOR protection period, the PDP, and the benign period, there might be the fourth region that has not be covered so far. Figure 2.4 shows that the whole Stable Period of S_i could be divided into four or three zones, depending on different timing parameters. Specifically, Fig. 2.4a shows if $nT + T_{DS} - t_{pd} < nT - t_{cd}$, then a SEU occurring in the interval of $(nT + T_{DS} - t_{pd}, nT - t_{cd})$ may fail to propagate into the detectable period, thereby resulting in detection "Blind Zone". Unlike the XOR protection period, this trouble can not be eliminated unless another dedicated stability checker is set for S_i, at considerable expense of implementation overhead. Fortunately, we propose a new approaches: Contamination Delay Optimization, by which the "Blind Zone" can be eliminated by some timing manipulations.

Contamination Delay Optimization Clearly, the "Blind Zone" can be naturally eliminated if

$$nT - t_{cd} < nT + T_{DS} - t_{pd} \tag{2.8}$$

is satisfied, as Fig. 2.4b illustrates. The SEU happening in $(nT - T_{GB} - t_{cd}, nT + T_{DS} - t_{pd})$ is either propagated into a Stability Violation detectable zone of

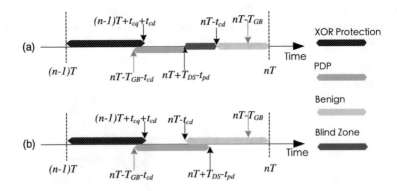

Fig. 2.4 Variety of timing period for S_i

corresponding S_o, or has nothing detrimental effect due to residing in benign period. From (2.8), we derive the contamination delay should meet

$$t_{cd} > t_{pd} - T_{DS} \tag{2.9}$$

In addition, given that the terminal time of XOR protection zone should meet

$$nT - T_{GB} - t_{cd} < (n-1)T + t_{cd} + t_{cq};$$

otherwise another "blind zone" would emerge; thus, we have

$$t_{cd} > \frac{1}{2}(T - T_{GB} - t_{cq}). \tag{2.10}$$

Lastly, considering $T_{DS} < t_{cq} + t_{cd}$ should always holds, that is

$$t_{cd} > T_{DS} - t_{cq}. \tag{2.11}$$

From (2.9), (2.10), and (2.11), we derive that t_{cd} should meet the requirement:

$$t_{cd} > \max\{t_{pd} - T_{DS}, \ \frac{1}{2}(T - T_{GB} - t_{cq}), \ T_{DS} - t_{cq}\} \tag{2.12}$$

Generally, (2.12) requires the contamination delay of the combinational logic reaches up to about a half cycle period. The same requirement is needed to be satisfied in some previous studies [55] to address "short path effects" [63]. Actually, It is consistent with the goal of many timing optimization strategies [11, 73], and therefore not a substantial limitation.

2.1.3.4 Available Precharge Period

Figure 2.4b sheds light on when the precharge can be scheduled: within $(nT - T_{GB} - t_{cd}, \ nT - T_{GB})$ the precharge can be conducted without sacrificing fault coverage. Additionally, to avoid the precharge intruding Detection Slack, the actual available start point of the precharge stage should be

$$\max\{nT - T_{GB} - t_{cd}, \ (n-1)T + T_{DS}\}; \tag{2.13}$$

therefore, the available precharge period is

$$(\max\{nT - T_{GB} - t_{cd}, \ (n-1)T + T_{DS}\}, \ nT - T_{GB}). \tag{2.14}$$

From (2.14), the available precharge duration τ can be calculated by

$$\tau = \begin{cases} t_{cd} & \text{if } t_{cd} < T - T_{GB} - T_{DS}, \\ T - T_{DS} - T_{GB} & \text{otherwise.} \end{cases}$$

To sustain normal operations, there is a minimum precharge duration τ_0, which is determined by the intrinsic RC constant. Clearly, $\tau > \tau_0$ needs to be satisfied. It is not difficult to meet this requirement. Experimental results show that for 65 nm CMOS, 1 GHz, τ_0 is merely 40 ps, while τ is at the magnitude of hundreds of picoseconds. More detail can be found in next Section.

To sum up, we can use only one stability checker, with the assistant XOR protection, for soft errors, aging delay, and delay faults detection for S_i and S_o. All we have to do is to ensure (2.12) and (2.14).

As the end of this section, the following exemplifies an empirical analysis of the above constrains.

Example Generally, T_{DS} is determined by the maximum width of SET pulses, commonly conservatively being set to a half cycle period, that is $T_{DS} = 0.5 \times T$. T_{GB} originally is determined by the aging detection interval—the time interval between two aging detection action (the aging sensor does not need to be always on). T_{GB} is much larger than 5% of cycle period, as suggested by [8], but should be less (or not much larger) than the reserved timing margin. Since commonly 10% timing margin is reserved to combat PVT variations, the cycle period dose not need to be increased to reserve extra time margin for T_{GB}. The propagation delay t_{pd} hence is $T \times (1 - 10\%) = 0.9T$. We omit the term of t_{cq} because comparing with other timing parameters, t_{cq} is marginal. Then, based on (2.12) we need to figure out the minimal t_{cd} since smaller t_{cd} implies that smaller compensation effort and associated area overhead to pay. We suggest use the results: $t_{cd} = 0.45T$, $T_{DS} = 0.45T$, $T_{GB} = 0.09T$ because this configuration is competent enough in detecting SET faults, delay faults, and aging delays with modest compensation effort.

2.1.4   On-Line Fault Detection Architecture

Figure 2.5a shows the top view of the whole fault detection scheme. Note that the XOR (NXOR actually) output needs to be gated outside of the XOR protection period where an XOR-flagged alarm can unintentionally discharge the detection unit if leave un-gated. The detailed timing relations and associate clock configurations is shown in Fig. 2.5b, where CLKS is used to control precharge-evaluation, and CLKG is the gating clock for XOR output.

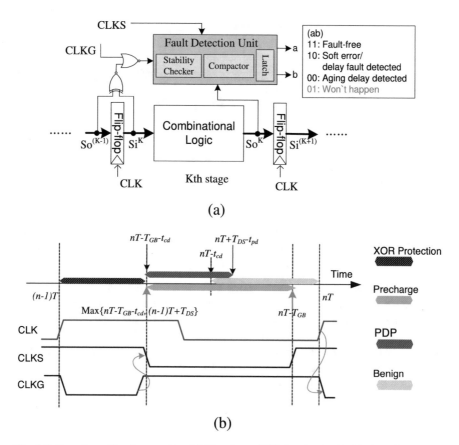

Fig. 2.5 Top view of implementation. (**a**) Top view of SVFD scheme. (**b**) Timing of precharge clock and XOR-protection gating clock

2.1.4.1   Circuit Design

Figure 2.6 shows the transistor level design of SVFD scheme. A detection unit consists of two key components: a stability checker (Fig. 2.6b) and an output compactor (Fig. 2.6c).

The basic stability checker can be derived from a sensing circuit for on-line delay fault detection [25], in which the signal integrity is verified by a pair of consistent charge/discharge nodes, a delay fault will trigger one of the nodes to be discharged/chargeed and thereby causes states inconsistent between them. The same fundamental detection principle is employed to design a sensor dedicated for aging prediction, referred as Aging Resistant Stability Checker (ARSC) [8]. Based on the same principle, we design a new stability checker. Compared with ARSC, the checker has several new features which can improve the robustness and reduce the overhead. The following explains how does the circuit work and then presents the new features.

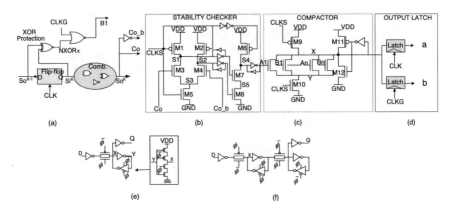

Fig. 2.6 SVFD implementation. (**a**) Host circuit and XOR protection. (**b**) Stability checker. (**c**) Cehcker outputs Compactor. (**d**) Output latch. (**e**) Latch. (**f**) Flip-flop

During precharge period, both nodes $S1$ and $S2$ in the stability checker are charged up to HIGH. Then, the circuit starts evaluation, one of the two nodes is pulled down, while the other one floats at HIGH because the gate signal of M3 is always complemented with that of M4 (a weak keeper can help the floated node stick to HIGH). Hence, the node $S1$ and $S2$ are always exclusive during fault-free time, which will make the node $S4$ stick to HIGH because the high-impedance path between S4 and GND always exists. When a Stability Violation is committed by S_i (out of the XOR protection period) or S_o, the violation will trigger the discharge of the node that has charged up to HIGH. Eventually both nodes are discharged, and thereby the node S4 is pull down to LOW. Then, the node X in output compactor will be discharged, which flags a fault being detected. The compacted result X needs to be latched twice: CLK-latched for indicating aging delay and CLKG-latched for indicating soft error or delay fault (Fig. 2.6d). The reason will be explained in Sect. 2.1.5.1.

There are two new features in the detection unit:

1. The NOR logic for combining the states of S1 and S2 is realized with a dynamic logic (M6, M7, and M8), which can improve the robustness of the checker and reduce the area overhead and switch power dissipation. Unlike the stability checker in ARSC [8], where the checker output, a static NOR gate, is directly driven by a floated HIGH node during fault-free time, our checker's output is generated by a dynamic NAND gate. This change is based on that both the node S1 and S2 are pulled up to HIGH during precharge, and consequently both M7 and M8 are turned off; thereby no short path existing when precharge. So the foot transistor for the dynamic NAND is eliminated. Note that due to the precharge RC delay of S1 and S2, the M6's precharge clock should be delayed by a precharge delay constant to avoid transient shot current in the NAND gate.
2. The outputs are compacted with a dynamic NOR for reducing the number of output latches. Usually, it is not necessary to identify which signals commits the

SV for most aging-aware and fault tolerant designs. So the distributed detection results can be "compacted" to reduce the number of output latches. We use a wide dynamic NOR to implement the compactor, in which the M11 and M12 serve as a level restorer for node X.

2.1.4.2 Low-Overhead Deployment

Given a target circuit, each output signal S_o needs to be monitored by a stability checker whose output is fed to a compactor, as Fig. 2.5a shows. In addition, each XOR-protected signal gated by CLKG is also fed to a compactor. We present two deploying techniques to reduce the overhead coming from the checkers, compactors, and latches.

Compacting S_o Using XOR-Trees With XOR-Trees, we can enable checker-sharing mechanism among multiple output signals, as Fig. 2.7a shows, thereby

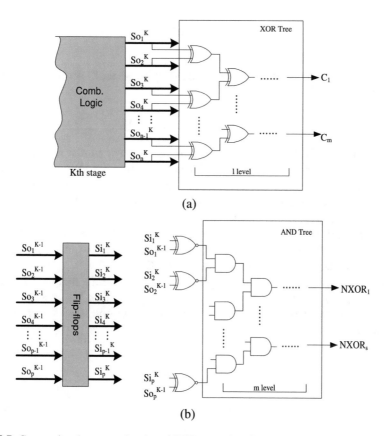

Fig. 2.7 Compacting the output signals and XOR-protection signals. (**a**) XOR tree. (**b**) AND tree

reducing the number of checkers. The rationale behind the XOR-Trees based compactor is the fact that for a XOR gate the non-simultaneous transitions of inputs can result in output transitions. This can be explained with the following example:

Suppose there are two signals S_a and S_b, and signal $C = S_a \text{XOR} S_b$; clearly, one or two non-simultaneous transitions of S_a and S_b can be exactly represented as or two transitions of C. This fact implies that if S_a or S_b imposes stability violations, then C must commit stability violations, too.

One side effect of XOR-Trees is that the compactor may hide some faults that happen to induce simultaneous transitions on the primary inputs of a XOR-Tree. For example, if S_a happens to switch from HIGH to LOW, while at the same time S_b from LOW to HIGH, then C may keep staying at HIGH. Fortunately, the possibility of such negative cancellation effect can be minimized by separating the S_o from the same logic cone to different XOR-Trees, since it is rare for multiple faults happen in the same spot at the same time, especially for soft errors.

Figure 2.7a illustrates an application of a set of XOR-Trees which compacts n output signals $So_1^K, So_2^K, \ldots, So_n^K$ into m checker-monitored signals $C_1, C_2, \ldots, C_m$. We have

$$m = \frac{n}{2^l}. \tag{2.15}$$

The number of required XOR-gate used to implement an XOR-Tree can be easily calculated by

$$N_{xor} = n \times (1 - (1/2)^l). \tag{2.16}$$

Compacting S_i Using AND-Trees The similar strategy can be used to compact the XOR-protection results with AND-Trees. If one or more SEUs strike the set of flip-flops, then corresponding inputs of the set of AND-Trees will be pulled down to LOW, and then pull down the outputs of corresponding AND-Trees, denoted by NXORx in Fig. 2.7b.

Unlike XOR-Trees for compacting output signals, AND-Trees won't suffer form the cancellation effect because one or more SEUs yield the same effect: pulling down the corresponding AND-Tree's output to LOW.

With the two deployment optimizations, we can derive the number of required checkers $N_{checker}$, compactors $N_{compactor}$, and output latches N_{latch}. Suppose for a circuit with n flip-flops, l-level XOR-Trees and m-level AND-Trees are employed, then we have

$$N_{checker} = \frac{n}{2^l}; \tag{2.17}$$

$$N_{compactor} = \frac{n}{BW}(\frac{1}{2^m} + \frac{1}{2^l}), \tag{2.18}$$

where BW (bandwidth) is the number of input signals of a compactor;

$$N_{latch} = 2N_{compactor}. \tag{2.19}$$

Timing Implication of XOR-Trees and AND-Trees The delay implication of the AND-Tree and XOR-Tree should be considered. The CLKG has to be postponed to accommodate the delay of the AND-Tree, denoted by t_{and}. The CLKS should also be postponed by the delay of $\min\{t_{and}, t_{xor}\}$, where t_{xor} denotes the delay of the XOR-Tree. The impact of the two delays is the increased detection latency. In the worst-case, the detection unit needs extra $\max\{t_{and}, t_{xor}\}$ time to complete, but this increase in latency will not substantially impair the effectiveness of the fault detection as long as output latch time is also postponed accordingly. Specifically, the first latch's clock CLK (Note, not the main flip-flop clock) is delayed by $\max\{t_{and}, t_{xor}\}$ and the second latch's clock CLKG by t_{and}.

Of course, one should also keep the delay of the AND-Trees and XOR-Trees from being the new critical paths in the target circuit. The empirical analysis of delay can be achieved based on classical logic effort theory [32]. Empirically, given a m-level AND-tree (each logic gate is two-input), the path logic effort is $(4/3)^m$; the path electric effort is $5/4$ because the load of the output signal is only a NOR gate. Then the path effort is $(4/3)^m \times 5/4$. The path parasitic delay is $2m$. Hence, the minimum delay D_{and_min} can be given by

$$D_{and\_min} = m \times ((4/3)^m \times 5/4)^{1/m} + 2m \tag{2.20}$$

Based on (2.20), we find the optimized AND-Tree delay is a quasi-linear function of m. For a 3-level AND-Tree, the delay is about 2 Fo4, even for a up to 10-level AND-Tree, the delay does not exceed 7 Fo4.

For an XOR-Tree with the same levels, the minimum delay D_{xor_min} is about $3D_{and\_min}$ because the logic effort for an XOR gate is three times larger than that of an XOR gate [32]. Therefore, the delay constraint on the XOR-Trees will be much stringent than that on the AND-Trees. Given the $10\sim18$ Fo4 clock period of today's pipelined processors [86], for example, the maximum level of each XOR-Tree should be no more than four levels.

A major drawback to adopting such AND-Trees and XOR-Trees is the degraded detection resolution—when a checker flag an alarm, we can not precisely identity the fault spot in the target circuit because the AND-Trees and XOR-Trees can exponentially expend the "region-under-control" of a specified fault detection unit. However, this issue is trivial since we only focus on efficient fault detection—which serves as the primary step for most backward error recovery schemes.

2.1.4.3 Clock Variation Consideration

The delayed clocks can be generated from locally delaying the system clock CLK, as prior work [8] did, or obtained from a DLL. To ease the implementation worry, the following cites some industry data to show that generating the clocks with well-defined intentional skew should not be a substantial problem. DLLs have been widely used to reduce the clock skew across clock domains [41, 58, 93]. The detailed design of a DLL is beyond the scope of this book. Many industry practices have shown that implementing clocks with only 10-picosecond skew is practical. For example, even in conventional tree-based clock networks across $500\,mm^2$ processor die with frequency up to 2.5 GHz, the unintended clock skew can be efficiently limited to less than 10 ps [23]. While previous study [8] shows that a reasonable T_{GB} is usually around 100 ps for a 1 GHz system. Therefore, generating the CLK, CLKS, and CLKG with well-defined intentional skew should not be a substantial problem. The sophisticated variation-resilient clocking scheme is beyond the scope of this book.

Another practice, Razor II [19], can also back up the feasibility of clocks used in SVFD. Razor II also relies on strict clocks. An auxiliary clock, called DC, is employed. The deployment of CLKG in our SVFD scheme is not harder than that of DC in Razor II scheme. Hence, we believe that implementing the supportive clocks is practical.

2.1.5 Experiment Result Analysis

The experiments consist of two parts. The first is dedicated for evaluating a basic fault detection unit in terms of detailed timing verification, area overhead, power, and performance. The results are obtained by using the Hspice targeting the next-generation 32 nm Predictive Technology Model [89] for High-performance applications. The second shows an application to a fully pipelined FPU, with emphasis on analysis of chip-level area and power overhead and comparisons with other solutions.

2.1.5.1 Evaluating SVFD Unit

Figure 2.8 shows the detail timing of a SVFD unit in consecutive five cycles. The topmost shows the system clock CLK, the precharge-evaluation clock CLKS, with which the guard-band defined. The second shows the monitored signals S_o. The third illustrates the XOR-protection signal and corresponding gating clock. The fourth shows the state transitions of the two most important internal node S1 and S2. The fifth shows the signals A1—the output of the stability checker, and B1—the gated output of XOR protection unit. Both are fed to the same compactor. The bottom most shows the detection result generated by the compactor.

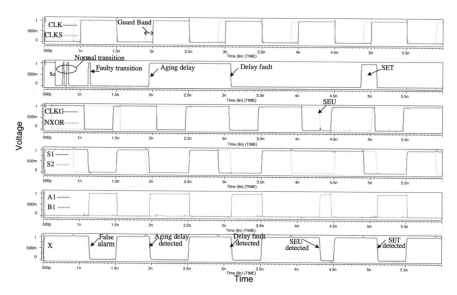

Fig. 2.8 Hspice simulated signal state transitions

During the first cycle (0–1 ns), S_o presents some normal transitions. In the first half of the second cycle (1–1.5 ns), an unexpected glitch, which is supposed to simulate a benign SET fault, occurs; then in the guard band of the second cycle, an aging delay is simulated. A delay fault is simulated in the third cycle. In the fourth cycle, a SEU fault is simulated by pulling down the NXOR signal.

From the bottom figure, we can see that all the SV shown in the second and third waveforms are successfully detected, represented by LOW state of node X.

We zoom in the figure to extract some useful timing information (the zoomed figures are omitted due to space limitation): (1) the critical precharge time τ_0 is about 40 ps, while the available precharge time is about 400 ps—one order of magnitude larger than τ_0. Hence, the precharge time will not be a limitation when we manipulate the related timings. (2) The detection delay is just about 40 ps which is merely 2 Fo4 delay in 32 nm technology. (3) The maximum undetectable glitch width is about 18 ps, which is even less than most soft error induce glitch width in 32 nm technology, so the robustness of SET detection should not be in question.

Table 2.1 shows the tradeoff comparisons between SEFF [72], LOWCOST [55], ARSC [8], CSWPFF [17], and SVFD. we use the number of transistors as the area overhead metric, as many circuit-level studies adopted.

To conduct comparisons between variety schemes, a baseline latch and flip-flop design needs to be determined. Figure 2.6e and f shows the adopted baseline design. The similar latch design is used by Intel as a standard datapath latch [45]. The flip-flops is used in PowerPC603 processor [28]. In addition, an XOR gate consumes at least 12 transistors when computing the number of transistors (eight transistors for the core XOR logic and another four for generating the inverter versions of

Table 2.1 Comparing Tradeoffs with other schemes

Overhead	SEFF[72]	LOWCOST [55]	ARSC [8]	CWSPFF [17]	SVFD
Transistor	14	36	24	46	36
Power	1.00	>1.00	>0.10[b]	N/A	1.16
performance	0	N/A	<1%	<1%	<1%
Clock	1	2	2	2	3
Applicability	Limited[a]	Limited	General	General	General

N/A: Not applicable

[a] The scheme needs support from a specific scannable flip-flop

[b] ARSC uses a different metric of power overhead

input signals). For fairness, only the checker and its input generating logics are considered; the subcomponents that can be shared among checkers (i.e. output compactor, and output latches) are not taken into account though such amortization will make the area overhead of SVFD more attractive.

Area As Table 2.1 indicates, SEFF is most economic scheme in term of area overhead; however, this benefit has to be based on a dedicated scannable flip-flop design in which each functional flip-flop has a replica, called shadow flip-flop, to support scan test. This heavy reliance on the specific scannable flip-flop, though greatly facilitate an area-efficient design, limits the applicability of SEFF, since not all designs use the same design-for-test techniques and implementation. LOWCOST can be regarded as a mutation of SEFF, but with a delay between the functional flip-flops and its' shadow counterpart. Thus, LOWCOST face the same issue of limited applicability. Clearly, if the shadow flip-flops are treated as overhead transistors, then the total transistors overhead must be much higher than that shown in Table 2.1.

Power We use a relative power penalty R_p to evaluate the power:

$$R_p = \frac{\text{Power of a detection unit}}{\text{Power of a flip-flop}}. \tag{2.21}$$

We compare the power of the detection unit against that of a standard flip-flop, respectively, with the same input signal and frequency. The input signal changes value every cycle. The Hspice results show that the stability checker is relatively power-hungry—16% higher than the power of a flip-flop. This is mainly because the checker is implemented with dynamic circuit style. The Compactor logic, however, is much power-saving—a 8-input compactor only consumes 40% power of a flip-flop; this because when fault-free, all input signals fed to a compactor won't discharge it. The power of output latches even drop to only 10% of a flip-flop because there no state transition happens to the latch during fault-free state, thus no dynamic power consumed.

As for other solutions, SEFF's power is doubled ($R_p = 1$), as [72] shows, since a redundancy flip-flop is enabled. Similar modification is conducted in LOWCOST, and moreover an extra lath is employed; hence the power of LOWCOST must be slightly larger than that of SEFF ($R_p > 1$).

Note that our checker seems much more power-hungry than ARSC. That is because the power overhead metric in [8] is different with ours. In ARSC, the power overhead is calculated as the whole logic (include both the flip-flop and combinational logic) power increase. Because the combinational logic's power is relatively constant, so the actual sensor power consumption compared with a flip-flop should be much higher.

Performance The performance mainly depends on the flip-flops time overhead and the critical path delay. In SVFD, there is no modification to the flip-flops and the critical path is not changed as well. The only timing penalty results from several extra gate capacitances drived by the S_i and S_o. Our experiment result shows this penalty is less than 1% for a special combinational logic: 8-inverter chain. In fact, the other SEFF, LOWCOST, ARSC, and CWSPFF face the same situation, but no one get hurt from it.

Clock We compare the number of clock (phase) used by these schemes. For example, SEFF dose not need any extra clock; LOWCOST, ARSC, CWSPFF, need one extra clock skewed with respect to the system clock. while SVFD needs two extra clocks: CLKS and CLKG. This is a negative attribute of SVFD since the extra clocks could potentially increase the complexity; as a tradeoff, however, the SVFD's detection capability is the most versatile over the other four schemes according to the comparison in Table 2.2.

Applicability The SEFF and LOWCOST need the support from a particular type of scannable flip-flop, but the other three schemes do not suffer from this limit.

2.1.5.2 Case Study: An Application of SVFD

We use a case study to demonstrate the main considerations when deploying SVFD, with emphasizing on area and power implications.

The pipelined FPU adopted by OpenSPARC T1 [79] is used as our target circuit which implements the SPARC V9 floating-point instructions and supports all IEEE 754 floating-point data types. The FPU comprises three independent pipelines: Multiplier pipeline (MUL), Adder pipeline (ADD) and Divider pipeline (DIV). More design details can be found in [79].

The FPU was synthesized using Synopsys Design Compiler with UMC 0.18um technology, with performance as the synthesizing priority.

Experimental Setup First, several timing parameters are determined. Specifically,

- The cycle period T is defined according to t_{pd}; given 10% margin reserved, $T = 10/9 \times t_{pd}$. The critical path delay (t_{pd}) reported by PrimeTime is 1.7 ns, so $T = 1.87$ ns.
- The clock-to-q time t_{cq} depends heavily on a specific flip-flop design and technology. Given 180 nm technology for the design in Fig. 2.6f, t_{cq} is about 110 ps; Thus, we get $t_{cq} = 0.06T$.
- Next, t_{cd}, $T_D S$, and T_{GB} needs to be determined. We prefer minimize t_{cd} since larger t_{cd} implies more path compensation area needed to pay, while check whether T_{DS} and T_{GB} meets the common requirement, for example, $T_{DS} \approx 0.5T$ and $T_{GB} > 0.05T$ [8, 55]. From (2.12), we figure out the minimal t_{cd} is 0.79 ns (0.43T), at which $T_{GB} = 0.095T$, $T_{DS} = 0.48T$. Then, we check out that T_{GB} indeed meets the requirement: larger than $0.05T$ while less than timing margin (0.1T). T_{DS}, however, is slightly smaller than $0.5T$; considering such minor mismatch won't impose any substantial problem for delay fault and SET detection, we prefer to keep $T_{DS} = 0.48$ while paying the minimal path compensation overhead.

Second, at register transfer level (RTL), we integrated parts of the SVFD infrastructure—the XOR-Protection, XOR-Trees, AND-Trees—into the target FPU. It is difficult to integrate corresponding stability checkers and compactors because these logic are highly custom dynamic logic at transistor-level; however, since we focus on overhead evaluation, so this difficulty can also be resolved in an "indirect" way. The area overhead imposed by these dynamic logic is estimated based on the data in Table 2.1. The short-path compensation is realized by imposing a timing constraints when conducting RTL synthesis. After the compensation process, we conduct the post-simulation to verify pipelines functionality and timing.

Third, we use PrimePower (a gate-level power simulation and analysis tool provided by Synopsys for power evaluation. The modified FPU are exercised with random input operands for 100,000 cycle, at the same time, dump the according VCD (Value Change Dump) format data for power evaluation. The power of checkers and compactors are still evaluated with Hspice. We wrote a C++ program to convert the output of the XOR-Trees and AND-Trees (VCD format) into PWL voltage sources which are recognizable for Hspice version checker and compactor to conduct a transistor-level power evaluation. Then, the Hspice-reported power is scaled to fit PrimePower-reported power based on R_p, thereby obtaining the overall power consumption.

Experimental Results The configurable parameters are (1) the level of XOR-Tree (L_{xor}), (2) the level of AND-Tree (L_{and}), and (3) the bandwidth of the compactor (BW). We first study the overhead at the tentative configuration: $L_{xor} = 3$, $L_{and} = 3$, $BW = 8$, and then seek to optimize it. Figure 2.9 shows the corresponding experimental results.

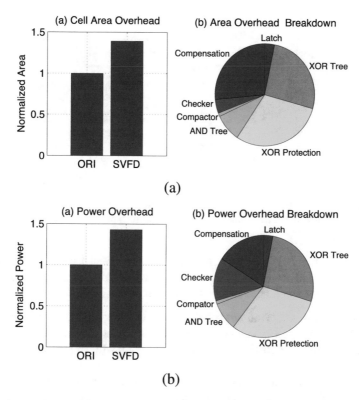

Fig. 2.9 Area and power with configuration: $L_{xor} = 3$, $L_{and} = 3$, $BW = 8$. (**a**) Area overhead and associated overhead breakdown. (**b**) Power overhead and associated overhead breakdown

Figure 2.9a compares the SVFD's area, denoted by SVFD, against that of the original FPU, denoted by ORI. The total cell area overhead is about 40%. This overhead comes from (1) compensating the short path to meet the t_{cd} requirement, (2) the stability checkers and associated compactors and latches, (3) the AND-Trees and XOR-Trees, and (4) the XOR-gates for XOR protection. Among these breakdowns of area overhead, "compensation" and "XOR Protection" are constant for a given target circuit because the former is determined by the minimal contamination delay and the later by the number of flip-flops; however, the other portions are configuration-specific. The corresponding power implication is shown in Fig. 2.9b. The overall power overhead is 43%. In addition, two significant implications, which can guide to a more efficient configuration, can be drawn from these results:

1. The checker's area and power are unproportionate: 4% area overhead contributing to 14% power penalty. Hence, reducing the number of checkers should be an effective way to optimize the overall power penalty.

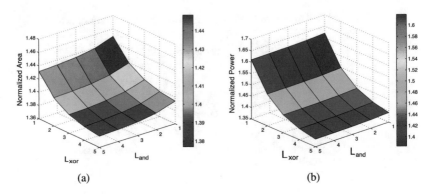

Fig. 2.10 Implication of L_{xor} and L_{and} on area and power, $BW = 8$. (**a**) Implication of L_{xor} and L_{and} on area overhead. (**b**) Implication of L_{xor} and L_{and} on power overhead

2. Increasing the BW of compactors has very marginal benefit to reducing the overall area and power since the area and power of the compactors and associated output latches together take only 4% and 3%, respectively.

One way to reduce the number of checkers is to adopt the XOR-Trees with higher levels. The same strategy can be considered to optimize the overhead imposed by AND-Trees. Figure 2.10 shows the overhead trends with different L_{xor} and L_{and} configurations.

The first perception gained from this figure is the power issue is much more crucial than the area issue: the worst-case power penalty can reach up to $1.62\times$ while the area is only $1.45\times$. In addition, the headroom for area optimization is limited comparing with that of power optimization. Hence, prioritizing the power optimization should be much effective for reaching an optimum design tradeoff. In SVFD scheme, power optimization actually does not conflict with area optimization.

Second, both the area and power trends are more sensitive to L_{xor} than to L_{and}. In particular, as Fig. 2.10b shows, the impact of L_{and} to the power is almost negligible. Note that although increasing L_{xor} and L_{and} seems facilitate more area- and power-efficient deployment, we should keep the delay implication of the XOR-Tree and AND-Tree in mind. For the pipelined FPU implemented with 180 nm technology, the T is about 17 Fo4 (≈ 1.9 ns/110 ps). We suggest configuring the XOR-Tree with fours levels, and the AND-Tree with five levels. With this configuration, the following will compare SVFD with several recently proposed solutions from cell area and power aspects.

2.1.5.3 Comparison with Other Schemes

Figure 2.11 gives the comparison results. SCAN denotes the scannable version of the original pipeline. In SCAN, all pipeline flip-flops are substituted by a scannable flip-flops in [72]. DMR represents the traditional dual-module-redundancy (we

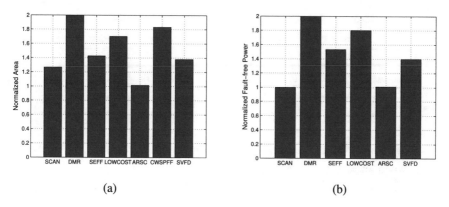

Fig. 2.11 Comparison with other solutions in terms of cell area and power, $L_{xor} = 4$, $L_{and} = 5$, $BW = 8$

simply double the original area and power to show DMR's overhead implication. In fact, for any meaningful DMR, other synchronous overhead such as output comparison should be also imposed). SEFF is implemented by substituting the scannable flip-flops for a self-checking flip-flops [72]. LOWCOST is substitute the scannable flip-flops with another modified flip-flops in which the clock of shadow flip-flop is skewed from that of the functional flip-flops; in addition, an output latch is also inserted [55]. CWSPFF is also based on a slightly modified DFF and additional Equivalence checker, another shared logic whose overhead can be amortized by the other logics [17], but even we neglect the amortizable logics, we believe that this solution is also not overhead-economic, given the results indicated in Table 2.1. ARSC is dedicated for only aging delay detection [8].

Figure 2.11a shows different total cell area required to deploy these solutions. In which, ARSC presets to be the most area-economic, this mainly because the ARSC logic only need to be deployed in the timing critical portions in terms of aging delay detection. The same reason, combined with the fact that the ARSC logic does not need to be always-on, makes the chip-level power overhead of ARSC negligible [8], as "ARSC" bar in Fig. 2.11b shows.

We bar SCAN in Fig. 2.11 is not because it can facilitate some fault detection or recovery (actually it incapable for any fault detection), but it can be viewed as the foundation of SEFF and LOWCOST.

Figure 2.11 shows that the overhead imposed by SVFD is very comparable with that of other schemes: the area overhead is 39%, and the power penalty is 40%—both are superior to that of SEFF scheme, while SEFF can only handle SEU faults. Given that SVFD can cope with SEUs, SETs, delay faults, aging delays; therefore, we conclude that the versatile SVFD is more promising.

Note that we omit the CWSPFF's power implication in Fig. 2.11 is because re-implementing this scheme in our target pipeline is very labor-intensive and time-consuming. But considering the complexity of the CWSPFF logic and associated deployment, the power overhead should not superior than that of SEFF. In addition,

Table 2.2 Comparison of detection capability

	SEFF [72]	LOWCOST [55]	ARSC [8]	CWSPFF [17]	SVFD
SEU	Yes	Yes	No	No	Yes
SET	No	Yes	No	No	Yes
Aging delay	No	No	Yes	No	Yes
Delay fault	No	Yes	No	Yes	Yes

compared with SVFD's versatile capability, CWSPFF can only handle SET faults as shown in Table 2.2.

2.1.6   Discussion

2.1.6.1   On SVFD Application

With the increasing impacts of soft errors and transistor aging under the relentless CMOS scaling, we believe SVFD will be increasingly promising. In part is because SVFD is far more area efficient than traditional DMR based schemes, in part for its versatile capability for fault detection. But SVFD does not suppose to totally take the place of existing approaches, especially ECC based schemes. The following will discuss how to apply SVFD efficiently and why SVFD is a significant complement to existing schemes.

Modern processor includes two types of structures: logic-dominated structures such as execution units and memory-dominated structures such as register file, caches [50]. Using SVFD for logic-dominated structures, as the FPU in our experimental study, are cost-efficient. Since such type of structures usually are so non-regular that engineers mostly have to resort to coarse-grained DMR, thereby imposing more area and power overhead. Moreover, the SVFD can also indicate the aging process, which is an essential benefit that the traditional DMR can hardly achieve.

As for protecting the regular memory-dominated structures from in particular soft errors, ECC has been proven to be a highly cost-effective approach. SVFD can not beat ECC in terms power and area overhead, though SVFD can also detected soft errors in memory-dominated structures since soft errors induced perturbations can also results in stability violation in primary outputs. The prior research shows that, with extensive architectural hits such as register lifetime prediction [59], selective placement [56], ECC-based approach commonly dictates about 30% area overhead. This overhead is comparable with that of SVFD. While one ECC's benefit that SVFD does not possess is error correction—the commonly used ECC is able to correct single-bit fault and detect two-bit fault. Hence, we think ECC is still the preferred option for memory-dominated structures in a microprocessor.

But SVFD scheme offers aging prediction that ECC-based doesn't. The aging process of SRAM cells exhibits by increased read-out and write-into delay. The read delay is more critical than write delay because the read path usually serves as the critical path [83]. While for the SVFD sensors the degraded read operations behave the same with the degrade critical delay in logics, and hence can also be handled by a simplified SVFD sensors that are only for aging prediction—as Agarwal et al. proposed previously [8].

Hence, we conclude that SVFD is a cost-efficient application for protection logic-dominated structures; combined with ECC based approaches which can already handle soft errors, SVFD can also provided additional capability for aging prediction for memory-dominated structures.

2.1.6.2 Variation and Aging Considerations

Just as DMR cannot be free from false positive, SVFD face the same situation. The systematic variation hurts little to SVFD unit as well as other fault detection infrastructures because it statistically exhibits distinct spatial locality and correlation. If the SVFD suffers from the systematic variation, so does the host circuits in the same silicon spots. But random variation in some corner cases can invalid the SVFD unit. As shown in Fig. 2.6, for example, if the leakage of M3 is overly large due to random variation, and at the same time the keeper for S1 happens to be too weak to compensate the escaped charge through M3, then a false alarm will be flagged. In other words, if S1's keeper does not happen to be that weak, the SVFD unit is highly probable to work. The same situation comes to M4. Therefore, on one hand, these keepers can help cancel out part of negative effects of random variation; on the other hand, we can properly size the transistors on the discharge paths to obtain more robustness against random process variation.

As the transistors in host circuits, the transistors in the SVFD unit also wear out over time. While the other hardware-based fault detection schemes such as LOWCOST and DMR suffer from the same situation. But the core logics, i.e. stability checker (Fig. 2.6b) and compactor (Fig. 2.6c) are relatively resistant to NBTI—one of the major aging mechanisms, because all of the PMOS transistors in the two logics are timing non-critical, while all the timing critical transistors are NMOS transistors which intrinsically are free from NBTI. Hence, we believe SVFD units have good chance to stand longer than the host circuits due to the better NBTI resilient characteristics.

2.1.6.3 Distinguish Detection Results

It is useful to distinguish the aging delay caused detection positive from the rest of detection results, because the detected aging delay rate is used as the input for some aging-aware designs.

SVFD implicitly apply a rule for distinguish the detected results. That is: If a stability violation is detected in Guard Band, then this violation is viewed as aging delay induced; the stability violation detected in other region is viewed as soft error or delay fault induced. Figure 2.6d is used to implement this rule. However, this might degrade the confidence level of detected aging delay rate since if a stability violation takes place within the Guard Band, SVFD can not determine whether this violation is caused by a soft error or an aging delay.

Fortunately, this confidence degradation incurred by this implementation is negligible. To quantitatively evaluate the miss rate, we define the miss as: a soft error induced stability violation is misjudged as an aging-fault stability violation.

Suppose that the raw soft error rate (SER), $R_{softerror}$, is uniformly distributed over time. The detectable SER is $\alpha R_{softerror}$, where the α is a constant ($0 < \alpha < 1$) related to the three masking effects [75]. The aging fault rate is denoted as R_{aging}.

The misjudgment rate R_{miss} can be expressed as

$$R_{miss} = 1 - \frac{R_{aging}}{R_{aging} + \alpha R_{softerror} \times \frac{T_{GB}}{T_{DS}+T_{GB}}}$$

Practically, the Guard Band should not be larger than the timing margin to avoid extra timing penalty. A typical timing margin is 10%. Assume that $\alpha = 0.5$, and $R_{softerror} = 0.1 \times R_{aging}$ (actually, after some detectable aging effects of devices begin emerging, the assumptions of α and raw SER are heavily conservative), $T_{GB}/T_{DS} = 0.2$ then R_{miss} is not large than 1%. Therefore, we can safely conclude that the imperfect distinguishing capability will not impose any substantial problem.

2.2   On-Chip Path Delay Measurement

We present a novel on-chip path delay measurement architecture for efficiently detecting and debugging of delay faults in the fabricated integrated circuits. Several delay stages are employed in the proposed on-chip path delay measurement (OCDM) circuit, whose delay ranges are increased by a factor of two gradually from the last to the first delay stage. Thus, the proposed OCDM circuit can achieve a large delay measurement range with a small quantity of delay stages. A calibration circuit is incorporated into the proposed on-chip path delay measurement technique to calibrate the delay range of the delay stage under process variations. In addition, delay calibration for import lines is conducted to improve the precision of path delay measurement. Experimental results are presented to validate the proposed path delay measurement architecture.

2.2.1   Path Delay Measurement and Fault Tolerance

With the scaling of semiconductor process technology, the performance of modern VLSI chips improves significantly. We have seen operating frequencies of integrated circuits reach multi-gigahertz, resulting in more rigorous timing requirements [1, 95]. Timing related defects originated from manufacturing process-related problems, such as resistive opens and shorts, metal mouse bites, via voids, etc., will become more common [30]. Consequently, delay faults caused by these physical defects, which prevent the circuit from meeting the timing requirements, are of growing concern in nanometer technologies [46]. Moreover, it should be noted that the manufacturing process is becoming more difficult to be controlled with the increasing complexity of modern VLSI chips. Therefore, electrical parameters, such as saturation current, gate capacitance, threshold voltage, etc., may vary from one device to another. As a result, the delay of gates and timing-critical paths will have large variations and can hardly be predicted during the design stage due to the imprecision of verification models [7, 14]. Furthermore, the circuit timing would also be impacted by the application environment conditions such as temperature, supply voltage noise, etc. In order to improve the quality of shippable products, there is an urgent need to conduct effective delay testing for ascertaining the correct operation of chips at the rated frequency [46, 54].

2.2.1.1 Challenges for Path Delay Measurement

Traditionally, at-speed delay testing is implemented to check the satisfiability of circuit timing by only considering whether the circuit under test (CUT) passes delay testing under the applied test vector pairs or not. However, under the process and environment variations, it requires to test the chip at different worst case timing scenarios to ensure the circuit's timing correctness [26, 47, 96]. For example, for a circuit path with a very small slack, even though it passes a test under the at-speed test clock frequency, it possibly fails another test that induces larger capacitive coupling or power supply noise.

The small delay defect (SDD), which introduces only a small extra delay over its normal value, may fail to be detected by at-speed delay testing due to the observability limitation for a large timing slack. However, the detection for SDDs is increasingly important to ensure the chip's quality and reliability [9, 57]. The first important reason is that a timing failure can be occurred in the circuit during functional application caused by the increment of small delay on paths with small timing slacks [48]. The second important reason is that the SDDs hidden in the circuit may become one of the major reliability limiters [64, 81]. In addition to the imperative requirement for SDD detection, it is well known that in order to improve the yield and reduce the time-to-market of chips, design-related failures and performance limiters need to be identified and rectified as early as possible during first silicon debug [12]. However, it is very expensive to use external high-speed automatic test equipment (ATE) for post-silicon debug of modern high-performance chips. Moreover, the frequency of test clock generated by external ATE would be affected by factors such as parasitic capacitance, resistance of probe and tester skew, etc. [80]. In addition, for a complex SoC, the internal circuit modules are limited to be accessed by the external ATE to conduct silicon debug.

The on-chip path delay measurement techniques have been gained many attentions for researchers in recent years, for it can provide a cost-effective alternative
way to perform delay defect detection and silicon debug in modern VLSI chips.
Rather than testing the chip with all possible worst-case test vectors and process
corners, it is better to measure the delays of paths and to check if the slacks are large
enough to tolerate all the possible delay variations. Therefore, high complexity for
finding the worst case test vectors considering different sources of variations can be
avoided and high test confidence can be obtained. Moreover, by on-chip measuring
the delays of selected paths in the actual silicon, precise path timing information
can then be obtained for circuit under actual operating conditions. As a result,
whether there are SDDs on a path can be analyzed based on the measured path
delay. Further, the amount of timing violations in the failing paths can be obtained
under certain environment conditions [20, 21]. Valuable information, which points
the performance limiter and source to circuit failure, can hence be obtained by the
on-chip path delay measurement technique with a much higher confidence.

2.2.1.2 Prior Path Delay Measurements

Several on-chip architectures have already been proposed for delay testing and
silicon debug in literatures. Ghosh et al. [29] presented a built-in delay-sensing
circuit to improve the delay fault coverage of the CUT. The delay of the path
under test is converted to a certain voltage height by using a saw-tooth waveform
generated from the reference clock signal. By comparing the converted voltage with
the reference voltage, delay fault of the target path can then be detected. The same
technique is also used in [68] for speed binning of the high performance chips
based on the delay measurement results for circuit's critical paths. Hsiao et al. [82]
proposed a built-in parametric measurement circuit for time-interval measurement
based on the dual-slop technique. The capacitor is first charged by the input voltage
with a high slope, and then the capacitor is discharged with a known lower slope.
Therefore, the time-interval can be derived from the discharging time based on the
proportional relationship between the discharging time and input voltage. Wang et
al. [92] proposed a ring oscillator based scheme for path delay measurement. By
configuring the path under measurement (PUM) and the returning loop into a ring
oscillator, delay of the target path can be translated into oscillation period. Tayade
et al. [82] utilize a programmable capture generator to obtain a fast capture signal
to conduct faster-than-at-speed testing. Small delay defects can then be efficiently
detected by this approach. Moreover, delays of the selected paths in circuit can also
be measured by sweeping the capture clock frequency. Datta et al. [20] proposed
an on-chip timing characterization scheme based on the skewed inverter delay line.
First a pulse is generated by the triggered transitions of the start and end points
of the PUM using the test vector, and then the width of pulse is recorded into
the latching circuits by using pulse shaping technique. Datta et al. [22] proposed
a modified vernier delay line (VDL) technique for path delay measurement. By
using a balanced delay line, high-resolution capability for delay measurement can

be provided. Based on the same principle of VDL technique, the delay scan chain is proposed in [21] to reuse the existing scan chain for path delay measurement. Tsai et al. [85] proposed a built-in delay measurement circuit consisting of coarse and fine blocks, which is an extension of the modified VDL technique. However, the above VDL based techniques require lots of delay stages to achieve a large measurement range [66]. Moreover, the delays of the import lines, which connect the chosen PUM into the path delay measurement unit, are not considered, thereby posing a significant influence on the precision of path delay measurement.

2.2.2 Path Delay Measurement Circuits

In this section, we present the design of OCDM for path delay testing and silicon debug. As mentioned above, the previous VDL based delay measurement techniques need lots of stages to achieve a large delay measurement range under the pre-determined delay measurement resolution. Consequently, the goal of the proposed OCDM circuit is to reduce the number of delay stages in the VDL, thus to achieve a significantly less hardware overhead as well as less delay measurement time.

2.2.2.1 Basic Structure and Operation

The basic structure of the proposed OCDM circuit is shown in Fig. 2.12, which can convert the path delay of the PUM into a series of digital values that can be stored in the flip-flops of the VDL chain. Each delay stage consisted in the VDL chain is constructed by a positive edge triggered D-type flip-flop, four multiplexes, and several buffers. In the proposed OCDM circuit, we assumed that the input x is fed by the output of the PUM, while the input y is fed by the input of the PUM. So y always switches earlier than x does during the delay measurement period. In order to explain the operation of the OCDM circuit, let's consider the case that both the input and output signals of the PUM are rising transitions.

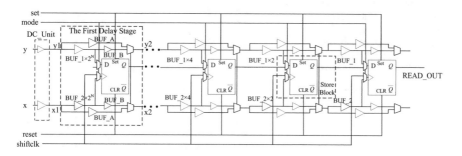

Fig. 2.12 Proposed on-chip delay measurement circuit

The upper delay unit (UDU) refers to the buffer chain that starts at the input of the delay stage at which the transition signal is propagated from node y, and ends at the input of the multiplexer whose output is connected to the data input of the flip-flop in each delay stage of the OCDM circuit. The lower delay unit (LDU) is similar to UDU, except that it starts at the input of the delay stage at which the transition signal is propagated from node x, and ends at the input of another multiplexer whose output is connected to the clock input of the flip-flop in each delay stage.

The delay range is defined as the delay difference between the two delay units in each delay stage of the OCDM circuit. For example, in the last stage of the OCDM circuit, the delay of UDU (named BUF_1), D_{buf_1}, is designed larger than that of LDU (named BUF_2), D_{buf_2}. Thus, the delay range of the last stage, R_{last}, is the delay difference between D_{buf_1} and D_{buf_2}, i.e.,

$$R_{last} = D_{buf\_1} - D_{buf\_2}. \tag{2.22}$$

From the last stage to the first stage of the OCDM circuit, the delay range of each stage is increased by a factor of two. The DC_Unit cell, as shown in Fig. 2.12, is used for delay compensation, and will be explained in detail later. Two rising input transitions from the PUM pass through the DC_Unit firstly, and then go into the inputs of the first delay stage of the OCDM circuit, respectively.

Let us explain the function of each delay stage by considering the operation of the first delay stage for the sake of clarity for illustration without loss of generality. Suppose the input and output signals of the upper delay chain in the first delay stage are $y1$ and $y2$, respectively, accordingly, $x1$ and $x2$ are assumed for the lower delay chain. All flip-flops of the OCDM circuit are initialized to logic ZERO values by asserting the reset signal. The delay measurement mode is activated by asserting the mode signal. As $x1$ and $y1$ signals propagate through their respective delay units, the time difference between the two signals will be reduced. As shown in Fig. 2.13a, assuming that $x1$ signal lags the $y1$ signal by enough time (i.e., $y1$ switches much earlier), and hence a logic-high value will be hold in the flip-flop. As a result, $y2$

Fig. 2.13 Relation between time difference of two input signals ($x1$, $y1$) and that of two output signals ($x2$, $y2$) in the first delay stage. (**a**) Logic ONE in the flip-flop. (**b**) Logic ZERO in the flip-flop

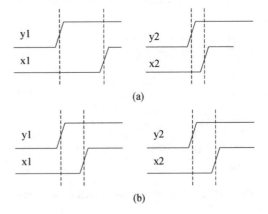

will be the signal that passes through the UDU and the buffer BUF_B in the upper delay chain from $y1$, while $x2$ will be the signal that passes through the LDU and the buffer BUF_B in the lower delay chain from $x1$. The delay of BUF_B is large enough to ensure that a stable logic high value can be stored in the flip-flop before the two transition signals arrive at the inputs of the multiplexers whose outputs are connected to the inputs of the next delay stage. Clearly, the time difference between $x2$ and $y2$ is reduced by an amount which equals the delay range of this delay stage.

The buffer named BUF_A in each delay stage has a delay value that is larger than the cumulative delay of the path that contains LDU and BUF_B of the same delay stage. Likewise, if the time difference of $y1$ and $x1$ is smaller than the delay range, the flip-flop will hold a logic ZERO value. Therefore, the signals propagating through BUF_A are then selected by the multiplexers. As a result, the time difference between $y2$ and $x2$ will be equal to that of $y1$ and $x1$, as shown in Fig. 2.13b.

Consequently, the principle of the OCDM circuit is that if the time difference between the two inputs of each delay stage is lager than the delay range of the same stage, a logic ONE value will be stored in the flip-flop of the delay stage. The time difference between the two output signals will be updated by simply subtracting the delay range from that between the input signals of the delay stage. Otherwise, the flip-flop of the delay stage will hold a logic ZERO value, and the time difference between the output signals will keep the same as that between the input signals of the delay stage.

Note that there exists a setup time in the store block of each delay stage as shown in Fig. 2.13, which consists of a D flip-flop and two multiplexers. If the time difference between the two inputs of the store block is smaller than the setup time (about 33 ps in the experiment), an error logic value may be hold in the flip-flop. Therefore, in order to provide better delay measurement precision, the DC_Unit cell constructed by two buffer lines is proposed for delay compensation, which means that the upper and lower delay units of DC_Unit are designed such that the delay difference between them is approximately equal to the setup time. Meanwhile, if half of the delay range in the last delay stage is also compensated in the delay difference of the upper and lower delay units of DC_Unit cell, the OCDM circuit can improve the delay measurement resolution by 50%. The values stored in the delay line can be shifted out serially using the clock signal shiftclk in the shift mode by de-asserting the mode signal. The delay of the PUM can then be obtained.

2.2.3   Delay Range Calibration

The delay range of each delay stage in the OCDM circuit would be varied due to the prominent process variations. It is thus necessary to calibrate the delay ranges to assure the precision of path delay measurement result before using the OCDM circuit [7, 14, 20, 85]. Figure 2.14 shows the basic structure of the calibration circuit [20, 85], which can be embedded into the OCDM circuit for delay range calibration.

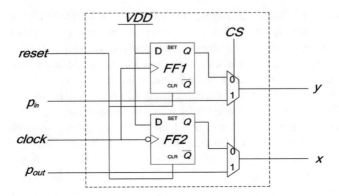

Fig. 2.14 Calibration circuit

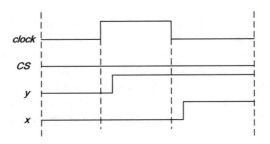

Fig. 2.15 Simplified timing waveform for calibration circuit

The outputs of the calibration circuit, denoted as y and x, are directly connected to the inputs with the same notations of the OCDM circuit, respectively.

Two inputs of the calibration circuit, denoted as P_{in} and P_{out}, are fed by the input and output of the PUM, respectively. Clearly, when the CS signal is set to 1, the generated transitions at the P_{in} and P_{out} can be sent into the OCDM circuit for delay measurement. When the CS signal is set to 0, the delay range calibration process is conducted.

The simplified timing waveform for the delay range calibration is shown in Fig. 2.15. The FF1 and FF2 are rising and falling edge triggered flip-flops respectively. First, the flip-flops of FF1 and FF2 are initiated with logic ZERO by the reset signal. Then, logic ONE will be loaded into the FF1 and FF2 by the rising and falling edges of the clock signal respectively. Clearly, the time difference between the generated rising transitions at y and x is equal to the width of the positive half cycle of the clock signal. The time period of the clock signal can be programmed deterministically with high resolution using the on-chip clock generator from [44].

Assuming the number of delay stages in the OCDM circuit is m. The following presents the calculation method for obtaining the delay range of each delay stage, which is described by Eq. 2.23:

$$
\begin{cases}
a_{11}x_1 + a_{12}x_2 + \ldots + a_{1m}x_m = b_1 \\
a_{21}x_1 + a_{22}x_2 + \ldots + a_{2m}x_m = b_2 \\
\ldots \\
a_{m1}x_1 + a_{m2}x_2 + \ldots + a_{mm}x_m = b_m
\end{cases}
\tag{2.23}
$$

Let

$$
A =
\begin{bmatrix}
a_{11} & a_{12} & \ldots & a_{1m} \\
a_{21} & a_{22} & \ldots & a_{2m} \\
\ldots \\
a_{m1} & a_{m2} & \ldots & a_{mm}
\end{bmatrix}
\tag{2.24}
$$

$$
X =
\begin{bmatrix}
x_1 \\
x_2 \\
\ldots \\
x_m
\end{bmatrix}
\tag{2.25}
$$

$$
B =
\begin{bmatrix}
b_1 \\
b_2 \\
\ldots \\
b_m
\end{bmatrix}
\tag{2.26}
$$

The we can get Eq. 2.27.

$$
AX = B
\tag{2.27}
$$

where $x_j \in (1 \leq j \leq m)$ in vector X represents the delay range of the jth delay stage to be calculated, $b_i \in (1 \leq i \leq m)$ in vector B represents the width of the positive half cycle of signal clock for the ith calibration process, a_{ij} in matrix A represents the measured value (0 or 1) for the jth delay stage during the ith calibration. Clearly, by selecting appropriate values for vector B in each calibration process, it is easy to conclude the delay range for each stage by solving Eq. 2.27.

For example, assuming there are four delay stages in the OCDM circuit and we know their nominal designed delay ranges. After we choose 70, 55, 40, and 25 for b_i in four calibration processes respectively, the obtained values for matrix A is listed as follows:

$$A = \begin{bmatrix} 1 & 1 & 1 & 0 \\ 1 & 0 & 1 & 1 \\ 1 & 0 & 0 & 0 \\ 0 & 1 & 0 & 1 \end{bmatrix} \qquad (2.28)$$

Hence, after solving Eq. 2.27, the delay ranges are found to be 40, 20, 10, and 5 from the first to the last stage, respectively.

Note that the value of b_i in the vector B, which is the width of the positive half cycle of the clock signal, may not be exactly equal to the expected value because of the clock jitter, and hence may induce error delay ranges for the delay stages. However, this can be compensated by multiple calibrations under each value because the clock jitter is a zero-mean random variable [40].

For example, if for the second calibration process is set to 55, the values in the second row of matrix A are then expected to be equal to (1, 0, 1, 1) respectively. This can be represented by Eq. 2.29.

$$55 = x_1 + x_3 + x_4 \qquad (2.29)$$

However, if the width of the positive half cycle of the clock signal is varied from the expected value and is 50 or 60 due to the clock jitter, then the second row of matrix will get (1, 0, 1, 0) or (1, 1, 0, 0), respectively. Hence, the second row of matrix is replaced to Eq. 2.30 or Eq. 2.31 as follows:

$$55 = x_1 + x_3 \qquad (2.30)$$

$$55 = x_1 + x_2 \qquad (2.31)$$

Therefore, error values would be calculated for the delay ranges of the delay stages by using Eq. 2.30 or Eq. 2.31. However, since the clock jitter is a zero-mean random variable [40], we can calibrate the delay ranges using the same expected b_i value for multiple calibration times. Though neither Eq. 2.30 nor Eq. 2.31 can be used to obtain the delay ranges correctly, the sum of the expressions obtained by multiple calibrations would be qualified. For example, by summing up Eqs. 2.29, 2.30, and 2.31, we can conclude Eq. 2.32.

$$165 = 3x_1 + x_2 + 2x_3 + x_4 \qquad (2.32)$$

As mentioned above, the delay ranges are 40, 20, 10, and 5 from the first to the last stage, respectively, and can verify the correction of Eq. 2.32. Hence, the delay range of each delay stage can be calibrated by the process mentioned above. The calibration errors caused by the clock tuning resolution and measurement resolution are small and can be ignored. They can also be compensated by multiple calibrations using multiple number of b_i values.

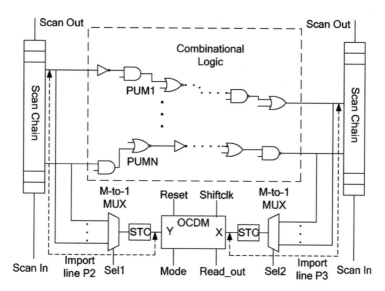

Fig. 2.16 Path delay measurement architecture

2.2.4 Path Delay Measurement Architecture

The architecture of the proposed path delay measurement scheme using the OCDM circuit is shown in Fig. 2.16. The paths selected for delay measurement can be timing-critical paths whose delays exceed the specified timing threshold under static timing analysis (STA) or statistical STA [27, 31]. Based on the selected timing-critical paths, the method proposed in [49] provides an effective way to further find an optimal path set for measurement, while the delays of all the selected timing-critical paths can be obtained either by direct measurement or by calculation from the measured delays. We mainly focus on the design of the path delay measurement architecture. Two M-to-1 multiplexers are included aiming to select a particular path into the OCDM circuit for delay measurement.

2.2.4.1 Signal Transition Conversion (STC)

As mentioned in the previous section, the OCDM circuit works well only when the input and output of the PUM are rising transitions. However, there are other three additional cases possibly to activate the worst case delay of a circuit path, such as a path in which the input is a rising transition and the output is a falling transition. It is thus better to transfer the output signal into the signal with rising transition for facilitating path delay measurement regardless of the transition direction of the original signal.

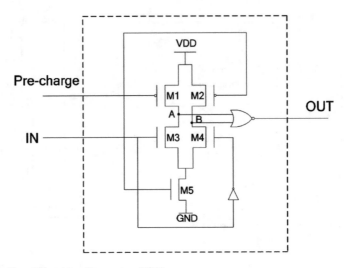

Fig. 2.17 Signal Transition Conversion (STC)

The STC block shown in Fig. 2.16 is used to handle this problem. Therefore, rising transitions which are derived from the start and end points of PUM can be fed into the inputs and of the OCDM circuit, respectively. Figure 2.17 shows the basic structure of the STC block, which is previously designed for signal stability violation detection in [8, 25, 94]. The simplified timing waveform for the STC block is shown in Fig. 2.18a and b, respectively. When the pre-charge signal is low, denoted as the pre-charge period, both the nodes and are charged up to logic high values. Hence the OUT signal keeps a logic low value.

Clearly, as shown in Fig. 2.18a, if a rising transition is generated at the IN signal when the pre-charge signal is high, both the node A and node B are discharged to logic low values after the arrival of the rising transition of IN. Therefore, a rising transition is generated at the OUT signal. Likewise, as shown in Fig. 2.18b, a rising transition would also be generated at the OUT signal after the arrival of a falling transition of the IN signal. Hence, by using the STC block, the input signal with arbitrary transition direction can be converted into a rising transition signal for facilitating path delay measurement.

2.2.4.2 Delay Measurement

The proposed on-chip delay measurement flow can be divided into eight steps as follows:

1. Select the paths for delay measurement;
2. For each PUM, the input and output transition signals of the PUM can be fed into the OCDM circuit for delay measurement by using the two M-to-1 multiplexes;

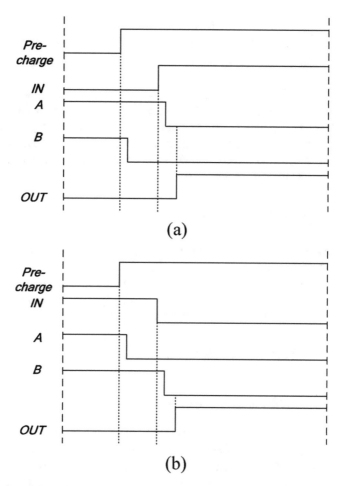

Fig. 2.18 Simplified timing waveform for signal transition converter. (**a**) A rising transition at IN. (**b**) A failing transition at IN

3. The first vector of the test vector pair for the PUM is applied to initialize the internal logic of the circuit to a stable state;
4. All flip-flops of the OCDM circuit are initialized to logic ZERO values by asserting the reset signal;
5. The delay measurement mode is activated by asserting the mode signal;
6. The second vector of the test vector pair is applied to the circuit, and hence a transition signal can be launched at the input of the PUM, and propagated to the output of the PUM; consequently, the delay difference of the two transition signals is measured by the OCDM and recorded into the delay line;
7. After the completion of delay measurement, the OCDM circuit is configured into shift mode by de-asserting the mode signal. Therefore, the values stored in the

delay line can be shifted out serially using clock signal shiftclk. Consequently, the path delay of the PUM can be calculated from the values read out.

All paths can be selected for delay measurement by repeating the above steps 2–7.

After the values stored in the delay line have been read out, the delay of the PUM can then be obtained. Suppose the total number of delay stages in the OCDM circuit is N, the delay measurement resolution of the OCMD circuit is M_{res}, which is half of the delay range in the last delay stage D_{las}, and the values stored in the flip-flop from the first delay stage to the last delay stage of the OCDM circuit are D_N to D_1, respectively. Then the path delay can be calculated as follows:

$$\text{Delay of Measurement} = \sum_{i=1}^{i=N} D_i \times 2^{i-1} \times D_{las}.$$

The range of the path delay is then given as $\sum_{i=1}^{i=N} D_i \times 2^{i-1} \times D_{las} - M_{res} <$ Path Delay $\sum_{i=1}^{i=N} \times D_i \times 2^{i-1} \times D_{las} + M_{res}$.

The calculated path delay value of the PUM is then compared with the expected delay value for timing validation and silicon debug. The maximum delay measurement range of the OCDM circuit can also be obtained as follows.

$$\text{Maximum measurement range} = \sum_{i=1}^{i=N} \times 2^{i-1} \times D_{las}.$$

2.2.4.3 Delay Calibration for Import Lines

In order to obtain the delay of the PUM with high precision, the delay of import lines P_2 and P_3 for feeding the start and end transitions of the PUM into the OCDM circuit, as shown in Fig. 2.16, should be taken into account. The reason is that it is difficult to mutually cancel the delays of the import lines P_2 and P_3 during physical design. Even though a careful custom layout can be conducted to balance the import lines P_2 and P_3 serving for one PUM, it can be hardly to satisfy this restriction for the import lines for all the PUMs. Moreover, the delays of import lines P_2 and P_3 would also be affected by the process variations and hence would bring a precision loss of the delay measurement. In order to address this problem, a 2-to-1 multiplexer is added for the flip-flop which is the end point of the PUM.

Figure 2.19 redraws the architecture of the path delay measurement scheme shown in Fig. 2.16, which includes a 2-to-1 multiplexer with data inputs, respectively, connected to the data-input and data-output of the flip-flop at the end point of the PUM to calibrate the delay difference of import lines.

When the MS signal is set to 1, the path delay measurement architecture is configured into the delay measurement mode. Hence the input and output of PUM1 are selected into the OCDM for delay measurement. The delay measurement result

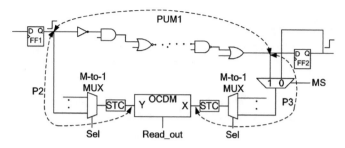

Fig. 2.19 Delay calibration for import lines

of PUM1 without considering the delay difference of import lines and can be represented as follows:

$$\text{Delay measurement result} = D_1 + D_3 - D_2$$

where the D_1, D_2, and D_3 represent the delays of $PUM1$, P_2, and P_3, respectively. However, in order to obtain the delay of the PUM with high precision, the delay value of $D_3 - D_2$ should be obtained firstly. The delay of P_3 is typically larger than that of P_2 for the insertion of a multiplexer. When the MS signal is set to 0, the import line's delay difference calibration mode is configured.

For the first case, if the PUM is started at one flip-flop and ended at another flip-flop, then either rising or falling transition can be simultaneously generated at the outputs of the start and the end flip-flops by shifting the test vector with specific values into them. Hence the transitions generated at the outputs of the start and end flip-flops will pass through and into the OCDM circuit, respectively. Therefore, the delay difference of P_3 and P_2 can be obtained by the OCDM circuit under the import line's delay difference calibration mode. For the second case, if the PUM is started and ended at the same flip-flop, then this scenario is even simpler. Either a rising or a falling transition generated at the output of the flip-flop can simultaneously pass through P_2 and P_3 into the OCDM circuit, respectively.

Consequently, by calibration the delay difference of the import lines for feeding the start and end transitions of the PUM into the OCDM circuit first, a high precision of path delay measurement can then be obtained.

2.2.5 Experiment Result Analysis

For validation, we implemented the proposed on-chip path delay measurement scheme using SMIC 0.18 μm CMOS technology. The experimental results consist of the following five main parts: (1) simulated delay range for each delay stage of the OCDM circuit; (2) simulated results for measuring the delays of circuit paths using the proposed scheme; (3) validation of the effectiveness of the proposed scheme

Table 2.3 Delay range of each delay stage

Delay stage	1	2	3	4	5	6
Delay range (ps)	409.7	205.1	102.84	51.59	25.91	13.23

under process variations; (4) the hardware and timing overheads of the proposed scheme; and (5) comparisons with previous works.

2.2.5.1 Experiment I

In this experiment, six delay stages were designed in the OCDM circuit, making the maximum path delay measurement range of the OCDM achieves about 800 ps, while the delay range of the last stage is about 13 ps. The number of delay ranges in the OCDM circuit can be easily extended to achieve a much larger delay measurement range if required.

The experimental result of the nominal delay range for each delay stage is reported in Table 2.3, which is obtained using HSPICE simulation. The delay range of each delay stage is approximately increased by a factor of two from the last to the first delay stage within a small margin of error. This ignorable error of delay range may be caused by the unbalanced load of each delay stage and the precision of HSPICE simulator. However, due to the fact that the delay measurement range of the OCDM circuit can be expanded exponentially by increasing the number of delay stages, thus we only need a small quantity of delay stages to achieve the required delay measurement range. Therefore, this error induced in the path delay measurement can be acceptable.

2.2.5.2 Experiment II

In the second experiment, two different lengths of paths are chosen from ISCAS85 C880 benchmark to verify the effectiveness of the proposed on-chip path delay measurement scheme under the typical process corner.

The delay difference of the import lines can be obtained by the proposed on-chip delay measurement technique under the import line's delay difference calibrationmode. In order to measure the delays of PUMs, path delay test vector pairs should be generated for the corresponding paths firstly. A transition is then launched at the input of the particular path which has been chosen for delay measurement using the generated test vector pair. The test vector generation method is beyond the scope of this book.

Figures 2.20 and 2.21 show the delay measurement results for the two paths obtained using HSPICE simulation, respectively. As shown in Fig. 2.20a, the delay of Path1 is 149.24 ps from HSPICE simulation. Figure 2.20b shows the simulated delay difference of the import lines, which are used to feed the start and end

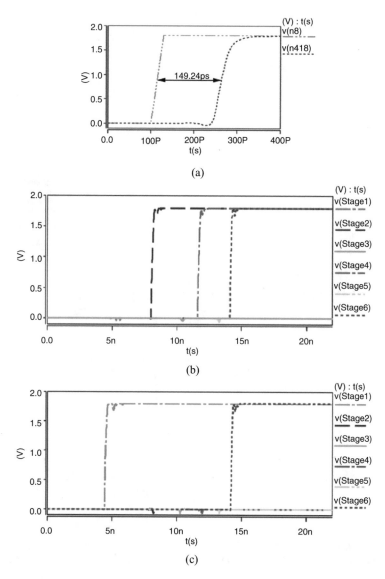

Fig. 2.20 Simulated waveform for delay measurement of Path 1. (**a**) Delay from HSPICE simulation. (**b**) Delay difference of the import lines. (**c**) Delay measurement result of PUM

transitions of Path1 into the OCDM circuit. Every delay stage holds the initial logic ZERO value except for stage 2, stage 4, and stage 6 when the delay measurement is completed. Thus, the measured delay difference of the import lines is the sum of delay ranges in stage 2, stage 4, and stage 6, which can be calculated from Table 2.3, i.e., 270 ps in this case. Figure 2.20c shows the delay measurement result of Path1 for not considering the delay difference of import lines. Likewise, this delay

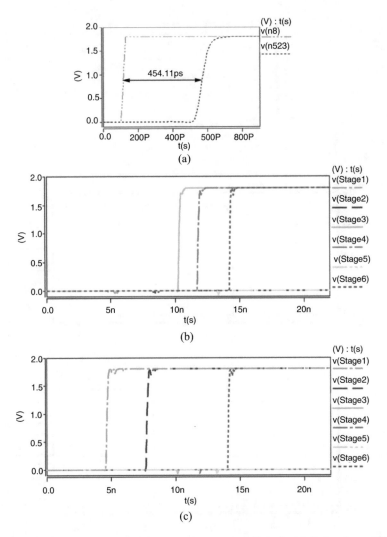

Fig. 2.21 Simulated waveform for delay measurement of Path 2. (**a**) Delay from HSPICE simulation. (**b**) Delay difference of the import lines. (**c**) Delay measurement result of PUM

measurement result can be obtained by summing the delay ranges of stage 1 and stage 6. Hence, the actual delay of Path1 can be obtained by subtracting the delay difference of import lines as obtained in Fig. 2.20b from the path delay measurement result as obtained in Fig. 2.20c. As a result, the actual path delay of Path1 obtained by the proposed on-chip path delay measurement technique is 153 ps.

It can be observed from Fig. 2.21a that the simulation delay of Path2 is 454.11 ps using HSPICE simulation. Under the import line's delay difference calibration mode, the delay difference of the import lines which feed the start and end transition of Path2 into the OCDM circuit can be measured. The delay stage 3, stage 4, and stage 6 hold final stable logic ONE values after the import line's delay difference calibration as shown in Fig. 2.21b. Hence the delay difference for the import lines is 167 ps. Likewise, the delay measurement result of Path 2, in which the delay difference of import lines is not taken into account, can be obtained by summing the delay ranges of stage 1, stage 2, and stage 6 as shown in Fig. 2.21c. Hence, the actual path delay measurement result for Path 2 can be obtained and is 460 ps. Through the aforementioned results, we have shown that the proposed on-chip path delay measurement scheme works well. It is worthy of note that the errors between the delay measurements and simulation values for the two paths are only 3.76 and 5.89 ps, respectively, and can be ignored.

2.2.5.3 Experiment III

The circuit parameters are apparently prone to fluctuations caused by the significant process variations in sub-micro technologies. Hence the delays of circuit paths, import lines, and the delay ranges of the delay stages in OCDM circuit are thus unavoidable to suffer from undesirable variations. In this experiment, HSPICE Monte Carlo simulations are conducted to analyze the effectiveness of the proposed on-chip path delay measurement method in the presence of process variations. It is well known that the gate length variation poses a dominant impact on the gate delay [6, 61]. In our analysis, the inter-die and intra-die gate length variations are considered to have Gaussian distributions, $N(\mu_L, \delta_1)$ and $N(\mu_L, \delta_2)$, respectively [81, 92]. The δ_1 and δ_2 represent the standard deviations of gate length for inter-die and intra-die variations respectively, while μ_L represents the transistor channel length obtained from the typical technology library.

Figure 2.22a and b shows the waveform of delay measurement results for Path1 and Path2, which are obtained from 50 Monte Carlo iterations considering both intra-die and inter-die variations. The variations considered in the Monte Carlo simulations are $3\delta_1 = 0.05\mu_L$ and $3\delta_2 = 0.05\mu_L$.

The panel indicated as Simulation in Fig. 2.22a shows the simulation delay results of Path1 using HSPICE Monte Carlo method. Note that the delay of Path1 without considering process variations is 149.24 ps as shown in Fig. 2.20. The delays of the import lines for feeding the start and end transitions of Path1 into the OCDM circuit would also be impacted by process variations. The panel indicated as Calibration in Fig. 2.22a shows the delay measurement results of the delay difference between the corresponding import lines. The panel indicated as Measurement in Fig. 2.22a shows the delay measurement results of Path1 without considering the delay difference of import lines P_2 and P_3. The panel indicated as Error in Fig. 2.22a shows the errors between the delay measurement and simulation results for Path1 in the 50 Monte Carlo iterations, respectively. Likewise, the corresponding experimental results for Path2 are shown in Fig. 2.22b. Clearly, as shown in Fig. 2.22, the error of path delay measurement conducted by the proposed

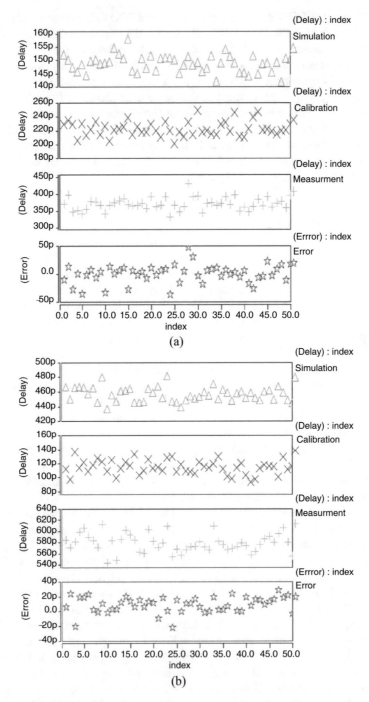

Fig. 2.22 Simulated waveform for delay measurement obtained from 50 Monte Carlo iteration with $3\delta_1 = 0.05\mu_L$ and $3\delta_2 = 0.05\mu_L$ (**a**) for Path1 (**b**) for Path2

scheme is very small, which demonstrates the effectiveness of the proposed path delay measurement scheme under process variations.

Figure 2.23a and b shows the Monte Carlo simulation results of delay measurement for Path1 and Path2 considering $3\delta_1 = 0.1\mu_L$ and $3\delta_2 = 0.1\mu_L$. It is clearly shown from Fig. 2.23 that although much larger delay variations are occurred as compared to the case in Fig. 2.22, the error of path delay measurement results conducted by the proposed scheme is still very small, all within the range of 50 ps.

2.2.5.4   Area and Timing Overhead

In this experiment, the proposed path delay measurement architecture was incorporated into several IWLS 2005 full-scan based benchmark circuits to evaluate its hardware and timing overheads. The area overheads reported in this chapter are obtained by using a commercial synthesis tool targeting the SMIC 0.18 μm CMOS technology. The benchmark circuits' profiles and the area overhead of the proposed approach incorporated into the benchmark are presented in Table 2.4. The circuit's name of the benchmarks and the numbers of the flip-flops are given in column 1 and column 2, respectively. The column under "Circuit Area (μm^2)" reports the area of the benchmark circuits without implementing the proposed delay measurement architecture, while the sub-columns "Total", "NoComb", "Comb" represent the corresponding total, sequential, and combinational part's area, respectively. Due to the different delay measurement requirements pursued by test experts, various path sets with totally different sizes and path delays may be selected for delay measurement. We only focus on the delay measurement architecture rather than how to select the circuit paths targeting for delay measurement. Hence, we evaluate the area overheads of the proposed delay measurement architecture considering different numbers of path endpoints, even in the worst case where all the flip-flops are acted as the endpoints of paths for delay measurements. The columns "20%M", "60%M", and "100%M" represent three cases in which 20%, 60%, and 100% of the flip-flops are the endpoints of paths under measurements. For each of these flip-flops, a multiplexer is added to calibrate the delay difference of import lines. The sub-columns "Area (μm^2)" and "Area (%)" under the three cases report the area overhead of the proposed delay measurement architecture and its percentage against that of the original benchmark circuit.

As is clearly shown in the Table 2.4, even in the worst case, the hardware overhead of the proposed delay measurement architecture can be acceptable. In practice, this scenario may be much more optimistic. For instance, Table 2.5 reports the hardware overhead of the proposed architecture for des perf benchmark circuit, where all the critical paths that can be single-path sensitized are selected for delay measurement. As shown in Table 2.5, the clock period of the des perf circuit is synthesized to 2.6 ns by using a commercial synthesis tool, which guarantees a slack of 10% the clock period for the longest path of the circuit under static timing analysis. The number of the selected critical internal paths is 1164, which is obtained by using a commercial timing analysis tool by specifying the path slack of which

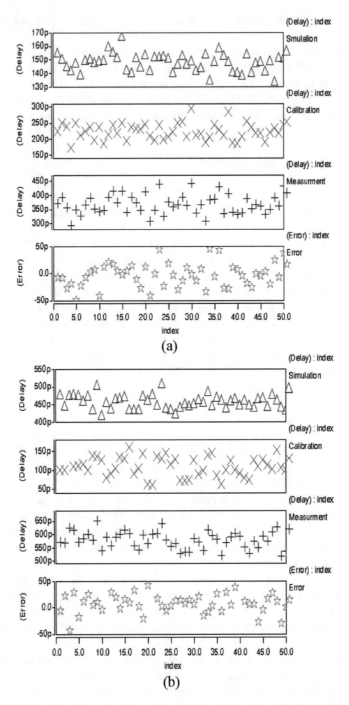

Fig. 2.23 Simulated waveform for delay measurement obtained from 50 Monte Carlo iteration with $3\delta_1 = 0.1\mu_L$ and $3\delta_2 = 0.1\mu_L$, (**a**) for Path1 (**b**) for Path2

Table 2.4 Area overhead of the proposed delay measurement architecture

Circuit	# of FFs	Circuit area (μm^2)			Area overhead of the proposed scheme					
		Total	No Comb.	Comb.	20% M		60% M		100% M	
					Area (μm^2)	Area (%)	Area (μm^2)	Area (%)	Area (μm^2)	Area (%)
des_perf	8808	1,196,203	585,978	610,225	57,037	4.77%	150,794	12.61%	244,550	20.44%
wb_conmax	578	230,776	48,243	182,533	13,235	5.74%	19,388	8.40%	25,540	11.07%
aes_core	530	202,325	38,699	163,626	12,980	6.42%	18,621	9.20%	24,263	11.99%
pci_bridge32	3313	396,500	264,226	132,274	27,792	7.01%	63,057	15.90%	98,322	24.80%
ac97_ctrl	2229	237,119	174,892	62,227	22,022	9.29%	45,749	19.29%	69,475	29.30%
mem_ctrl	1126	158,606	92,866	65,740	16,152	10.18%	28,138	17.74%	40,123	25.30%
usb_funct	1741	242,305	127,228	115,077	1945	8.02%	37,957	15.66%	56,489	23.31%
systemcaes	670	139,789	55,894	83,895	13,725	9.82%	20,857	14.92%	27,989	20.02%

Table 2.5 Experiment
results of DES_Perf circuit

Benchmark	Des_perf
# of FFs	8808
Clock period (ns)	2.6
# of circuit critical paths	1164
# of single path sensitization	779
# of critical endpoint	253
Area overhead (μm^2)	16,892
Area overhead (%)	1.41%

is less than 20% of the clock period. For the selected critical internal paths, the number of paths that can be detected under the single path sensitization criterion is 779, which is obtained by using a commercial test generation tool and can then be sensitized for delay measurement. Clearly, multiple critical paths may be ended at the same endpoint. The number of endpoints for these paths suitable for delay measurement is 253. Therefore, only 253 endpoints should be inserted with the multiplexers to support the proposed delay measurement architecture. The area overhead of the whole proposed delay measurement architecture is $116,892\,\mu m^2$, and its percentage against that of the original benchmark circuit is only 1.41%.

Due to the application of the proposed delay measurement architecture, the delay of circuit paths may be impacted. Hence, the timing overhead of the delay measurement architecture to the critical path, which impacts the circuit performance, should be evaluated. Table 2.6 evaluates the timing impact of the proposed delay measurement architecture to the delay of the longest circuit internal path in each benchmark circuit. The experimental circuit's names and clock domains are listed in the column 1 and column 2, respectively. The columns under "Longest internal path delay (before)" and "Longest internal path delay (after)" represent the delays of the longest internal path before and after the incorporation of the delay measurement architecture for the considered clock domain. The column under "Delay increase" represents the delay increase of the longest path caused by incorporation of the proposed architecture. The column under "Timing overhead" represents the percentage of delay increase against the delay of the longest internal path before incorporation of the delay measurement architecture. As shown in Table 2.6, the timing impact of the proposed delay measurement architecture to the sample circuit is less than 0.7% of the longest internal delay and can be negligible.

2.2.5.5 Comparison A

To compare with previous works, the delay measurement circuits using the proposed OCDM method and the method from [22] which employed a modified VDL with equal delay range value in each stage are implemented respectively. Table 2.7 compares the experimental results of the two methods. Note that the proposed OCDM circuit needs only 3.3% of the delay stages to achieve even larger maximum

Table 2.6 Timing overhead

Circuit	Clock domain	Longest circuit internal path delay (before) (ns)	Longest circuit internal path delay (after) (ns)	Delay increase (ps)	Timing Overhead (%)
des_perf	clk	2.0280	2.0377	9.7	0.48%
wb_commax	clk_i	1.9256	1.9644	11.8	0.60%
aes_core	clk	2.7504	2.7588	8.4	0.31%
pci_bridge32	pci_clk_i	1.7575	1.7656	8.1	0.46%
ac97_ctrl	clk_i	2.0684	2.0790	10.6	0.51%
mem_ctrl	clk_i	2.0788	2.0931	14.3	0.69%
usb_funct	phy_clk_pad_i	1.8180	1.8261	8.1	0.44%
systemcaes	clk	3.0745	3.0813	6.8	0.22%

delay measurement range compared to the delay measurement circuit using the method from [22], while the delay measurement resolution of the proposed OCDM circuit is only 49% of that for the delay measurement circuit using the method from [22]. As mentioned earlier, when the delay measurement is completed, the values stored in the flip-flops of the OCDM circuit should be shifted out serially using slow shift clock. If we assume the frequency of shift clock is 1 GHz, then the time for scanning out the measurement values is only 8 ns for the proposed OCDM circuit, but is up to 245 ns for the delay measurement circuit using the method from [22] according to Table 2.7.

The area overheads of the two delay measurement circuits are obtained using a commercial synthesis tool. It can be seen that the combinational, non-combinational, and the total area overheads of the proposed OCDM circuit are only 35.5%, 3.3%, and 22.3% of that for the delay measurement circuit using the method from [22] respectively. It seems unfair to compare only the hardware overhead of the OCDM circuit of the proposed delay measurement architecture with the delay measurement circuit using the method from [22] without considering the hardware overhead of the insertion of multiplexers at the endpoints of the PUMs. However, it should be noted that the OCDM circuit provides the same path delay measurement ability with that of the method from [22], while the purpose of the insertion for 2-to-1 multiplexers to the end points of the PUMs is to calibrate the delay difference of import lines. Thereby, a higher precision of delay measurement results for the PUMs can be obtained by the proposed method as compared to the method from [22].

2.2.5.6 Comparison B

By considering the delay difference of the import lines in the proposed scheme, and considering the returning loop delay in the Path-RO scheme [92], both the proposed scheme and the Path-RO scheme can provide a high precision for path delay measurement. However, as compared to the Path-RO technique, the proposed technique provides a more effective way to measure the delay of a path. This is mainly due to the following reasons.

1. A multiplexer is required to be inserted into the critical PUM in the Path-RO technique, which reduces the speed of high performance circuit. Clearly, in the proposed path delay measurement architecture, no extra cell has to be inserted in the PUM, while only a small overload from one input of the multiplexer is added in the PUM. Hence, the proposed technique has a weak impact to the delay of a critical path as compared to the Path-RO technique.

2. The Path-RO technique can only measure either the delays of paths that begin at a clocked flip-flop or the delays of paths that end at this clocked flip-flop. The reason is that the flip-flop which is the start point of the PUM has to be modified to a calibration launch flip-flop (CLFF), while the flip-flop which is the end point of the PUM has to be modified to a calibration capture flip-flop

Table 2.7 Measurement circuit comparison

Circuit	Stage numbers	Resolution	Maximum measurement range	Area (μm²)		
				Combinational	No combinational	Total
Proposed OCDM	8	6.62 ps	3295 ps	9547	612	10,159
[22]	245	13.45 ps	3295 ps	26,894	18,744	45,638

(CCFF) with a different circuit structure. However, the delay of each circuit path chosen for delay measurement can be obtained by the proposed on-chip path delay measurement technique.

3. In order to measure the delay of a path by using the Path-RO technique, one and two extra multiplexers are required to be added in the flip-flops which are stood at the input and output of the PUM, respectively. However, only one extra multiplexer is required to be added for the flip-flop which is the endpoint of the PUM in the proposed path delay measurement technique. Hence, the proposed method suffers from a significant lower hardware overhead as compared to the Path-RO technique.

4. By using the Path-RO technique, only the delay of a path on which the number of inverting logics is odd can be measured due to the use of the oscillation technique. Otherwise, one inverter is required to be added to the PUM, which will further increase the design complexity to the path delay measurement architecture. Moreover, the delay of the returning loop might not be calibrated to a clock period because the first requirement of the calibration process is to assure that the PUM is configured to be able to oscillate. Hence, the precision of the path delay measurement would be influenced. Clearly, no such extra restrictions are posed into the proposed on-chip path delay measurement technique when measuring the delay of a chosen circuit path.

2.2.6 Discussion

We have presented a novel on-chip path delay measurement technique for timing characterization and silicon debug. In the proposed OCDM circuit, the delay range of each delay stage is set to increase by a factor of two gradually from the last to the first delay stage. In addition, by conducting delay compensation, both improved delay measurement resolution and measurement precision can be provided when compared to the previous VDL based delay measurement schemes. The delay difference of the import lines for feeding the start and end transitions of the PUM into the OCDM circuit is also considered in the proposed technique, which can further provide a high precision for path delay measurement. Experimental results show that the proposed on-chip path delay measurement scheme works well. A small quantity of delay stages in OCDM circuit can obtain a large delay measurement range, and hence can provide a significant reduction in delay measurement time. Moreover, the area overhead of the proposed method is also significantly reduced as compared to previous works.

2.3 Lifetime Fault-Tolerant Circuit Design

In the past decades, the device and reliability communities have devoted much efforts to lifetime projection [10, 76], but less to design for lifetime reliability. This situation would be changed because the lifetime reliability is seriously challenged by the aggressive technology scaling [15, 34]. One of the major impending (above 22 nm) challenges comes from MOS transistor wearout [34]; NBTI (negative bias temperature instability) and TDDB (time dependent dielectric breakdown) draw the most attentions over a wide variety of transistor aging mechanisms [34]. Both aging mechanisms can gradually degrade the performance of transistors over time [8, 36] due to elevated threshold voltage [13, 91] or degraded integrity of gate oxide [3, 43, 70].

To guarantee the chips' lifetime reliability, a common practice is reserving conservative timing margin—just like that for process variations [71]. However, the effectiveness of such approaches is diminishing, given that up to 10–20% guard band has to be reserved to safely accommodate the aging-induced performance degradation—which can even offset the performance benefit from one-generation of technology advancement.

Many researches have been conducted at different levels: device level [18, 87], circuit level [90, 91], and (micro)architecture level [35, 74, 77]. Particularly, Blome et al. proposed an online wearout detection approach through sensing the aging-induced delay [36]. Agarwal et al., based on the same observation, proposed a sensor design dedicated for aging failure prediction [8]. Yan et al. presented a more versatile and cost efficient sensor design [94] which can also be used for aging detection.

Although the prior sensor designs prepare a ground for aging-aware designs, few researches are conducted so far to study how to effectively use them; this work aims to serve this purpose. The lifetime of a chip is governed by the "weakest-link principle"—usually only a minority of transistors suffer large aging degradation reflected in excessive path delay. The aging sensors can capture this change; however, previous solutions such as turning voltage and/or frequency [77], reducing individual core utilization [4], and duplicating hardware resources [39, 78] do not use such fine-grained detection capability sufficiently. Although those architecture- and application-level approaches are somewhat effective to remedy the aged chips, these coarse-grained solutions trading either performance or hardware resources for lifetime may be far from efficient due to the blindness to the minority of fine-grained "weakest links" which can be identified by the aging sensors.

Above analysis motivates us to propose a new approach to exploiting fine-grained aging adaptability. Unlike those coarse-grained approaches, the fine-grained approach can cope with the "weakest-links" more locally and efficiently, thereby making it possible to improve lifetime reliability while without compromising with the architectural performance and coarse-grained hardware resources. In particular, we make three contributions:

1. We propose ReviveNet, a hardware-implemented aging-aware and self-adaptive architecture, to improve lifetime reliability. Aging-awareness is realized by deploying dedicated aging sensors, and "self-adaptive" is achieved by employing a group of synergistic adaptation agents.
2. To support ReviveNet, we present a localized timing adaptation mechanism, with which the aged critical paths can be locally coped with. The fine-grained adaptability results from timing imbalance between consecutive timing paths. The lifetime can be extended significantly through exploiting such "path-grained" adaptability.
3. We propose an evaluation model to quantitatively study the ReviveNet-enhanced reliability.

The effectiveness of ReviveNet has been evaluated through incorporating it into an industrial pipelined floating-point co-processor. Experimental results show that ReviveNet can improve the MTTF by 48.7% without compromising with architectural performance, only at about 9.5% area and small power overhead.

2.3.1   Aging Symptoms and Aging Sensors

The aging-induced delay is a suitable symptom candidate [8, 36, 51]. For example, Blome et al. took the TDDB induced delay as the symptom for wearout detection [36]. Agarwal et al., took the NBTI induced delay as the symptom for aging failure prediction [8, 51]. We also take aging delay as the symptom in this work.

Aging-awareness can be realized by employing some dedicated aging sensors. The fundamental working principle of sensors is on-line delay fault detection. The only difference between the aging sensing and traditional delay fault detection is that the former takes place in a safe timing interval called "Guard band" [8], while the latter takes place in the interval after the effective clock edge called "Detection slack" [94]. As Fig. 2.24 shows, initially, in fresh state, no signal transitions occur in guard band, but after suffering form aging, some transitions could be delayed into guard band. Since the signal should have been stabilized before entering the guard band, we call the event of such a "faulty" transition in guard band as a Stability Violation [94]. It is worthy to note that the detected aging delay, unlike conventional delay faults, won't cause any timing fault (a.k.a. Timing violation).

The detection for aging delay is actually to detect the stability violations in guard band. We can use stability checker—the key component in aging sensor—to fulfill this purpose. The basic stability checker can be derived from a sensing circuit for on-line delay fault detection, in which the signal integrity is verified by a pair of consistent charge/discharge nodes, the delay transitions will trigger one of the charged nodes to be discharged and thereby causes state inconsistence between them. More specifically, as shown in Fig. 2.25, during precharge period,

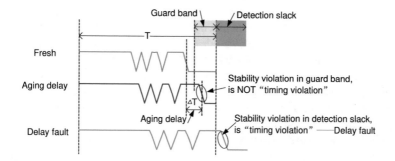

Fig. 2.24 The timing of aging delay and delay fault

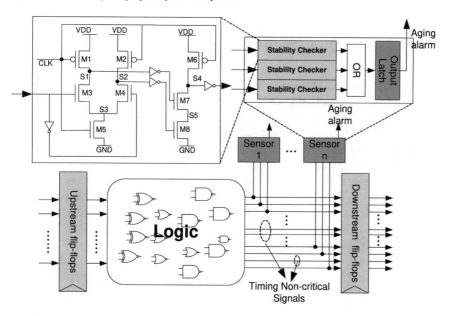

Fig. 2.25 Sensor setup

both nodes $S1$ and $S2$ in the stability checker are charged up to HIGH. The circuit starts evaluation when entering the guard band; one of the two nodes is pulled down, while the other one floats at HIGH because the gate signal of M3 is always complemented with that of M4. Hence, the node $S1$ and $S2$ are always exclusive during fault-free time, which will make the node $S4$ stick to HIGH because the high-impedance path between S4 and GND always exists. When aging delay happens, the stability violation will trigger the discharge of the node that has charged up to HIGH. Eventually both nodes are discharged, and thereby the node S4 is pull down to LOW—which flags aging delay being detected. Please refer to [94] for more details.

One sensor consists of multiple stability checkers, one wide dynamic OR gate, and one output latch [94]. To reduced overhead, multiple stability checkers share one output latch through a wide dynamic OR gate, as shown in Fig. 2.25.

The aging sensors are deployed to monitor critical paths. As an example, Fig. 2.25 shows a setup for a stage of logic, where each sensor handles three signals. If some aged transistors in the logic or upstream flip-flops result in stability violations in the guard band—aging delay, the corresponding sensors can tell that an aging failure is impending.

With the "awareness" of aging, the next essential problem is how to accommodate the impending aging failures indicated by these alarms. The ReviveNet aims to address this problem.

2.3.2 Lifetime Fault-Tolerant Architecture

Figure 2.26 illustrates the ReviveNet architecture. Each stage is monitored by a set of periodically-invoked aging sensors. The adaptation to each stage is implemented with a set of adaptation agents which are fed by not only the local stage's aging sensors but also the next stage's agents, thereby enabling bidirectional adaptation—*backward timing adaptation* (BTA) and *forward timing adaptation* (FTA). BTA is using the $(K + 1)$st stage's timing slack to accommodate the aging emergencies in the Kth stage, while FTA is using the $(K - 1)$st stage's slack to accommodate the emergencies in the Kth stage. With the bidirectional adaptation mechanism, ReviveNet offers more adaptation freedom and performs more effectively.

Let's explain the basic idea of ReviveNet with a simple example. Figure 2.27 shows a part of a pipeline, where each arrow denotes a timing path and the length of it represents corresponding delay; in particular, the critical path in the middle stage is denoted by a bold arrow. After experiencing some aging, suppose that the

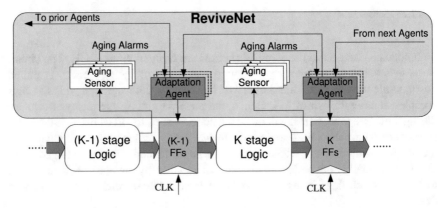

Fig. 2.26 ReviveNet architecture

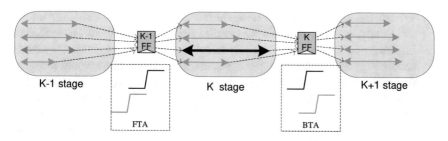

Fig. 2.27 Example of adaptation

delay of the critical path is going to exceed the clock period—an impending aging failure, an aging sensor monitoring this path detects the impending failure [8, 94] and flags an aging alarm; then, three local adaptation options can be enabled to tolerate this aging delay: (1) backward skew the clock of Kth flip-flop—BTA, (2) forward skew the clock of $(K-1)$st flip-flop—FTA, or (3) both FTA and BTA. The specific adaptations are governed by a finite state machine, referred to agent.

The above conceptual example can just convey a very basic idea of ReviveNet; we can gain more insights into the ReviveNet's operations and underling design tradeoffs by answering the following questions:

(1) Why are BTA and FTA feasible?

Clearly, BTA or FTA can help tolerate the aging delay of the target critical path only if there is timing imbalance between the corresponding paths, i.e. all upstream paths of $(K-1)$st flip-flop, or all downstream paths of Kth flip-flop are non-critical. We call such imbalance as path-grained (or, localized) adaptability. We will use a case study (Sect. 2.3.3.2) to show that the potential of such localized adaptability, which ReviveNet aims to exploit, is quite attractive.

(2) Where the sensors and agents should be deployed?

This problem is trivial if both the critical paths and aging impacts can be well-predicted: every critical path that is prone to suffer aging impacts should be monitored by a sensor. Unfortunately, though the critical paths can be somewhat distinguished from non-critical paths with some sophisticated SSTA (statistical static timing analysis) approaches, many researches have been evident that the aging degree of individual transistor highly depends on the physical geometries, defect density and the stress states during working mode. In other words, the aging degree of individual transistor is highly unpredictable; hence it seems hopeless to identify the aging-prone critical paths. We take an engineering way to tackle this problem: conservatively put all critical paths under monitor. Thought it is not an theoretically optimum option, the experimental results show that such engineering way is still cost-efficient (Sect. 2.3.7).

Deploying agents is based on the sensors deployment and specific circuit topology. The detail can be found in (Sect. 2.3.4.5).

(3) **What's the adaptation logic of agents?**

Usually, one sensor is able to monitor multiple critical paths to reduce the implementation overhead. The side-effect is decreased "resolution"—when a sensor flags an aging alarm, the agent actually cannot immediately recognize that which path (or paths) causes this alarm; hence the agent needs to follow a policy to efficiently identify the root of the alarm. Given that the aging is a progressive process and thus does not need to be in realtime accommodated, we propose a round-robin trial adaptation mechanism—the agent travels across a set of prioritized adaptation states to track back the source of the alarm and then tries the best to accommodate it (Sect. 2.3.4.1).

(4) **How to implement the intentional clock skew?**

The intentional skew is used to enable BTA and FTA. One way to obtain the intentional skew is by inserting delay buffers [5]. However, the drawback of such delay-buffer based design is poor controllability. For example, suppose that during the early years of service life almost no adaptation is required, but these buffers still suffer from aging, contribute to leakage power, and so on. We propose a new implementing scheme to obtain the skewed clocks in a highly controllable way, while minimizing the side effects to the adaptation-free period (Sect. 2.3.5.1, 2.3.5.2).

(5) **What if the infrastructure of ReviveNet, sensors and agents, fail to work due to aging?**

ReviveNet is relatively aging resistant because it does not need to be always-on; most of lifetime it is power-off. Thus, the transistors' aging rate in sensors and agents, statistically, is much slower than that in host logics. We shall give more detailed discussion in next section.

(6) **How much extended lifetime can be achieved?**

This question is hard to answer due to lack of accurate models that capture the relationship between a variety of aging mechanisms and aging delay. To quantitatively study the MTTF (Mean-Time-To-Failure) improvement, we propose a ReviveNet-enhanced reliability model in which the relationship is condensed to a hypothetical function δ (Sect. 2.3.6). Then, we instantiate the function based on the well-studied NBTI mechanism (Sect. 2.3.7) to show the effect of ReviveNet, though the reliability model can also be applied to other aging mechanisms that need more intensive studies in the future. Experimental results show that up to 48.7% MTTF improvement can be achieved.

Figure 2.28 qualitatively shows the ReviveNet-enhanced lifetime. When ReviveNet is too exhausted to make any effective adaptation—if any of the agents fails to accommodate an impending aging failure, the chip is judged reaching the end of lifetime. ReviveNet can also readily indicate the "incurable" failure; then, one can proactively take actions, such as replacing the aged chips, degrading the architectural performance, to minimize the impacts of failure.

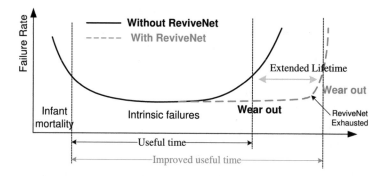

Fig. 2.28 Anticipated effect of ReviveNet

2.3.3 Self-adaptive Fault-Tolerant Pipeline

2.3.3.1 Timing Imbalance

We describe the timing imbalance that can be exploited to tolerate the aging delay through characterizing pipeline flip-flops. A pipeline flip-flop can be categorized according to the slack values of related upstream and downstream paths. Specifically, suppose a flip-flop FF serves as the end point of m paths with slack values $e_1, e_2, \ldots, e_m$, and the start point of n paths with slack values $s_1, s_2, \ldots, s_n$. Given a threshold, TH, which distinguishes the (potential) critical paths ($slack \leq TH$) from others ($slack > TH$), the flip-flop must fall into one of the four classes:

- Generous Flip-flop (GFF): $\forall e_i \in \{e_1, e_2, \ldots, e_m\}$, s.t. $e_i > TH$, and $\forall s_j \in \{s_1, s_2, \ldots, s_n\}$, s.t. $s_j > TH$ (say, "Generous" with timing margin).
- Backward Adaptable Flip-flop (BAFF): $\exists e_i \in \{e_1, e_2, \ldots, e_m\}$, s.t. $e_i \leq TH$, but $\forall s_j \in \{s_1, s_2, \ldots, s_n\}$, s.t. $s_j > TH$.
- Forward Adaptable Flip-flop (FAFF): $\forall e_i \in \{e_1, e_2, \ldots, e_m\}$, s.t. $e_i > TH$, but $\exists s_j \in \{s_1, s_2, \ldots, s_n\}$, s.t. $s_j \leq TH$.
- Unadaptable Flip-flop (UAFF): $\exists e_i \in \{e_1, e_2, \ldots, e_m\}$, s.t. $e_i \leq TH$, and $\exists s_j \in \{s_1, s_2, \ldots, s_n\}$, s.t. $s_j \leq TH$.

In the following cases can yield critical paths:

1. start with a FAFF and end with a BAFF, or
2. start with a FAFF and end with a UAFF, or
3. start with a UAFF and end with a BAFF, or
4. start with a UAFF and end with a UAFF.

A critical path in case (2) and (3) can gain extra $TH/2$ slack (note that we let the slack-providing paths still hold at least $TH/2$ slack); that in case (1) can gain extra $TH/2 + TH/2$ slack; while that in case (4) cannot gain any extra slack.

Threshold TH is a key factor affecting the design tradeoffs. On one hand, the larger TH, the higher percentage of UAFFs, thus more critical paths will be rendered unadaptable; on the other, the larger TH can facilitate more aggressive time stealing on adaptable paths. In (Sect. 2.3.7), we will show that neither over-large nor over-small TH can lead to an optimum design tradeoff.

2.3.3.2 Self-Adaptive Design Example

As a case study, the following investigates the intrinsic timing imbalance in a industry design.

We took a pipelined FPU adopted by OpenSPARC T1 [79] processor as our target circuit. This FPU is synthesized using Synopsys Design Compiler with UMC $0.18\,\mu$m technology, and its' path timing is analyzed with PrimeTime. We set the performance as the synthesizing priority to smooth the distribution of path delay as much as possible. The timing analysis results are shown in Fig. 2.29.

Figure 2.29 shows the breakdowns of flip-flops with different type of adaptability, under six TH configurations: 0.05 (T_{max}), 0.1, 0.15, 0.2, 0.25, and 0.3, where T_{max} represents the most critical path delay. When TH=0.05, all of the critical paths are adaptable due to no UAFF appears. With TH increasing, some GFFs fall into the groups of BAFFs or FAFFs, even UAFFs, but GFFs, BAFFs and FAFFs always take considerable percentage—that is the "potential" (localized adaptability) which ReviveNet can exploit.

2.3.4 Self-adaptive Agent

The agents are responsible for controlling the localized adaptations. Before delving into the implementation details, let's first suppose that such localized adaptations can be realized by selecting a clock from multiple available clocks skewed from

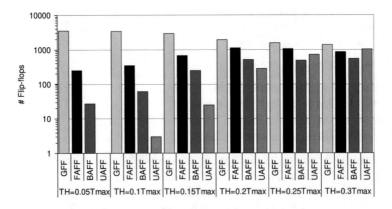

Fig. 2.29 Distribution of flip-flops at different TH

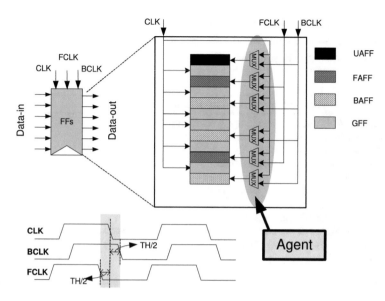

Fig. 2.30 Example of adaptive clock assignment (agent is responsible for generating the clock-steering signals)

each other, as Fig. 2.30 shows. The adaptability of each flip-flop has been identified beforehand with a static timing analysis tool. The GFFs' and UAFFs' clocks are kept intact, and each FAFF's, BAFF's clock is individually controllable. Dealing with UAFFs in this way is because no favorable time margins can be exploited without hurting the timing of other critical paths, so we would rather keep them intact than take tentative adaptations which cannot guarantee any reliability benefits. A FAFF is clocked by either original clock (CLK) or forward skewed clock (FCLK) to enable FTA; a BAFF is clocked by either CLK or backward skewed clock (BCLK) to enable BTA.

In Fig. 2.30, suppose that a sensor is deployed to monitor all of UAFFs and BAFFs, when the sensor flags an aging alarm, how does the corresponding agent perform the clock steering? One way is to enable all of the BAFFs (the FAFFs are enabled by the next stage's agent and discussed later); however, such "brutal" way may significantly sacrifice the timing margins of the innocent paths, thus not complying with the principle of "localized adaptation". The following presents a trial-based approach to address this problem.

2.3.4.1 Round-Robin Trial Adaptation (RRTA)

When a sensor raises an aging alarm, it could be traced back to single or multiple critical paths. Fortunately, given that circuit aging usually is a gradual process, the response of an intended adaptation does not need to be in realtime. This allowable adaptation latency can justify the proposed RRTA approach below.

RRTA performs in an "identify-then-adapt" manner. Each trial represents an adaptation state—the value of clock-steering signals of related flip-flops. Algorithm 1 presents the procedure of RRTA.

Algorithm 1: Round-Robin trial adaptation (K)

Data: The Kth Agent receives an aging emergency;
1 **for** *each adaptation state candidates* **do**
2   conduct a trial adaptation;
3   **if** *the emergency is eliminated* **then**
4   break;
          // Adaptation succeeded!
5   **else**
6   Recover this trial adaptation;
7   **if** *all the adaptation states have been reached* **then** break;
          // Adaptation failed!
8   **end**
9 **end**

The following clarifies how to define the set of adaptation states (related to line 1 in Algorithm 1). Generally, each agent is fed by an aging alarm and a request from another agent (as shown in Fig. 2.26). For agent A_K and a set of flip-flops FF, the aging alarms only trigger the backward adaptations to BAFFs, and the requests triggers the forward adaptations to FAFFs. The adaptation states are described with the following example.

Example For the Kth stage with downstream flip-flops $FF_k=\{f_1^k, \ldots, b_1^k, b_2^k, b_3^k, u_1^k\}$ and upstream flip-flops $FF_{k-1}=\{f_1^{k-1}, f_2^{k-1}, f_3^{k-1}, f_4^{k-1}, b_1^{k-1}, \ldots, u_1^{k-1}, \ldots\}$, where f, b, and u denote FAFF, BAFF, and UAFF, respectively. Agent A_K and A_{K-1} handles FF_k and FF_{k-1}, respectively. Clearly, only $\{b_1^k, b_2^k, b_3^k\}$ and $\{f_1^{k-1}, f_2^{k-1}, f_3^{k-1}, f_4^{k-1}\}$ can contribute to the Kth stage's adaptations. Furthermore, suppose that only $f_1^{k-1}, f_2^{k-1}, f_3^{k-1}, f_4^{k-1}$ are related inputs to b_1^k, b_2^k, b_3^k. The correspondence of related FAFFs and BAFFs is easy to identify with logic core generation algorithms which has been well-studied and widely used on ATPG (Automatic Test Patten Generation) [88].

The candidates of backward adaptation states (BAS) are denoted by $BAS=BAS_0 \cup BAS_1 \cup BAS_2 \cup BAS_3$ where each term is a set of states corresponding to b_1^k, b_2^k, and b_3^k, as follows:

$$BAS_0 = \{000\};$$

$$BAS_1 = \{001, 010, 100\};$$

$$BAS_2 = \{011, 101, 110\};$$

$$BAS_3 = \{111\}.$$

BAS_0 is an initial state representing no adaption conducted. BAS_1, BAS_2, and BAS_3 represent 1-bit, 2-bit, and 3-bit backward adaptations conducting on b_1^k, b_2^k, and b_3^k, respectively. The agent, for example, conducts a "001" adaptation, means that BCLK for b_3^k is enabled, while keeping the b_1^k, b_2^k intact. Clearly, the perturbation level to the circuit is elevated from BAS_1 to BAS_3 because more bits adapted implies more perturbations introduced.

On the other hand, if A_K receives an aging alarm, there should be another option: forward adapting the FAFFs in FF_{k-1}. To do so, A_K needs to cooperate with A_{K-1}. The corresponding candidates of forward adaptation states (FAS), similarly to BAS, can be defined as $FAS=FAS_0 \cup FAS_1 \cup FAS_2 \cup FAS_3 \cup FAS_4$, where

$$FAS_0 = \{0000\};$$

$$FAS_1 = \{0001, 0010, 0100, 1000\};$$

$$FAS_2 = \{0011, 0101, 1001, 0110, 1010, 1100\};$$

$$FAS_3 = \{0111, 1011, 1101, 1110\};$$

$$FAS_4 = \{1111\}.$$

Priority of Adaptation States   These adaptation states have to be prioritized to make the adaptations agree with "perturbation-least" principle. We have explained that the priority of states in BAS is $BAS_1 > BAS_2 > BAS_3$. Clearly, for the same reason, the FAS should meet: $FAS_1 > FAS_2 > FAS_3 > FAS_4$. It is preferred to enable one or multiple BAFFs in FF_k since this is the most direct and effective way to accommodate an aging emergency. So BAS_1 to BAS_3 are given the top priority. And the states in FAS_1 to FAS_4 are given lower priority since these states involve FAFFs which just can indirectly contribute to the aging delay tolerance. Then the overall priority over these states can be presented as: $BAS_1 > BAS_2 > BAS_3 > FAS_1 > FAS_2 > FAS_3 > FAS_4$.

Adaptation Latency   The worst case adaptation latency in number of trials for the above example is 22 (sum of adaptation states). In fact, in the early period of aging, the number of trials will be much smaller than the worst case since most aging alarms would be easily accommodated with high priority states. The situation cannot become much worse with the gradually exacerbated aging process because many high-priority states have been used in the early stage, thereby gradually shrinking the set of available states. In addition, the worst case will not exponentially increase with the increasing number of flip-flops because in the same stage, there can be multiple independent agents and each of them works under limited complexity. Furthermore, in Sect. 2.3.4.4, we present two optimizing approaches to further reduce the hardware overhead.

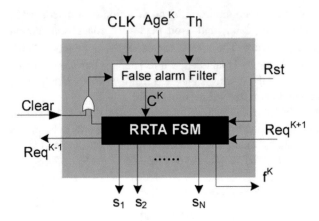

Fig. 2.31 Adaptation agent

2.3.4.2 Agent Implementation

Figure 2.31 shows the top view of an agent architecture. The agent can send a request Req^{K-1} to an agent in the $(K-1)$st stage to enable forward adaptation for the Kth stage logics, and can also receive Req^{K+1} coming from an agent in the $(K+1)$st stage to enable forward adaptation for the $(K+1)$st stage logics. A failure signal (f^K) is asserted if an aging alarm still appears after the agent has traveled the all adaptation states.

Each agent consists of a RRTA unit and a False Alarm Filter; the RRTA is a finite state machine (FSM), and the filter is a counter. Signal Age^K, which is an aging alarm signal coming from an aging sensor, is cycle-updated. The adaptation process, however, should not be triggered at the same pace, otherwise it could incur useless adaptations due to the presence of *false alarms*.

2.3.4.3 False Alarm Filter

The false alarms are caused by subtle dynamic variations [15] such as power noise, temperature fluctuation. But aging can still be reliably detected even in the presence of these dynamic variations. The main reason is that the locations of aged paths generally won't change over time. This is very different from the power noise which mainly results from the time-varying current demand and exhibits much randomness in both spatial and temporary dimensions. Hence, the aging alarms traced back to the same spots are more "repetitive", by contrast to the more random dynamic variations. By exploiting the repetitiveness, we can filter the most, if not all, false alarms.

Identifying the "repetitiveness" can be realized with a counter, which records the number of alarms in a specified span of time. A confident aging alarm (C^K) is asserted only when corresponding counter reaches a threshold (Th) that has

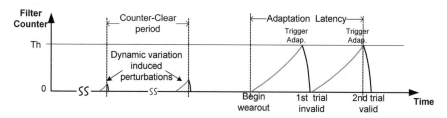

Fig. 2.32 Example of filter counter change

been calibrated according to some alarm statistics. To eliminate the aggregate effect of these false alarms, after each period of trial adaptation, the counter should be cleared.

Figure 2.32 exemplifies the change of a filter counter over time. The normal perturbations (false alarms) have little chance to trigger adaptations; two adaption trials are conducted: the first fails, thus the counter still keeps growing after the invalid adaptation, while the second succeeds and the counter does not increase any more.

2.3.4.4 Complexity Analysis and Two Critical Optimizations

In Example 9, for agent A_K handling 7-bit clock-steering signals (3 bit for BAFFs and 4 bit for FAFFs), there are up to 22 ($2^3 - 1 + 2^4 - 1$) candidate states. Furthermore, each agent owns a private filter, which could incur non-negligible area overhead. Fortunately, with the following two optimizations the potential complexity can be decreased significantly.

Many adaptation state candidates can be removed with little loss of adaptability. The following shows how to use "logic cones" analysis to

1. remove those low-effective states for loose-couple logic cones, or
2. merge them for tight-couple logic cones.

Example Figure 2.33 exemplifies a stage of logic covered in two logic cones without overlap—loose-couple, referred to case (a) and with some overlap—tight-couple, referred to case (b). Suppose that flip-flop F1, F2, F3, and F4 are FAFFs and F5, F6 are BAFFs.

For case (a), the basic adaption states for F5 and F6 are {01, 10, 11}. Clearly, the state "11" is effective only in the case: (at least) one aged path in each logic cone causes aging alarm at the same time. Such "coincidence", however, hardly happens; thus, we can safely remove the "11" from the adaptation state candidates. Similarly, the forward adaption states (for F1, F2, F3, F4) can be simplified from {0001, 0010, ..., 1111} to {0001, 0010, 0100, 1000, 0011, 1100}.

For case (b), the overlap can reduce some efficiency of such optimization. Removing state "11" for F5 and F6 may be problematic since an aging alarm could

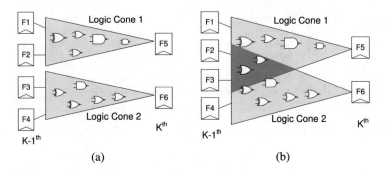

Fig. 2.33 Logic cones. (**a**) Loose-couple logic cones. (**b**) Tight-couple logic cones

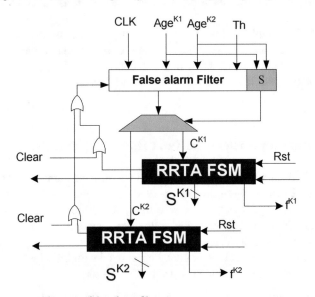

Fig. 2.34 Two agents share one false alarm filter

be raised at F5 and F6 simultaneously if aging happens in the overlap zone. For the same reason, the forward adaptation states should not be removed. However, since these two logic cones is tightly coupled, using 1-bit state for F5 and F6 should be reasonable. Then the backward adaptation states can be reduced from $\{01, 10, 11\}$ to $\{1\}$. Similarly, the forward adaptation states can be simplified to $\{001, 010, 100, 011, 110, 111\}$ (for F1, $<F2, F3>$, F4).

Each agent owning a private false-alarm filter is cost-inefficient, since such private filter is only necessary in such case: all the agents are active at the same time—that is a quite small probability event. Enabling filter sharing can be readily implemented by appending selection-indicating bits S to original filter. Figure 2.34 shows an example of two agents sharing one filter.

The above have described the individual agent design and functionality; the following will detail how to deploy the agents and corresponding sensors with respect to the correspondence of BAFFs, FAFFs, and UAFFs.

2.3.4.5 Deploy Agents and Sensors

Suppose that the Kth stage with downstream flip-flops

$$FF_k = \{f_1^k, \ldots, b_1^k, \ldots, b_s^k, u_1^k, \ldots, u_t^k, g_1^k, \ldots\},$$

and upstream flip-flops

$$FF_{k-1} = \{f_1^{k-1}, \ldots, f_r^{k-1}, b_1^{k-1}, \ldots, u_1^{k-1}, \ldots, g_1^{k-1}, \ldots\}.$$

Among these flip-flops, only $\{b_1^k, \ldots, b_s^k\}$ and $\{f_1^{k-1}, \ldots, f_r^{k-1}\}$ can contribute to the adaptation in the Kth stage. We explain the policy of deployment with the following example:

Figure 2.35 shows the Kth stage's upstream and downstream flip-flops that can contribute to adaptation, and each sensor is assumed to handle eight signals at the most. Sensor $S_1, \ldots, S_n$ are assigned to $b_1, \ldots, b_s$, and $S_{n+1}, \ldots, S_m$ to $u_1, \ldots, u_t$. Furthermore, suppose that the upstream flip-flops can be divided into three loose-couple groups: $f_1, \ldots, f_p$ are relevant inputs to $b_9, \ldots, b_{16}$, $f_{p+1}, \ldots, f_q$ to $b_{17}, \ldots, b_s$, and $f_{q+1}, \ldots, f_r$ to $b_1, \ldots, b_8$. Three polices can be used to guide the deployment:

1. The agents are not required for the UAFFs, e.g. $u_1, \ldots, u_t$; but sensors is required, i.e. $S_{n+1}, \ldots, S_m$.
2. The agents assigned to FAFFs, unlike that assigned to BAFFs, are triggered by the downstream agents, rather than by any sensors (so false alarm filters are not necessary for the FAFFs' agents).
3. The connecting relations between upstream agents and downstream agents is determined by the target circuit topology which can be obtained by conducting logic cones analysis (the ultimate goal of using logic cones analysis for

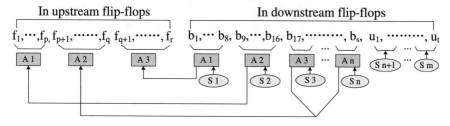

Fig. 2.35 Deploying sensors and agents

ReviveNet is to extract all loose-couple logic cones, and merging all tight-coupling logic cones).

The number of required sensors N_{sensor} for the Kth stage is

$$N_{sensor} = \frac{s}{BW_{sensor}}, \tag{2.33}$$

where BW_{sensor} denotes the maximum number of nodes that each sensor can handle.

The number of required agents N_{agent} is

$$N_{agent} = N_{agent}^{dn} + N_{agent}^{up}, \tag{2.34}$$

where N_{agent}^{dn} denotes the number of downstream agents and N_{agent}^{up} denotes that of upstream agents. Generally, each downstream agent is assigned a sensor and has the same bandwidth with the associated sensor, so

$$N_{agent}^{dn} = N_{sensor}. \tag{2.35}$$

The number of upstream agents and its' bandwidth, however, is circuit topology-specific; thus the area of each upstream agents are not constant. For instance, the upstream A1, A2, and A3 in Fig. 2.35 may handle different number of FAFFs (different bandwidth).

Base on the above analysis, we present a typical organization of agents for a N-stage pipeline in Fig. 2.36 (no filter sharing illustrated for simplicity), where Age^K is a set of aging alarm signals from the Kth stage and S^K is a set of clock-steering signals to enable localized adaptations.

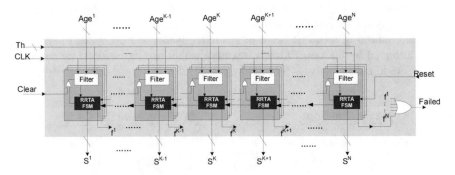

Fig. 2.36 A group of synergistic agents for a n-stage pipeline

2.3.5 Architecture Implementation

2.3.5.1 Clock Generation and Overhead Analysis

ReviveNet needs two extra clocks, FCLK and BCLK, with intentional skew from CLK. These clocks can be generated by using a DLL (delay-locked loop). DLLs are widely used to reduce the clock skew across clock domains [41, 58, 93]. The detailed design of a DLL is beyond the scope of this book. A major concern is whether those PVT (process, voltage, and temperature) variations can spoil the intentional skew. Fortunately, many industry practices have shown that implementing clocks with only picoseconds of skew is very practical. For example, even in conventional tree-based clock networks across $500\,mm^2$ processor die with frequency up to 2.5 GHz, the unintended clock skew can be efficiently limited less than 10 ps [23]. Thus, it can be extrapolated that for relatively spatial concentrated pipeline logics with less die area, the unintentional skew can be further optimized. In fact, even "10 ps" is generally one order of magnitude smaller than the intentional skew. Moreover, the power consumption of a processor's DLLs, commonly, is less than 2% [24], and the hardware overhead is very limited. Hence, with the state-of-the-art clocking techniques, we believe that generating the adaptation clocks won't be a major obstacle.

In our scheme, we point out that although ReviveNet needs two extra clocks, our evaluation results show that on average the load of each of them is only about 20% of CLK's. This is because only BAFFs and FAFFs need to be deployed with extra clocks, while the proportion of the two types of flip-flops takes only about 19%. That means more than 80% clock distributions are kept intact. This implies that (1) the clock power will not be tripled but far less than that (Sect. 2.3.7.2), and (2) the routing complexity will not be significantly increased. So, the overall design complexity should be in check.

2.3.5.2 ReviveNet-Supported Clock Gating

Since aging adaptations usually are conducted on minority aging-prominent logics, so for the rest logics, It's better to keep the associated standby clocks off.

ReviveNet can readily support a high-efficient clock gating to further reduce the extra power consumed by the additional FCLK and BCLK. Figure 2.37 shows ReviveNet's clock network. The basic clock routing for CLK can be found in [24]. Usually, the pipeline will not suffer from aging in the early phase of lifetime, so FCLK and BCLK do not need to be enabled during that period. Two "root" clock gates, A and B, are employed to totally cut FLCK and BCLK off the DLL; thereby no power is consumed on the extra clock networks. If some parts of the pipeline need to be adapted, the corresponding root gate and branch gate can be switched on on-demand, while the unrelated clock branches are still kept off.

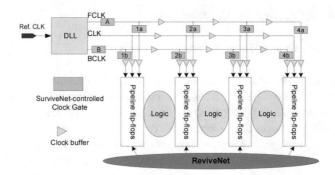

Fig. 2.37 ReviveNet-supported clock gating

2.3.5.3 Implication of Multi-Cycle Paths

Since a multi-cycle path usually consist more logic gates, the timing margin that a single-cycle path is able to share is likely to be inadequate. For example, suppose the cycle period is 1 ns, for a 5-cycle path with fresh path delay 4.7 ns. Then 10% degradation yields 5.17 ns ($4.7 + 4.7 \times 10\%$), which must violate the 5-cycle path timing requirement. But a single-cycle path can only contribute 0.075 ns ($1 \times 15\%/2$) slack (suppose $TH = 0.15$). Hence, although this slack, if exploited, can partially alleviate the aging delay, we had better not rely on single-cycle paths to salvage multi-cycle paths.

For multi-cycle paths, especially for "many-cycle" paths, we think a more effective way is to resort to some logic optimizations. For example, re-organize the 5-cycle paths into 6-cycle paths, to naturally gain more aging tolerability, though this approach usually needs to interact with some microarchitecture implications (which are supposed to beyond the scope of this book).

2.3.5.4 Impact of ReviveNet Wearout

Aging can indeed affect all logics on the chip, including aging sensors, adaptation agents, and even clocks networks.

Among them, the adaptation agents are relatively timing-non-critical; the latency of each adaptation, for example, increase from 1 cycle to 2 cycles should not be critical for an effective adaptation. This implies that, to protect these agents from the impact of aging, we can "over-design" the agents; that is to reserve conservative timing margins for these agents. For the clock networks, aging may results skew drift. Since skew-controlling actually is one of the primary objectives in many traditional clock optimizations, and we suppose that is beyond the scope of this book. The sensor degradation, however, can impair the effectiveness of the proposed ReviveNet; after all, we cannot count on the adaptations triggered by unreliable sensors.

Fortunately, because the sensors' area and power overhead are small ($<5\%$ and 1%, respectively), so we can also over-design those sensors by using such as transistor-sizing techniques [65]. Usually, transistor-sizing impose about 9% area overhead [65], the overall extra overhead, therefore, should be very small.

2.3.6 Model Based Reliability Analysis

2.3.6.1 Reliability Model

Commonly, the reliability of semiconductor is modeled with Weibull distribution [67]. Given a circuit, the reliability at time t is given by

$$R(t) = \exp[-(\frac{t}{\alpha})^\beta] \qquad (2.36)$$

where α is the characteristic time-to-failure and β is the shape parameter [67]. The MTTF is calculated by

$$MTTF = \int_0^\infty R(t)\,dt. \qquad (2.37)$$

Suppose that there are n critical paths in the target circuits. The reliability of the ith path at time t can be expressed as

$$R_i(t) = P(T_i(t) < T) \qquad (2.38)$$

where, $T_i(t)$ denotes the delay of the ith path at time t; T is the clock cycle period. Let's further assume that these paths are independent to each other, as Bowman et al. assumed in [16]. Then, $R(t)$ can be put in another way:

$$R(t) = \prod_{i=1}^n R_i(t) = \prod_{i=1}^n P(T_i(t) < T). \qquad (2.39)$$

Moreover, we treat each critical path as a "mini-component", then $R_i(t)$ can be expressed as

$$R_i(t) = P(T_i(t) < T) = \exp[-(\frac{t}{\alpha_i})^{\beta_i}], \qquad (2.40)$$

then we have

$$R(t) = \prod_{i=1}^n \exp[-(\frac{t}{\alpha_i})^{\beta_i}] = \exp[-\sum_{i=1}^n (\frac{t}{\alpha_i})^{\beta_i}]. \qquad (2.41)$$

The corresponding MTTF can be calculated by

$$MTTF = \int_0^\infty \exp[-\sum_{i=1}^n (\frac{t}{\alpha_i})^{\beta_i}] \, dt. \tag{2.42}$$

The above general analysis has not taken the effect of ReviveNet into account yet, and the following will involve it. When considering ReviveNet, the group of $\mathcal{R} = \{R_1(t), R_2(t),\ldots, R_n(t)\}$ can be divided into three groups according to the adaptability of each critical path:

- Group 1: the set of critical paths in case (2) and (3) (Sect. 2.3.3.1) which can only be backward or forward adapted by $TH/2$;
- Group 2: the set of critical paths in case 1) which can not only be backward, but also forward adapted by $(TH/2 + TH/2) = TH$;
- Group 3: the set of critical paths in case 4) which are unadaptable.

Suppose that there are l paths in Group 1, m paths in Group 2, and the other $(n - l - m)$ in Group 3. Without loss of generality, denote the first group as $\mathcal{R}_u = \{R_1(t), R_2(t), \ldots, R_l(t)\}$, the second group as $\mathcal{R}_b = \{R_{l+1}(t), \ldots, R_{l+m}(t)\}$, and the third group as $\mathcal{R}_n = \{R_{l+m+1}(t), \ldots, R_n(t)\}$. Then we have the ReviveNet-involved reliability term $\widetilde{R}_i(t)$, as follows:

$$\widetilde{R}_i(t) = \begin{cases} P(T_i(t) < T + TH/2) & \text{if } i = 1, 2, \ldots, l, \\ P(T_i(t) < T + TH) & \text{if } i = l + 1, \ldots, l + m, \\ P(T_i(t) < T) & \text{if } i = l + m + 1, \ldots, n. \end{cases} \tag{2.43}$$

The enhanced MTTF can be obtained:

$$MTTF_R = \int_0^\infty \prod_{i=1}^n \widetilde{R}_i(t) \, dt. \tag{2.44}$$

We define a relative MTTF improvement, EX (short for "EXtension of lifetime"), denoted by

$$EX = \frac{MTTF_R}{MTTF} \tag{2.45}$$

to evaluate the effect of ReviveNet.

To calculate EX we have to figure out the relations: $\alpha_i = \alpha_i(T)$, and $\beta_i = \beta_i(T)$. Figure 2.38 shows the qualitative relations; the following describes how to figure out the two relations.

In Weibull distribution,

$$\beta = \frac{1.38}{\ln(t_{50}/t_{16})}, \quad \text{and } \alpha = \frac{t_{50}}{ln(2)^{1/\beta}} \approx t_{63} \tag{2.46}$$

Fig. 2.38 Weibull failure rate
in wearout period

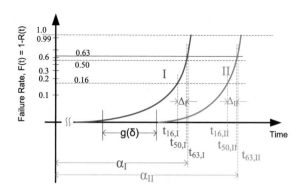

where t_x means the lifetime at the failure rate $x\%$ [67], as shown in Fig. 2.38.
Intuitively, given a critical path, if more margin is reserved for it, then the wearout
should be also postponed, as curve I and II show. ReviveNet can provide margin
for some critical paths, thereby postponing the onset of wearout. In the following,
relying on the assumption: the curve I and II are same in "shape", can greatly
simplify the discussion, although the actual failure rate in the wearout region for
I and II may slightly differ from each other.

Figure 2.38 also reveals the effect of ReviveNet for a specific critical path can be
reflected by the parameter α and β. Let $t_{50} = t_{16} + \Delta$, and commonly, $\Delta \ll t_{16}$ then

$$\beta = \frac{1.38}{\ln(1 + \Delta/t_{16})} \approx \frac{1.38}{\Delta/t_{16}} \tag{2.47}$$

For the both curves, because $\Delta_I = \Delta_{II}$, so

$$\frac{\beta_I}{\beta_{II}} = \frac{t_{16,I}}{t_{16,II}}, \quad \frac{\alpha_I}{\alpha_{II}} = \frac{t_{63,I}}{t_{63,II}} \tag{2.48}$$

Furthermore, let

$$t_{16,II} = t_{16,I} + g(\delta) \text{ and } t_{63,II} = t_{63,I} + g(\delta) \tag{2.49}$$

where $g(\delta)$ denotes the lifetime extension contributed by tolerating δ aging delay; δ
can be 0, $TH/2$, or TH, determined by the specific adaptability of paths. Clearly,
function $g(\delta)$ is highly dependent to specific aging mechanisms. Unfortunately,
no such function proposed so far that can accurately reflect the performance
degradation over time under a variety of aging mechanisms (some of them such as
dielectric breakdown even have not been well-understood by the community [37]).
In the following case study, we just use the relatively well-studied NBTI, one of the
major reliability challenge, as target aging mechanism to evaluate the ReviveNet.
We expect the physical community to contribute a much more versatile $g(\delta)$ in the
near future.

Fig. 2.39 NBTI degradation

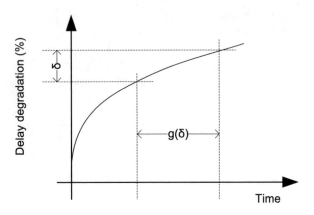

Paul et al. proposed a NBTI circuit delay model that capture the relation ship between the threshold voltage change and resultant delay degradation [13]: the NBTI degradation is much fast at the early years, and then slowed down later, as the trend shown in Fig. 2.39. Moreover, Fig. 2.39 also shows the relation between δ and g; we obtain $g(\delta)$ by regressing the results in [91]. More details are presented in Sect. 2.3.7.2.

2.3.6.2   Implication of TH

Equation (2.43) implies an essential tradeoff behind ReviveNet. Note that the critical paths in Group 3 is free from ReviveNet; only the Group 1 and Group 2 can contribute to the lifetime improvement. However, given a target circuits, the sizes of the three groups are depends on the TH: on one hand, larger TH can result higher percentage of UAFFs, and thereby more critical paths in Group 3, and thus leads to fewer adaptable critical paths; on the other, the larger TH implies that more aggressive tolerability to aging delay on those adaptable critical paths. Hence, given a circuit, there should be an optimum TH that can maximize the EX.

2.3.7   Case Study and Discussion

2.3.7.1   Experiment Setups

We took a fully pipelined FPU [79] as our target circuit which implements the SPARC V9 floating-point instructions and supports all IEEE 754 floating-point data types. The FPU comprises three independent pipelines: Multiplier pipeline (MUL), Adder pipeline (ADD) and Divider pipeline (DIV). We used the largest MUL, which takes up to 50% area of the FPU, as the target pipeline. More design details can be found in [79].

The FPU was synthesized using Design Compiler with UMC 0.18 μm technology. We set the performance as the synthesizing priority to smooth the distribution of path delay as much as possible. Then, the path delay was analyzed with PrimeTime.

First, we identify the adaptability of each pipeline flip-flop, based on the STA results. Then, the deployment of sensors and agents can be determined as follows: for each flip-flops i, find the upstream flip-flops that in the same logic cone; this can be done by matching the start points of paths ended with the flip-flop i. The number of required sensors and agents can be figured out by using Eqs. (2.33) and (2.34). Then, we evaluate the MTTF improvement (EX) by using the proposed reliability model. Finally, we present the overhead in terms of area, power, and performance.

2.3.7.2 Results and Discussions

Lifetime Improvement Analysis We conduct the lifetime evaluation based on the 65 nm technology (the STA results actually are based on a 180 nm technology due to lack of 65 nm compiler libraries. To match the following analysis, we scale the STA results to 65 nm based on scaling theory [42]). The NBTI degradation results are from [91]. The lifetime is studied at different configurations: without ReviveNet, and with ReviveNet, at $TH = 5\%$ (of the delay of the most critical path), 10%, 15%, 20%, 25%, 30%, respectively. The necessary $g(\delta)$ at these TH is as follows:

$$
\begin{aligned}
g(0.05) &= 876(\text{hours}); & g(0.1) &= 8760(\text{hours}); \\
g(0.15) &= 21,900(\text{hours}); & g(0.2) &= 43,800(\text{hours}); \\
g(0.25) &= 87,600(\text{hours}); & g(0.3) &= 131,400(\text{hours}).
\end{aligned}
\tag{2.50}
$$

For example, $g(0.05) = 876$ (hours) means that the 5% tolerability to delay degradation can translate to 876 hours lifetime extension. The above results faithfully reflect that NBTI degradation which is much faster at the early years and slowed down over time.

Next, the Weibull parameter α and β is calculated as follows: we use empirical data: $t_{16} = 35,040$ hours (4 years) and $t_{63} = 39,420$ hours (4.5 year) (thus $\Delta = 4380$ hours). Then, from Eq. (2.46), we have the original α and β for a critical path is $\alpha = 39,420$ (hours), $\beta = 11.04$. Then, combined Eq. (2.50) with Eq. (2.49) and then put it into Eq. (2.48), the new α and β at different TH can be obtained. When calculating MTTF, we assume that the critical paths with the same adaptability have the same α and β.

Finally, base on the STA results, the three path groups $\mathcal{R}_u$, $\mathcal{R}_b$, and $\mathcal{R}_n$ at different TH configurations can be determined, respectively.

With the above preparation, the original and improved MTTF can be calculated with Eqs. (2.42) and (2.44); Fig. 2.40 shows the detailed results that offer a significant insight: larger TH does not necessarily results higher improvement in lifetime reliability. The underling reason is on one hand larger TH can facilitate more aggressive timing stealing, thereby improving more reliability for adaptable

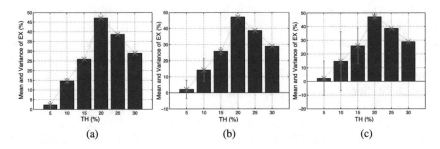

Fig. 2.40 MTTF improvement at different TH and clock skew variations. (**a**) Skew variation: 1%. (**b**) Skew variation: 3%. (**c**) Skew variation: 5%

paths; on the other, larger TH will definitely results more UAFFs and thereby more unadaptable paths. In other words, the overall MTTF is determined not only the reliability benefit of individual path, but also the population of paths governed by ReviveNet. At the optimum configuration, $TH = 20\%$, MTTF can be improved by 48.7%.

Impact of Clock Skew Variation The effectiveness of ReviveNet, as concerned in Sect. 2.3.5.1, is also impacted by the variation in clock skew (measured by $skew/cycle\_period$). The impact actually results in corresponding variation in "effective" TH. We find that the degradation can only be marginally impacted if the adaptation clocks are kept beyond a large interval, say, $TH > 0.2$. Specifically, Fig. 2.40a, b, and c shows the EX variation under different clock skew variations: 1%, 3%, and 5%, respectively. Two trends can be clearly identified: (1) the degradation in effectiveness reduces with TH increasing, and (2) the larger clock skew variation results in more variation in MTTF improvement. Hence, the worst-case efficacy under overly "weak" adaptation intensity, i.e. $TH < 0.1$, can be significantly reduced under 3% skew variation, and even totally diminished under 5% skew variation, as shown in Fig. 2.40b and c. However, the optimal design point is around $TH = 0.2$ where the impact of clock skew is marginal.

In addition, it is practical to keep the clock skew below 3% by using the state-of-the-art clocking techniques (for example, 10 ps skew variation for 2.5 GHz Itanium processor [23]). This can further justify the effectiveness of ReviveNet.

Overhead Analysis We evaluate ReviveNet's overhead from three aspects: silicon area, power, and performance. The overhead largely depends on the parameter TH.

1. Area Overhead.

Sensor Configuration The number of sensors for each stage depends on specific sensor design [8, 94]; we take the configuration of one sensor handles eight signals.
Agent Configuration Agents are configured as follows: 6-bit False Alarm Filter which can filter as much as 64 false alarms during one adaptation period. We study the area overhead with different degrees of Filter sharing: no sharing, two agents sharing one filter, four agents sharing one filter, and eight agents sharing one filter.

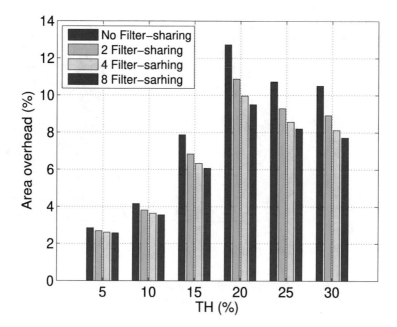

Fig. 2.41 Area overhead with different sharing configurations

The sensor and agents are insert into the original MUL netlist, and re-synthesized using the same technology. Figure 2.41 shows the overall area overhead under different configurations. Generally, the area overhead is small: only 9.5% at the recommended $TH = 0.2$.

2. Power Overhead.

Power overhead mainly comes from ReviveNet logics (sensors and agents) and extra clock networks. That is

$$P_{overhead} = P_{logic} + P_{clk} = (P_{sensor} + P_{agent}) + P_{clk}.$$

The following results show that P_{logic} is negligible, and the major power overhead results from P_{clk}.

(1) Logic Power. We use PrimePower to evaluate P_{logic}. Evaluation results show that even in the worst case—each sensor raises an aging alarm in every cycle—the power overhead caused by the sensors and agents is negligible. Figure 2.42 shows that a typical logic power overhead ($TH = 0.2$) is less than 5%.

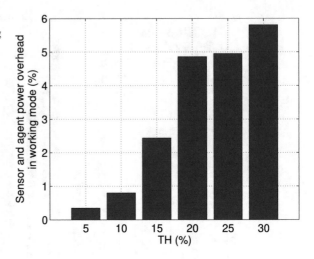

Fig. 2.42 Power overhead of sensors and agents in working mode

(2) Clock Power. The worst case overhead of clock power, P_{clk}, is more significant than that of logics. In ReviveNet, the clock power can be calculated as

$$P_{clkall} = P_{pipeffs} + P_{DLL} + P_{buf} + P_{wire} + P_{mux}\ [24]$$

where $P_{pipeffs}$ and P_{DLL} is the power consumed by pipeline flip-flops and DLL, and P_{buf}, P_{wire}, and P_{mux}, are power consumed by clock buffers (drivers), clock wires, and clock multiplexers, respectively. $P_{pipeffs}$ and P_{DLL} stay unchanged because little modifications are made to them. The clock buffers which take the most proportion, 56%, in the original pipelines, increase by 32% to support FCLK and BCLK networks (the increase in buffers is proportion to the increase in clock load). P_{wire} almost triples, but it takes only about 10% in original pipelines. Compared with the other proportions, P_{mux} is ignorable. Overall, the clock power increases by 38%.

The previous study [24] shows generally for a pipelined processor, the clock power is about the 30~40% (denoted by η) of the total power, so this increase contribute to the overall power overhead is calculate by

$$[(1 - \eta) + \eta \times (1 + 38\%)] - 100\%.$$

Since η is about 30~40%, the overall overhead should be between 11.4~15.2%. Note that this overall power overhead is in the *Worst Case*—all the drivers of FCLK and BCLK are turned on. However, little power overhead is imposed in the early period of lifetime, because few of the extra logics and clock networks need to be turned on due to little appreciable aging delay. Moreover, we believe with ReviveNet-supported clock gating, the overall power overhead can be significantly reduced even after the onset of wearout.

3. Performance Overhead.

ReviveNet needs some sensors. From circuit design perspective, these sensors can cause some capacitance load to the target pipelines. This concern, however, will not be substantial because the performance penalty imposed by such capacitance load is less than 1% [8, 94].

ReviveNet improves the lifetime reliability only by tolerating the aging delay, which may not be comprehensively enough. In addition, ReviveNet does not suppose to handle some "abrupt" wearout which in reality is possible due to some mechanical stress induced failures. In addition, ReviveNet is not designed for coping with all corner cases, but for average case; in other words, ReviveNet is statistically effective, rather than deterministic.

2.3.8 *Discussion*

The proposed ReviveNet architecture, without compromising with the nominal architectural performance, can efficiently hide the aging induced delay, thereby improving the lifetime reliability. The weakest links of lifetime can be locally and efficiently remedied by enabling a path-grained adaptation mechanism; ReviveNet employs a group of collaborative cost-efficient agents to achieve this purpose. A new reliability model is also proposed to quantitatively evaluate the effect of ReviveNet. Evaluation results based on a case study show that the ReviveNet can improve the MTTF by 48.7%, at the expense of about 9.5% area overhead, and about 4.9% power increase during aging-free period.

2.4 Summary

In ultra-deep submicrometer technology, soft errors and device aging are two of the paramount reliability concerns. To achieve an optimum performance-cost trade-off, we propose a unified fault detection called SVDF, which grounds on stability violation, derived from analysis of signal behavior. SVDF is an unified fault detection scheme that handles the soft errors, aging delay, and delay faults. Experimental results show that SVFD has more versatile fault detection capability for fault detection than several schemes recently proposed at comparable overhead in terms of area, power, and performance.

With the scaling of semiconductor process technology, the performance of modern VLSI chips improves significantly. The on-chip path delay measurement is one of the effective performance evaluation techniques that provides a cost-effective alternative way to perform delay defect detection and silicon debug in modern VLSI chips. To help to reduce hardware overheads and delay measurement time, we propose a novel on-chip path delay measurement architecture, OCDM, for path delay testing and silicon debug. OCDM employs several delay stages, whose delay ranges are increased by a factor of two gradually from the last to the first delay stage. Thus, the proposed OCDM circuit can achieve a large delay measurement range with a small quantity of delay stages.

The device and reliability communities have devoted much efforts to lifetime projection, but less to design for lifetime reliability. To tackle this problem, we propose a hardware-implemented aging-aware and self-adaptive architecture, ReviveNet, to exploiting fine-grained lifetime reliability. We use a localized timing adaptation mechanism to locally cope with the aged critical paths. Therefore, the lifetime can be extended significantly through exploiting such "path-grained" adaptability.

References

1. International Technology Roadmap for Semiconductors, July 2009. http://pulic.itrs.net.
2. J.R. Black. Electromigration—A brief survey and some recent results. *IEEE Trans. on Electron Devices*, 16(4):338–347, 1969.
3. A. Avellan, and W.H. Krautschneider. Impact of soft and hard breakdown on analog and digital circuits. *Transactions on Device and Materials Reliability*, 4(4):676–680, 2004.
4. A. Tiwari and J. Torrellas. Facelift: Hiding and Slowing Down Aging in Multicores. In *2008 41st IEEE/ACM International Symposium on Microarchitecture*, pages 129–140, 2008.
5. A. Tiwari, S. R. Sarangi, and J. Torrellas. ReCycle: Pipeline Adaptation to Tolerate Process Variation. In *Proceedings of the 34th Annual International Symposium on Computer Architecture*, pages 323–334, 2007.
6. Aseem Agarwal, David Blaauw, and Vladimir Zolotov. Statistical timing analysis for intra-die process variations with spatial correlations. In *ICCAD-2003. International Conference on Computer Aided Design (IEEE Cat. No. 03CH37486)*, pages 900–907, 2003.
7. Aseem Agarwal, Vladimir Zolotov, and David T Blaauw. Statistical timing analysis using bounds and selective enumeration. *IEEE Transactions on Computer-Aided Design of Integrated Circuits and Systems*, 22(9):1243–1260, 2003.
8. Mridul Agarwal, Bipul C Paul, Ming Zhang, and Subhasish Mitra. Circuit failure prediction and its application to transistor aging. In *25th IEEE VLSI Test Symposium (VTS'07)*, pages 277–286, 2007.
9. Nisar Ahmed, Mohammad Tehranipoor, and Vinay Jayaram. A novel framework for faster-than-at-speed delay test considering ir-drop effects. In *Proceedings of the 2006 IEEE/ACM international conference on Computer-aided design*, pages 198–203, 2006.
10. Atmel Corporation. Quality & Reliability Handbook. *Section 6*, pages 6.1–6.5, 2004.
11. B. Taskin, I.S. Kourtev,. Delay insertion method in clock skew scheduling. *IEEE Transactions on Computer-Aided Design of Integrated Circuits and Systems*, 25(4):651–663, 2006.
12. Hari Balachandran, Kenneth M Butler, and Neil Simpson. Facilitating rapid first silicon debug. In *Proceedings. International Test Conference*, pages 628–637, 2002.
13. B.C. Paul, K. Kunhyuk, H. Kufluoglu, M. A. Alam, K. Roy. Impact of NBTI on the temporal performance degradation of digital circuits. *IEEE Electron Device Letters*, 26(8):560–562, 2005.
14. David Blaauw, Kaviraj Chopra, Ashish Srivastava, and Lou Scheffer. Statistical timing analysis: From basic principles to state of the art. *IEEE transactions on computer-aided design of integrated circuits and systems*, 27(4):589–607, 2008.
15. S. Borkar. Designing reliable systems from unreliable components: the challenges of transistor variability and degradation. *IEEE MICRO*, 25(6):10–16, 2005.

16. K.A. Bowman, S.G. Duvall, and J.D. Meindl. Impact of die-to-die and within-die parameter fluctuations on the maximum clock frequency distribution for gigascale integration. *IEEE Journal of Solid-State Circuits*, 37(2):183–190, 2002.

17. C. Nagpal, R. Garg, S.P. Khatri. A Delay-efficient Radiation-hard Digital Design Approach Using CWSP Elements. In *2008 Design, Automation and Test in Europe*, pages 354–359, 2008.

18. G. Chen, K. Y. Chuah, M. F. Li, D. S. H. Chan, C. H. Ang, J. Z. Zheng, Y. Jin, and D. L. Kwong. Dynamic NBTI of PMOS transistors and its impact on device lifetime. In *2003 IEEE International Reliability Physics Symposium Proceedings, 2003. 41st Annual*, pages 196–202, 2003.

19. D. Blaauw, S. Kalaiselvan, K. Lai, W.H. Ma, S. Pant, C. Tokunaga, S. Das, and D. Bull. Razor II: In Situ Error Detection and Correction for PVT and SER Tolerance. In *Proceedings of the IEEE International Solid-State Circuits Conference*, pages 400–401, 2008.

20. Ramyanshu Datta, Gary Carpenter, Kevin Nowka, and Jacob A Abraham. A scheme for on-chip timing characterization. In *24th IEEE VLSI Test Symposium*, pages 6–pp, 2006.

21. Ramyanshu Datta, Antony Sebastine, and Jacob A Abraham. Delay fault testing and silicon debug using scan chains. In *Proceedings. Ninth IEEE European Test Symposium, 2004. ETS 2004*, pages 46–51, 2004.

22. Ramyanshu Datta, Antony Sebastine, Ashwin Raghunathan, and Jacob A Abraham. On-chip delay measurement for silicon debug. In *Proceedings of the 14th ACM Great Lakes symposium on VLSI*, pages 145–148, 2004.

23. B. Doyle, P. Mahoney, E. Fetzer, and S. Naffziger. Clock distribution on a dual-core, multi-threaded itanium/spl reg/family microprocessor. In *2005 International Conference on Integrated Circuit Design and Technology, 2005. ICICDT 2005*, pages 292–293, 599, 2005.

24. D.E. Duarte, N. Vijaykrishnan, and M.J. Irwin. A clock power model to evaluate impact of architectural and technology optimizations. *IEEE Transactions on Very Large Scale Integration (VLSI) Systems*, 10(6):844–855, 2002.

25. Michele Favalli and Cecilia Metra. Sensing circuit for on-line detection of delay faults. *IEEE transactions on very large scale integration (VLSI) systems*, 4(1):130–133, 1996.

26. Xiang Fu, Huawei Li, Yu Hu, and Xiaowei Li. Robust test generation for power supply noise induced path delay faults. In *2008 Asia and South Pacific Design Automation Conference*, pages 659–662, 2008.

27. Xiang Fu, Huawei Li, and Xiaowei Li. Testable critical path selection considering process variation. *IEICE transactions on information and systems*, 93(1):59–67, 2010.

28. G. Gerosa, S. Gary, C. Dietz, Dac Pham, K. Hoover, J. Alvarez, H. Sanchez, P. Ippolito, Tai Ngo, S. Litch, J. Eno, J. Golab, N. Vanderschaaf, and J. Kahle. A 2.2 w, 80 mhz superscalar risc microprocessor. *IEEE Journal of Solid-State Circuits*, 29(12):1440–1454, 1994.

29. Swaroop Ghosh, Swarup Bhunia, Arijit Raychowdhury, and Kaushik Roy. A novel delay fault testing methodology using low-overhead built-in delay sensor. *IEEE Transactions on Computer-Aided Design of Integrated Circuits and Systems*, 25(12):2934–2943, 2006.

30. Charles Hawkins, Ali Keshavarzi, and Jaume Segura. View from the bottom: nanometer technology ac parametric failures-why, where, and how to detect. In *Proceedings 18th IEEE Symposium on Defect and Fault Tolerance in VLSI Systems*, pages 267–276, 2003.

31. Zijian He, Tao Lv, Huawei Li, and Xiaowei Li. Fast path selection for testing of small delay defects considering path correlations. In *2010 28th VLSI Test Symposium (VTS)*, pages 3–8, 2010.

32. I. Sutherland, R.F. Sproull, and David Harris. *Logical Effort: Designing Fast CMOS Circuits*. Morgan Kaufmann, San Mateo, CA, USA, 1999.

33. International SEMATECH, Inc. Critical Reliability Challenges for The International Technology Roadmap for Semiconductors (ITRS). pages 1–37, March 2003.

34. ITRS. PROCESS INTEGRATION, DEVICES, AND STRUCTURES. 2007.

35. J. Abella, X. Vera, and A. Gonzalez. Penelope: The NBTI-Aware Processor. In *40th Annual IEEE/ACM International Symposium on Microarchitecture (MICRO 2007)*, pages 85–96, 2007.

36. J. Blome, S. Feng, S. Gupta, and S. Mahlke. Self-calibrating Online Wearout Detection. In *40th Annual IEEE/ACM International Symposium on Microarchitecture (MICRO 2007)*, pages 109–122, 2007.
37. J. H. Stathis. Reliability limits for the gate insulator in CMOS technology. *IBM J. RES. & DEV*, 46(2/3):265–265., 2002.
38. J. Han, J. Gao, Y. Qi, P. Jonker, and J.A.B. Fortes. Toward Hardware-Redundant, Fault-Tolerant Logic for Nanoelectronics. *IEEE Design & Test of Computers*, 22(4):328–339, 2005.
39. J. Shin, V. Zyuban, P. Bose, and T.M. Pinkston. A Proactive Wearout Recovery Approach for Exploiting Microarchitectural Redundancy to Extend Cache SRAM Lifetime. In *2008 International Symposium on Computer Architecture*, pages 353–362, 2008.
40. M Rabaey Jan, Chandrakasan Anantha, Nikolic Borivoje, et al. Digital integrated circuits: a design perspective, 2002.
41. Young-Jin Jeon, Joong-Ho Lee, Hyun-Chul Lee, Kyo-Won Jin, Kyeong-Sik Min, Jin-Yong Chung, and H.-J. Park. A 66-333-MHz 12-mW register-controlled DLL with a single delay line and adaptive-duty-cycle clock dividers for production DDR SDRAMs. *IEEE Journal of Solid-State Circuits*, 39(11):2087–2092, 2004.
42. J.M. Rabaey, A. Chandrakasan, and B. Nikolic. *Digital Integrated Circuits, A design perspective, Second Edition, Chapter 9*. Pearson Education Asia Limited and Tsinghua University Press, Beijing, China, 2004.
43. Ben Kaczer, Robin Degraeve, Ph Roussel, and Guido Groeseneken. Gate oxide breakdown in FET devices and circuits: From nanoscale physics to system-level reliability. *Microelectronics Reliability*, 47(4-5):559–566, 2007.
44. Shunichi Kaeriyama, Mikihiro Kajita, and Masayuki Mizuno. A 1-to-2ghz 4-phase on-chip clock generator with timing-margin test capability. In *2007 IEEE International Solid-State Circuits Conference. Digest of Technical Papers*, pages 174–594, 2007.
45. T. Karnik, B. Bloechel, K. Soumyanath, V. De, and S. Borkar. Scaling trends of cosmic ray induced soft errors in static latches beyond 0.18/spl mu. In *2001 Symposium on VLSI Circuits. Digest of Technical Papers (IEEE Cat. No. 01CH37185)*, pages 61–62, 2001.
46. Angela Krstic and Kwang-Ting Cheng. *Delay fault testing for VLSI circuits, 1st edition*. Springer, Boston, MA, 1998.
47. Angela Krstic, Jing-Jia Liou, Yi-Min Jiang, and Kwang-Ting Cheng. Delay testing considering crosstalk-induced effects. In *Proceedings International Test Conference 2001 (Cat. No. 01CH37260)*, pages 558–567, 2001.
48. Bram Kruseman, Ananta K Majhi, Guido Gronthoud, and Stefan Eichenberger. On hazard-free patterns for fine-delay fault testing. In *2004 International Conference on Test*, pages 213–222, 2004.
49. Jean Davies Lesser and John J. Shedletsky. An experimental delay test generator for LSI logic. *IEEE Transactions on Computers*, 29(03):235–248, 1980.
50. Xiaoyao Liang, Gu-Yeon Wei, and David Brooks. Revival: A variation-tolerant architecture using voltage interpolation and variable latency. *IEEE Micro*, 29(1):127–138, 2009.
51. M. Agarwal, et al. Optimized Circuit Failure Prediction for Aging: Practicality and Promise. In *2008 IEEE International Test Conference*, pages 1–10, 2008.
52. M. Nicolaidis. Design for Soft Error Mitigation. *IEEE Transactions on Device and Materials Reliability*, 5(3):405–418, 2005.
53. M. Zhang, S. Mitra, T.M. Mak, N. Seifert, N.J. Wang, Q. Shi, K.S. Kim, N.R. Shanbhag, and S.J. Patel. Sequential Element Design With Built-In Soft Error Resilience. *IEEE Transactions on Very Large Scale Integration (VLSI) Systems*, 14(12):1368–1378, 2006.
54. TM Mak, Angela Krstic, K-T Cheng, and Li-C Wang. New challenges in delay testing of nanometer, multigigahertz designs. *IEEE Design & Test of Computers*, 21(3):241–248, 2004.
55. Mojtaba Mehrara, Mona Attariyan, Smitha Shyam, Kypros Constantinides, Valeria Bertacco, and Todd Austin. Low-cost protection for SER upsets and silicon defects. In *2007 Design, Automation Test in Europe Conference Exhibition*, pages 1146–1157, 2007.
56. Mojtaba Mehrara and Todd Austin. Exploiting selective placement for low-cost memory protection. *ACM Transactions on Architecture and Code Optimization (TACO)*, 5(3):1–24, 2008.

57. Sreekumar Menon, Adit D Singh, and Vishwani Agrawal. Output hazard-free transition delay fault test generation. In *2009 27th IEEE VLSI Test Symposium*, pages 97–102, 2009.
58. K. Minami, M. Mizuno, H. Yamaguchi, T. Nakano, Y. Matsushima, Y. Sumi, T. Sato, H. Yamashida, and M. Yamashina. A 1 GHz portable digital delay-locked loop with infinite phase capture ranges. In *2000 IEEE International Solid-State Circuits Conference. Digest of Technical Papers (Cat. No. 00CH37056)*, pages 350–351, 2000.
59. Pablo Montesinos, Wei Liu, and Josep Torrellas. Using register lifetime predictions to protect register files against soft errors. In *37th Annual IEEE/IFIP International Conference on Dependable Systems and Networks (DSN'07)*, pages 286–296, 2007.
60. N. Oh, E.J. McCluskey. Error Detection by Selective Procedure Call Duplication for Low Energy Consumption. *IEEE Transactions on Reliability*, 51(4):392–402, 2002.
61. Sanil Nassif. Delay variability: sources, impacts and trends. In *2000 IEEE International Solid-State Circuits Conference. Digest of Technical Papers (Cat. No. 00CH37056)*, pages 368–369, 2000.
62. M. Nicolaidis. Time redundancy based soft-error tolerance to rescue nanometer technologies. In *Proceedings 17th IEEE VLSI Test Symposium (Cat. No. PR00146)*, pages 86–94, 1999.
63. Michael Nicolaidis. Graal: a new fault tolerant design paradigm for mitigating the flaws of deep nanometric technologies. In *2007 IEEE International Test Conference*, pages 1–10, 2007.
64. Phil Nigh and Anne Gattiker. Test method evaluation experiments and data. In *Proceedings International Test Conference 2000 (IEEE Cat. No. 00CH37159)*, pages 454–463, 2000.
65. Bipul C Paul, Kunhyuk Kang, Haldun Kufluoglu, Muhammad Ashraful Alam, and Kaushik Roy. Temporal performance degradation under NBTI: Estimation and design for improved reliability of nanoscale circuits. In *Proceedings of the Design Automation & Test in Europe Conference*, volume 1, pages 1–6, 2006.
66. Songwei Pei, Huawei Li, and Xiaowei Li. A low overhead on-chip path delay measurement circuit. In *2009 Asian Test Symposium*, pages 145–150, 2009.
67. R. Doering, and Y. Nishi. *Handbook of Semiconductor Manufacturing Technology (2nd edition), Chapter 30*. CRC Press, Boca Raton, FL, USA, 2017.
68. Arijit Raychowdhury, Swaroop Ghosh, and Kaushik Roy. A novel on-chip delay measurement hardware for efficient speed-binning. In *11th IEEE International On-Line Testing Symposium*, pages 287–292, 2005.
69. Richard Blish, Noel Durrant. *Semiconductor Device Reliability Failure Models*. International SEMATECH, May 2000. http://ismi.sematech.org/docubase/abstracts/3955axfr.htm.
70. R. Rodriguez, J.H. Stathis, and B.P. Linder. Modeling and experimental verification of the effect of gate oxide breakdown on CMOS inverters. In *2003 IEEE International Reliability Physics Symposium Proceedings, 2003. 41st Annual*, pages 11–16, 2003.
71. S. Borkar, T. Karnik, S. Narendra, J. Tschanz, A. Keshavarzi, and V. De. Parameter Variations and Impact on Circuits and Microarchitecture. *DAC*, pages 338–342, 2003.
72. S. Mitra, N. Seifert, M. Zhang, Q. Shi, and K.S. Kim. Robust System Design with Built-In Soft-Error Resilience. *IEEE Computer*, 38(2):43–52, 2005.
73. N.V. Shenoy, R.K. Brayton, and A.L. Sangiovanni-Vincentelli. Minimum padding to satisfy short path constraints. In *Proceedings of 1993 International Conference on Computer Aided Design (ICCAD)*, pages 156–161, 1993.
74. Jeonghee Shin, Victor Zyuban, Zhigang Hu, Jude A. Rivers, and Pradip Bose. A framework for architecture-level lifetime reliability modeling. In *37th Annual IEEE/IFIP International Conference on Dependable Systems and Networks (DSN'07)*, pages 534–543, 2007.
75. P. Shivakumar, M. Kistler, S.W. Keckler, D. Burger, and L. Alvisi. Modeling the effect of technology trends on the soft error rate of combinational logic. In *Proceedings International Conference on Dependable Systems and Networks*, pages 389–398, 2002.
76. SONY SEMICONDUCTOR. Quality and Reliability HandBook. *Chapter 4*, pages 120–152, Oct. 2000.
77. J. Srinivasan, S.V. Adve, P. Bose, and J.A. Rivers. The case for lifetime reliability-aware microprocessors. In *Proceedings. 31st Annual International Symposium on Computer Architecture*, pages 276–287, 2004.

78. Jayanth Srinivasan, Sarita V Adve, Pradip Bose, and Jude A Rivers. Exploiting structural duplication for lifetime reliability enhancement. In *32nd International Symposium on Computer Architecture (ISCA'05)*, pages 520–531, 2005.
79. Sun Microsystem Inc. OpenSPARC T1 Microarchitecture Specification. pages 1.1–10.26, August 2006.
80. Stephen Sunter. Bist vs. ate: Need a different vehicle? In *Proceedings International Test Conference 1998 (IEEE Cat. No. 98CH36270)*, page 1148, 1998.
81. Rajeshwary Tayade and Jacob Abraham. Small-delay defect detection in the presence of process variations. *Microelectronics journal*, 39(8):1093–1100, 2008.
82. Rajeshwary Tayade and Jacob A Abraham. On-chip programmable capture for accurate path delay test and characterization. In *2008 IEEE International Test Conference*, pages 1–10, 2008.
83. Radu Teodorescu, Jun Nakano, Abhishek Tiwari, and Josep Torrellas. Mitigating parameter variation with dynamic fine-grain body biasing. In *40th Annual IEEE/ACM International Symposium on Microarchitecture (MICRO 2007)*, pages 27–42, 2007.
84. T.N. Vijaykumar, I. Pomeranz, and K. Cheng. Transient-Fault Recovery Using Simultaneous Multithreading. In *Proceedings of the 29th Annual International Symposium on Computer Architecture (ISCA)*, pages 87–98, 2002.
85. Ming-Chien Tsai, Ching-Hwa Cheng, and Chiou-Mao Yang. An all-digital high-precision built-in delay time measurement circuit. In *26th IEEE VLSI Test Symposium (VTS 2008)*, pages 249–254, 2008.
86. V. Zyuban, D. Brooks, V. Srinivasan, M. Gschwind, P. Bose, P.N. Strenski, and P.G. Emma. Integrated Analysis of Power and Performance For Pipelined Microprocessors. *IEEE Transactions on Computers*, 53(8):1004–1016, 2004.
87. R. Vattikonda, Wenping Wang, and Yu Cao. Modeling and minimization of PMOS NBTI effect for robust nanometer design. In *2006 43rd ACM/IEEE Design Automation Conference*, pages 1047–1052, 2006.
88. S. Venkataraman and S.B. Drummonds. Poirot: applications of a logic fault diagnosis tool. *IEEE Design & Test of Computers*, 18(1):19–30, 2001.
89. W. Zhao, and Y. Cao. New generation of Predictive Technology Model for sub-45nm early design exploration. *IEEE Trans. on Electron Devices*, 53(11):2816–2823, 2006.
90. Wenping Wang, Vijay Reddy, Anand T. Krishnan, Rakesh Vattikonda, Srikanth Krishnan, and Yu Cao. Compact modeling and simulation of circuit reliability for 65-nm cmos technology. *IEEE Transactions on Device and Materials Reliability*, 7(4):509–517, 2007.
91. Wenping Wang, Shengqi Yang, Sarvesh Bhardwaj, Rakesh Vattikonda, Sarma Vrudhula, Frank Liu, and Yu Cao. The impact of NBTI on the performance of combinational and sequential circuits. In *Proceedings of the 44th annual Design Automation Conference*, pages 364–369, 2007.
92. Xiaoxiao Wang, Mohammad Tehranipoor, and Ramyanshu Datta. Path-RO: A novel on-chip critical path delay measurement under process variations. In *2008 IEEE/ACM International Conference on Computer-Aided Design*, pages 640–646, 2008.
93. T. Xanthopoulos, D.W. Bailey, A.K. Gangwar, M.K. Gowan, A.K. Jain, and B.K. Prewitt. The design and analysis of the clock distribution network for a 1.2 GHz alpha microprocessor. In *2001 IEEE International Solid-State Circuits Conference. Digest of Technical Papers. ISSCC (Cat. No.01CH37177)*, pages 402–403, 2001.
94. Guihai Yan, Yinhe Han, and Xiaowei Li. A unified online fault detection scheme via checking of stability violation. In *2009 Design, Automation Test in Europe Conference Exhibition*, pages 496–501, 2009.
95. PETER M ZEITZOFF, JAMES A HUTCHBY, and HOWARD R HUFF. MOSFET and front-end process integration: Scaling trends, challenges, and potential solutions through the end of the roadmap. *International journal of high speed electronics and systems*, 12(02):267–293, 2002.
96. Minjin Zhang, Huawei Li, and Xiaowei Li. Multiple coupling effects oriented path delay test generation. In *26th IEEE VLSI Test Symposium (VTS 2008)*, pages 383–388, 2008.

Chapter 3
Fault-Tolerant General Purposed Processors

Abstract With the continuous decrease of CMOS feature size and threshold voltage, microprocessors are expected to see increasing failure rates due to intermittent faults, in company with soft errors and hard faults. With intermittent faults gradually becoming a major source of failures, a simple and quantitative metric is needed to guide reliable design for microprocessors. Having such a metric will help designers analyze which part of a microprocessor is more vulnerable to intermittent faults, and then select optimal protection techniques at an early design stage. To tackle this problem, we propose a metric intermittent vulnerability factor (IVF) to represent the probability that an intermittent fault in a structure will manifest itself in an observable program output. We also propose several IVF computation algorithms considering three intermittent fault models: intermittent stuck-at-1 and stuck-at-0 fault model, intermittent open and short fault model, and intermittent timing fault model. To further improve system reliability, accurately quantify the degradation of a given core is often of critical importance. We propose a novel core-level degradation quantification scheme, CoreRank, to facilitate the management. We first develop a new degradation metric, called "healthy condition", to capture the implication of performance degradation of a core with specific degraded components. Then, we propose a performance sampling scheme by using micro-operation streams, called snippet, to statistically quantify cores' healthy condition. We find that similar snippets exhibit stable performance distribution, which makes them ideal micro-benchmarks to testify the core-level healthy conditions. We develop a hardware-implemented version of CoreRank based on bloom filter and hash table. Unlike the traditional "faulty" or "fault-free" judgement, CoreRank provides a key facility to make better use of those imperfect cores that suffered from various progressive aging mechanisms such as negative bias temperature instability (NBTI), hot carrier injection (HCI).

3.1 Challenges of Fault-Tolerant Processor Design

3.1.1 Processor Vulnerability Characterizing

With the continuous decrease of CMOS feature size and threshold voltage, micro-processors are expected to see increasing failure rates due to intermittent faults, in company with soft errors and hard faults [16, 36, 42]. Intermittent faults are hardware errors which occur frequently and irregularly for a period of time, commonly due to manufacturing residuals or process variation, combined with voltage and temperature fluctuations [15, 77]. Soft errors, namely transient faults, are caused by energetic particles such as alpha particles from packaging material and neutrons from the atmosphere. Hard faults reflect irreversible physical changes, mainly caused by manufacturing defects, such as contamination in silicon devices or wear-out of materials. Conventionally, soft errors and hard faults have been considered as the major factor of program failures, and the effects of these faults have been extensively analyzed [29, 61]. Nevertheless, field collected data and failure analysis show that intermittent faults also become a major source of failures in new-generation microprocessors [17]. Without protection techniques, the microprocessor failure rates due to these faults will greatly increase with the exponential growth in the number of transistors.

To improve system reliability, prior work has proposed a variety of techniques to deal with these faults from circuit level to architecture level. Optimal protection techniques should meet a predefined reliability budget while with minimal per-formance, area, and energy penalties. As the number of ways that different faults manifest are likely to rise, leading to a consequential increase in the complexity and overhead of the techniques to tolerate them. Traditional protection techniques, for example, dual or triple modular redundancy results in at least 100% hardware and energy overhead [64, 78]. Solutions such as full redundant multithreading (RMT) and various partial redundancy schemes based on RMT also lead to about 30% performance degradation [45, 49, 56, 63]. In a recent workshop, an industry panel converged on a 10% area overhead target to handle all sources of chip errors as a guide for microprocessor designers [40]. Therefore, designers should evaluate the pros and cons of different protection techniques. Heavyweight protection techniques (such as strict hardware duplication) can ensure system reliability but incur unnecessary overheads, while lightweight protection (such as partial software redundancy) techniques can reduce the protection overheads but may be hard to satisfy the desired reliability goal.

Researchers have utilized several metrics to guide microprocessor reliability design. Two most widely used metrics are mean time to failure (MTTF) and failures in time (FIT). MTTF and FIT are used as metrics to describe component reliability, but are incapable of explicitly characterizing the inherent masking effect of hardware structures to a fault and the utilization of different structures. Recently, researchers have proposed several architecture level metrics to characterize the vulnerability of microprocessor structures to soft errors and hard faults. Mukherjee et al. [46] propose architecture vulnerability factor (AVF) to describe the probability that a soft error in a structure leads to an external visible error. Sridharan et al. [66, 67] propose two metrics program vulnerability factor (PVF) and hardware vulnerability factor (HVF) to characterize the masking effect of soft errors at architecture level and microarchitecture level, respectively. Bower et al. [7] introduce hard-fault architectural vulnerability factor (H-AVF) to help designers to compare various hard-fault tolerance methods. Since intermittent faults are very different from soft errors and hard faults, existing evaluation metrics can not accurately reflect the vulnerability of microprocessor structures to intermittent faults. With intermittent faults gradually becoming a major source of failures, a simple and quantitative metric is needed to guide reliable design for microprocessors. Having such a metric will help designers analyze which part of a microprocessor is more vulnerable to intermittent faults, and then select optimal protection techniques at an early design stage. However, characterizing the vulnerability to intermittent faults is far from mature.

In the first part of this chapter, we propose a metric intermittent vulnerability factor (IVF) to represent the probability that an intermittent fault in a structure will manifest itself in an observable program output. We analyze IVFs for two representative microprocessor structures: reorder buffer and register file. We then propose several IVF computation algorithms considering three intermittent fault models: intermittent stuck-at-1 and stuck-at-0 fault model, intermittent open and short fault model, and intermittent timing fault model. We exploit a cycle-accurate simulator Sim-Alpha to implement the proposed IVF computation algorithms and use SPEC CPU2000 integer benchmark suite as the workload.

3.1.2 Sick Processor Management

The growing integration density of transistors has been escorted by progressive semiconductor technologies for the past three decades. Unsurprisingly, the scale and complexity of modern microprocessors have reached a unprecedented level, and 1000-core processor will not be a buzz word but reality [6]. Unfortunately, we still face grand challenges to drive such powerful processor with a sea of computing cores to work efficiently.

One of the looming challenges is core management, which directly determines the harvestable performance of the powerful hardware substrate. This challenge in essence comes from the core-to-core heterogeneity, either *intentional* due to architectural innovations such as "bigLITTLE" architectures [28], or *unintentional* due to process variation [9, 58], aging [5, 12, 68, 79], and core salvaging [34, 62], i.e. decoupling some faulty microarchitectural components for reliability reasons. Such core-to-core heterogeneity results in functionally equivalent cores with different performance levels. Intel and ARM demonstrated adaptive RISC core designs to tolerate such dynamic variations, at the expense of performance degradation [10, 74]. In the near future, we believe that the core-level unintentional heterogeneity

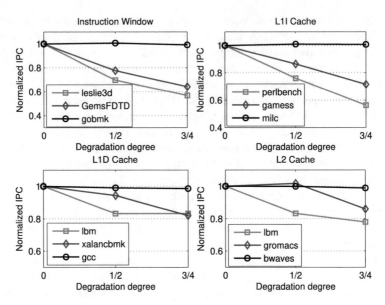

Fig. 3.1 Performance degradation vs. defect degrees of inst. window (UL), L1 inst. cache (UR), L1 data cache(LL), L2 cache(LR)

would be more significant, given the faulty components and aging effects would be more prevalent and prominent in smaller technology nodes [5]. We call such aging-induced performance degradation as "Sick Silicon" problem. Therefore, *instead of simply ruling out those cores salvaged from various defects, we should try to hide the imperfections.*

An obvious solution to this problem is always prioritizing the cores with the least "degradation". However, we find that it's not that intuitively simple to quantify the degradation. First, the performance degradation depends on both applications and defect degrees, as Fig. 3.1 shows. The results show the performance responses of cores under various types of degradations. The cores are salvaged from instruction window defects, or L1 instruction/data cache defects, or L2 cache defects, respectively [53]. For simplicity, we don't show the more complicated compound defects. The degradation degree of "0" indicates defect-free, and 1/2 indicate a half resource unavailable, and so on. The results show that performance response not only depends on degradation degrees, but also exhibits to be highly application-specific. For example, the gobmk in the Fig. 3.1 (UL) shows to be very resilient to the instruction window degradation, but, by contrast, the leslie3d and GemsFDTD are very sensitive to it. Such complexity is never unique for instruction window only, but also to other resources, as exemplified in the other three sub-figures. Hence, even though the defect and associate defect degree are accessible to operating system (OS), we still have no ways to figure out how much performance impact such degradation to the running applications. Second, the performance degradation of different phases can also change significantly, even on the same core.

Hence, the degradation measured in coarse-grained application may underestimate the impact of core-to-core heterogeneity. For example, assume an application is divided into two phases, Phase 1 and Phase 2. The execution time of the two phases on Core A is 100 and 200 ms, denoted by

$$T (\text{Core A, Phase 1}) = 100 \text{ ms}, \, T (\text{Core A, Phase 2}) = 200 \text{ ms}.$$

Suppose that the execution time of the same application on Core B, which is salvaged from a different defect component, is

$$T (\text{Core B, Phase 1}) = 200 \text{ ms}, \, T (\text{Core B, Phase 2}) = 100 \text{ ms}.$$

Clearly, the performance of Core A and Core B have no difference for this application because both cores take the same time, i.e. 300 ms, to finish. An obvious defect-hiding optimization is to schedule Phase 1 to Core A, and Phase 2 to Core B, the execution time can be reduced to 200 ms. However, this opportunity is invisible if oblivious to the phase-specific degradation to heterogeneous cores.

In view of the above two observations, we claim that to maximally hide the defect-induced performance degradation, the prerequisite is to know how much degradation the phases of running application to specific cores. We use the term "healthy condition" to capture the function that a core performance is both phase- and defect-specific, denoted by $H(core_i | phase_j)$. Unfortunately, it is challenging to dynamically figure out $H(core_i | phase_j)$ because of the stochastic characteristics of application performance, which will be elaborated in Sect. 3.3.1. Simply put, how can we know which core can deliver the best performance for the coming phase of an in-flight application?

In the second part of this chapter, we propose a statistical core ranking mechanism, called "CoreRank", to dynamically quantify individual core's healthy condition. CoreRank indicates the OS to avoid the unhealthy cores as much as possible, and always prioritize the healthier ones. Since the healthy condition can be reflected by the performance responses, and quantifying healthy condition is not very timing critical, we can sample sufficient runtime performance statistics to infer each core's healthy condition. These statistics can be obtained by performance counters. Note that the inference is not one-time procedure, but in a progressive way. CoreRank never finishes its mission even all cores are testified, but periodically invoked to keep tracking them over the lifetime to capture the in field degradations. CoreRank establishes two principles: First, unlike distinguishing between faulty and fault-free cores in the realm of design for reliability, healthy condition should be a "conditional" probability, given a core's healthy condition is highly workload dependent. For example, a core with a faulty branch predictor shows to be healthier when comes to branch-non-intensive applications than to branch-intensive ones. The application-dependent characteristic implies that the healthy condition should be conditionally defined. Second, CoreRank should not be tied with any specific applications. Quantifying healthy condition towards different applications is less useful because (1) the applications can be extremely diversified, and (2) the impact of inter-application interference on a highly parallel architecture is sporadic and hard to quantify. CoreRank quantifies healthy condition towards more specific phase representations, called "snippets", which are dynamic micro-operation streams and oblivious to all of the software level interferences. The snippet can be readily characterized by build-in performance counters, without any instrumentation to running workloads.

3.2   Processor Vulnerability Evaluation

3.2.1   Vulnerability Analysis Methods

Our work is related to several recent researches on characterizing the vulnerability of microprocessor structures to soft errors and hard faults. Architecture vulnerability factor (AVF) is a widely used metric to characterize the masking effect of soft errors both from microarchitecture level and architecture level [3, 24, 46]. A structure's AVF is the probability that a soft error in it causes an external visible error. The AVF can be calculated as the average-over-time percent of architecturally correct execution (ACE) bits in a structure. The ACE bits are those if been changed will affect the final output of a program, and on the contrary, un-ACE bits are those if been changed will not propagate to program output. For example, the AVF of a storage cell is the percentage of cycles the cell contains ACE bits; the AVF of a function unit is the percentage of cycles the unit processes ACE bits or ACE instructions. ACE bit analysis is carried out with a performance level simulator during program execution. Equation (3.1) describes how to compute a structure's AVF through ACE bit analysis, where B is the total bits in a hardware structure, T is the execution cycles of a program, and N_{ACE}^t is the number of ACE bits in the structure at a specific cycle t.

$$AVF = \frac{\sum_{t=0}^{T} N_{ACE}^t}{B \times T} \tag{3.1}$$

Another method to compute AVF is through statistical fault injection [73, 76]. Fault injection experiments are performed on a register transfer level (RTL) model of microprocessors. After injecting a fault, the architecture state of the fault injected simulator will be compared with a golden model to determine whether the injected fault results in an external error. After a huge number of fault injections, the percentage of faults leading to external errors is taken as AVF. Statistical fault injection is able to simulate any execution path and allows for high accuracy estimation. Most recently, Walcott et al. [75] use linear regression to identify the correlation between AVF and several key performance metrics (such as instructions per cycle and reorder buffer occupancy), and then use the predictive model to compute AVF dynamically during program execution. Duan et al. [21] propose an alternative prediction method to compute AVF across different workloads and microprocessor configurations using boosted regression trees and patient rule induction method.

Prior works also demonstrate that AVF varies significantly and highly depends on microarchitecture structures and architecture programs [48]. In order to characterize the vulnerability of a program independent of microarchitecture structures, Sridharan et al. [66] propose PVF to evaluate the masking effect of soft errors at architecture level. They use A-bits (like ACE bits) and architecture resources (the structures which can be seen from the perspective of programmers, such as register file and arithmetic logic unit) to compute PVF. Equation (3.2) is utilized to compute an architecture resource's PVF where B represents the total bits in the architecture resource, I represents the total number of instructions in the program and N^i_{A-bit} represents the number of A-bits in instruction i. PVF can be used to quantitatively estimate the masking effect of a program to soft errors and to express the behavior of AVF when executing a program. There are also several practical uses of PVF, such as choosing proper algorithms and compiler optimizations to reduce the vulnerability of a program to soft errors. Recently, Sridharan et al. [67] propose another metric HVF to analyze the vulnerability to soft errors only from microarchitecture level.

$$PVF = \frac{\sum_{i=0}^{I} N^i_{A-bit}}{B \times I} \tag{3.2}$$

AVF, PVF, and HVF, all of them are focusing on the masking effect of soft errors. Bower et al. [7] propose a metric named H-AVF for hard faults. H-AVF allows designers to compare alternative hard-fault tolerance schemes. For a given program, a structure's H-AVF can be computed as Eq. (3.3) where N_i represents the total number of instructions in the program, N_f represents the total number of fault sites in the structure, and $inst_{error}$ represents the number of instructions that will be corrupted due to hard faults. The purpose of H-AVF is to evaluate whether a particular sub-structure in microprocessors will benefit from hardening. It can also be used to compare hard-fault tolerance designs thus to provide a quantitative basis for comparison of alternative designs. Besides, Pellegrini et al. [51] propose a resiliency analysis system called CrashTest. CrashTest is capable of orchestrating and performing a comprehensive design resiliency analysis by examining how the design reacts to faults during program execution. This method mainly considers the impact of hard faults and soft errors on program execution.

$$H - AVF = \frac{1}{N_i} \times \frac{1}{N_f} \times \sum_{\forall fault} \sum_{\forall inst} inst_{error} \tag{3.3}$$

Unlike soft errors and hard faults, intermittent faults have many uncertain causes and their behaviors vary significantly. However, the vulnerability of microprocessor structures to intermittent faults is rarely considered. We propose a metric IVF to characterize the vulnerability of microprocessor structures to intermittent faults. We compute IVFs for different microprocessor structures considering three intermittent fault models: intermittent stuck-at-1 and stuck-at-0 faults, intermittent open and short faults, and intermittent timing faults.

3.2.2 Intermittent Fault Oriented Analysis

This section first describes our IVF evaluation algorithms for different intermittent fault models, and then presents the equations for IVF computation. A structure's IVF is defined as the probability that an intermittent fault in the structure leads to an external visible error. The higher IVF, the more a structure is vulnerable to intermittent faults. In modern microprocessors, reorder buffer and register file are two of the most important hardware structures.

Figure 3.2a shows a baseline pipeline used in this work. Reorder buffer is used for out-of-order instruction execution, which allows instructions to be committed in-order. It keeps the information of in-flight instructions and allows for precise exceptions and easy rollback for control of target address mispredictions. The entry in reorder buffer is allocated in a round-robin order. Figure 3.2b further shows typical fields contained in an entry of reorder buffer [59]. These fields have different functions. The busy flag, issued flag, finished flag, speculative flag, and valid flag are control signals, while PC denotes the address of the current instruction, and rename register shows the renamed register for the destination register of an instruction. For register file, it is an array of processor registers and will be used to provide operation data during program execution. Each register in it contains 64 bits. If any

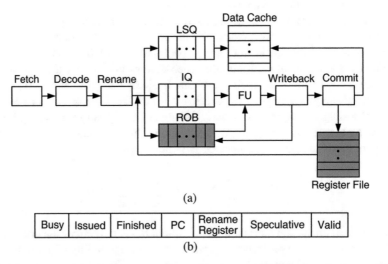

(a)

| Busy | Issued | Finished | PC | Rename Register | Speculative | Valid |

(b)

Fig. 3.2 (a) Schematic diagram of a baseline microprocessor. The two gray units are the structures under analyzing; (b) Reorder buffer entry [59]

of these two structures is affected by an intermittent fault, the probability resulting in a visible error is very high. We compute IVFs for these two representative structures in this work.

Before IVF computation, the following two questions should be carefully answered.

1. How to determine whether an intermittent fault affects program execution?
2. In order to describe intermittent faults, how to set these three key parameters: burst length, active time, and inactive time appropriately?

For the first question, to evaluate the impact of an intermittent fault on program execution, we need to determine whether the fault propagates to a storage cell and changes ACE bits during its lifetime. For intermittent stuck-at faults, as they only affect a single location, we should check whether the affected location contains an ACE bit, and then analyze whether the ACE bit is upset during the fault's active time. Only the case when the affected location contains an ACE bit and the ACE bit is changed will affect program execution. For intermittent open and short faults, they may corrupt two adjacent bit lines. When such a fault occurs, we need to determine whether the fault propagates to a storage cell and change ACE bits. While for intermittent timing faults, they may cause timing violations and affect write operations. Only when an intermittent timing fault has been captured by a storage structure and changes ACE bits, it will affect program execution.

For the second question, the parameters of an intermittent fault should follow the characteristics of an actual fault. As intermittent faults may be caused by different factors, the duration of intermittent faults could vary across a wide range of timescale. To set appropriate values for these key parameters, we analyze one kind of intermittent timing faults caused by significant voltage variation. The situation when supply voltage variation across a allowed voltage threshold is called a voltage emergency [35]. Voltage emergencies will lead to timing violations by slowing logic circuits. Figure 3.3 shows an example of intermittent timing faults caused by voltage emergencies. As can be seen, intermittent timing faults caused by voltage variations usually last on the order of several to tens of nanoseconds. Prior works also show the similar duration of an intermittent fault [27, 65, 70]. According to the observation,

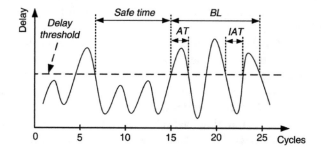

Fig. 3.3 Example of intermittent timing faults caused by voltage emergencies

we set the burst length of an intermittent fault in the range of 5 cycles to 30 cycles in our experiments. Both active time and inactive time are set to 2 cycles. The number of activations will be changed according to burst length, but the 50% duty cycle is kept constant. For an instance, if burst length is 30-cycle, the number of activations is 8. Besides, as the appearance time of intermittent faults cannot be predicted, their start time are randomly generated during program execution.

Based on the above analysis, the first step for IVF computing is to determine ACE bits in a structure during program execution; the second step is to check whether ACE bits are changed when an intermittent fault occurs. As reorder buffer is used to support out-of-order instruction execution, we analyze ACE bits in it by monitoring instructions when these instructions go through all stages of the pipeline. Meanwhile, register file is used to store and provide operation data for in-flight instructions, we analyze ACE bits in it based on its related operations, such as read, write, and evict. Following we present IVF computation algorithms for intermittent stuck-at faults, intermittent open and short faults, and intermittent timing faults, respectively.

3.2.2.1 Intermittent Stuck-at Faults

Intermittent stuck-at faults include intermittent stuck-at-1 faults and intermittent stuck-at-0 faults. As the analysis methods for these two kinds of faults are similar, for the sake of brevity, we take intermittent stuck-at-1 faults as an example in this section.

1. Reorder Buffer: We illustrate the IVF computation algorithm for reorder buffer at first. Unlike a soft error only existing for a single cycle, an intermittent fault will last for a while and repeatedly appear during its lifetime. Figure 3.4 shows a 3-D perspective of a simplified reorder buffer. The X-axis represents the number of entries in the structure, the Y-axis represents the number of bits in each entry, and the Z-axis represents the time of program execution. For the example structure, it has two entries and each entry contains two bits. The small black parallelograms and white parallelograms are used to indicate ACE bits and un-ACE bit, respectively. For this example, we assume an intermittent stuck-at-1 fault occurs. The burst length is set to 2 cycles, while both active time and inactive time are 1 cycle.

    The gray part of the cube shows the possible affected region by the fault. The parallelograms in the X-Y plane are planar representation of ACE bits and un-ACE bits for the gray part. For a specific bit, if it contains an ACE bit during the fault's active time and its value is changed by the fault, the projection of that bit in X-Y plane is an ACE bit, otherwise, the projection will be an un-ACE bit. As can be seen in Fig. 3.4, during the fault's active time, B_1 and B_2 contain ACE bits and will be affected by the fault. Though B_1 and B_3 contain ACE bits in the fault's inactive time, they will not be affected by the fault. To generate bit projection, we further need to analyze whether the values in and will be changed.

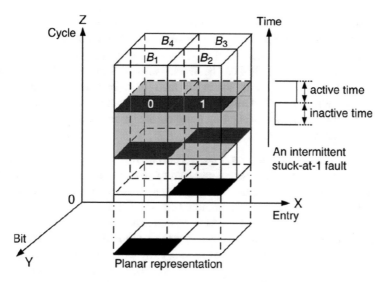

Fig. 3.4 ACE bits and un-ACE bits projection for IVF computing

For the intermittent stuck-at-1 fault, only if an ACE bit is supposed to be a logic value "0", it will actually be corrupted. Figure 3.4 shows the values of B_1 and B_2 during the active time. As the fault in-question is an intermittent stuck-at-1 fault, only the projection of B_1 is an ACE bit and other three bits are un-ACE bits. In this case, the probability that the fault leads to an external visible error is 25%, which means the IVF is 25%. With the above ACE bit analysis and bit projection, we can quickly determine whether an intermittent stuck-at fault affects program execution and further compute IVF for reorder buffer.

2. Register File: Unlike reorder buffer, the ACE bits analysis for register file is a little different. The ACE bits in register file are analyzed according to the related operations on each physical register. During the execution of a program, if the microprocessor decodes an in-flight instruction with a destination register, it will allocate a free physical register for the instruction, creating a new register version [44]. The lifetime of a register version is shown in Fig. 3.5. During the lifetime of

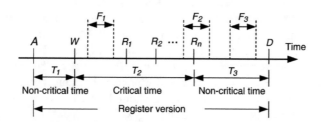

Fig. 3.5 Lifetime of a register version with related operations. F_1, F_2, and F_3 are three intermittent stuck-at faults occurring at different time

a register version, the possible operations include allocation (A), write (W), read (R), and deallocation (D). A register version can only be written once but can be read several times during its lifetime. The lifetime of a register version is from allocation to deallocation and can be divided into three intervals: from allocation to write (A to W), from write to the last read (W to R_n), and from the last read to deallocation (R_n to D). Only the interval from write to the last read is critical time and other two intervals belong to noncritical time. During the critical time, all bits in the register are ACE bits.

If an intermittent stuck-at-1 fault occurs during the critical time, these ACE bits with logic value "0" will be affected and lead to an external visible error (like fault F_1). If the fault occurs during noncritical time, it will always be masked (like fault F_3). A complicated situation is that a fault may start from a critical time region and end at a noncritical time region (like fault F_2). For this kind of fault, if its residency time in critical time region overlaps its active time, the fault can be handled like F_1; if there is no overlap, the fault will be masked. Only when an intermittent stuck-at-1 fault occurs during critical time and changes ACE bits will affect program execution. With the above analysis, the IVF for reorder buffer and register file considering intermittent stuck-at faults can be expressed as Eq. (3.4) where B represents the total number of bits in the structure under analysis, s represents a location in the structure, D represents the burst length of an intermittent stuck-at fault, and $U^D_{ACE}(s)$ represents whether an ACE bit in location will be changed by the fault; if it is, the value is assigned to one; otherwise, the value is assigned to zero. The numerator adds the total number of ACE bits that will be affected during the lifetime of an intermittent stuck-at fault.

$$IVF_{sa} = \frac{\sum_{s=1}^{B} U^D_{ACE}(s)}{B} \tag{3.4}$$

3.2.2.2   Intermittent Open and Short Faults

Intermittent open and short faults have different behaviors depending on where they occur. They also can be taken as intermittent stuck-at faults or intermittent timing faults for some cases. Intermittent bridging faults, one kind of intermittent short fault, are different from intermittent stuck-at faults and intermittent timing faults. Intermittent bridging faults describe the cases when two signal wires are shorted together. They can be divided into four types: wired-AND, wired-OR, dominant-AND, and dominant-OR. For intermittent wired bridging faults, the logic value of the shorted nets is modeled as a logical AND or OR of the logic values on the shorted wires, while for intermittent dominant bridging faults, one wire is modeled to dominate the logic value on the shorted nets. The wired bridging faults were originally developed for bipolar circuits, while dominant bridging faults were for CMOS devices. Since CMOS technology is widely used for microprocessor manufacturing, we only analyze the dominant bridging faults in this work. An

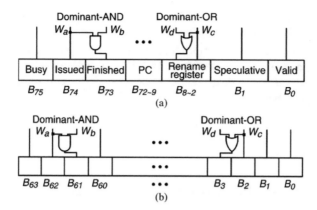

Fig. 3.6 Intermittent dominant-AND and dominant-OR bridging faults (**a**) in reorder buffer and (**b**) in register file

intermittent dominant bridging fault will corrupt two adjacent bit lines which produce two-bit of corruption.

Figure 3.6a, b show intermittent dominant-AND and dominant-OR bridging faults in the metal interconnect wires to reorder buffer and register file, respectively. and are aggressor wires, while and are victim wires. The logic value of the victim wire is dominated by the AND operation or OR operation of the logic value of the aggressor wire and its own value. For intermittent dominant-AND and dominant-OR faults, their controlling values are logic value "0" and logic value "1", respectively. These two kinds of faults also have similar analysis methods, for the sake of brevity, we only take dominant-AND bridging faults as an example. The intermittent open and short faults refer to intermittent dominant-AND bridging faults if not specifically mentioned in the following analysis. When an intermittent dominant-AND bridging fault occurs, the value of the victim wire will be changed only when the victim wire has a logic value "1" and the aggressor wire has a logic value "0". The corrupted data of the victim wire then propagates during program execution. If the corrupt data propagates to a storage cell, we further need to determine whether the affected bit is an ACE bit or not. If it is an ACE bit, then the fault will result in an external visible error; otherwise, the fault is said to be masked.

To compute IVFs of reorder buffer and register file for intermittent dominant bridging faults, we also need to analyze the data fields in them. As can be seen in Fig. 3.6a, if the control bit in a reorder buffer entry has been corrupted, the instruction will be in a wrong state, and may lead to a fatal error. If the destination register tag is affected, the instruction result will be written to a wrong register. The bits in a register [shown in Fig. 3.6b], however, make no difference to the data if been affected, there is no need to further differentiate them. We only check the value containing in two adjacent lines and determine whether the fault changes ACE bits in that register.

With the above analysis, the IVF for reorder buffer and register file considering intermittent dominant bridging faults can be expressed as Eq. (3.5) where NUM represents the total number of intermittent dominant bridging faults, P_{ACE}^e represents whether a fault e propagates to reorder buffer or register file and finally affects ACE bits. If true, P_{ACE}^e will set to one. Otherwise, P_{ACE}^e will set to zero and the fault is said to be masked.

$$IVF_{bf} = \frac{\sum_{e=1}^{NUM} P_{ACE}^e}{NUM} \tag{3.5}$$

3.2.2.3 Intermittent Timing Faults

Unlike intermittent stuck-at faults which transform the correct value to a constant value, intermittent timing faults will affect data propagation and leads to capture wrong data to storage structure at entry level.

Before presenting the algorithm to compute IVF for intermittent timing faults, we need to know when a fault will affect program execution. To determine the impact of an intermittent timing fault, two steps are needed. First, analyze whether the fault is captured by a storage cell; second, check whether ACE bits in the storage cell have been affected. Only when an intermittent timing fault propagates to storage cells and changes ACE bits, it will affect the final program output. Otherwise, the fault will not manifest itself in external output and is said to be masked. In this work, we assume an intermittent timing fault only cause timing violations during its active time. If a write operation occurs during the active time of an intermittent timing fault, we assume the fault propagates to the structure. If no write operations occur or write operations only occur during inactive time, the fault is said to be masked and will not affect program execution. We use an example to further explain for this. Figure 3.7 illustrates whether an intermittent timing fault will lead to capture a wrong data to a storage cell. As can be seen, write operation W_1 occurs during the active time of $Fault_1$, the fault will propagate to a storage cell. While write

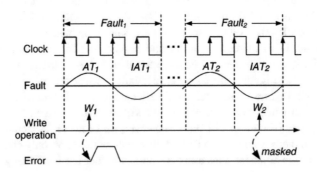

Fig. 3.7 Intermittent timing fault results in writing a wrong data to a storage cell

operation W_2 occurs during the inactive time of $Fault_2$, the fault will not affect the data propagation.

With the above analysis, the frequency of write operations has strong correlation with the vulnerability of a structure to intermittent timing faults. During the lifetime of an intermittent timing fault, a structure with high write frequency is more vulnerable because the probability a fault propagating to the structure is very high. On the contrary, a structure with low write frequency is less vulnerable. To compute the IVF for different structures, we then need to determine whether a write operation is taken during the active time of an intermittent timing fault. For reorder buffer, the related write operations occur when the state of an instruction in it changes. For register file, the related write operations take place when an instruction commits or when a value is loaded from memory. The related write operations will be recorded for IVF computation during program execution.

When a wrong data has been captured by a structure, we need to further analyze whether ACE bits in that cell have been changed by the fault. If ACE bits are upset, the fault will affect the external visible output. Otherwise, it is said to be masked at architecture level. There are mainly two scenarios that an intermittent timing fault will be masked during program execution: first, the data in a storage structure is proved to be a dead value; second, the captured data only changes un-ACE bits. If an intermittent timing fault is in either of the two scenarios, it will not affect program execution. Which scenario occurs is determined by analyzing ACE bits and un-ACE bits in different structures. For example, Fahs et al. [23] found that about 14% instructions are dead instructions during executing SPEC CPU2000 benchmarks. Dead instructions are those instructions whose results will not be used by any other instructions in the future. If the result of a dead instruction is changed by an intermittent timing fault, even if an incorrect data has been written to register file, the fault will not affect program execution. By analyzing ACE bits and un-ACE bits in different structures during program execution, we can determine which scenario occurs.

Only an intermittent timing fault propagates to a storage cell and changes ACE bits, it will contribute to IVF computation. The IVF considering intermittent timing faults can be expressed as Eq. (3.6) where NUM represents the total number of intermittent timing faults during executing a program; P_{NUM} represents the number of intermittent timing faults propagating to the structure; N_{dead} represents the number of faults only affecting dead values; N_{un-ACE} represents the number of faults only changing un-ACE bits. With this equation, we can compute IVF_{tf} for different microprocessor structures.

$$IVF_{tf} = \frac{P_{NUM} - (N_{dead} + N_{un-ACE})}{NUM} \tag{3.6}$$

3.2.2.4   Statistical Significance

In this work, we use statistical sampling to study the characteristics of intermittent faults. To make the evaluation having statistical significance, a large number of faults should be analyzed during a simulation. After trying different number of faults, we set the fault number as 1000 to make a tradeoff between accuracy and analysis time. Besides, the burst length and the number of activations in an intermittent fault have significant impact on IVF computation. During executing different benchmarks, the two parameters will be changed to make our analysis more comprehensive, and the final IVF of a structure is the average result across all faults under analysis.

With the above introduced Eqs. (3.4)–(3.6), we can quickly compute IVFs for reorder buffer and register file. Furthermore, our proposed IVF estimation methodology also can be extended to other structures, such as issue queue, load/store queue, and L1/L2 caches. As the analysis of ACE bit in issue queue and load/store queue is also based on tracking the ACE bits in instructions when these instructions go through the pipeline, which is similar to the ACE analysis of reorder buffer. Besides, the analysis of ACE bit in L1/L2 caches is based on dividing the lifetime of a data block into critical time and noncritical time, which is similar to the ACE analysis of register file. Therefore, our IVF estimation methodology is also suitable for these structures. As all the above mentioned storage structures may occupy more than 60% area of modern microprocessors [69], our proposed evaluation methodology provides a generic metric for reliability estimation.

3.2.3   Experiment Result Analysis

3.2.3.1   Experiment Setups

All of our experiments are conducted on the Sim-Alpha simulator [19]. Sim-Alpha is a validated execution-driven simulator for Alpha 21264 microprocessor [37]. It can execute instructions down the mis-speculated path, in the same way as an actual microprocessor would execute them. In this work, Sim-Alpha is heavily modified to support IVF computing for reorder buffer and register file. We use all the twelve SPEC CPU2000 integer benchmarks to evaluate our method. Since the simulator cannot accurately simulate the floating-point pipeline, the floating-point benchmarks are not included in our experiments. All the benchmarks are compiled for the Alpha ISA. In order to reduce simulation time, we use Simpoint tool [60] to pick the most representative simulation point for each benchmark and each benchmark is fast-forwarded to its representative point before detailed performance simulation takes place. Each benchmark is evaluated for 100 million instructions using the full reference input set. The baseline configuration of the simulator is further summarized in Table 3.1. As we focus on the integer pipeline, only the integer pipeline resources are shown in the table. Besides, to analyze the impact

Table 3.1 Simulated microprocessor configuration

Configuration parameter	Value
Pipeline stages	7
Fetch/slot/issue/commit width	4/4/4/11 instruction/cycle
Branch-predictor type	Hybrid, 4K global + 2-level 1K local + 4K choice
Integer register file size	80 entries
Integer issue queue size	20 entries
Reorder buffer size	80 entries
Unified load/store queue size	64 entries
Integer ALUs	4, 1-cycle latency
Integer multipliers/dividers	–
L1 data cache	64 KB, 2-way, 64 byte line-size, 1-cycle latency
L1 instruction cache	64 KB, 2-way, 64 byte line-size, 3-cycle latency
L2 unified cache	2 MB, direct mapped, 64 byte line-size, 7-cycle latency
I-TLB/D-TLB	128-entry, full-associative

of different microarchitecture design parameters on IVF computation, we further change the number of fetch/slot/issue width, commit width, reorder buffer size, and register file size in our experiments.

3.2.3.2 IVF Computation for Different Intermittent Fault Models

We first present IVF of reorder buffer and register file considering different intermittent fault models, and then compute IVF by changing microarchitecture parameters and program phases. Finally, we introduce several IVF guided protection techniques to improve system reliability. In our experiments, we compute IVF with different fault configurations by changing the key parameters of intermittent faults. The burst length of each intermittent fault is assigned to 6 cycles, 10 cycles, and 22 cycles, respectively. Both active time and inactive time are assigned to 2 cycles. The start time of each intermittent fault is randomly generated during program execution.

1. Intermittent Stuck-at Faults: For intermittent stuck-at faults, as the value of ACE bits will affect IVF evaluation, we compute IVF_{sa1} in terms of intermittent stuck-at-1 fault model and IVF_{sa0} in terms of intermittent stuck-at-0 fault model, respectively.

   Figures 3.8 and 3.9 show IVF_{sa1} and IVF_{sa0} for reorder buffer and register file during executing different benchmarks. The average IVF_{sa1} for reorder buffer and register file vary from 21 to 37% and from 21.4 to 31.5%, respectively. The average IVF_{sa0}, however, vary from 5.8 to 10.3% and from 1.1 to 1.6%, respectively. As can be seen, the longer burst length, the more ACE bits been affected, which leads to a higher IVF_{sa1} and IVF_{sa0}. For a same burst length, the average IVF_{sa1} is much higher than IVF_{sa0}. This is because during executing different benchmarks, the number of ACE bits containing logic value

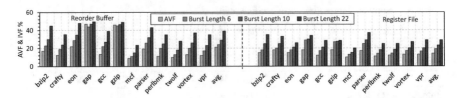

Fig. 3.8 Reorder buffer (left part) and register file (right part) AVFs considering soft errors and IVF_{sa1} considering intermittent stuck-at-1 faults

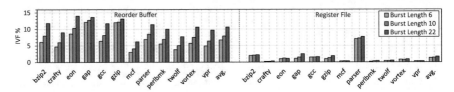

Fig. 3.9 Reorder buffer (left part) and register file (right part) IVF_{sa0} considering intermittent stuck-at-0 faults

"0" is much more than these containing logic value "1", especially in register file. ACE bits with logic value "0' are vulnerable to intermittent stuck-at-1 faults, but not to intermittent stuck-at-0 faults. Meanwhile, both IVF_{sa1} and IVF_{sa0} of reorder buffer are much higher than that of register file. The reason is that the residency time of an instruction in reorder buffer is very long, from issue stage till commit stage. Register file, however, will be written very frequently, making its vulnerable time much shorter than that of reorder buffer.

We also present the AVFs of reorder buffer and register file considering soft errors in Fig. 3.8. Compared to IVF_{sa1}, their AVFs are much lower. As an intermittent stuck-at-1 fault has longer duration than soft errors and most ACE bits contain logic value "0" in the two structures, which makes the probability an intermittent stuck-at-1 fault affecting final program execution is much higher. Therefore, intermittent stuck-at-1 faults have much more serious impact on program execution than soft errors if occur. The situation for intermittent stuck-at-0 faults, however, is just on the contrary. The reason is that soft errors can flip all the ACE bits while intermittent stuck-at-0 faults only affect these ACE bits with logic value "1".

2. Intermittent Open and Short Faults: Fig. 3.10 shows IVF_{bf} for reorder buffer and register file considering intermittent dominant-AND bridging faults. As can be seen, for different burst length, the average IVF_{bf} for reorder buffer and register file vary from 14.8 to 23% and from 11.5 to 22.8%, respectively. These two structures have relatively low vulnerability to intermittent dominant bridging faults. When an intermittent dominant bridging fault occurs, only the case that the aggressor wire holds a controlling value and the victim wire holds a non-controlling value, the fault can propagate during program execution. With the same burst length, reorder buffer has a little higher than that for register file. The

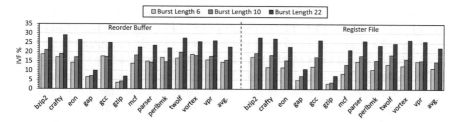

Fig. 3.10 IVF_{bf} for reorder buffer (left part) and register file (right part) considering intermittent dominant-AND bridging faults

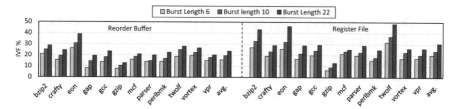

Fig. 3.11 IVF_{tf} for reorder buffer (left part) and register file (right part) considering intermittent faults

explanation is as follows: for reorder buffer, the control bits are more sensitive to intermittent dominant bridging faults; while for register file, however, it contains many narrowvalues during program execution. A value is categorized as narrow only if its leading bits are all zeros or ones. Kumar et al. [38] show about 50% of the produced results could be categorized as narrow values. For the narrow values in register file, they have higher masking rates to intermittent dominant bridging faults, which results in a lower IVF_{bf}.

3. Intermittent Timing Faults: We further present IVF_{tf} results for reorder buffer and register file considering intermittent timing faults. Figure 3.11 shows the IVF_{tf} for reorder buffer and register file during executing different benchmarks. As can be seen, the average IVF_{tf} for reorder buffer and register file are from 15.8% to 23.7% and from 19.7% to 30.6%, respectively. The longer burst length, the more write operations will be affected, which leads to higher IVF_{tf} results. From Fig. 3.11, we can tell that the average IVF_{tf} of register file is a little higher than that of reorder buffer, this is because register file provides operands for each instruction and has higher write frequency than reorder buffer. There is also a notable exception during executing two benchmarks gap and gzip. As for these two benchmarks, they have much higher cache miss rates than other benchmarks. During the time a cache miss occurs, the write operation for reorder buffer and register file will reduce dramatically, which leads to a much lower IVF_{tf} at that time. The widely used method to tolerate timing violations is to set a wider timing margin [2]. Only the intermittent timing faults occurring at critical paths and resulting in timing margin violation are what need to be considered.

4. Comparisons: Figs. 3.8, 3.10, and 3.11 have shown IVFs of reorder buffer and register file for three intermittent fault models. We then give a comparison of the impact of these faults. From these figures, it is easy to tell that intermittent stuck-at-1 faults have most serious impact on program execution during executing most benchmarks. For all these fault models, when the burst length of an intermittent fault increases, the probability to cause external errors is also increase, which means a structure's IVF will increase. Besides, for a same fault model, the IVFs of reorder buffer and register file also vary significantly. Reorder buffer is more sensitive than register file to intermittent stuck-at faults and intermittent open and short faults, while less sensitive to intermittent timing faults. Utilizing the proposed IVF evaluation methodology, designers can quantitatively analyze the masking effect of intermittent faults and guide system reliability design during the early design stage.

In this work, we focus on the impact of intermittent faults, while Pellegrini et al.'s work CrashTest [51] analyzes the impact of hard faults and soft errors on program execution. Their experimental results shows that about 80% of stuck-at faults will cause errors, while only 40% of path-delay faults have adverse effects on program execution. Soft errors have the least impact on the correct functionally of the design and on average less than 10% of them cause an error. Comparing their results with our experimental results, it is easy to knowthat hard faults have most serious impact on program execution, followed by intermittent faults, and finally soft errors. Pellegrini et al.'s work combined with our work provides a global reliability picture for designers to understand the impact of different kinds of faults on program execution.

3.2.3.3   IVF Computation for Different Microprocessor Configurations and Program Phases

We have computed IVF for different intermittent fault models under a specified microprocessor configuration. In this subsection, we further extend our proposed methodology to address different microprocessor configurations. We choose four microarchitecture design parameters (fetch/slot/issue width, commit width, reorder buffer size, and register file size) which are believed to have impact on IVF computation. We change the size of these parameters to generate different microprocessor configurations. Tables 3.2 and 3.3 show four different microprocessor configurations for reorder buffer and register file, respectively. Of these configurations, rob_base and reg_base are the baseline configurations. We compute reorder buffer's and register file's IVF for each configuration shown in Tables 3.2 and 3.3. Burst length is set to 10 cycles in the following experiments.

Figures 3.12, 3.13, 3.14, and 3.15 present our computed IVF results for different intermittent fault models. Each figure represents the result for one configuration. As can be seen, for configurations rob_c1 and reg_c1, reorder buffer's and register file's IVFs are much higher than the results of the baseline configuration. That is

Table 3.2 Different microprocessor configurations for computing IVF of reorder buffer

	Fetch/slot/issue width	Commit width	Reorder buffer size	Simulated workloads
rob_base	4	11	80	All twelve SPEC CPU2000 integer benchmarks
rob_c1	4	11	40	
rob_c2	4	11	120	
rob_c3	2	5	80	

Table 3.3 Different microprocessor configurations for computing IVF of register file

	Fetch/slot/issue width	Commit width	Reorder buffer size	Simulated workloads
reg_base	4	11	80	All twelve SPEC CPU2000 integer benchmarks
reg_c1	4	11	60	
reg_c2	4	11	120	
reg_c3	2	5	80	

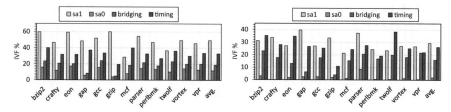

Fig. 3.12 Reorder buffer's IVF on configuration rob_base (left) and register file's IVF on configuration reg_base (right)

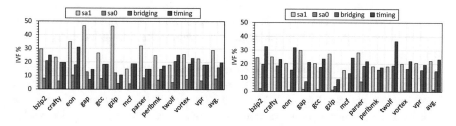

Fig. 3.13 Reorder buffer's IVF on configuration rob_c1(left) and register file's IVF on configuration reg_c1(right)

because when reduce a structure's size, its occupancy increases greatly and the structure will be more vulnerable to intermittent faults. For configurations rob_c2 and reg_c2, on the contrary, the occupancy of a structure will reduce, which results in IVF reduction. While for configurations rob_c3 and reg_c3, though we reduce instruction fetch width and commit width, their IVFs also decrease significantly.

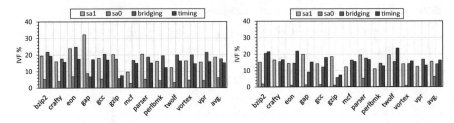

Fig. 3.14 Reorder buffer's IVF on configuration rob_c2 (left) and register file's IVF on configuration reg_c2 (right)

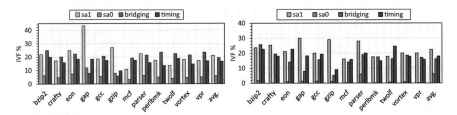

Fig. 3.15 Reorder buffer's IVF on configuration rob_c3 (left) and register file's IVF on configuration reg_c3(right)

This is due to both the number of in-flight instructions and the number of ACE bits in the pipeline reduces sharply during program execution. The experimental results reflect that a structure's IVF varies across different microprocessor configurations and has high correlation with its size and the number of in-flight instructions. Besides, we can tell that intermittent stuck-at-1 faults have most serious impact while intermittent stuck-at-0 faults have minimal impact on program execution for most benchmarks. Our proposed IVF evaluation methodology can be easily extended to evaluate IVF for different microprocessor configurations and can be used to choose appropriate microarchitecture parameters during the early design stage.

Furthermore, we compute IVF_{sa1} of reorder buffer and register file for different program phases. All program phases are chose by Simpoint [60] and each contains 1 million instructions. Figures 3.16 and 3.17 show IVF_{sa1} of reorder buffer and register file during executing several benchmarks. As can be seen, IVF varies significantly across different program phases and is heavily depended on the characteristics of a program. This phenomenon can be exploited to select proper protection techniques during program execution. We can use heavier protection (strict redundant multithreading) during highly vulnerable phases and lighter protection (partial or no redundant multithreading) during less vulnerable phases. With the dynamic tuning of protection, designers can achieve system reliability while minimize performance and/or energy overhead. The dynamic tuning of protection scheme also has been exploited to protect microprocessors from soft errors [75].

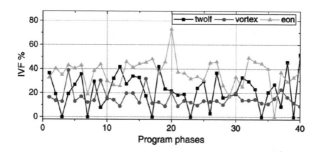

Fig. 3.16 IVF_{sa1} of reorder buffer for different program phases during executing twolf, vortex, and eon

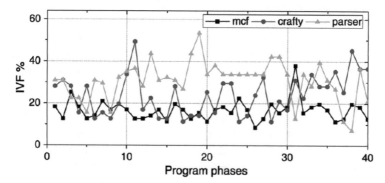

Fig. 3.17 IVF_{sa1} of register file for different program phases during executing mcf, crafty, and parser

3.2.3.4 IVF Guided Reliable Design

Our experimental results show that IVFs of reorder buffer and register file varies significantly, implying that these structures have different vulnerability to intermittent faults. Designers can exploit IVF information to determine which parts in microprocessors are most cost-effective to protect. For those structures with high IVFs, some heavyweight protection techniques are needed. We further introduce several possible techniques to improve system reliability.

For intermittent stuck-at faults or intermittent open and short faults, a feasible protection scheme is to harden these high IVF structures with fault detection techniques (such as ECC or parity code). As intermittent faults occur in burst at the same location, if a fault in a storage cell has been detected for a predefined times, we can deduce that an intermittent fault has happened. At that time, a flag bit in the entry will be set to busy, and the entry will be unused for a while to avoid the influence of the intermittent fault. After then, the entry can be used again when the intermittent fault disappears, for example, when the power delivery subsystem returns to its steady-state voltage. The partial protection technique ParShield proposed in [44] also can be used to protect register file from intermittent faults. Meanwhile, for intermittent timing faults, a prior proposed technique Razor [22] can be combined to these storage cells in critical paths of the most vulnerable structures, for example, Razor can be used to protect architecture registers as they are more vulnerable to intermittent timing faults. Besides, we can exploit architecture level masking of intermittent timing faults to improve system reliability [47].

The above introduced techniques seek to tolerate intermittent faults at fine-granularity. A coarse-granularity technique can be used to deal with intermittent faults in nowadays multi-core or many-core microprocessors. With inherent redundancy in these microprocessors, if a core sustains an intermittent fault, it should be suspended for a period of time, or operating system should transfer threads executing in the faulty core to other spare cores. Once the intermittent fault disappears later, the affected core can be used again.

Besides, we also show that a structure's IVF varies across different microprocessor configurations and program phases. This phenomenon can be exploited to select microarchitecture design parameters and tune protection schemes online. With the guide of IVF, designers can select appropriate protection techniques for these most vulnerable structures or program phases, which satisfies system reliability design goal while minimize implementation overheads. Nevertheless, combining our IVF evaluation methodology with these protection techniques is beyond the scope of this book, we plan to exploit protection techniques to detect and recover from intermittent faults in our future work.

3.2.4 Discussion

Intermittent faults are emerging as a big challenge to reliable microprocessor design. We propose a metric IVF to quantitatively characterize the vulnerability of microprocessor structures to intermittent faults. The IVF evaluation methodology contains the following aspects:

- analyze the physical causes of intermittent faults;
- classify intermittent faults into different fault models based on their behaviors;
- set key parameters for an intermittent fault and determine when the intermittent fault results in a visible error;
- for a specific microprocessor structure, propose IVF computation algorithms for different intermittent fault models;
- implement IVF computation algorithms in a high-level performance simulator, with which to compute IVF for the specific structure.

With the IVF evaluation methodology, we compute IVFs for reorder buffer and register file in terms of intermittent stuck-at faults, intermittent open and short faults, and intermittent timing faults. Experimental results show that intermittent stuck-at-1 faults have most serious adverse impact on program execution among these three types of intermittent faults. Besides, IVF varies noticeably across different microprocessor structures and program phases. Our experimental results imply partial protection of the most vulnerable structures and program phases to enhance system reliability. With the guide of IVF evaluation methodology, we also discuss several possible intermittent fault detection and recovery techniques which can be used to improve system reliability.

3.3 Multi-Core Processor Salvaging

According to recent ITRS report, reliability issue due to progressive aging mechanism has notched one of the top five near-term (by 2020) challenges [33]. These aging mechanisms, such as TDDB (Time-Dependent Dielectric Breakdown), NBTI (Negative Bias Temperature Instability), PBTI (Positive Bias Temperature Instability), HCI (hot carrier injection), RTN (Random Telegraph Noise), can cause processor degradations, and are blamed for "Sick Silicon". The circuit-level impact can be measured by aging sensors [71, 80].

There are two types of core salvaging approaches which inevitably result in core-to-core heterogeneity:

- Decoupling the faulty components [53]. As shown in Fig. 3.18, for example, the Core A and Core B suffered from pipeline defect and L1 I-cache defect, respectively; the defect-affected partitions, marked as dark parts, are decoupled from the rest to make each core functionally right, but in a degraded manner.

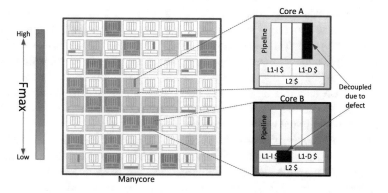

Fig. 3.18 Core-to-core heterogeneity due to core salvaging

Table 3.4 Degradation
models

Degradation component		Decoupled capacity
Front end	Branch predictor	1/4 : 1/2 : 3/4
	Inst. window	1/4 : 1/2 : 3/4
Back end	Issue width	1/4 : 1/2 : 3/4
Memory	L1 data cache	1/4 : 1/2 : 3/4
	L1 inst. cache	1/4 : 1/2 : 3/4
	L1 D-Cache	1/4 : 1/2 : 3/4
	L2 cache	1/4 : 1/2 : 3/4

- Adaptive voltage-frequency setting [74] and timing recycling [1, 79]. For example, the cores initially have the same max frequency, $Fmax$, but with the in-field dynamic variations such as aging effects, the $Fmax$ of the cores can differ from each other, as the $Fmax$ distribution indicated with the color bar.

The impact of $Fmax$ is relatively simple because the performance is always positively correlated with it; however, the impact from decoupling of faulty components is much more subtle. Take the Core A and Core B for example, clearly, we cannot conclude whether Core A outperforms Core B, or not. So, we will focus on the defect-decoupling style of core salvaging.

The degradation models used in experiments are listed in Table 3.4. The degradation terminology is borrowed from [52]. Basically, the degradation is roughly divided into three categories: (1) front-end degradation, involving branch predictor, instruction window; (2) back-end degradation, reflected by throttling the issue width; (3) memory degradation, involving private L1, private L2 caches. For each component, we assume three degradation degrees: Mild, Median, and Severe, corresponding to 1/4, 1/2, 3/4 capacity disabled. The degradation models exclude the extreme cases of 0 and 1, corresponding to defect-free and totally out-of-operation components that cannot be salvaged, respectively.

Why Application-Level Quantification Is not Good? As exemplified in Fig. 3.1, a core's performance degradation is determined by not only the hardware defect degrees, but also the target applications. An intuitive approach to quantify the core-level performance is using benchmark applications. The performance of core i running application j, denoted by $Perf(core_i|app_j)$, can be measured by the wall time of execution. However, directly using the per-application approach is less effective for OS maximizing the chip-wide performance. Besides the drawback of obliviousness to phase-specific performance variations as described in Sect. 3.1.2. There are two additional major reasons, detailed as follows:

First, $Perf(core_i|app_j)$ usually behaves as a random variable with wide and sporadic distribution [13]. For example, Fig. 3.19a illustrates the performance distribution of an application on two cores salvaged from different defects. The distributions are obtained by sampling multiple runs. Even though the sporadic distribution tends to become gaussian with a large enough number of runs, e.g. 1000 runs, given the central limit theorem (CLT), such brutal exercise is not applicable for a system in service.

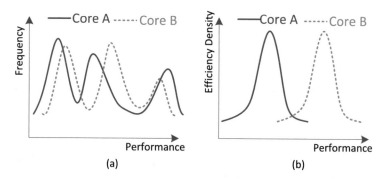

Fig. 3.19 Performance distribution. (**a**) Distribution in reality. (**b**) Gaussian distribution

Second, the measured performance may not faithfully reflect the performance of cores, but also other hardware and software subsystems such as memory bandwidth, interconnect, thread synchronization, etc. The performance bottlenecks in these subsystems can underestimate the difference between cores. Hence, it's unreliable using the applications to testify which core is "healthier". For example, it's impossible to judge a core's healthy condition if the core is stalled for a long time in the evaluation window.

Many previous researches have study variation-aware optimization problems [20, 32, 41, 72, 82]. However, most of them assume the variation is known and static, process variation for example. Our primary goal is to provide a way to quantify the performance impact of variation, especially in the filed dynamic variation. Therefore, CoreRank serves as a fundamental facility for other optimization procedures.

3.3.1 Dynamic Sick Core Ranking

We take a new approach to characterizing the core-level performance. There are two unique perspectives that diverge from conventional performance measurements. (1) Rather than building dedicated benchmarks, we use the ordinary workloads as the benchmarks which are readily accessible in the field. (2) Rather than using the user visible system-level performance, we use microarchitectural-level operations (uops) to testify the core's performance. The rational is that the uop throughput of a core can more faithfully reflect the core's capacity, even though these uops may come from different applications. The uops statistics can be obtained by build-in performance counters.

We define a segment of uops as a "snippet" characterized by the frequency of different types of uops. For example, the snippet $s = [fmul : 60, fadd : 35, branch : 5]$ represents a 100-uop snippet comprised of 60 floating point (FP) multiply operations, 35 FP add operations, and 5 branch operations. A snippet servers as the basic micro-benchmark to testify a core's healthy condition. Many

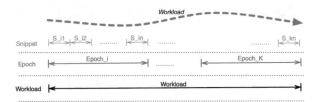

Fig. 3.20 Temporal granularities of snippet, epoch, and workload

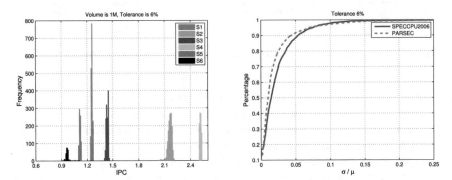

Fig. 3.21 Exemplifying the variation of six snippet classes (L) and the CDF of 10^3 snippet classes (R)

snippets constitute an epoch which corresponding to a OS scheduling interval. A workload is comprised of many epochs. The basic temporal granularity in CoreRank is shown in Fig. 3.20. Note that a valid snippet should not undergo the two types of stalls due to (1) uncore resources contentions, such as memory bandwidth, network congestions, and (2) threading synchronization, such as barriers, locks. These stalls can mislead the quantification of core healthy conditions because they are not caused by core defects.

In the following, we first give an overview definition of healthy condition, and then describe how to use snippets to quantify it, followed by the validation of snippets.

3.3.1.1 Healthy Condition Definition

The healthy condition (H) of core i (c_i) is defined as a such metric that measures the degradation of core's performance (P) on snippet m (s_m), $P(c_i|s_m)$, compared with a reference (degradation-free) core (c_{ref}), denoted by

$$H(c_i|s_m) = \frac{P(c_i|s_m)}{P(c_{ref}|s_m)}. \qquad (3.7)$$

Given healthy condition is reflected by the performance, we can directly use the performance as the proxy to healthy condition, that is

$$H(c_i|s_m) = P(c_i|s_m), \tag{3.8}$$

where, $P(c_i|s_m)$ behaves like a random variable, but we find the randomness can be regulated well under properly defined snippets.

3.3.1.2 Snippet Definition

Snippet is used to characterize the dynamic streams of micro-operations; hence it is a microarchitecture-specific representation and aims to faithfully reflect the activity of various microarchitectural components. Because a micro-operation is directly associated with the opcode of corresponding instruction (for complex instructions in CISC architectures, the micro-operation is referred to those decoded sub-instructions from the complex instructions), the snippet therefore is characterized by the combinations of various opcodes and associate frequencies. Mathematically, a snippet can be represented as the following vector:

$$s = [op_{(1)} : f_{(1)}, op_{(2)} : f_{(2)}, \cdots, op_{(n)} : f_{(n)}], \tag{3.9}$$

where $op_{(i)}$ is the identification of the type (i)'s active micro-operation, and $f_{(i)}$ is the associate frequency of occurrence.

The definition of snippet holds two merits: (1) the popularity of different snippets exhibits prominently exponential distribution, which implies that we only need to study a set of "basis" snippet to cover most operation streams in reality. (2) The degradations of the same snippet to the same core approximate to each other is context-insensitive, which implies we can use the combination of basis snippets to calculate the performance impact of virtually any streams of uops. Before delving into the detail validation, we first introduce three key attributes characterizing a valid snippet.

- **Volume**: Snippet volume is defined as the total number of uops of the target snippet, i.e. $\sum_{i=1}^{n} f_{(i)}$. If two snippets, s_1 and s_2, are comprised of the same types of active operations and each type with the same frequencies, then we call the two snippets belong to the same class S, denoted by $S = \{s_1, s_2\}$; otherwise they belong to different classes.
- **Capacity**: The number of snippets of a class, i.e. $|S|$, is defined as the class capacity. If we view S as a random variable, then s is actually a sample of S. Therefore, Eq. (3.8) can be represented as

$$H(c_i|s_m) = P(c_i|S_m), \tag{3.10}$$

where $P(c_i|S_m)$ is the expectation performance of core i on random variable S_m.

- **Tolerance**: In reality, we may relax the classification requirement by allowing a tolerance η in frequency variations. For example, $\eta = 10\%$ means that the frequency of the same active uops with $\pm 5\%$ variation can be viewed as equivalent.

3.3.1.3 Snippet Characterization

In this section, we study the snippets performance distributions, population distribution, and the impacts of snippet volume and tolerance.

Snippet Performance Distribution Is Narrowly Distributed Snippet classes can serve as ideal reagents to testify the healthy condition of cores because they are narrowly distributed, or called "stable" in performance, no matter which application these snippets come from. As an example, we demonstrate the performance distribution of six snippet classes in Fig. 3.21(L). The performance (measured by instructions per cycle, IPC) with volume of 10 million uops and tolerance of 6%. With such narrowly distribution, the mean value (μ) of S on core i can serve as a reasonable approximation to $P(c_i | S_m)$.

In fact, this merit of performance stability is not a coincidence but holds for majority of the snippet classes. The stability can be reflected by the ratio of performance standard deviation and mean (σ/μ). The smaller σ/μ implies higher performance stability. We demonstrate stability of snippet classes with SPECCPU2006 and PARSEC benchmarks, which represent the multi-program and multi-thread workload, respectively. The result in Fig. 3.21(R) shows that the σ/μ is no more than 5% for more than 90% snippet classes, when $\eta = 6\%$.

Note that we do not emphasize that the distribution of S has to be gaussian, even though it always tends to be as long as the **Capacity** is large enough. This trend is guaranteed by CLT (Central Limit Theorem).

Exponential Distribution of Snippet Population The reader may be wondering how many snippet classes, empirically, do the running applications have? For example, for Intel Nehalem microarchitecture, there are about 1125 types of uops, and the possible number of S could be astronomical! Fortunately, we find two exponential distributions can safely reduce the complexity, as shown in Fig. 3.22.

First, the "hot" uops usually are only small part of the whole number of uops. As Fig. 3.22(L) shows, the most frequently used top 80 uop types can cover over 97% of uop streams.

Second, the "hot" snippet classes also are small part of the whole space. As Fig. 3.22(R) shows, the top 0.1 million snippets can be classified into about 50 and 200 classes for PARSEC and SPEC benchmarks, but more than 80% classes contain a few snippets less than 10, compared to the top hot classes with thousands of snippets. Hence, we can ignore those snippets classes with a small number of snippets.

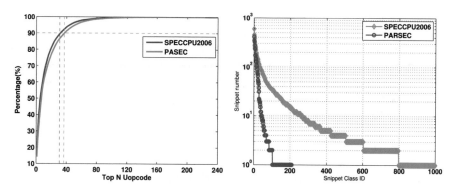

Fig. 3.22 The uops frequency distribution (L) and snippet occurrence distribution (R)

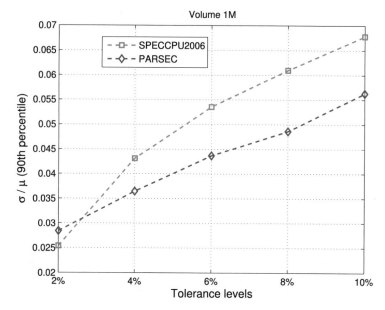

Fig. 3.23 The impact of tolerance to stability

Impact of Tolerance to Performance Stability To reinforce stable performance, the tolerance plays a critical role. Generally, the tighter tolerance threshold, the higher performance stability, because tighter threshold leads to less frequency variation in each active uop. Figure 3.23 shows the σ/μ value at 90 percentile across a rang of tolerance. We can see the stability degrades roughly linearly with increasing tolerance threshold.

Impact of Volume   The volume size is a design tradeoff. If the volume is too large, then a snippet will experience high possibility to be invalid, due to uncore resources contentions or threading synchronization, but the overhead of snippet scheduling will be amortized well. However the volume smaller than the snippet scheduling interval is also unnecessary because the OS cannot exploit so fine-grained phase variations. Given the minimal Linux scheduling time slice is 10 ms [18], we set the volume to 10 millions of uops because its execution time is comparable to a time slice.

3.3.1.4   Different Snippets Susceptible to Different Defects

Clearly, different snippet classes may stress different core microarchitectural components. Hence, the healthy condition of cores will be snippet-specific, rather than conventional judgement "faulty" or "fault-free". Figure 3.24 clearly confirms this implication. As an example, we compare the performance of seven snippet classes on a fresh core (no degradation) against a degraded core (with half private L2 cache decoupled). The S2, S3, S4, and S6 shows to be resilient to this degradation, while S1 and S5 affected by this degradation. We call such phenomenon as snippet-specific healthy condition.

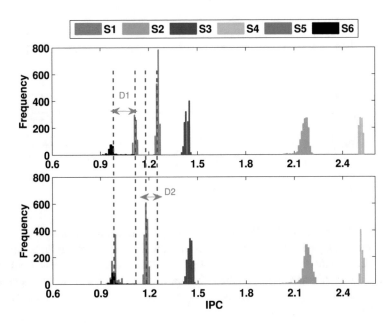

Fig. 3.24   Snippet-specific healthy condition

3.3.1.5 Dynamic Healthy Condition Quantification

So far, we can obtain the healthy condition of any cores on any target S by Eq. (3.10). These information can be logically organized into a matrix, denoted by $\mathcal{H}$

$$\mathcal{H} = \begin{bmatrix} H(c_1|S_1) & H(c_1|S_2) & \ldots & H(c_1|S_m) \\ H(c_2|S_1) & H(c_2|S_2) & \ldots & H(c_2|S_m) \\ \vdots & \vdots & \ddots & \vdots \\ H(c_n|S_1) & H(c_n|S_1) & \ldots & H(c_n|S_m) \end{bmatrix} \tag{3.11}$$

where the element $H(c_i|S_j)$ represents the healthy condition of c_i on S_j.

With the snippet-specific healthy condition, we can virtually calculate the healthy condition of a target core on any workloads. Suppose an epoch (E) of a workload consists of N_{S_i} snippets of class S_i, $i = 1, 2, \cdots, m$, that is

$$E = [N_{S_1}, N_{S_2}, \cdots, N_{S_m}], \tag{3.12}$$

then the healthy condition of c_i on E can be calculated by

$$H(c_i|E) = \frac{\mathcal{H}(i, :) \times E^T}{\sum_{i=1}^{m} N_{S_i}}, \tag{3.13}$$

where $\mathcal{H}(i, :)$ is the ith row vector of $\mathcal{H}$; E^T is the transpose of vector E. By characterizing the workload epoch by epoch, the OS is able to maximally hide the degradation of defective cores by judicious epoch scheduling between them.

As a key intelligence of CoreRank, $\mathcal{H}$ is not static but dynamically refined to faithfully capture the cores' degradation. S_i $(i = 1, \ldots, m)$ is dynamically updated by organizing the valid snippets in a FIFO (first in, first out) approach. We find that empirically using the capacity of 200 snippets is a good choice to average out the small randomness, given $H(c_i|S_j)$ behaves as a random variable (even though with a narrow distribution).

3.3.1.6 Validation of Healthy Condition (H)

In fact, according to definition, the healthy condition (H) can be interpreted as a kind of performance model measuring CPI (cycle per instruction). To explicitly demonstrate the effectiveness of CoreRank model, we compare the performance obtained by CoreRank and the real performance on degraded cores. To make a fair comparison, we assume the threads wont be suspended or stalled, because, as explained in Sect. 3.3.1.3, those snippets undergo suspension/stalls are categorized as invalid micro-benchmarks and therefore cannot be used to testify the cores healthy conditions. The performance is translated to average IPC of a randomly chopped phase with 1 billion instructions from SPEC CPU2006 benchmark suit.

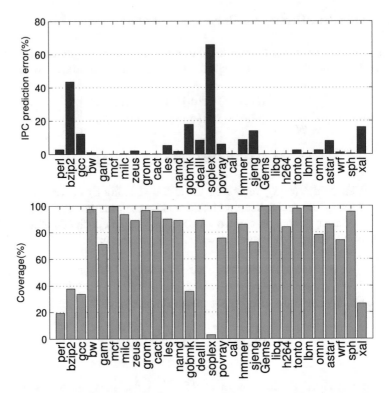

Fig. 3.25 Validation of CoreRank in performance prediction accuracy (U) on a salvaged core with half L2 cache disabled, and corresponding workload coverage (L) by valid snippet classes

The error is defined as $\frac{|IPC_{real} - IPC_{pred}|}{IPC_{real}} \times 100\%$, where IPC_{real} is measured value and IPC_{pred} is obtained by CoreRank. As shown in Fig. 3.25 (U), the IPC prediction errors for most of the benchmarks are no more than 5%. Although the worst-case error reach up to unacceptable 60% for soplex, such large error is not the limitation of CoreRank itself, but mainly because the valid snippet classes cannot cover this workload due to insufficient snippets obtained in our experiment, as indicated in Fig. 3.25 (L). The same reason also applies to other high-error workloads such as bzip2, gobmk, and xal. However, this is not a substantial limitation of CoreRank because in reality the coverage can very close to 100% with sufficient snippet samples.

3.3.1.7 Impact of Dynamic Management

According to the definition of healthy condition H, a core's H is inferred from the statistics of sampled snippet performance. However, the actual performance, measured in million instructions per second (MIPS) for example, may change because of engaging dynamic management for controlling thermal [30], saving power [14], or hiding aging effects[79]. An effective way to implement such dynamic management is through dynamic frequency (and corresponding voltage) adaptations (there is a large body of related references, just to name a few [14, 30, 79, 81]).

The actual core's performance, under dynamic frequency scaling, may mislead the H inference, since the low (high) performance may attribute to under-clock (over-clock) the core, rather than bad (good) healthy conditions. This problem can be solved by rectifying the performance statistics to a reference case. Specifically, the original H definition (Eq. (3.7)) is revised to

$$H(c_i|s_m) = \frac{P((c_i, f_{act})|s_m)}{P((c_{ref}, f_{ref})|s_m)} = \frac{P(c_i|s_m)}{P(c_{ref}|s_m)} \times \eta, \quad (3.14)$$

where η is the performance speedup attributing to frequency tuning from f_{ref} to f_{act}. It can be obtained by online [81] or offline regressions. The most naive η can be approximated by f_{ref}/f_{act} (more sophisticated η can provide more accurate inference; the detail is beyond the scope of this section). By incorporating parameter η, the framework of CoreRank can be applied to systems with dynamic management.

3.3.1.8 Handling Failed Cores

Even though this section focuses on the core progressive degradation, i.e. the cores still functionally work in the presence of salvageable defects in field [53]. Dealing with failed cores, or "dead" cores, is relatively easy by simply disabling them, i.e. all elements of the corresponding row vector of $\mathcal{H}$ are set to "0". The core salvaging can be implemented by exploiting the natural microarchitectural redundancy. The technical details of diagnosis [8, 31, 39] and salvaging [53, 54] are beyond the scope of this chapter.

3.3.2 Core Ranking Implementation

CoreRank works like a high frequency sampling system. A software-implemented version can cause performance overhead if the snippet volume is small. Suppose snippets with one million uops volume are encoded with 256 bytes, then the estimated sample frequency is about 2 KHz at 1 GHz core frequency and two uops per cycle, which generates 512 KB/s per core. For a processor with 100 active cores, the peak bandwidth to move out these sample data can reach up to 50 MB/s, even without considering the performance counter reading overhead which will burden the IO bandwidth. But a software-implementation is possible when taking larger snippet volume on manycores with small core counts.

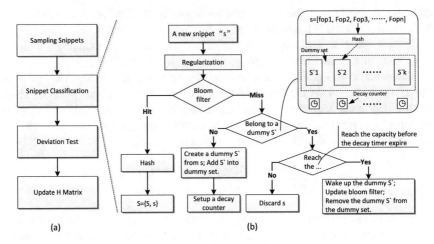

Fig. 3.26 CoreRank implementation. (**a**) CoreRank mechanism. (**b**) Snippet classification

We propose a hardware-implemented version which provides the OS core healthy information to make better resource management. The overview of CoreRank is shown in Fig. 3.26. The only modification to current performance counter scheme is to log the opcode information, and build a hash table with hundreds of buckets storing the information of $\mathcal{H}$. To minimize the hardware overhead, we design a Time Division Multiplexer (TDM) style CoreRank, as shown in Fig. 3.27, where each CoreRank handles 16 cores. This TDM hardware optimization exploits the fact that the process of quantifying healthy condition is timing non-critical.

The basic CoreRank mechanism can be divided into four steps, as shown in Fig. 3.26a. First, we sample the uops streams with a set of performance counters which log the uops types and associated frequency, and clock cycles. These data is encapsulated as snippets. Then, these snippets are classified to build snippet classes S. Because a qualified S should possess small deviations, so we make a deviation test in step three. The S passed the deviation test is qualified to update the healthy matrix $\mathcal{H}$. Among the four steps, the classification is the most complicated in hardware implementation. Traditionally, the classification is computationally difficult (NP-hard). We develop a novel efficient classification approach, detailed as follows.

3.3.2.1 Classification

When a new snippet is collected, we first regularize it by filtering those "minority" uops whose frequency percentages are smaller than a predefined threshold, 0.5% of the volume for example. These minority uops have little impact on the overall performance, but can greatly complicate the classification. By doing so, the dimension of snippets can be significantly reduced.

Fig. 3.27 Time division multiplexer (TDM) style CoreRank to reduce the hardware overhead

The classification allows a tolerance in frequency variation, which can be easily implemented by ignoring the least-significant bits in frequency of each type of uops. The main decision-making process is shown in Fig. 3.26b. We use a bloom filter to quickly decide whether this snippet belongs to an already existing snippet class S. If yes, this snippet goes through a hash table to find the associate classes and update it with the new sample. Otherwise, we cannot simply discard this snippet, but have to carefully decide whether this snippet belongs to a new class that has not existed so far. Our solution is to build a dummy class S' for this snippet, and then enable a decay timer. A dummy class will be allowed to change into a qualified class as long as its capacity can reach a threshold in one counting period of the decay timer; otherwise, this snippet and associate dummy class S' can be safely discarded.

There are two key hardware components in the implementation: a Bloom filter and a Hash table. Bloom filter is a time-efficient and hardware-implemented friendly structure used to test whether an element (s) is a member of a set (S). The basic principle can be explained with Fig. 3.28 which illustrates a bloom filter with m-bit signature vector and n hash functions. If a snippet s has been proven not a minority, then, the bloom filter needs to be updated: the n hash functions map the s into n-bit of the signature vector and set the corresponding bit into 1. In filter mode, if the

Fig. 3.28 Bloom filter in snippet classification

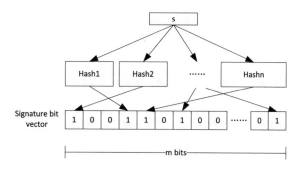

n-bit signature of a new snippet s has been set in the signature vector, called a "hit" in the bloom filter, this s belongs to a qualified S; otherwise called a "miss".

3.3.2.2   Deciding Design Parameters

Bloom filter [4] has a good merit of no false negative, but may suffers from false positive, i.e. erroneously claim that s belongs to a class S. The probability of false positive is given as $P_{fp} = (1 - e^{-nk/m})^n$, k is the number of classes successfully mapped into the m-bit signature vector. The optimal number of hash functions can be calculated by

$$n = \lceil \frac{m}{k} ln2 \rceil. \tag{3.15}$$

We can see from Fig. 3.22b, empirically setting k to 400 should be enough, then P_{fp} and optimal n would be functions of m, as shown in Fig. 3.29. The result shows that a bloom filter configured with at least 5000-bit signature vector and 9 hash functions can keep the false positive rate below 0.5%, and therefore is a recommend design point. In implementation, we use a 8192-bit (2^{13}) signature vector and 10 hash functions.

The snippet classes are managed with a hash table, as Fig. 3.30 exemplifies. The set of uops types and associated frequency of a S serve as the key. Each class is associated with a bucket storing the corresponding IPC of each snippet in that

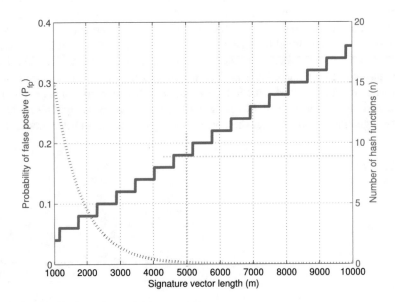

Fig. 3.29 Bloom filter design space

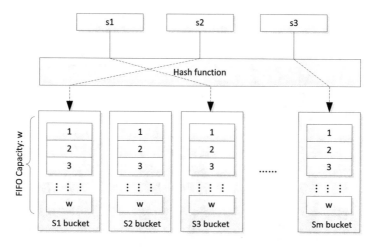

Fig. 3.30 Hash table

class. The bucket is organized as a FIFO buffer to capture the most up-to-date core degradation degree.

3.3.2.3   Choosing Appropriate Hash Functions

We have two types of hash functions, one for the 8192-bit bloom filter, and another for a hash table. The bloom filter uses MD5 [57] as the hash function. MD5 is a powerful hash function producing a 128-bit hash value. We divide the 128-bit hash value into 10 13-bit sub-hash values (the right-most sub-hash is padded with two "0" bits) to set corresponding bits in signature vector; each sub-hash value behaves as a different hash function mapping to individual location in the 8192-bit signature vector.

However, managing the snippet classes is more tricky. We find it requires very low, even not zero, collision rate because a snippet class polluted by other snippets out of that class is probably rejected by the deviation test. Hence, a perfect hash is virtually necessary. However, we find it's hard to design any even close-to-perfect hash function resulting in negligible collision rate. We have testify three types of hash functions, Segment Hash (i.e. split the original keys into segments, then map each segment to an integer, and finally combine the integers to map to a bucket.), Pearson Hash [50], and Modulo Hash [26], but none performs good enough. As Fig. 3.31 shows, even we map the classes into a 1024-bucket hash table, the collision rate is still as high as 10%.

Therefore, we use direct map approach to achieve the effect of perfect hash. The detail is using the MD5 signature to directly tag each bucket. When encounter a new class, we assign a free bucket to the new class and tag the bucket with its MD5 signature. The MD5 signatures have no collisions, so does the corresponding bucket

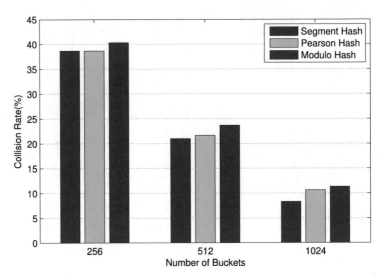

Fig. 3.31 Collision rate of different hash functions

assignments. The overhead is the search complexity. However, the complexity is affordable because we only need to manage several hundreds of buckets and it is no more complex than indexing a cache with comparable number of cache blocks.

3.3.2.4   Handling Sparsity of $\mathcal{H}$

The healthy matrix $\mathcal{H}$ is progressively built and updated. So, some elements of $\mathcal{H}$ may be unavailable until the qualified snippet classes are obtained from the corresponding cores. We use a "default-first" policy to assign the default value to those unavailable elements. According to this policy, the unavailable elements are assigned positive infinite value $(+\infty)$, which implies the healthy condition is so well that the cores tend to be activated to work immediately. This policy is helpful to quickly explore the cores and reduce the sparsity as soon as possible.

3.3.2.5   Hardware Overhead

The main hardware overhead comes from the bloom filters and MD5 hash function. From Fig. 3.22b, we can figure out a 512-bucket hash table should be enough. The detailed overhead includes hash functions, bloom filters, MD5 registers, and some associative search logics. We implemented the CoreRank logic into RTL with verilog, and synthesized it with Altera Quartus tool. The overhead is shown in Table 3.5. The results show that a CoreRank imposes about 1.7M logic gates and 21KB storage. This overhead is small compared to a processor with billion

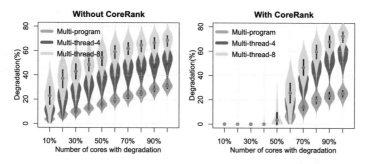

Fig. 3.32 Performance comparison between processors without (L) and with CoreRank (R)

	Component	Comb. logic gates (K)	Storage (KB)
Table 3.5 CoreRank hardware overhead	MD5	76	0.1
	Bloom filter	1582	12.6
	Pearson Hash	0.62	0.6
	Bucket	0.38	7.3
	Others	61.2	0.2
	Total	1720	20.8

transistors. Furthermore, with TDM mechanism, the overhead can be further amortized.

3.3.3 Experiment Result Analysis

3.3.3.1 Experimental Setup

We evaluate CoreRank scheme with Sniper [11], a multi-core simulator based on the interval core model[25] and Graphite[43] simulation infrastructure. Sniper can accurately simulate x86 architecture at a speed of serval MIPS. Sniper uses Intel Pin tool (version 61147) to dynamically profile the stream of uops of each cores, which provides us a easy way to collect snippets in the experiments. We use a 12x12 manycore as the baseline to evaluate the performance.

We run through SPECCPU2006 and PARSEC benchmark suits, which generates over ten thousands of snippets under different core degradation models. We assume each core, if has defect, only suffers from a single type of defects to make the time-consuming experiment affordable. We configure the core according to Intel Nehalem microarchitecture which has 1125 types of uops. Table 3.6 shows the basic core configuration. In terms of snippet, otherwise specified, the snippet volume is 10M, the capacity of each snippet class is 200, with tolerance of 6%.

Table 3.6 Core
configuration

Parameter	Value
Frequency	1 GHz
L1 I/D cache 32 KB	Cache line 64 B, associativity 4
L2 cache 512 KB	Cache line 64 B, associativity 8
Issue width	4
Branch predict entry	1024
Instruction window	96

3.3.3.2 Workloads

We build two types of workloads: SPEC CPU2006 for multi-program workloads, and PARSEC to multi-thread workloads. The manycore is always fully loaded with the synthesized workloads. For example, for multi-program workload, we randomly chose 12x12 benchmarks from the SPEC benchmark suite to feed the manycore. For multi-thread workloads, we use 4-thread and 8-thread configurations, respectively. Note that a specific benchmark can be repetitively chosen from the benchmark suites. To make diversity, each benchmark is fast-forward to different phases before sampling the snippets.

Application Mapping Policy To demonstrate the application of CoreRank, we have to fairly compare the performance between processors with and without CoreRank. The performance is measured by summing up all of the active core IPC within the same time window. When measuring the performance degradation, we use the geometric mean of slowdown of all cores. For processor without CoreRank, it's reasonable to assume that applications are randomly mapped to the cores with different degradations, since we have no way to distinguish which core is superior to another. By contrast, for that with CoreRank, we assume a policy that maximizes the overall performance. This can be achieved by using Eq. (3.13). With this equation, we can figure out which core is the best for a given workload. For experiment, we assume w can be predefined by a perfect profiling. But in reality, w should be dynamically predicted. In addition, when comparing the performance, we neglect the scheduling overhead because the execution time of a snippet is very comparable to a Linux OS time slice in reality.

3.3.3.3 Result Analysis

Performance Comparison First, we study the performance degradation with obliviousness to core healthy conditions. Figure 3.32(L) shows the normalized performance degradation under gradually increased percentage of unhealthy cores. The degradation model for each core is randomly chosen from the degradation models listed in Table 3.4, with "median" degradation degree. We run 500 workloads to highlight the statistical trend, presented by violin plot.[1]

The Impact Of Unhealthy Cores The result confirms the unhealthy cores can dramatically degrade the system performance. Specifically, the multi-thread workloads are more sensitive than multi-program workloads to core degradations, because of more prominent "cask-effect" in multi-thread workloads. The more thread-level parallelism, the more sensitive to core degradation. Also, we find the performance degradation goes relatively slowly, especially when the population of degraded cores exceeds 60%, this is because every multi-thread workload has high possibility to be slowed down by at least one unhealthy core. Given the prevalent big-data processing today dominated by multi-thread programming model (MapReduce for example) and algorithms, the impact of unhealthy cores should not be underestimated.

The situation can be alleviated greatly with CoreRank, as Fig. 3.32(R) shows. We assume an oracle scheduling policy, which directly uses CoreRank output to guide application mapping. The result shows that even the population of unhealthy cores is 50%, the performance declines no more than 10% even for the most susceptible 8-thread workloads, compared to the around 55% degradation when oblivious to the cores' healthy conditions shown in Fig. 3.32(L). This is not surprising because the CoreRank can maximally hide the negative impact of unhealthy cores.

The Effectiveness of CoreRank CoreRank can successfully hide defects if the number of salvaged cores are less than 50%. Comparing the Fig. 3.32(L) and (R), we also conclude that it is impractical to expect CoreRank helping revive a "terribly sick" processor, i.e. majority cores are salvaged. As Fig. 3.32(R) shows, when the unhealthy core population goes beyond 50%, the performance degradation climbs quickly. The performance benefit is very slim when the population of unhealthy cores crosses over 70%. Nevertheless, below 50%, the processor, even with unhealthy cores, can provide performance very close to a fresh one.

An Implication About Processor Retirement Since not all defective cores can be hidden, a key problem is when the unhealthy processor should be retired. Based on the above result, we arrive at an interesting conclusion: the time when the salvaged cores take 50% of a target processor probably can be used to define the lifetime of a manycore processors, because below this percentage the salvaged cores can be hidden well.

Impact of Various Degradation Degree The above results have studied the impact of median degradation degree. In this experiment we study how CoreRank responds to different degradation degrees. Figure 3.33 shows the results of performance under *mild*, *median*, and *severe* degradation, respectively. Unexpectedly, we find the performance under mild and median shows very similar: the difference is merely 3~5% at each unhealthy populations. This is because most of the applications actually cannot fully exercise even the *median* cores, so the *mild* and *median* make

---

[1] Violin plot is a statistical illustration of a group of values; the density of each value is reflect by the width on corresponding notch.

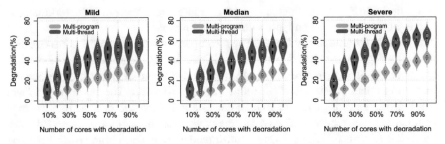

Fig. 3.33 Performance degradation on processors with mild(L), median(M), and severe(R) degradation models, without CoreRank, 4-thread for multi-thread workloads

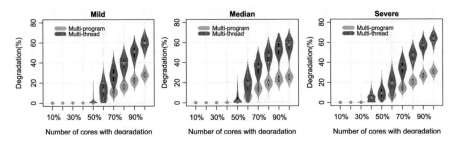

Fig. 3.34 Performance degradation on processors with mild(L), median(M), and severe(R) degradation models, with CoreRank, 4-thread for multi-thread workloads

a little difference in performance. But *severe* causes more appreciable performance degradation.

An interesting difference emerges when we enable CoreRank. Figure 3.34 shows that even though all of the performance drops similarly to that discussed in Fig. 3.32(R), the takeoff points of degradation are different from each other. The severer degradation, the earlier appearance of the takeoff point. For example, for *mild*, the performance won't drop until around 50% unhealthy cores reached. While for *severe*, 30∽40% unhealthy core can cause performance degradation.

3.3.3.4 Comparing with Defect-Aware Scheme

To compare our scheme with a baseline that can be aware some defects by some means, we carefully set up another baseline, called Defect-aware, and a new set of experiments. We assume that a microprocessor has core-wise built-in fault-register which indicates which components suffer from defect during runtime. The OS, by reading these registers, is able to prioritize the degradation-free cores when mapping jobs. In this comparison, the Defect-aware baseline follows the policy: picks the defect-free cores first, then the cores with less degree of degradations, till all cores are put to use. In this experiment, we assume the core utilization is 50%, i.e. only half of the cores are active. The defective cores suffer random defects as listed in

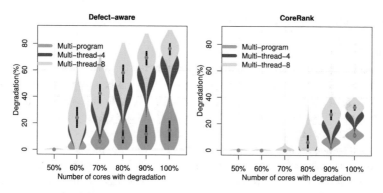

Fig. 3.35 Performance comparison between conventional defect-aware scheme (L) and CoreRank (R)

Table 3.4. The results are shown in Fig. 3.35. We can see if the defective cores take less than half of the core count, the Defect-aware scheme can always pop up the defect-free cores, so there will no performance degradation compared to the oracle case. However, with the increase of number of defective cores, the Defect-aware scheme cannot hide the defective cores well, even though it still prioritizes the core with mildest degradations. By contrast, CoreRank shows to be more resilient to the escalating of defective cores by taking the workload-dependent characteristics.

Note that, without CoreRank, Defect-aware baseline still has no ways to figure out which types of defects are more affectional to a given workload, i.e. Defect-aware baseline cannot quantify how different degradations affect the resultant performance, for various workloads. Take the degradation in issue width for example, Defect-Aware baseline can be aware the core with issue width degradation, so the job is better to be mapped to a defect-free core, or at least, to a core with less degree of issue degradation, if possible. However, as we know, the core with issue width defect shows to be resilient when running a workload with poor intrinsic IPC. Therefore, assigning a thread with poor intrinsic IPC to such a core should not be much problematic. Such case-sensitive phenomena also happen to other microarchitectural components, such as cache, instruction window, and so on. By doing so, we can save healthy cores for those threads more sensitive to certain types of defects. In other words, it is not enough to only know whether a core suffers from what types of defects.

CoreRank is designed to bride this gap. In CoreRank framework, it's more important to know how a defective core performs on a given workload, than to know which defect the core suffers from. The former, i.e. the key idea of this article, focuses on how to make best use of the imperfect cores, while the later focuses on how to isolate the defects to ensure correctness (and has been intensively studied in the reliability community).

3.3.3.5   Comparing with Heterogeneity-Aware Scheme

CoreRank serves as a bottom mechanism to gain variability awareness. Rangan et al. proposed an approach to maximize throughput in the presence of variation-induced heterogeneity in multi-core processors [55], where the heterogeneity refers to the various core frequencies. The key contribution is a scheduling algorithm, called Throughput-Driven Scheduling (TDS) targeting maximum chip throughput, which is in line with our objective to demonstrate the effectiveness of CoreRank.

The difference from our approach is that TDS employes last-value predictor to serve as the fundamental mechanism to support epoch-by-epoch thread scheduling. TDS uses BIPS over a prediction period of 100K cycles as the proxy of core performance level, and maps the applications, according to their computing intensities, to the cores with accordant performance levels; a more computing bounded application is assigned a core with higher performance level. In our scheme, similar to cores with lower frequency due to process variation, the defective cores deliver lower performance, which serves as the ground for comparison.

Figure 3.36 shows the comparison between TDS and CoreRank, on multi-program workloads. Unsurprisingly, CoreRank outperforms TDS in hiding the degradation. The key reason is that simply using the sampled BIPS to serves as the performance level, as TDS adopted, is not alway reliable, because the BIPS is not only determined by the core itself, but also the threads executed. So, even the algorithm aims to maximize the throughput, but the sub-optimal scheduling is unavoidable due to unreliable core-level performance prediction.

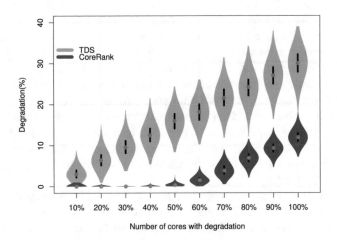

Fig. 3.36 Performance comparison between throughput-driven scheduling (TDS) (L) and CoreRank (R)

3.3.4 Discussion

Quantifying the performance response of cores with degradation is a fundamental problem to make best use of the manycore processors suffered from "sick silicon". We find that the core performance depends on not only applications, but also specific hardware components with degradation. We therefore develop a new metric, healthy condition, to capture this implication. Then, we propose CoreRank to quantify the core-level healthy condition. CoreRank samples the uops streams to build micro-benchmarks, called snippets, to testify cores with different degradation. We also propose a detailed implementation of CoreRank. Experimental results show that with CoreRank, the performance degradation of a manycore can be reduced significantly. We believe that CoreRank is instructive to other dynamic performance optimizations for future large-scale manycore processors.

3.4 Summary

Intermittent faults are emerging as a big challenge to reliable microprocessor design. We propose a metric IVF to quantitatively characterize the vulnerability of microprocessor structures to intermittent faults. With the IVF evaluation methodology, we compute IVFs for reorder buffer and register file in terms of intermittent stuck-at faults, intermittent open and short faults, and intermittent timing faults. Experimental results show that intermittent stuck-at-1 faults have most serious adverse impact on program execution among these three types of intermittent faults. Besides, IVF varies noticeably across different microprocessor structures and program phases. Our experimental results imply partial protection of the most vulnerable structures and program phases to enhance system reliability. With the guide of IVF evaluation methodology, we also discuss several possible intermittent fault detection and recovery techniques which can be used to improve system reliability.

Quantifying the performance response of cores with degradation is a fundamental problem to make best use of the manycore processors suffered from "sick silicon". We develop a new metric, healthy condition, to capture the impact of both applications and hardware component degradation of core performance. Additionally, we propose CoreRank to quantify the core-level healthy condition. Experimental results show that CoreRank helps to reduce the performance degradation of a manycore. Therefore, it is concluded that CoreRank is instructive to other dynamic performance optimizations for future large-scale manycore processors.

References

1. A. Tiwari, S. R. Sarangi, and J. Torrellas. ReCycle: Pipeline Adaptation to Tolerate Process Variation. In *Proceedings of the 34th Annual International Symposium on Computer Architecture*, pages 323–334, 2007.
2. Murali Annavaram, Ed Grochowski, and Paul Reed. Implications of device timing variability on full chip timing. In *2007 IEEE 13th International Symposium on High Performance Computer Architecture*, pages 37–45, 2007.
3. Arijit Biswas, Paul Racunas, Razvan Cheveresan, Joel Emer, Shubhendu S Mukherjee, and Ram Rangan. Computing architectural vulnerability factors for address-based structures. In *32nd International Symposium on Computer Architecture (ISCA'05)*, pages 532–543, 2005.
4. Burton H. Bloom. Space/time trade-offs in hash coding with allowable errors. volume 13, pages 422–426, 1970.
5. S. Borkar. Designing reliable systems from unreliable components: the challenges of transistor variability and degradation. *IEEE MICRO*, 25(6):10–16, 2005.
6. Shekhar Borkar. Thousand core chips: a technology perspective. In *Proceedings of the 44th Annual Design Automation Conference*, pages 746–749. ACM, 2007.
7. Fred A Bower, Derek Hower, Mahmut Yilmaz, Daniel J Sorin, and Sule Ozev. Applying architectural vulnerability analysis to hard faults in the microprocessor. In *Proceedings of the joint international conference on Measurement and modeling of computer systems*, pages 375–376, 2006.
8. FRED A. BOWER, DANIEL J. SORIN, and SULE OZEV. Online diagnosis of hard faults in microprocessors. *ACM Trans. Archit. Code Optim.*, 4(2):Article 8, 32 pages, 2007.
9. K.A. Bowman, S.G. Duvall, and J.D. Meindl. Impact of die-to-die and within-die parameter fluctuations on the maximum clock frequency distribution for gigascale integration. *IEEE Journal of Solid-State Circuits*, 37(2):183–190, 2002.
10. David Bull, Shidhartha Das, Karthik Shivshankar, Ganesh Dasika, Krisztian Flautner, and David Blaauw. A power-efficient 32b arm isa processor using timing-error detection and correction for transient-error tolerance and adaptation to pvt variation. In *2010 IEEE International Solid-State Circuits Conference - (ISSCC)*, pages 284–285, 2010.
11. T.E. Carlson, W. Heirman, and L. Eeckhout. Sniper: Exploring the level of abstraction for scalable and accurate parallel multi-core simulation. In *International Conference for High Performance Computing, Networking, Storage and Analysis (SC),*, pages 1–12, 2011.
12. Liu Changze, Zou Jibin, Wang Runsheng, Huang Ru, Xu Xiaoqing, Liu Jinhua, Wu Hanming, and Wang Yangyuan. Towards the systematic study of aging induced dynamic variability in nano-mosfets: Adding the missing cycle-to-cycle variation effects into device-to-device variation. In *IEEE International Electron Devices Meeting (IEDM)*, pages 25.4.1–25.4.4.
13. Tianshi Chen, Yunji Chen, Qi Guo, O. Temam, Yue Wu, and Weiwu Hu. Statistical performance comparisons of computers. In *IEEE 18th International Symposium on High Performance Computer Architecture (HPCA),*, pages 1–12, 2012.
14. Ryan Cochran, Can Hankendi, Ayse K. Coskun, and Sherief Reda. Pack amp; cap: Adaptive dvfs and thread packing under power caps. In *2011 44th Annual IEEE/ACM International Symposium on Microarchitecture (MICRO)*, pages 175–185, 2011.
15. Cristian Constantinescu. Impact of deep submicron technology on dependability of vlsi circuits. In *Proceedings International Conference on Dependable Systems and Networks*, pages 205–209, 2002.
16. Cristian Constantinescu. Trends and challenges in vlsi circuit reliability. *IEEE micro*, 23(4):14–19, 2003.
17. Cristian Constantinescu. Intermittent faults and effects on reliability of integrated circuits. In *2008 Annual Reliability and Maintainability Symposium*, pages 370–374, 2008.

18. Kenzo Van Craeynest, Aamer Jaleel, Lieven Eeckhout, Paolo Narvaez, and Joel Emer. Scheduling heterogeneous multi-cores through performance impact estimation (pie). In *Proceedings of the 39th Annual International Symposium on Computer Architecture*, pages 213–224, 2012.

19. Rajagopalan Desikan, Doug Burger, Stepen W Keckler, and Todd Austin. Sim-alpha: a validated execution driven alpha 21264 simulator. Technical report, Technical Report TR-01-23, Department of Computer Sciences, University of Texas at Austin, 2001.

20. Jianbo Dong, Lei Zhang, Yinhe Han, Guihai Yan, and Xiaowei Li. Variation-aware scheduling for chip multiprocessors with thread level redundancy. In *IEEE Pacific Rim Dependable Computing Conference*, pages 17–22.

21. Lide Duan, Bin Li, and Lu Peng. Versatile prediction and fast estimation of architectural vulnerability factor from processor performance metrics. In *2009 IEEE 15th International Symposium on High Performance Computer Architecture*, pages 129–140, 2009.

22. D. Ernst, Nam Sung Kim, S. Das, S. Pant, R. Rao, Toan Pham, C. Ziesler, D. Blaauw, T. Austin, K. Flautner, and T. Mudge. Razor: a low-power pipeline based on circuit-level timing speculation. In *Proceedings. 36th Annual IEEE/ACM International Symposium on Microarchitecture, 2003. MICRO-36.*, pages 7–18, 2003.

23. Brian Fahs, Satarupa Bose, Matthew Crum, Brian Slechta, Francesco Spadini, Tony Tung, Sanjay J Patel, and Steven S Lumetta. Performance characterization of a hardware mechanism for dynamic optimization. In *Proceedings. 34th ACM/IEEE International Symposium on Microarchitecture. MICRO-34*, pages 16–27, 2001.

24. Xin Fu, Tao Li, and José Fortes. Sim-soda: A unified framework for architectural level software reliability analysis. In *Workshop on modeling, benchmarking and simulation*, volume 2006, 2006.

25. Davy Genbrugge, Stijn Eyerman, and Lieven Eeckhout. Interval simulation: Raising the level of abstraction in architectural simulation. In *IEEE International Symposium on High-Performance Computer Architecture (HPCA)*, pages 307–318, 2010.

26. Marc Girault. Hash-functions using modulo-n operations. In *Proceedings of the 6th Annual International Conference on Theory and Application of Cryptographic Techniques*, pages 217–226, 1987.

27. Joaquin Gracia, Luis J Saiz, Juan Carlos Baraza, Daniel Gil, and Pedro J Gil. Analysis of the influence of intermittent faults in a microcontroller. In *2008 11th IEEE Workshop on Design and Diagnostics of Electronic Circuits and Systems*, pages 1–6, 2008.

28. Peter Greenhalgh. *big.LITTLE Processing with ARM Cortex-A15 & Cortex-A7 (White paper)*. ARM, September 2011.

29. Anoop Gupta, Andrew Tucker, and Shigeru Urushibara. The impact of operating system scheduling policies and synchronization methods of performance of parallel applications. In *Proceedings of the 1991 ACM SIGMETRICS conference on Measurement and modeling of computer systems*, pages 120–132, 1991.

30. Heather Hanson, Stephen W. Keckler, Soraya Ghiasi, Karthick Rajamani, Freeman Rawson, and Juan Rubio. Thermal response to dvfs: analysis with an intel pentium m. In *Proceedings of the 2007 international symposium on Low power electronics and design (ISLPED '07)*, pages 219–224, 2007.

31. Siva Kumar Sastry Hari, Man-Lap Li, Pradeep Ramachandran, Byn Choi, and Sarita V. Adve. mswat: Low-cost hardware fault detection and diagnosis for multicore systems. In *2009 42nd Annual IEEE/ACM International Symposium on Microarchitecture (MICRO)*, pages 122–132, 2009.

32. Sebastian Herbert and Diana Marculescu. Variation-aware dynamic voltage/frequency scaling. In *2009 IEEE 15th International Symposium on High Performance Computer Architecture*, pages 301–312, 2009.

33. ITRS. Process integration, devices, and structures summary, 2013.

34. J. Shin, V. Zyuban, P. Bose, and T.M. Pinkston. A Proactive Wearout Recovery Approach for Exploiting Microarchitectural Redundancy to Extend Cache SRAM Lifetime. In *2008 International Symposium on Computer Architecture*, pages 353–362, 2008.

35. Russ Joseph, David Brooks, and Margaret Martonosi. Control techniques to eliminate voltage emergencies in high performance processors. In *The Ninth International Symposium on High-Performance Computer Architecture, 2003. HPCA-9 2003. Proceedings.*, pages 79–90, 2003.
36. Tanay Karnik and Peter Hazucha. Characterization of soft errors caused by single event upsets in cmos processes. *IEEE Transactions on Dependable and secure Computing*, 1(2):128–143, 2004.
37. Richard E Kessler. The alpha 21264 microprocessor. *IEEE micro*, 19(2):24–36, 1999.
38. Sumeet Kumar and Aneesh Aggarwal. Reducing resource redundancy for concurrent error detection techniques in high performance microprocessors. In *The Twelfth International Symposium on High-Performance Computer Architecture, 2006.*, pages 212–221, 2006.
39. Man-Lap Li, Pradeep Ramachandran, Swarup K. Sahoo, Sarita V. Adve, Vikram S. Adve, and Yuanyuan Zhou. Trace-based microarchitecture-level diagnosis of permanent hardware faults. In *2008 IEEE International Conference on Dependable Systems and Networks With FTCS and DCC (DSN)*, pages 22–31, 2008.
40. Man-Lap Li, Pradeep Ramachandran, Swarup Kumar Sahoo, Sarita V Adve, Vikram S Adve, and Yuanyuan Zhou. Understanding the propagation of hard errors to software and implications for resilient system design. *ACM Sigplan Notices*, 43(3):265–276, 2008.
41. Xiaoyao Liang, Gu-Yeon Wei, and David Brooks. Revival: A variation-tolerant architecture using voltage interpolation and variable latency. *IEEE Micro*, 29(1):127–138, 2009.
42. Joseph W McPherson. Reliability challenges for 45nm and beyond. In *2006 43rd ACM/IEEE design automation conference*, pages 176–181, 2006.
43. J.E. Miller, H. Kasture, G. Kurian, C. Gruenwald, N. Beckmann, C. Celio, J. Eastep, and A. Agarwal. Graphite: A distributed parallel simulator for multicores. In *IEEE 16th International Symposium on High Performance Computer Architecture (HPCA)*, pages 1–12, 2010.
44. Pablo Montesinos, Wei Liu, and Josep Torrellas. Using register lifetime predictions to protect register files against soft errors. In *37th Annual IEEE/IFIP International Conference on Dependable Systems and Networks (DSN'07)*, pages 286–296, 2007.
45. Shubhendu S Mukherjee, Michael Kontz, and Steven K Reinhardt. Detailed design and evaluation of redundant multi-threading alternatives. In *Proceedings 29th annual international symposium on computer architecture*, pages 99–110, 2002.
46. Shubhendu S Mukherjee, Christopher Weaver, Joel Emer, Steven K Reinhardt, and Todd Austin. A systematic methodology to compute the architectural vulnerability factors for a high-performance microprocessor. In *Proceedings. 36th Annual IEEE/ACM International Symposium on Microarchitecture, MICRO-36.*, pages 29–40, 2003.
47. Songjun Pan, Yu Hu, Xing Hu, and Xiaowei Li. A cost-effective substantial-impact-filter based method to tolerate voltage emergencies. In *2011 Design, Automation & Test in Europe*, pages 1–6, 2011.
48. Songjun Pan, Yu Hu, and Xiaowei Li. Online computing and predicting architectural vulnerability factor of microprocessor structures. In *2009 15th IEEE Pacific Rim International Symposium on Dependable Computing*, pages 345–350, 2009.
49. Angshuman Parashar, Anand Sivasubramaniam, and Sudhanva Gurumurthi. Slick: slice-based locality exploitation for efficient redundant multithreading. *ACM SIGOPS Operating Systems Review*, 40(5):95–105, 2006.
50. Peter K. Pearson. Fast hashing of variable-length text strings. *Commun. ACM*, 33(6):677–680, 1990.
51. Andrea Pellegrini, Kypros Constantinides, Dan Zhang, Shobana Sudhakar, Valeria Bertacco, and Todd Austin. Crashtest: A fast high-fidelity fpga-based resiliency analysis framework. In *2008 IEEE International Conference on Computer Design*, pages 363–370, 2008.
52. Paula Petrica, Adam M. Izraelevitz, David H. Albonesi, and Christine A. Shoemaker. Flicker: a dynamically adaptive architecture for power limited multicore systems. In *Proceedings of the 40th Annual International Symposium on Computer Architecture*, pages 13–23, 2013.

53. Michael D. Powell, Arijit Biswas, Shantanu Gupta, and Shubhendu S. Mukherjee. Architectural core salvaging in a multi-core processor for hard-error tolerance. In *Proceedings of the 36th Annual International Symposium on Computer Architecture*, pages 93–104, 2009.
54. Shivakumar Premkishore, S. W. Keckler, C. R. Moore, and D. Burger. Exploiting microarchitectural redundancy for defect tolerance. In *ICCD*, pages 481–488.
55. K. K. Rangan, M. D. Powell, Wei Gu-Yeon, and D. Brooks. Achieving uniform performance and maximizing throughput in the presence of heterogeneity. In *2011 IEEE 17th International Symposium on High Performance Computer Architecture (HPCA)*, pages 3–14, 2011.
56. Steven K Reinhardt and Shubhendu S Mukherjee. Transient fault detection via simultaneous multithreading. In *Proceedings of 27th International Symposium on Computer Architecture (IEEE Cat. No. RS00201)*, pages 25–36, 2000.
57. RFC document. Rfc 1321: The md5 message-digest algorithm. In *Internet Engineering Task Force*, 1992.
58. S. Borkar, T. Karnik, S. Narendra, J. Tschanz, A. Keshavarzi, and V. De. Parameter Variations and Impact on Circuits and Microarchitecture. *DAC*, pages 338–342, 2003.
59. John Paul Shen and Mikko H Lipasti. *Modern processor design: fundamentals of superscalar processors*. Waveland Press, 2013.
60. Timothy Sherwood, Erez Perelman, Greg Hamerly, and Brad Calder. Automatically characterizing large scale program behavior. *ACM SIGPLAN Notices*, 37(10):45–57, 2002.
61. P. Shivakumar, M. Kistler, S.W. Keckler, D. Burger, and L. Alvisi. Modeling the effect of technology trends on the soft error rate of combinational logic. In *Proceedings International Conference on Dependable Systems and Networks*, pages 389–398, 2002.
62. Premkishore Shivakumar, Stephen W Keckler, Charles R Moore, and Doug Burger. Exploiting microarchitectural redundancy for defect tolerance. In *Proceedings 21st international conference on computer design*, pages 481–488, 2003.
63. Smitha Shyam, Kypros Constantinides, Sujay Phadke, Valeria Bertacco, and Todd Austin. Ultra low-cost defect protection for microprocessor pipelines. *ACM SIGARCH Computer Architecture News*, 34(5):73–82, 2006.
64. T.J. Slegel, R.M. Averill, M.A. Check, B.C. Giamei, B.W. Krumm, C.A. Krygowski, W.H. Li, J.S. Liptay, J.D. MacDougall, T.J. McPherson, J.A. Navarro, E.M. Schwarz, K. Shum, and C.F. Webb. Ibm's s/390 g5 microprocessor design. *IEEE Micro*, 19(2):12–23, 1999.
65. Jared C Smolens, Brian T Gold, James C Hoe, Babak Falsafi, and Ken Mai. Detecting emerging wearout faults. In *Proceedings of the IEEE Workshop on Silicon Errors in Logic - System Effects*, pages 1–6, 2007.
66. Vilas Sridharan and David R Kaeli. Eliminating microarchitectural dependency from architectural vulnerability. In *2009 IEEE 15th International Symposium on High Performance Computer Architecture*, pages 117–128, 2009.
67. Vilas Sridharan and David R Kaeli. Using hardware vulnerability factors to enhance avf analysis. *ACM SIGARCH Computer Architecture News*, 38(3):461–472, 2010.
68. Jayanth Srinivasan, Sarita V. Adve, Pradip Bose, and Jude A. Rivers. The impact of technology scaling on lifetime reliability. In *International Conference on Dependable Systems and Networks, 2004*, pages 177–186, 2004.
69. Blaine Stackhouse, Sal Bhimji, Chris Bostak, Dave Bradley, Brian Cherkauer, Jayen Desai, Erin Francom, Mike Gowan, Paul Gronowski, Dan Krueger, Charles Morganti, and Steve Troyer. A 65 nm 2-billion transistor quad-core itanium processor. *IEEE Journal of Solid-State Circuits*, 44(1):18–31, 2009.
70. James H Stathis. Physical and predictive models of ultrathin oxide reliability in cmos devices and circuits. *IEEE Transactions on device and materials reliability*, 1(1):43–59, 2001.
71. Kim Tae-Hyoung, R. Persaud, and C. H. Kim. Silicon odometer: An on-chip reliability monitor for measuring frequency degradation of digital circuits. *IEEE Journal of Solid-State Circuits*, 43(4):874–880, 2008.
72. Radu Teodorescu and Josep Torrellas. Variation-aware application scheduling and power management for chip multiprocessors. In *Proceedings of the 35th Annual International Symposium on Computer Architecture*, pages 363–374, 2008.

73. Emmanuel Touloupis, James A Flint, Vassilios A Chouliaras, and David D Ward. Study of the effects of seu-induced faults on a pipeline protected microprocessor. *IEEE Transactions on Computers*, 56(12):1585–1596, 2007.

74. James Tschanz, Keith Bowman, Shih-Lien Lu, Paolo Aseron, Muhammad Khellah, Arijit Raychowdhury, Bibiche Geuskens, Carlos Tokunaga, Chris Wilkerson, Tanay Karnik, et al. A 45nm resilient and adaptive microprocessor core for dynamic variation tolerance. In *2010 IEEE International Solid-State Circuits Conference-(ISSCC)*, pages 282–283, 2010.

75. Kristen R Walcott, Greg Humphreys, and Sudhanva Gurumurthi. Dynamic prediction of architectural vulnerability from microarchitectural state. In *Proceedings of the 34th Annual International Symposium on Computer Architecture*, pages 516–527, 2007.

76. Nicholas J Wang, Justin Quek, Todd M Rafacz, et al. Characterizing the effects of transient faults on a high-performance processor pipeline. In *International Conference on Dependable Systems and Networks, 2004*, pages 61–61, 2004.

77. Philip M Wells, Koushik Chakraborty, and Gurindar S Sohi. Adapting to intermittent faults in multicore systems. *ACM SIGOPS Operating Systems Review*, 42(2):255–264, 2008.

78. Alan Wood. *Data integrity concepts, features, and technology (White paper)*. Compaq NonStop®, 1999.

79. Guihai Yan, Yinhe Han, and Xaiowei Li. Revivenet: A self-adaptive architecture for improving lifetime reliability via localized timing adaptation. *IEEE Transctions on Computers*, 60(9):1219–1232, 2011.

80. Guihai Yan, Yinhe Han, and Xiaowei Li. SVFD: A versatile online fault detection scheme via checking of stability violation. *IEEE transactions on very large scale integration (VLSI) systems*, 19(9):1627–1640, 2010.

81. Guihai Yan, Yingmin Li, Yinhe Han, Xiaowei Li, Minyi Guo, and Xiaoyao Liang. Agileregulator: A hybrid voltage regulator scheme redeeming dark silicon for power efficiency in a multicore architecture. In *2012 IEEE 18th International Symposium on High Performance Computer Architecture (HPCA)*, pages 287–298, 2012.

82. Guihai Yan, Xiaoyao Liang, Yinhe Han, and Xiaowei Li. Leveraging the core-level complementary effects of pvt variations to reduce timing emergencies in multi-core processors. In *Proceedings of the 37th Annual International Symposium on Computer Architecture*, pages 485–496, 2010.

Chapter 4
Fault-Tolerant Network-On-Chip

Abstract Manycore systems are emerging for tera-scale computation and typically utilize Network-on-Chip (NoC) as the communication fabrics between the cores. Since a single routing node failure in NoC can destroy the connectivity of the entire manycore system, NoC is of essential importance to the manycore system. To improve the reliability of NoCs, we investigate fault-tolerant design approaches from different angles including fault-tolerant NoC architecture, fault-tolerant routing, and fault-tolerant circuits respectively. From the perspective of fault-tolerant NoC architecture, we propose a topology reconfiguration technique that re-defines a regular virtual topology on top of the original NoC with random faulty nodes. By introducing two new metrics, namely Distance Factor (DF) and Congestion Factor (CF), we can evaluate the performance of different virtual topologies efficiently. Moreover, We also propose Row Rippling Column Stealing-guided Simulated Annealing algorithm to determine the optimized virtual topology without affecting high-level parallel applications on the manycore system. From the perspective of fault-tolerant routing, we propose ZoneDefense routing that helps to find the faulty blocks in advance and route around the faulty routers. Unlike prior fault-tolerant routing algorithms that generally disable a set of routers directly or indirectly affected by hardware faults because of deadlock routing rules, ZoneDefense can reduce a large number of sacrificed fault-free routers significantly. From the perspective of fault-tolerant circuit designs, we develop a novel salvaging scheme named RevivePath, which allows faulty NoC data paths to be functional. The basic idea is to have serial-to-parallel and parallel-to-serial circuits inserted between NoC data path components such as crossbar, link, and on-chip buffers such that hardware faults will not easily corrupt these data paths and routing algorithms. Hence, the salvaging circuits ensure highly resilient NoC architecture and graceful performance degradation given increasing hardware faults.

4.1   Introduction to NoC Fault Tolerance

Network-on-Chip (NoC) is envisioned to be a scalable communication substrate for building on-chip manycore systems [5, 11, 20, 23]. Many of the data transmitted in NoC can be critical data such as cache coherence protocol, so a single hardware fault which can either be persistent fault or transient fault can corrupt the data transmitted in NoC and destroy the communication protocol of the entire manycore system, which makes NoC particularly vulnerable to hardware faults. In addition, transistors with continuously shrinking feature sizes and lower power supply become more sensitive to working environments such as heavy particles and high temperature and suffer wear-out and process variations [9, 17]. Thereby, reliability of NoC turns out to be a key design metric and fault-tolerant design remains highly demanded [11, 17, 59].

In order to improve NoC reliability, there have been a variety of works proposed from different angles and they can be roughly divided into fault-tolerant NoC architecture, fault-tolerant routing, and fault-tolerant circuits. As for fault-tolerant NoC architecture, we mainly investigate how a faulty NoC can be virtualized as a regular topology to present a consistent view to high-level applications. Unlike prior fault-tolerant NoC architecture designs that mainly attempted to tolerate faults with architectural designs, the proposed NoC topology reconfiguration mainly seek to enhance the reusability of faulty NoCs from the perspective of high-level applications. For fault-tolerant NoC routing, many of the prior works have a set of routing rules to avoid routing deadlock [8, 30, 32, 93, 94, 97], but these rules can disable many of the fault-free routers in NoC and induce considerable hardware overhead of routers as well as the attached processing cores eventually. Different from these solutions that either disable all nodes of the faulty network edges or include all faults into one faulty block, we propose a ZoneDefense routing, which not only includes faults into convex faulty blocks but also spreads the faulty blocks' position information in corresponding columns. By broadcasting the positions of faulty blocks, routing packets can be aware of the faulty blocks and route around the faulty routers in advance to avoid network congestion and achieve higher performance. For the fault-tolerant circuits, many prior works mainly rely on redundancy schemes, i.e., introducing spare components to replace faulty ones [82, 91]. However, redundancy-based approaches usually incur expensive hardware overhead by at least 100%. Instead of using the redundancy-based approaches, we mainly explore the inherent redundancy in NoC data paths to tolerate the faults. The basic idea is to split the data path in NoC which takes up more than 90% chip area into multiple identical lanes and salvage the data path with a set of serial-to-parallel and parallel-to-serial converters. With the proposed data path salvaging based on time division multiplexer (TDM), NoC keeps functional as long as there are still fault-free lanes available.

4.1.1 Fault-Tolerant NoC Architecture

Using redundant components to tolerate fabrication faults in large array based architectures such as memory blocks and array processors has been widely adopted in practice and demonstrated to be successful in terms of yield improvement [90]. In fact, spare elements, i.e., redundant columns, rows, words or small blocks are added to repair faulty storage cells for almost all memories with relatively high capacity [46]. NoC as a typical array architecture can also benefit from the typical redundant architecture design approaches [90]. The objective of the redundancy architecture design approaches is essentially to choose the minimum number of spare rows or columns that can recover all the faulty elements of the array architecture. The 2D redundancy fault-tolerant design optimization problem has been proved to be NP-complete [56] and the processing time is also a crucial design factor accordingly. Hence, a number of research works have been dedicated to the above problems [6, 26, 45, 49, 62].

Typically, the fault-tolerance approaches for the array based architecture can be divided into two categories, namely redundancy approach and degradation approach. In redundancy approach, some of the processing elements in the array based architecture are dedicated as spare parts to replace faulty ones in the array to ensure a fully functional design. The chip will be discarded when it fails to recover all the faults using the spare ones. The fault recovery is essentially architecture reconfiguration and various reconfiguration algorithms have been proposed in [13, 50, 55, 89]. In the degradation approach, all elements are treated equally to derive a fault-free sub array, whose size is flexible. Two metrics including *harvest* and *degradation* are commonly used to evaluate the efficiency of fault-tolerant reconfiguration algorithms [36, 48, 61]. Note that *harvest* represents how effective the fault-free elements are utilized to construct a functional sub array while *degradation* measures the performance penalty of the remaining sub array over the original processing array.

On top of the above metrics of fault-tolerant reconfiguration of the array based architecture, NoC based manycore systems also need to maintain the same physical topology as much as possible and present a consistent view to high-level applications which cannot be aware of the underlying hardware reconfiguration. The main reason is that high-level applications typically assume a determined manycore architecture such as mesh and assign parallel processing tasks based on the topology of the system for the sake of more efficient communication and higher performance accordingly. For instance, tasks with massive data transmission will be put on neighboring processing elements of the processing array to ensure minimum communication overhead. In this case, when the fault-tolerant reconfiguration approach changes the physical topology of the processing arrays, the same optimized high-level application can suffer dramatic performance degradation due to the lack of the information about the underlying topology of the array based architecture. Thereby, topology similarity of the array based architecture is also critical and needs to be considered in fault-tolerant NoC architecture reconfiguration.

To further quantify the fault-tolerant reconfiguration quality for the array based architectures, we utilize network embedding to formulate this problem. The idea of constructing a virtual topology based on a physical topology for a certain purpose has been widely applied in many research areas. A famous application is the overlay networks [25], which create a structured virtual topology above the basic transport protocol level to facilitate deterministic content search. Virtual neighbor nodes in overlay networks are defined by identifiers derived from the stored contents. In this subsection, we briefly review the network embedding research problems that are closely related to our topology reconfiguration problem for an NoC based manycore system.

The network embedding problem, which has been studied extensively, is widely used for simulations between networks with different topologies. By embedding a G(uest) network topology into a H(ost) topology, parallel programs could have better portability. This is because one can automatically transform any parallel algorithms developed for the multiprocessor system with topology G into an algorithm for the system with topology H. Cong et al. [15] focused on embedding of any arbitrary network into its optimum complete binary trees. Kim and Hur [51] proposed a new approach to embed a given torus into another given torus. Liu and Xu [60] studied the embedding of rings and 2D mesh into a RP(k) network.

An application of network embedding in parallel computing is the mapping from virtual process topology to physical processor topology. The virtual process topology is the abstract of communications among processes or tasks, in which each vertex represents process, and an edge represents the communication between two processes. To execute a parallel program, its process topology should be constructed effectively based on the underlying processor topology. The virtual process topology is also supported by MPI libraries [33, 68] discussed the mapping problem in switch-based cluster systems with irregular topology. Bauch and Maehle [3] presented techniques to reconfigure application topology in an octagonal 2D mesh machine topology when faults occur.

The topology reconfiguration problem we studied, and the network embedding problem belong to a more general problem of graph embedding, i.e., constructing a guest graph based on a host graph. As the same class of problems, however, they are applied at different levels and should be analyzed from different perspectives.

Topology reconfiguration lies in the hardware level. From the perspective of manycore processor architecture, they reconfigure a virtual topology to isolate various underlying physical topologies so that they can transparently provide OS and programmers a unified interface to ease task dispatching scheduling and application optimization. Network embedding, however, lies in the application level. From the perspective of application programmers, they assume that the underlying system topology is fixed, and then embed their application topology based on the given physical topology to optimize the software performance. If chip architects do not provide a unified (virtual) topology, application programmers should have to handle various embedding problems from their application topology to different chip physical topologies.

It should be noted that, network embedding problems use *dilation* and *congestion* to evaluate the performance of virtual topologies [51]. *Dilation* of a virtual edge *e* in the guest topology is the length of the corresponding physical path in the host topology. *Congestion* of an edge *e* in the host topology is the number of virtual edges that include that edge. *Dilation* and *congestion* consider the worst case scenario for the guest topology. However, we use different evaluation metrics in the topology reconfiguration problem in NoC-based manycore systems, i.e., DF and CF. When there are a wide range of applications running on the NoC-based manycore systems, it is difficult to evaluate the effect of virtual topologies on various applications at the chip architecture design stage. As a result, we evaluate the performance of virtual topologies themselves. The primary evaluation metric DF, i.e., the average hop count determines the zero-load latency of a virtual topology while the auxiliary metric CF reflects the distribution of traffic load and thus could affect network latency and throughput.

4.1.2   Fault-Tolerant NoC Routing

When there are faults on routers and links of NoC, many of the routing paths can break and the connectivity of NoC is destroyed. To address this problem, many prior works leverage fault-tolerant routing to circumvent the faulty routing paths which can potentially make best use of the faulty NoC. However, the constrained routing in NoC can cause deadlock problems and stall the entire network soon. While virtual channels in routers can be utilized to constrain the routing paths of different packets in NoC while reusing the same links in TDM, a number of virtual channel based fault-tolerant routing algorithms such as [8, 41, 44, 94] have been explored. The major challenge is that virtual channels are usually constructed with registers and can consume substantial hardware overhead. In addition, fault-tolerant routing may require additional virtual channels and the imbalanced workload in faulty NoC can result in severe underutilization of the virtual channels, which further deteriorate the hardware overhead. There are also some flow control techniques that can be used to avoid deadlock, such as the bubble flow control [74] and the one proposed in [93]. Typically, they have specific constrains added to virtual channels, which limits the NoC parameter setups and affects NoC performance.

Different from the virtual channel based fault-tolerant routing, stochastic routing algorithms enhance NoC reliability by sending multiple replicated packets through redundant routes, such as the probabilistic gossip flooding algorithm [27] and N-Random walk algorithm [73], or by deflection, such as [69, 87]. Although stochastic routing algorithms can be highly resilient, they also face some design challenges, such as high energy and bandwidth consumption.

On top of the virtual channel based fault-tolerant routing algorithms, there are also many fault-tolerant routing algorithms designed for lightweight NoCs without virtual channels. They can be further categorized into two classes, turn model-based and segment-based. For example, Glass and Ni [40] proposed a non-minima version of negative-first routing [39]. Wu proposed a fault-tolerant routing based on odd–even turn model [92]. Zhang et al. [97] proposed a reconfigurable router to tolerate one faulty block. Fick et al. [30, 31] proposed a distributed algorithm to reconfigure the routing table. Fu et al. [34] proposed a multiple-round dimension-order routing. Segment-based routing classifies networks into subnets, and subnets into segments [64]. By placing a bidirectional turn restriction in each segment, the network can be guaranteed deadlock free. Cooperating with the logic-based distributed routing [32] or universal LBDR [76], segment-based routing provides a way to improve the reliability of NoCs.

We should note that fault-tolerant routing algorithms are expected to be high resilience, high performance, high scalability, and low cost. However, these objectives are somewhat conflicting. Therefore, trade-offs among these metrics need to be considered in fault-tolerant routing. For example, algorithms relying on off-line analysis with global fault information, such as those segment-based routing algorithms [34, 64, 76], can tolerate more faults. However, for NoCs which cannot afford virtual channels, collecting and dumping global fault information is usually too expensive. Routing table provides the flexibility to reconfigure the network in the presence of faults. However, algorithms relying on a routing table, such as [29, 30], are not suitable for large-scale NoCs, especially for those without virtual channels, due to the cost problem [32].

Logic-based fault-tolerant routing algorithms, such as in [40, 92, 97], is low cost. However, the main problem in [40] and [97] is that only one fault can be tolerated. Zhang et al. [97] claimed that their algorithm can be extended to tolerate multiple faults by including them into one convex faulty block. However, this usually leads to a large number of disabled fault-free nodes. The main problem in [92] is the way that is used to handle the faults locating on four network edges as well as the two columns that are adjacent to the left and right network edges. For example, if a fault appears at these places, nodes of the corresponding edge or column are all disabled, which disables a number of fault-free routers and causes considerable hardware overhead and performance penalty.

In this chapter, we mainly focus on the cost-effective NoCs without virtual channels and select the logic-based fault-tolerant routing algorithms, such as [92] and [97], as the baseline algorithms. The major difference between the proposed ZoneDefense routing and previous work [92], [97] is the use of defense zones, which can reduce the number of disabled fault-free routers significantly.

4.1.3 Fault-Tolerant NoC Circuits

With the continuous advancements of semiconductor technologies, transistor feature sizes scales down substantially and the supply voltage is getting close to the threshold voltage, which enhances the performance and energy efficiency significantly. However, the probability of transistor failures including both transient errors and permanent errors also grows and the manufacturing induced failures become inevitable for large-scale VLSI designs especially manycore designs and NoCs [28, 73]. In order to address the problems, enormous efforts from both industry and academia have been devoted [41, 69, 87].

Constantinides et al. [27] proposed a component-level diagnose and redundancy-based reconfiguration strategy to improve the reliability of general VLSI designs. The authors leverage an automatic cluster and decomposition algorithm to balance the chip area overhead of the fault-tolerant design and the overall system resilience. Specifically, larger granularity of fault-tolerant design requires smaller hardware overhead because less interface signals are exposed to the fault detection and reconfiguration modules for the redundancy-based protection, but the reliability of the overall system can be lower because the large redundant components are more likely to fail at the same time. Hence, the redundancy granularity is the key to the optimized fault-tolerant design and intensively explored in this work. Since it is a general fault-tolerant design approach and there is a lack of NoC architectural information, there are still space left for further improvement for fault-tolerant NoC designs. Koibuchi et al. [74]. presented a lightweight fault-tolerant mechanism based on default backup paths (DBPs). This approach adds some DBPs instead of complete hardware duplication, so it consumes much less chip area compared to the standard redundancy approaches. However, DBP remains rather expensive and the network will soon degrade to a unidirectional ring when more DBPs are added under relatively higher error rate, which leads to dramatic network bandwidth degradation. Fick et al. [93] combined ECC (error correcting code), port-swapping, and a crossbar bypass to mitigate wear-out induced hard faults. They mainly exploited inherent redundancy of NoCs such as error bypassing and redundancy-based fault-tolerant design similar to DBP to improve NoC reliability with less hardware overhead. However, this approach generally targets at router ports and crossbars, and fails to address faults on buffers and links.

On top of the fault recovery approaches, fault detection that is utilized to determine the location of hardware faults is also essential to a fault-tolerant NoC design and it is particularly critical to handle runtime faults. Built-in Self-Test (BIST) [92] or other on-chip fault detection techniques [29, 32, 58, 76] are general fault-diagnosis approaches targeting at arbitrary VLSI designs and can be applied for NoC fault diagnosis as well. In addition, some classical fault detection error codes (DEC) can also be utilized to locate hardware faults on links and buffers. A variety of different DEC such as Berger code, parity, Reed Solomon code and other commonly-used CRC can also be adopted based on specific error rate and the target reliability design goals.

In summary, there have been quite some works improving the reliability of VLSI designs from the perspective of circuits, which generally shows promising results and inspires fault-tolerant NoC design at circuit layer. Although redundancy-based fault-tolerant circuit design approaches can be generic and potentially applied to various designs including processors and NoCs, they typically require substantial hardware overhead without being aware of features of the target hardware architecture. In contrast, the approaches that mainly explore the inherent fault tolerance of NoCs are more attractive especially for resource-constrained scenarios. In this chapter, we will also introduce a novel fault-tolerant design approach for NoCs at circuit layer and explore the inherent fault tolerance of NoC data paths such as links, buffers, and crossbars for hardware-efficient protection of NoCs.

4.2 NoC Fault Tolerance with Topology Reconfiguration

As technology advances, industry has started to employ multiple cores on a single silicon die in order to improve performance through parallel execution, which has the benefits of power-efficiency and short time-to-market [38]. Significant research has been undertaken on tera-scale computing that is able to integrate tens to hundreds of homogeneous processing cores on a single chip to process massive amounts of information in parallel[10], [1]. For example, an 80-core tera-flop processor prototype was demonstrated at Intel Developer Forum 2006 [57]. Such processors containing a large number of cores are called manycore processors (note the difference from multicore processors that contain a small number of cores). In terms of communication infrastructure, NoC is generally regarded as the most promising interconnect solution for Giga-scale Integrated Circuits (ICs) such as manycore processors [20, 24], in which the topology determines the ideal performance of the on-chip network whereas the routing algorithm and the flow control mechanism determine how much of this potential is realized. As a result, Operating System (OS) should understand the topology of NoC-based manycore systems to dispatch and schedule tasks to multiple cores more effectively; while programmers should also be aware of the topology to improve the performance of parallel applications [66, 84].

There are many challenges for the architecture design of these NoC-based manycore systems, in which fabrication yield is one of the most serious concerns because an IC's profitability depends heavily on it [52, 53]. With the ever-increasing circuit density, obtaining high fabrication yield solely through improving the manufacturing process is increasingly difficult and will become un-affordable in the near future. For example, as stated in [83], it would have been lucky to get yield in the range of 10–20% for the Cell processor if architectural help is not provided. A more practical solution is therefore to provide defect tolerance capabilities on-chip by incorporating redundant circuits. For example, Memory Built-In-Self-Repair (MBISR) techniques have been widely utilized in the industry and proved to be very effective to keep the high fabrication yield of memory circuits. Such techniques should be extended to other types of VLSI circuits as well [54].

However, tolerating defects in the microprocessor is quite different from tolerating defects in memory because the processor's internal structure is not as regular as memory cells, and previous attempts in this domain mainly focused on introducing microarchitecture-level redundancy (e.g., [78, 81]). This is appropriate for multicore chips (e.g., a quad-core processor) in order to keep the overhead small. When the number of on-chip cores increases to a point that single core becomes inexpensive when compared to the entire chip (e.g., a 64-core processor), however, it is not necessary to tolerate defective cores at the microarchitecture level. Instead, it is more appropriate to employ core-level redundancy in such case to reduce the complexity associated with microarchitecture-level redundancy.

For NoC-based manycore systems with core-level redundancy, faulty cores are replaced by spare ones placed on-chip. Therefore, it is possible that the topology of the target design is modified and different fabricated chips may have different underlying topologies. This is a big burden for programmers because an optimized program for one topology may not work well for a different one and the programmers are facing various topologies when optimizing their parallel programs.

To address the above problem, the concept of virtual topology is reintroduced from prior network embedding problem. A virtual topology is isomorphic with the topology of the target design but is a degraded version. From the viewpoint of OS and programmers, they always see a unified virtual topology regardless of the various underlying physical topologies. This eases the dispatching and scheduling tasks for OS and facilitates the optimization of parallel programs. The above issue was briefly discussed in [95]. When compared to [95], we re-define the problem by introducing two new metrics, namely Distance Factor (DF) and Congestion Factor (CF), to evaluate the performance of different virtual topologies. We also introduce new algorithms to tackle the problem, and conduct extensive simulation experiments to verify the effectiveness of the proposed solution.

4.2.1 NoC Topology Reconfiguration

4.2.1.1 Core-Level Redundancy in Homogeneous Manycore Processors

As the internal structure is not as regular as memory cells, previous research work on defect tolerance in microprocessors mainly focused on introducing microarchitecture-level redundancy. Redundancy improves yield while at the same time may reduce the chip performance. Researchers thus evaluate the effectiveness of various redundancy mechanisms using performance averaged yield (Y_{PAV})[81] or Yield-Adjusted Throughput (YAT) [78]. Performance degradation is measured by the relative Instructions Per Cycle (IPC), i.e., the ratio of the reduced IPC to the maximum IPC of the perfect version.

For multicore and manycore processors, the chips themselves naturally have regularity and redundancy as they contain a number of cores. As a result, core-level redundancy could be employed besides microarchitecture-level redundancy. Microarchitecture- and core-level redundancy are named intra- and inter-processor redundancy respectively in [81]. In the former case, a core can be in any degraded states, but the entire chip is considered bad once the available intra-processor redundancy is exhausted in even one of its cores. In the latter case, a core becomes useless if it contains any faults. However, as long as enough of the remaining cores are functional, the chip is considered to be operational.

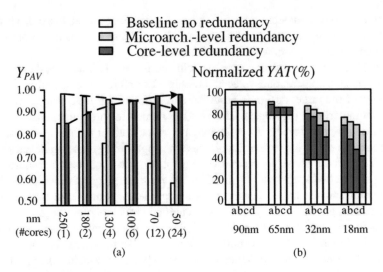

Fig. 4.1 Comparison between microarchitecture- and core-level redundancy. (**a**) comparison redrawn from [81] with the permission of the author. (**b**) YAT comparison redrawn from [78] with the permission of the author

Various types of microarchitecture-level redundancies are considered with core-level redundancy by using poisson yield model in [81]. SPEC2000 and a speech recognition benchmark are chosen to get the IPC reduction. The results are reproduced and shown in Fig. 4.1a. The x-axis shows the feature size and the number of cores per chip at each technology. As can be seen in the figure, although there are significant benefits by using microarchitecture-level redundancy when compared to baseline model, Y_{PAV} drops from 98% at 250 nm to 91.3% at 50 nm. Core-level redundancy covers the entire area of the chip and therefore Y_{PAV} increases uniformly from 85.4% to 98%. The yield benefits offered by microarchitecture-level and core-level redundancy crossover at 100 nm.

The authors in [78] proposed a novel defect tolerant microarchitecture (namely *Rescue*). Core-level redundancy (called "core sparing" in their work), is used to compare with *Rescue* by using HotSpot model and negative binomial yield model. IPC reduction is evaluated by simulating 23 benchmark programs from SPEC2000. It also assumes a 20%(a), 30%(b), 40%(c), and 50%(d) growth of core complexity starting from one core per chip at the 90 nm. The results are redrawn and shown in Fig. 4.1b. Similarly, we can observe, as technology advances, YAT becomes increasingly lower without redundancy. At the same time, microarchitecture-level redundancy brings YAT improvement, but at a smaller scale when compared to core-level redundancy in newer technology generation. Microarchitecture-level redundancy shows greater improvement under larger core complexity growth, because the chip has fewer cores and each defective core disables a larger portion of the chip.

From the above analysis, we can conclude that, for manycore chips, because the number of on-chip cores is large and they are fabricated in latest technology, the probability of an embedded core being defective is quite small. Each degraded chip contains a majority of fully functional cores and a small number of defective ones. Therefor, it is not necessary to tolerate defective cores at the microarchitecture-level. Instead, it is more appropriate to employ core-level redundancy in such case to reduce the complexity associated with microarchitecture-level redundancy.

In fact, industry has started to employ core-level redundancy in their products recently. For example, while the Cell processor contains eight Synergistic Processing Elements (SPEs), Sony's PlayStation 3 video game console considers using only seven of them to increase the manufacturing yield [83]. This approach is also applied in Sun's UltraSPARC T1 processor [71], [86] and Azul's Vega2 chip [63].

There are two schemes to design homogeneous multicore or manycore chips with core-level redundancy, namely As Many As Available (AMAA) and As Many As Demand (AMAD). The AMAA scheme, adopted in the T1 processor, degrades a chip by disabling faulty cores only. For example, a fabricated quad-core processor can be a full version with 4 functional cores; or it can be degraded to a tri-core, dual-core or single-core processor depending on the number of faulty cores. In AMAD scheme, also denoted as "$N + M$" mechanism, adopted in the Cell processor ($N = 7, M = 1$), an -core processor is provided with redundant cores and we always provide customers with operational cores. That is, it is possible that there are fault-free cores left unused in AMAD.

It is preferred to employ the AMAA scheme in multicore to keep the overhead small. However, as the number of on-chip cores increases, the overhead of leaving a few redundant cores on-chip unused is acceptable because a single core is inexpensive compared to the entire chip as discussed above. In addition, with many cores implemented on-chip, we may get various types of degraded chips (with different number of faulty cores) after fabrication and the yield of the demanded-core processor cannot be promised in AMAA scheme. Finally, from a commercial point of view, it may cause some confusion in marketing with many different degraded versions. Therefore, for manycore processors, AMAD scheme is preferred and we mainly focus on this scheme.

Manycore processors typically use NoC as the communication infrastructure, in which the topology determines the ideal performance whereas the routing algorithm and the flow control mechanism determine how much of this potential is realized. However, in AMAD scheme, as the cores that are fabricated to be defective are not known a priori, when they are replaced by spare cores, the topology of the target design can be different. For example, suppose we want to provide 9-core processors with 3×3 2D mesh topology to customers, as shown in Fig. 4.2a. Also, suppose 3 redundant cores (1 column) are provided to improve the yield of these chips as shown in Fig. 4.2b. If some cores (no more than 3) are defective, we could still get 9-core processors. However, as shown in Fig. 4.2c, if faulty cores are replaced by spare cores, not only the topologies that we get are different from what we expect, but also the topologies of different chips can be distinct. These changed topologies become irregular and would cause performance degradation for manycore processors.

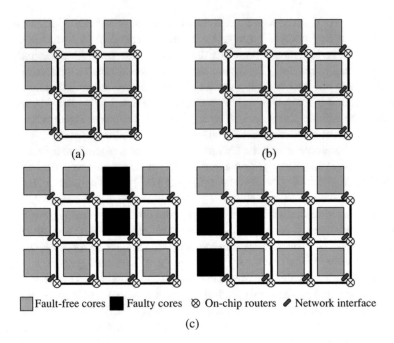

Fault-free cores ▇ Faulty cores ⊗ On-chip routers ✏ Network interface

(c)

Fig. 4.2 Faulty cores change the topology of target design. (**a**) What we expect. (**b**) What we implement. (**c**) What we get

4.2.1.2 Topology Impacts on NoC-Based Manycore Systems

In NoC-based homogeneous manycore systems, the performance of the on-chip communication significantly affects the efficiency of parallel applications. As a result, to minimize the communication overhead among threads or tasks, today's OS relies on explicit knowledge of the underlying topology [84]. For example in Microsoft Windows Server 2003, a so-called Advanced Configuration and Power Interface (ACPI) circuit is used to pass a description of the physical topology of the system to OS [66]. The topology information is stored in Static Resource Affinity Table (SRAT), and is used by Windows when dispatching and scheduling tasks. For example, a representative scheme, namely Gang Scheduling [42], divides processors into groups, in which processors of the same group have lower communication overhead. Tasks that frequently communicate with each other will be assigned to processors in the same group to minimize communication overhead.

In addition, from the parallel programmers' perspective, to optimize the performance of the application software, currently they need to know the underlying manycore's organization [72]. For example, topology information is provided to programmers through API functions in Windows Server 2003. This is the communication-exposed programming for NoC platforms [24]. Such tailored programs may be not portable to other processors due to different system architectures, such as the number of on-chip cores and their topology.

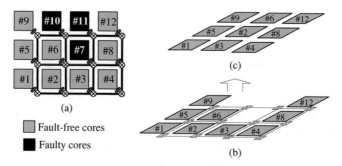

Fig. 4.3 Physical topology and virtual topology. (**a**) A chip with faulty cores. (**b**) The physical topology. (**c**) A virtual topology

4.2.1.3   Physical Topology and Virtual Topology

As shown in Fig. 4.2, faulty cores change the target topology and different chips may have distinct underlying topologies. It would be rather cumbersome for OS and programmers to face various different topologies and optimize them differently. To address this problem, we propose to provide a unified virtual topology regardless of the underlying one. Before introducing the details, we first define *Reference Topology* as the topology of the target design that we expect. For example, the 3 × 3 2D mesh topology in Fig. 4.2a is the expected reference topology.

For the illustrative "9 + 3" manycore processor shown in Fig. 4.2b, suppose the 7th, 10th and 11th cores are defective after fabrication as shown in Fig. 4.3a, these cores are considered to be removed out of the chip. The remaining fault-free cores and their interconnections construct a *Physical Topology* as shown in Fig. 4.3b. It should be emphasized that once a manycore processor is taped out, its physical topology is determined and cannot be changed during its lifetime. This is fundamentally different from board-level multiprocessor systems, which are much easier to be repaired since the target topology can be maintained by simply replacing the faulty processor with a good one.

Based on our AMAD scheme, a 9-core processor can still be provided but with different topology when compared to the reference topology. That is, we can construct a *Virtual Topology* of the chip based on the given physical topology, which is isomorphic with the reference topology. An example is shown in Fig. 4.3c, in which we construct a *virtual* 3 × 3 2D mesh topology.

With the above configuration, the 3rd, the 5th, the 6th and the 8th cores are four virtual neighbors of the 2nd core. The 3rd core is considered to be below the 2nd core virtually, although it locates at the 2nd core's right-hand side physically. In addition, while the 5th core is more than one hop away from the 2nd core, they are considered to be adjacent in the above virtual topology.

By using virtual topology, OS and programmers always see a unified topology that is isomorphic with the reference topology, no matter how the underlying cores are connected physically. This greatly simplifies task dispatching and scheduling duties for OS and also facilitates the optimization of parallel programs. In addition, a unified topology that isolates various physical topologies for different chips also significantly eases marketing process.

A similar idea has been applied in Cray T3E network [79]. If some processors fail during the operation of the system, one or more of them may not be physically contiguous. To continue providing applications with a contiguous range of virtual processor numbers, the routing table along with the logical "who am I" registers allows the nodes to be logically renamed, i.e., mapping from physical to virtual number. This kind of "hot swapping" is totally transparent to users. As mentioned above, the failure of nodes and the change of topologies in systems such as Cray T3E are temporary and can be easily recovered because a faulty processor is removed from the system and replaced while OS and user jobs are kept running on the healthy nodes. However, for manycore processors, defects are permanent and physical topologies cannot be recovered. It should be also noted that, depending on the architecture design of manycore processors, there are many ways to implement the mapping from various physical topologies to their corresponding virtual topology. For example, one possible solution is to add a firmware layer below OS to record mapping information which is obtained after fabrication test. This is similar to the CORE_AVAILABLE_REG used in UltraSPARC T1 processor [71, 86]. OS and programmers always work on the reference topology while the firmware is responsible for transformation.

4.2.2 NoC Topology Virtualization Formulation

On-chip faulty cores change the topology of the target design and cause performance degradation for parallel applications. To tackle this problem, we use virtual topology to provide a unified interface to OS and programmers, no matter how the underlying cores are connected physically. At the same time, however, as there can be many virtual topologies for a particular physical topology and they may affect applications differently, we should choose the one that results in the best performance.

Since there are a wide range of applications with different characteristics running on the NoC-based manycore systems and they may have different requirements on the construction of virtual topologies, it is difficult to evaluate the impact of virtual topologies on various applications at the chip architecture design stage. As a result, we evaluate the performance of virtual topologies themselves and mainly consider the average latency and throughput of different virtual topologies.

In order to do so, from the viewpoint of the NoC, two evaluation metrics are introduced in this section to model the performance degradation of different virtual topologies when compared to the reference topology, namely Distance Factor (DF) and Congestion Factor (CF). For the sake of simplicity, we assume the communication infrastructure to be fault-free in this research work. This assumption can be justified since the routers and links use much less hardware resources when compared to the cores and are thus less vulnerable to defects [36]. Also, it would not cause significant overhead to include fault-tolerant features such as Triple Modular Redundancy (TMR) to protect them.

Distance Factor The zero-load latency T_0 of a topology can be expressed as [21]: $T_0 = H \times t_r + D/v + L/b.$. It is composed of three terms. The router delay is $H \times t_r$ for a network with an average hop count of H and a delay of t_r through a single router. The time of flight is D/v for a network with an average distance of D and a propagation velocity of v. The last one is the serialization latency which is the time for a packet of length L to cross a channel with bandwidth b.

For a particular physical topology, virtual topologies differ from each other only in the average hop count H. When compared to reference topology, it is obvious that the average hop count of an irregular virtual topology becomes larger and thus the zero-load latency becomes longer. The distance factor is used to evaluate such degradation, in which $DF_{nn'}$ between two nodes n and n' is defined as the physical hops between them $\left(DF_{nn'} = Hops_{nn'}\right)$ and the distance factor of node n (DF_n) is defined as the average distance factor between node n and all its k virtual neighbors

$$DF_n = \frac{1}{k} \sum_{n'=1}^{k} DF_{nn'} \tag{4.1}$$

Finally, the distance factor of a virtual topology (DF) is defined as the average DF_n of all nodes

$$DF = \frac{1}{N} \sum_{n=1}^{N} DF_n \tag{4.2}$$

(There are in total N nodes in the virtual topology.)

The reference topology has the minimum DF as usually virtual neighbors are located next to each other physically. For example, DF is 1 in mesh and torus topologies, which means that each pair of virtual neighbors is exactly one hop away from each other. Larger value of DF means longer communication delay among virtual neighbors.

Congestion Factor For a given physical topology, it is likely that there are several virtual topologies with the same DF values, as shown in Fig. 4.4. We therefore use congestion factor to further evaluate the performance of virtual topologies. A virtual topology not only changes the average hop count among cores but also affects the distribution of channel load. Traffic may become unbalanced among different links. As the more balanced the channel load, the closer the throughput of the network is to the ideal case [21], a virtual topology that could balance traffic more evenly across all NoC links is preferred.

According to the previous discussion, traffic distribution in NoC-based manycore systems has the property of spatial locality, i.e., communication is more likely to happen between adjacent cores rather than distant ones. We thus only consider the case where a node only communicate with its virtual neighbors. We define the

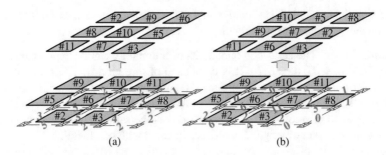

Fig. 4.4 CF comparison between two virtual topologies with the same DF (DF = 2) for a given physical topology. (**a**) Virtual topology I. (**b**) Virtual topology II

congestion factor of a physical link l (denoted as CF_l) as follows: for any nodes n and n', if they are virtual neighbors, and l is on one of the routing paths between them according to the NoC's routing mechanism (e.g., XY-routing [24]), we add CF_l by 1. For the two virtual topologies in Fig. 4.4, the CF_l values are shown above each physical links. It is clear that traffic in topology I is much balanced than the one in topology II. In topology II, some links are much congested ($CF_l = 11$) while some others are barely used ($CF_l = 0$).

Based on the above observation, we define the congestion factor (CF) of a virtual topology as the standard deviation of CF_l of all links to indicate the traffic distribution

$$CF = \sqrt{\frac{\sum_{l=1}^{L} \left(CF_l - \overline{CF_l}\right)^2}{L - 1}} \qquad (4.3)$$

(There are in total L links in the physical topology.)

CF of the reference topology is 0, which means that traffic can be more balanced across the network.[1] Greater CF means less even flow distribution. Please note that even though advanced routing algorithms can be introduced to balance channel load, CF can be an auxiliary performance metric to evaluate the raw flow distribution which reflects the quality of a virtual topology. With the above two metrics, the quality of different virtual topologies can be evaluated and compared. DF and CF might be conflicted with each other during optimization, hence we unify them together. The Unified Metric (UM) is defined as

$$UM = w_{DF} \times DF + w_{CF} \times CF \qquad (4.4)$$

---

[1] Please note, congested links are usually revealed around the middle of network even for uniform traffic pattern in practice, CF metric is mainly for comparison purpose and 0 is its ideal upper bound.

Fig. 4.5 System organization for manycore platform with "$N + M$" scheme

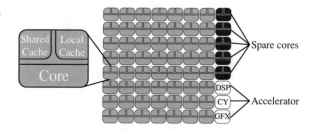

in which w_{DF} and w_{CF} are the optimization weights designated by users ($w_{\mathrm{DF}} + w_{\mathrm{CF}} = 1$).

Reconfiguration from physical to virtual topology is very complex and it depends heavily on the system organizations, such as the reference topology, the on-chip redundancy distribution, etc. We mainly focus on mesh and torus topologies, which are the most widely used ones in NoC-based manycore systems. We adopt a representative scalable manycore architecture proposed by Intel as our platform model, which integrates an array of tens to hundreds of streamlined processing cores and accelerators connected by a scalable NoC infrastructure [57], as shown in Fig. 4.5. We formulate the topology reconfiguration problem for 2D mesh/torus topology investigated as follows:

Topology Reconfiguration Problem (TRP) For an $R \times C$ homogeneous manycore processor with S redundant cores, suppose D cores ($D \leq S$) are faulty, construct $R \times C$ coordinates as follows:

$$
\begin{bmatrix}
(R-1,0) & (R-1,1) & \cdots & (R-1,C-1) \\
\cdots & \cdots & \cdots & \cdots \\
(1,0) & (1,1) & \cdots & (1,C-1) \\
(0,0) & (0,1) & \cdots & (0,C-1)
\end{bmatrix}
$$

Distribute these coordinates to ($R \times C + S - D$) fault-free cores to construct a virtual topology T_{virtual} , in which nodes with coordinates $(i+1, j), (i-1, j), (i, j+1)$ and $(i, j-1)$ are four virtual neighbors of node (i, j) , and nodes without being assigned coordinates are left unused, satisfying

$$\mathrm{UM\ of\ } T_{virtual} \mathrm{\ is\ minimized.}$$

Two example virtual topologies for a given physical topology are shown in Fig. 4.6. The values of DF and CF for these two virtual topologies are also shown in the figure. Clearly, new topology reconfiguration algorithm needs to be developed to select the best candidate topology. Before introducing our proposed algorithms, we firstly review prior related work in this area and then give some in-depth analysis of the above TRP problem in the following two sections.

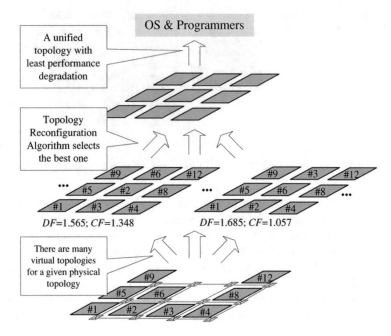

Fig. 4.6 Topology reconfiguration

4.2.3   NoC Topology Virtualization Optimization

The objective of TRP in essence is to find a map from virtual locations to physical cores with optimized performance. Considering the configuration shown in Fig. 4.3, as depicted in Fig. 4.7, the example virtual topology can be achieved according to the mapping table. For example, virtual location V is mapped to the 2nd physical core. In other words, the 2nd fault-free core is placed in virtual location V in the virtual topology. For the given physical topology in Fig. 4.7, there are 9! possible virtual topologies with different DF and CF values, because a fault-free core can be placed in any virtual locations.

The topology reconfiguration problem can be broken into two related subproblems, to minimize DF and to minimize CF, which we call TRP-I and TRP-II, respectively. In this section, we first recast these two problems from an optimization problem to a decision problem, and then show both of them are essentially instances of known NP-complete problems.

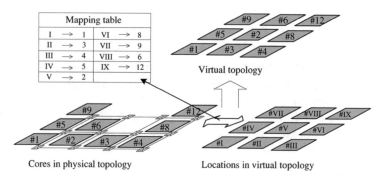

Fig. 4.7   The essence of TRP is to find a map from virtual locations to physical cores

4.2.3.1   TRP-I: An Instance of Quadratic Assignment Problem

According to the above analysis, the decision form of TRP-I can be formulated as follows:

TRP-I Virtual locations are numbered $\{1, 2 \ldots, n\}$, while physical cores are numbered $\{1, 2 \ldots, m\}, n \leq m$. d_{kl} is the distance (number of *hops*) between physical nodes k and l . $d_{kl} = \infty$ if k or l is defective. Is there a one-to-one function $f : \{1, 2 \ldots, n\} \rightarrow \{1, 2, \ldots, m\}$ to construct a virtual topology T, such that:$\mathrm{DF}(T) \leq B$ (bound $B \in Z^{+}$).

To ease analysis, suppose the reference topology is torus. Each virtual location i has four neighbors in torus. According to (4.1), the distance factor of i can be expressed as $\mathrm{DF}_i = (1)/(4) \sum_j d_{f(i)f(j)}$, in which j indicates four virtual neighbors of i and $d_{f(i)f(j)}$ represents the physical distance of node i and its virtual neighbors as mentioned above. The above formulation can be similarly applied for mesh topology, except that the coefficients for different nodes can be 1/2, 1/3, or 1/4, as a virtual node in mesh may have 2, 3, or 4 neighbors based on its position.

From the above, according to (4.2) the distance factor of the virtual topology T is

$$\mathrm{DF}(T) = \frac{1}{4n} \sum_{i=1}^{n} \sum_{j} d_{f(i)f(j)} \tag{4.5}$$

We now show that TRP-I is essentially an instance of Quadratic Assignment Problem (QAP), which is a well-known NP-complete problem [77]. QAP can be formulated as follows [43].

[QAP]   Non-negative integer cost: $c_{ij}, 1 \leq i, j \leq n$
distanced$_{kl}, 1 \leq k, l \leq m$
Is there a one-to-one $f : \{1, 2 \ldots, n\} \rightarrow \{1, 2 \ldots, m\}$
such that:$\sum_{i=1}^{n} \sum_{j=1}^{n} c_{ij} d_{f(i)f(j)} \leq B$

A QAP instance can be expressed as:

$$\{\langle c_{ij}, d_{kl}, B \rangle, c_{ij}, d_{kl}, B \in Z^+; 1 \leq i, j \leq n; 1 \leq k, l \leq m\}$$

The famous "backboard wiring" problem [85] is a typical application of QAP, which concerns how to place computer components to minimize the total amount of wiring required to connect them.

Considering a QAP instance $\{\langle c_{ij}, d_{kl}, B \rangle\}$, let i and j be virtual locations ($1 \leq i, j \leq n$) in torus, and d_{kl} is the distance between physical nodes k and l as defined in TRP-I. C_{ij} is defined as follows:

$$\begin{cases} c_{ij} = 1/4n, & \text{if } i \text{ and } j \text{ are virtual neighbors} \\ 0, & \text{otherwise.} \end{cases}$$

Then the objective of this QAP becomes

$$\frac{1}{4n} \sum_{i=1}^{n} \sum_{j} d_{f(i)f(j)} \leq B \qquad (4.6)$$

in which j are four virtual neighbors of i. According to (4.5) and (4.6), it is clear that the objective of the above QAP instance becomes to find a mapping function or in other words a virtual topology (T) with distance factor not exceeding B. As a result, TRP-I is an instance of the quadratic assignment problem.

4.2.3.2   TRP-II: An Instance of Vectorial Quadratic Assignment Problem

Similarly, the decision form of TRP-II can be formulated as follows:

TRP-II Virtual locations are numbered $\{1, 2 \ldots, n\}$, while physical cores are numbered $\{1, 2 \ldots, m\}, n \leq m$. Is there a one-to-one function $f : \{1, 2, \ldots, n\} \to \{1, 2 \ldots, m\}$ to construct a virtual topology T, such that: $\text{CF}(T) \leq B$(bound $B \in Z^+$).

In this subsection, we show that TRP-II is also an instance of quadratic assignment problem, but with a different form. To prove this, we first define a Vectorial Quadratic Assignment Problem (V-QAP) as follows:

V-QAP Non-negative integer cost: $c_{ij}, 1 \leq i, j \leq n$; P-dimensional non-negative vector $v_{kl}, 1 \leq k, l \leq m$, and bound $B_V = (A_1, A_2 \ldots, A_P)$. For two P-dimensional vectors V_1 and V_2 is defined as $|V_1| \leq |V_2|$. Is there a one-to-one function $f : \{1, 2 \ldots, n\} \to \{1, 2, \ldots, m\}$ such that:$\sum_{i=1}^{n} \sum_{j=1, j \neq i}^{n} c_{ij} v_{f(i)f(j)} \leq B_V$.

An instance of V-QAP can be expressed as $\{< c_{ij}, P, v_{kl}, B_V >, c_{ij} \in Z^+, v_{kl}$ and B_V are P-dimensional non-negative vectors, $1 \leq i, j \leq n, 1 \leq k, l \leq m\}$. It is easy to see that V-QAP is NP-complete because QAP is in fact one-dimensional

Fig. 4.8 Path vector examples

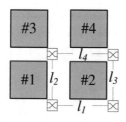

Path vector: $p_{rs}=(l_1, l_2, l_3, l_4)$	
$p_{12}=(1,0,0,0)$	$p_{31}=(0,1,0,0)$
$p_{13}=(0,1,0,0)$	$p_{32}=(0,0,1,1)$
$p_{14}=(1,0,1,0)$	$p_{34}=(0,0,0,1)$
$p_{21}=(1,0,0,0)$	$p_{41}=(0,1,0,1)$
$p_{23}=(1,1,0,0)$	$p_{42}=(0,0,1,0)$
$p_{24}=(0,0,1,0)$	$p_{43}=(0,0,0,1)$

V-QAP. We now show that TRP-II is an instance of V-QAP. Suppose the reference topology is 2D mesh or torus with L physical links, denoted as $l_1, l_2, l_3 \ldots, l_1$.

Definition 1 *Path Vector* p_{rs} is a L-dimensional vector $(l_1, l_2, l_3 \ldots, l_L)$. If $l_x(1 \leq x \leq L)$ is on one of the paths from physical node r to s according to the NoC's routing mechanism (e.g., XY-routing), l_x in p_{rs} is 1, otherwise l_x is 0. A simple example is shown in Fig. 4.8, in which XY-routing is used. For example, $p_{14} = (1, 0, 1, 0)$ because packets from 1st core to 4th core pass through links l_1 and l_3.

Definition 2 *Congestion Increment Vector* v_{rs} is defined as $v_{rs} = p_{rs} - I \times d_{rs}/L$, d_{rs} is the distance between physical node and as defined in TRP-I. I is the L-dimensional unit vector.

We now construct a V-QAP instance:
$\{< c_{ij}, L, v_{rs}, \sqrt{L-1} \times B_V >, 1 \leq i, j \leq n, 1 \leq r, s \leq m\}$, in which i and j are virtual locations, and c_{ij} is defined as

$$c_{ij} = \begin{cases} 1, & \text{if } i \text{ and } j \text{ are virtual neighbors} \\ 0, & \text{otherwise.} \end{cases}$$

According to the definition of V-QAP, we want to find a one-to-one function f : $\{1, 2 \ldots, n\} \rightarrow \{1, 2 \ldots, m\}$ such that $\sum_{i=1}^{n} \sum_{j=1, j \neq i}^{n} c_{ij} v_{f(i)f(j)} \leq \sqrt{L-1} \times B_V$.

As c_{ij} is 0 if i and j are not virtual neighbors, the objective then becomes $\sum_{i=1}^{n} \sum_{j} v_{f(i)f(j)} \leq \sqrt{L-1} \times B_V$, or in another form

$$\frac{1}{\sqrt{L-1}} \left| \sum_{i=1}^{n} \sum_{j} \left(p_{f(i)f(j)} - I \times \frac{d_{f(i)f(j)}}{L} \right) \right| \leq |B_V| \qquad (4.7)$$

in which i and j are virtual neighbors.

Based on the above definitions of path vector and the congestion factor of a link in Sect. 4.2.2, it is not difficult to derive: $\sum_{i=1}^{n} \sum_{j} p_{f(i)f(j)} = \left(\text{CF}_{l_1}, \text{CF}_{l_2} \ldots \text{CF}_{l_L} \right)$ and $(1)/(L) \sum_{i=1}^{n} \sum_{j} d_{f(i)f(j)} = \overline{\text{CF}}$. Then, we can conclude from (4.7) after substitution:

$(1)/(\sqrt{L-1}) \left| \left(\text{CF}_{l_1}, \text{CF}_{l_2} \ldots \text{CF}_{l_L} \right) - I \times \overline{\text{CF}} \right| \leq |B_V|$, i.e., $CF \leq |B_V|$.

It is clear that the above constructed instance of V-QAP is in fact to find a virtual topology(T) with congestion factor not exceeding $|B_V|$. As a result, we have proved that TRP-II is an instance of V-QAP.

To sum up, we point out that TRP is an instance of the quadratic assignment problem, one of the most complex combinatorial optimization problems. We therefore do not hold much hope for finding an exact polynomial time algorithm for its solution. Efficient and effective heuristics are therefore introduced to solve this problem, as shown in the following section.

On top of the above analysis, an advanced Simulated Annealing (SA) algorithm proposed for QAP is firstly adopted to tackle our TRP. This algorithm, however, is quite time-consuming. We therefore present a fast deterministic greedy algorithm, called Row Rippling and Column Stealing (RRCS). Finally, a gSA algorithm is proposed, which outperforms both SA and RRCS algorithms in terms of computing time and the quality of results. It should be noted that we mainly focus on the reconfiguration algorithms for 2D mesh/torus topologies. Other topologies (e.g., butterfly or fat tree topology) may require different optimization algorithms.

4.2.3.3   An Adopted Simulated Annealing Algorithm

Since we have proved that topology reconfiguration problem is an instance of the quadratic assignment problem, we can adopt previous heuristic approaches for QAP to tackle our TRP. One such approach that has yielded promising results is simulated annealing [7, 12, 16, 67]. We adopt one of the most efficient simulated annealing implementations proposed in [67] for QAP to tackle TRP.

Various simulated annealing algorithms generally differ with respect to neighborhood search, annealing schedule and termination criterion. The adopted SA algorithm uses (4.4) as the cost function and random virtual topologies as initial solutions. The neighborhood function employed is the widely used "2-exchange". For example, if the current solution is

$$\begin{bmatrix} (1,0) & \text{Faulty} & \text{unused} \\ (0,0) & (0,1) & (1,1) \end{bmatrix}$$

one of its neighbors by exchanging $(1,1)$ and 'unused' is

$$\begin{bmatrix} (1,0) & \text{Faulty} & (1,1) \\ (0,0) & (0,1) & \text{Unused} \end{bmatrix}.$$

The neighboring solutions are searched thoroughly in a fixed order, not randomly. For the above solution, $5 \times (5-1)/2$ trials are needed to explore all its neighborhood by the sequence $(1,0) \leftrightarrow$ 'unused', $(1, 0) \leftrightarrow (0, 0), \ldots$ 'unused' $\leftrightarrow (0, 0)$, 'unused' $\leftrightarrow (0, 1) \ldots$

The adopted SA algorithm uses the inhomogeneous annealing with oscillation schedules, i.e., temperature is reduced by a very small amount after every trial without any equilibrium test. In addition, temperature is decreased and increased periodically, i.e., reannealing instead of the straightforward annealing, which is the common practice of state-of-the-art simulated annealing algorithms. The SA algorithm in [67] uses an advanced formula to calculate the initial and final temperatures for each iteration, leaving two tuning control parameters, i.e., the initial (λ_1) and the final (λ_2) temperature factors, which can be used to control the cooling process effectively.

The algorithm terminates when the current iteration number exceeds Q , or in other words after $Qn(n-1)/2$ trials, in which n is the number of fault-free cores.

4.2.3.4 Row Rippling Column Stealing Algorithm (RRCS)

Simulated annealing is a kind of common technique that can be adopted to all combinatorial optimization problems. However, it does not consider any characteristics of the TRP problem, such as reference topology, system architecture, etc. Moreover, SA is quite time-consuming because it has to explore many random solutions before achieving a satisfactory result. As the configuration time has great impact on the chip cost, SA is not acceptable for large scale manycore systems. As a result,we proposed a fast deterministic greedy algorithm, called Row Rippling and Column Stealing (RRCS) [95].

RRCS is based on the observation that the performance degradation of a virtual topology is mainly caused by the physical irregularity of the virtual topology compared to the reference topology. Therefore, RRCS algorithm tries to maintain the physical regularity of the virtual topologies in row and in column unit.

To ease illustration, suppose in mesh or torus topology, there are one column of spare cores. If a row contains only one faulty core, i.e., faulty cores are no more than the spare ones in this row, Row Rippling is employed to reconfigure the row, in which a faulty core is replaced by its neighbor and the virtual position of the core used to replace the faulty one is transferred to the next neighboring core. This process continues until the spare one is used to replace the last element in the row. When a row contains more than one faulty cores, i.e., faulty cores are more than the spare ones in this row, the rightmost faulty core is replaced using rippling. The other faulty elements within the row, however, are replaced with the elements immediately beneath them. In other words, we "steal" a fault-free core from another row within the same column. This stolen core should be considered faulty when the row containing it is reconfigured. An example of using RRCS in a "16+4" processor with 4×4 mesh reference topology and one column redundancy is depicted in Fig. 4.9. To configure the uppermost row, which contains 3 faulty cores, we steal the

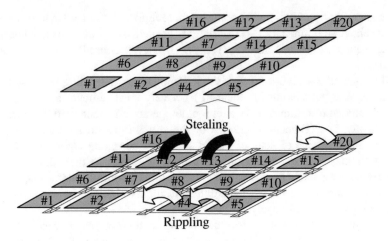

Fig. 4.9 An example of RRCS algorithm

12th and the 13th fault-free cores for the left two fault cores; while the rightmost one is rippling to the 20th core. Only Row Rippling is used to configure the lowermost row as it contains one faulty core. The achieved virtual topology is shown above the physical topology.

In the above discussion, we provide a column of redundant cores as an example. In practice, the number of redundant cores, i.e., M, for an N-core processor should be carefully determined by the designers in advance (e.g., using the analysis framework in [70]), and may be different from the column size. This however does not affect the working mechanism of the proposed RRCS algorithm as it only needs to compare the number of faulty cores N_f and spare cores on each row. We are able to generate an effective virtual topology as long as the number of faulty cores is less than M. In the worst case, i.e., all available cores in both the same row and the same column are exhausted, we simply choose a nearest core to replace the faulty one.

4.2.3.5   RRCS-Guided Simulated Annealing Algorithm

RRCS is very fast when compared to SA algorithm, but it does not directly consider DF or CF metrics during the optimization process. Moreover, RRCS may cause serious chain column stealing operations for certain physical topologies and result in undesirable virtual topologies.

For example, consider a physical topology with 6×6 2D mesh reference topology and 5 spare cores located on the righthand side and 5 faulty cores, as shown in Fig. 4.10a. The virtual topology achieved by RRCS is shown in Fig. 4.10b, in which the coordinates indicates the virtual locations for the corresponding cores. Reconfiguration begins from row R3, causing two stealing operations, i.e., the two CS1 from row R4. R4 then does not have enough available cores and has to steal

Fig. 4.10 Comparison between RRCS and SA. (**a**) Physical topology. (**b**) Virtual topology achieved by RRCS (DF = 1.660; CF = 1.428). (**c**) Virtual topology achieved by gSA (DF = 1.329; CF = 0.937)

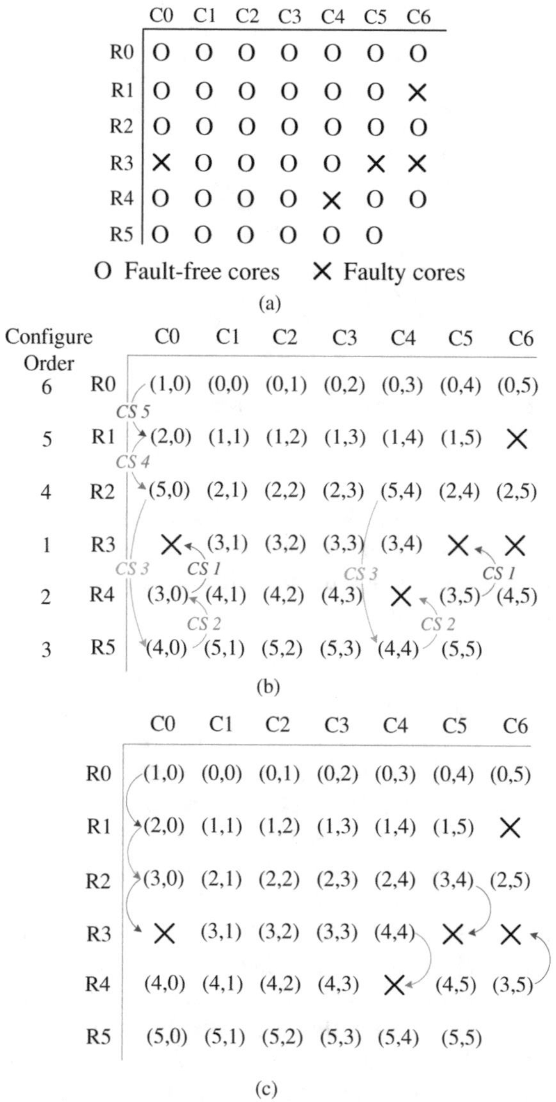

	C0	C1	C2	C3	C4	C5	C6
R0	O	O	O	O	O	O	O
R1	O	O	O	O	O	O	X
R2	O	O	O	O	O	O	O
R3	X	O	O	O	O	X	X
R4	O	O	O	O	X	O	O
R5	O	O	O	O	O	O	

O Fault-free cores   X Faulty cores

(a)

Configure Order		C0	C1	C2	C3	C4	C5	C6
6	R0	(1,0)	(0,0)	(0,1)	(0,2)	(0,3)	(0,4)	(0,5)
		CS 5
5	R1	(2,0)	(1,1)	(1,2)	(1,3)	(1,4)	(1,5)	X
		CS 4
4	R2	(5,0)	(2,1)	(2,2)	(2,3)	(5,4)	(2,4)	(2,5)
1	R3	X	(3,1)	(3,2)	(3,3)	(3,4)	X	X
		CS 3	CS 1			CS 3		CS 1
2	R4	(3,0)	(4,1)	(4,2)	(4,3)	X	(3,5)	(4,5)
			CS 2				CS 2	
3	R5	(4,0)	(5,1)	(5,2)	(5,3)	(4,4)	(5,5)	

(b)

	C0	C1	C2	C3	C4	C5	C6
R0	(1,0)	(0,0)	(0,1)	(0,2)	(0,3)	(0,4)	(0,5)
R1	(2,0)	(1,1)	(1,2)	(1,3)	(1,4)	(1,5)	X
R2	(3,0)	(2,1)	(2,2)	(2,3)	(2,4)	(3,4)	(2,5)
R3	X	(3,1)	(3,2)	(3,3)	(4,4)	X	X
R4	(4,0)	(4,1)	(4,2)	(4,3)	X	(4,5)	(3,5)
R5	(5,0)	(5,1)	(5,2)	(5,3)	(5,4)	(5,5)	

(c)

another two cores, i.e., CS2 from row R5. The process continues until the last row R0 is configured. Note that CS3 borrows relatively distant cores to configure faulty cores in row R5. These chain column stealing operations will generate an undesirable virtual topology.

At the same time, RRCS is very efficient, and it can arrange most part of the virtual topology in a good shape. We find that by applying several 2-exchange operations on top of the topologies achieved by RRCS, the quality of the results can be greatly improved. As a result, we propose to combine the algorithms of RRCS

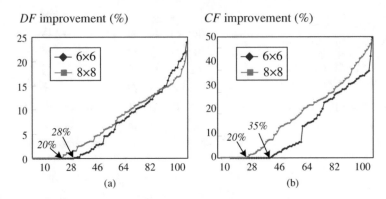

Fig. 4.11 gSA improvement over RRCS for different network size. (**a**) DF improvement. (**b**) CF improvement

and SA together. We use RRCS to quickly generate a good initial solution point, and then apply the adopted SA algorithm on top of it to explore its 2-exchange neighboring solutions. We call this strategy RRCS-guided Simulated Annealing (gSA) technique.

We use gSA ($w_{DF} = 0.9$, $w_{CF} = 0.1$) and RRCS working on 100 random physical topologies in 6×6 2D mesh with 5 spare and 5 randomly distributed faulty cores and 8×8 2D mesh with 8 spare and 8 random faulty cores respectively. The DF and CF improvement of gSA over RRCS are reordered from small to large and are shown in Fig. 4.11. For the DF metric in 6×6 array, RRCS generates the same results as gSA for the first 28 physical topologies, i.e., no improvement, while for the other 72 cases, gSA has different levels of improvement. When the network size increases to 8×8, gSA achieves greater improvement than in 6×6 for 80% cases. CF metric is similar. We can conclude that RRCS is efficient since for around 20%–35% cases, it generates results as good as gSA. However, for many circumstances due to chain column stealing operations, RRCS has very poor performance, and gSA can improve over RRCS greatly, especially for larger network size.

We then use SA algorithm with different parameters working on the above 100 physical topologies in 6×6 and 8×8 mesh. The initial and final temperature factors λ_1 and λ_2 are tuned and set to be 0.5 and 0.05 respectively. We choose 50 and 100 random solutions, i.e., SA-50 and SA-100 with different iteration numbers, i.e., $Q = 10$ and $Q = 20 \cdot w_{DF}$ and w_{CF} are set to be 0.9 and 0.1 respectively. The averaged results are shown in Table 4.1. It can be seen that, gSA outperforms SA in all cases with very little computational time. With more random solutions and more iteration numbers, SA improves a little but with great computing time overhead. This is because the quality of random initial solutions used by SA are much worse than RRCS, which is able to focus on a good solution point very fast.

Table 4.1 Comparison between gSA and SA from the perspective of computing time, DF, and CF

	SA-50 (Q = 10)	SA-100 (Q = 20)	gSA
	6 × 6 *2D mesh with 5 spare and 5 faulty cores*		
Time(s)	177.4	484.7	2.2
DF	1.538	1.483	1.319
CF	1.396	1.312	0.977
	8 × 8 *2D mesh with 8 spare and 8 faulty cores*		
Time(s)	484.4	3477.8	8.9
DF	1.782	1.473	1.296
CF	1.615	1.288	0.908

4.2.4 Experiment Result Analysis

4.2.4.1 Experimental Setup

We have implemented a manycore NoC simulation platform composed of classic pipelined virtual channel routers and cores which generate synthetic workload. The router pipeline has four stages, i.e., routing computation, virtual-channel allocation, switch allocation and switch traversal, in which each stage takes one clock cycle. Since we want to evaluate the performance of virtual topologies, other parameters should remain unchanged. In our experiments, each physical link has 8 virtual channels, and each virtual channel has 8 flit buffers. Credit-based flow control is used for buffer management. To reveal the performance of topologies themselves, the simple dimension-order routing is used which has the minimum impact on traffic distributions.

As execution-driven workload makes it difficult to isolate bottlenecks in the network design [21] and we concern more about the network performance, we use synthetic workload instead of execution-driven workload. Each core in our manycore NoC simulation platform is actually a traffic generator. As virtual topologies are constructed based on the spatial locality of communication, we adopt the neighboring traffic pattern in our experiments, in which a core only exchanges information with its neighbors. It is important to point out that the traffic patterns are applied to virtual topologies, not to physical topologies. That is, 1-hop communication between virtual neighbors may involve multiple physical hops.

Virtual topologies generated by reconfiguration algorithms are in XML format to be read by the simulation platform. Each core will then be assigned a name "$c\_vtx\_vty\_phx\_phx$", in which (vtx, vty) and (phx, phy) are its virtual and physical coordinates. Each time a core sends a packet, it reads its virtual location, looks up the mapping table stored in the simulator to find the physical locations of its virtual neighbors and then encapsulates in the packets as the destination address.

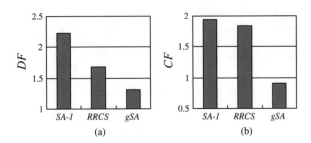

Fig. 4.12 Comparison between SA-1, RRCS and SA. (**a**) DF comparison. (**b**) CF comparison

4.2.4.2   Experiment I

In this experiment, we show how predictive of DF and CF metrics to real performance measurements. DF is the average hop count between virtual neighbors and thus should reflect the average delay and throughput of the network. While CF indicates traffic distribution across all the physical channels. We use SA-1 (1 random initial solution), RRCS and gSA ($w_{DF} = 0.9$, $w_{CF} = 0.1$) to work on 100 different physical topologies in 8×8 2D mesh with 8 spare cores and 8 randomly distributed faulty cores on-chip. We use SA-1 to keep the computational time comparable to gSA. We choose the physical topology on which gSA achieves the greatest improvement over SA-1 and RRCS in this experiment. The obtained DF and CF values are shown in Fig. 4.12.

Next, we import virtual topologies generated by these three algorithms into our manycore NoC platform to get the simulation performance measurements, i.e., average delay, throughput and average occupied time of all channels as shown in Fig. 4.13.

Average delay is the time required for a packet to traverse the network from source to destination. It can be observed from Fig. 4.13a, the latency of virtual topologies achieved by SA-1, RRCS and gSA are almost the same under light traffic load. When the network saturates, it is clear that the delay of gSA is better than RRCS, and RRCS is better than SA-1. Network throughput is the packets delivering rate for a particular traffic pattern. Figure 4.13b shows the throughput of saturation of the three algorithms. It is clear that the throughput of gSA is higher than RRCS, while RRCS is higher than SA-1. Compared with Fig. 4.12a, we show the effectiveness for DF as performance metrics.

Figure 4.13c shows the percentage of occupied time of all physical channels. More occupied time implies that more traffic passing through that channel. We reorder these values from small to large for easy comparison. It can be observed that the curve for gSA has the smallest slope, which means the differences between all channels are small, i.e., the traffic is more evenly distributed. RRCS is more steep than gSA, and SA-1 is more steep than RRCS. Compared with Fig. 4.12b, we show that the CF metric reflects real performance measurement.

From the above we can conclude that, gSA has better performance than RRCS and SA-1, not only in terms of DF and CF metrics but also in real performance

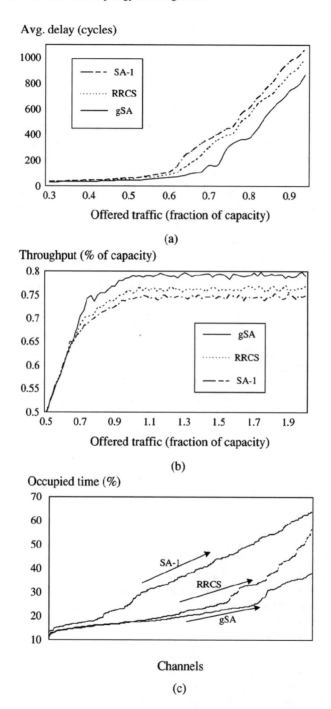

Fig. 4.13 Simulation measurements comparison between SA-1, RRCS and gSA. (**a**) Average delay. (**b**) Throughput. (**c**) Traffic distribution

measurements, i.e., latency, throughput and traffic distribution. In addition, the effectiveness of DF and CF as evaluation metrics is proved with this experiment.

4.2.4.3 Experiment II

In this experiment, we evaluate the effectiveness of the proposed gSA algorithm with the scale of network size. We use the 8×8 2D mesh topology with 8 spare cores and 8 randomly distributed faulty cores. We choose another larger configuration with 10×10 2D mesh reference topology, 12 spare cores and 12 random faulty cores for proportional scaling. We work on 100 random physical topologies in 8×8 and 10×10 respectively. The average improvement of gSA over RRCS for DF metric is 6.828% in 8 8 while 9.737% in 10×10 configurations. Regarding the CF metric, the improvement is 18.935% in 8×8 and 20.983% in 10×10 respectively. That means when network becomes larger, gSA achieves much better improvement over RRCS.

The average delay, throughput and traffic distribution are shown in Fig. 4.14. It is clear that gSA improves over RRCS for both network sizes. For smaller network size, i.e., 8×8, the averaged delay, throughput and traffic distribution of virtual topologies achieved by RRCS are much closer to that of gSA. For larger network size, i.e., 10×10, gSA achieves much better improvement in all measurements. Thus we can conclude that, firstly, when network size scales, gSA achieves better improvement; secondly, we further validate the effectiveness of DF and CF because the level of improvement for these two metrics and real performance measurements are similar.

4.2.4.4 Experiment III

In this experiment, we evaluate the impact of different number of faulty cores and spare cores on gSA algorithm.

Firstly, we use 8×8 2D mesh with one column spare cores. We vary the number of faulty cores from 2 to 8 (i.e., D2, D4, D6 and D8). Faulty cores are randomly distributed, leading to various physical topologies. Results are averaged and shown in the first two figures in Fig. 4.15.

It is clear that when the number of defective cores increases, the performance of virtual topologies achieved by gSA slightly becomes worse in terms of both DF and CF. This is expected because the increase of faulty cores limits the solution space of the proposed algorithm.

Next, we assume there are always 2 randomly distributed faulty cores in 8×8 2D mesh and we vary the number of spare cores from 2 to 10 (i.e., S2, S4, S6, S8 and S10). As expected, the increase of spare cores also increases the solution space of the gSA algorithm, and both DF and CF slightly becomes better. However, when the number of spare cores is increased from 8 to 10, we find that DF almost remains the same while CF becomes much worse as in Fig. 4.15. This is because there are many

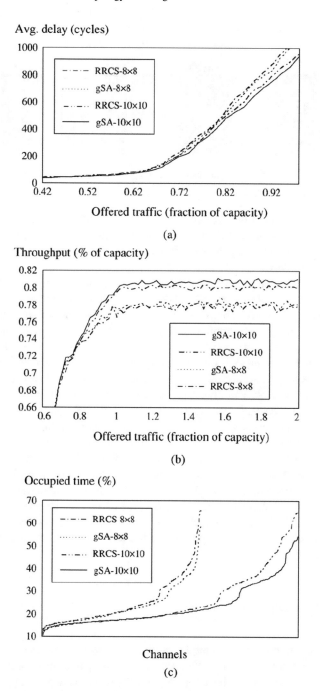

Fig. 4.14 Comparison between RRCS and *g*SA for different network size. (**a**) Average delay. (**b**) Throughput. (**c**) Traffic distribution

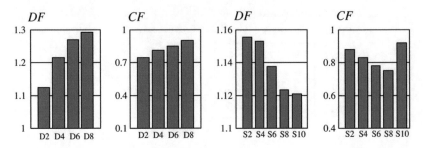

Fig. 4.15 The impact of different number of faulty cores and spare cores on gSA algorithm

cores and channels left unused on-chip, traffic distribution becomes much uneven. Therefore, we can conclude employing more-than-necessary number of spare cores does not facilitate to boost the NoC-based manycore systems' performance much after reconfiguration.

Effective defect tolerance techniques are essential to improve the yield of homogeneous manycore processors. We propose to employ core-level redundancy with AMAD scheme to address this issue. As defective cores change the topology of the target design, programmers may face various different topologies when optimizing their parallel programs. This is a big burden and may also cause confusion in marketing. We propose to address the above problem by providing a unified topology that is isomorphic with the target reference topology regardless of the various possible underlying physical topologies. We borrow the concept of virtual topology from network embedding problem and we propose two metrics to evaluate the performance of different virtual topologies. An effective heuristic, namely Row Rippling Column Stealing-guided Simulated Annealing algorithm is then presented to solve the topology reconfiguration problem. The proposed algorithm is evaluated on various topologies in a NoC-based manycore simulation platform. Experimental results not only show the effectiveness of the proposed gSA algorithm, but also show the effectiveness of the two evaluation metrics used in our algorithms, i.e., DF and CF. In our future work, we plan to investigate the topology reconfiguration problems for topologies other than mesh and torus (e.g., butterfly topology).

4.2.5 Discussion

Effective defect tolerance techniques are essential to improve the yield of homogeneous manycore processors. We propose to employ core-level redundancy with AMAD scheme to address this issue. As defective cores change the topology of the target design, programmers may face various different topologies when optimizing their parallel programs. This is a big burden and may also cause confusion in marketing. We propose to address the above problem by providing a unified topology that is isomorphic with the target reference topology regardless of the various possible underlying physical topologies. We borrow the concept of virtual topology from network embedding problem and we propose two metrics to evaluate the performance of different virtual topologies. An effective heuristic, namely Row Rippling Column Stealing-guided Simulated Annealing algorithm is then presented to solve the topology reconfiguration problem. The proposed algorithm is evaluated on various topologies in a NoC-based manycore simulation platform. Experimental results not only show the effectiveness of the proposed SA algorithm, but also show the effectiveness of the two evaluation metrics used in our algorithms, i.e., DF and CF.

In our future work, we plan to investigate the topology reconfiguration problems for topologies other than mesh and torus (e.g., butterfly topology).

4.3 NoC Fault Tolerance with Routing

Fault-tolerant routing is usually used to provide reliable on-chip communication for many-core processors. We focus on a special class of algorithms that do not use virtual channels. One of the major challenges is to keep the network deadlock free in the presence of faults, especially those locating on network edges. State-of-the-art solutions address this problem by either disabling all nodes of the faulty network edges or including all faults into one faulty block. Therefore, a large number of fault-free nodes will be sacrificed. To address this problem, the proposed ZoneDefense routing not only includes faults into convex faulty blocks but also spreads the faulty blocks' position information in corresponding columns. The nodes, which know the position of faulty blocks, form the defense zones. Therefore, packets can find the faulty blocks and route around them in advance. Exploiting the defense zones, the proposed ZoneDefense routing could tolerate many more faults with significantly reduced sacrificed fault-free nodes compared with the state-of-the-art algorithms. Furthermore, the ZoneDefense routing does not degrade the network performance in the absence of faults, and could get similar performance as its counterparts in the presence of faults.

4.3.1 Challenges of Fault-Tolerant NoC Routing

MANY-CORE processors usually utilize NoC to provide on-chip communication [21]. 2-D mesh topology is widely adopted since its planar structure facilitates the IC manufacturing. For example, TILE64 [4] and Godson-T [28] processors select an 8 × 8 mesh, and Intel Tera-scale prototype processor adopts an 8 × 10 mesh [88]. The performance of NoC depends heavily on the efficiency of routing algorithm, which is either deterministic or adaptive. Most many-core processors use deterministic routing, such as the X-Y routing, since it facilitates the design of efficient routers [4, 28, 88]. Unfortunately, X-Y routing is not fault-tolerant.

Faults can appear in cores, routers, and other components. Failed cores can be tolerated by redundancy [96], while failed routers are usually handled by fault-tolerant routing. One of the major challenges of designing fault-tolerant routing is to keep the network deadlock free. The wormhole switching technique and the absence of virtual channels make this problem more challenging. In addition, many-core processors usually use virtual networks to avoid protocol deadlock, where each virtual network is usually assigned with a separate virtual channel. Thus, no virtual channel could be used by the routing algorithm to avoid routing deadlock. From the routing algorithms' point of view, this kind of NoC is same with that does not have virtual channels.

In NoCs without virtual channels, turn models are usually used to avoid deadlock [14, 35, 39]. Chiu [14] has proved that a network is deadlock free if all rightmost columns are removed from the network. However, without rightmost columns, it is difficult to tolerate faults locating on the left network edge [40, 92, 97].

To address this problem, Glass and Ni [40], Wu [92], and Zhang et al. [97] have proposed their solutions. These solutions either tolerate only one fault [40] or disable a large number of fault-free nodes [92], [97]. One common feature of them is that packets do not know the faults until they are blocked. In our opinion, this is the major reason that causes the difficulties to keep the network deadlock free. Because packets should make a turn to route around faults. However, these turns are usually unexpected and make it difficult to avoid deadlock.

To address this problem, we propose to include faults into defense zones with which packets could find faults in advance. Based on the defense zones, we propose the ZoneDefense routing that can significantly improve the state-of-the art routing algorithms [40, 92, 97]in the following three aspects: (1) the number of sacrificed fault-free nodes, (2) the network reconfiguration time, and (3) the coverage of fault distributions.

4.3.2 Preliminaries of Fault-Tolerant Routing

4.3.2.1 2-D Meshes

As shown in Fig. 4.16, a 2-D mesh has $m \times n$ nodes, where m (resp., n) is the radix of dimension x (resp., y). Each node d has an address $d : (d_x, d_y)$, where $d_x \in 0, 1, 2, \ldots, m-1$ and $d_y \in 0, 1, 2, \ldots, n-1$. Two nodes $d : (d_x, d_y)$ and $e : (e_x, e_y)$ are connected in dimension x (resp., y) if and only if $|d_x - e_x| = 1|$ and $|d_y = e_y|$ (resp., $|d_y - e_y| = 1|$ and $d_x = e_x$). If two nodes are connected in dimension x (resp., y), they are connected by a bidirectional row (resp., column) channel. Each bidirectional row (resp., column) channel consists of two opposite physical channels: EW and WE (resp., NS and SN) channels. Particularly, EW (resp., WE, NS, and SN) channel is used to forward packet from east to west (resp.,

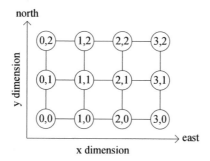

Fig. 4.16 Example of 4×3 mesh ($m = 4, n = 3$)

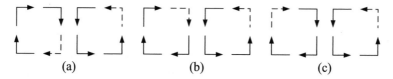

Fig. 4.17 Partially adaptive routing algorithms based on turn model. Forbidden turns are shown as dashed lines. (**a**) West-first. (**b**) Negative-first. (**c**) North-last

west to east, north to south, and south to north). Each $m \times n$ mesh has m columns and n rows. Each row (resp., column) consists of m (resp., n) nodes that has the same coordinate in dimension y (resp., x).

4.3.2.2   Turn Model

A packet moving toward direction A makes an AB turn if it turns to direction B, where $A, B \in E, W, N, S$ and E (resp., W, N, and S) refers to direction east (resp., west, north, and south). Note that most routing algorithms prohibit 180-degree turns. Thus, there are eight possible turns, which can form two abstract cycles, clockwise and counter-clockwise abstract cycles. The turn model avoids deadlock by prohibiting one turn in each abstract cycle [39]. Since there are four different turns in each abstract cycle, there are totally 16 different combinations to prohibit two turns. Of these 16 combinations, 12 combinations are legal and only three combinations are unique if rotation symmetry is considered. As shown in Fig. 4.17, they are named as west-first, negative-first, and north-last, resp.

4.3.2.3   Odd-Even Turn Model

The main idea of the odd-even turn model is preventing the formation of rightmost column segments of any circular waiting path [14]. As shown in Fig. 4.18, there are two kinds of rightmost column, clockwise column and counterclockwise column.

Fig. 4.18 Rightmost column
on the waiting path. (**a**)
Clockwise column. (**b**)
Counter-clockwise column

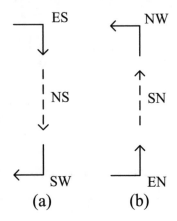

The clockwise rightmost column, as shown in Fig. 4.18a, consists of an ES turn, an SW turn, and several NS channels. To break the clockwise rightmost column, Chiu [14] proposed to prohibit ES turn in even columns and SW turn in odd columns. To break the counter-clockwise rightmost column, EN and NW turns are forbidden in even and odd columns, resp.

4.3.2.4 Fault Model

We adopt the convex block fault model [8], in which both node and link faults can be used. For example, a node fault can be modeled by declaring all links incident on it faulty, and a link fault can be used to model partial faults of routers. However, we only consider node fault for simplicity. Furthermore, we assume that faulty blocks do not share boundaries. If two faulty blocks share a boundary, a bigger faulty block covering the two original ones will be formed. Note that some new fault models, such as the MCC [8] and planar faulty blocks [47], were proposed to reduce the number of fault-free nodes sacrificed by block fault models. Since they are designed for 3-D (or higher dimensional) networks, we omit the detailed discussions.

Definition 3 A convex faulty block is a rectangular contiguous area that consists of danger nodes in 2-D meshes.

Definition 4 A node is danger if it is faulty or unsafe.

Definition 5 All fault-free nodes are safe initially, and a safe node changes to semi-safe if it has only one danger neighbor. Particularly, if the danger neighbor is in x-dimension (resp., y-dimension), it changes to semi-safe-x (resp., semisafe-y).

Definition 6 A safe or semi-safe node changes to unsafe if: (1) it has two danger neighbors, or (2) it has a danger neighbor in x-dimension (resp., y-dimension) and a semi-safe-y (resp., semi-safe-x) neighbor.

Fig. 4.19 Faulty blocks without shared boundary channels. Dark nodes represent faults and gray nodes indicate unsafe nodes

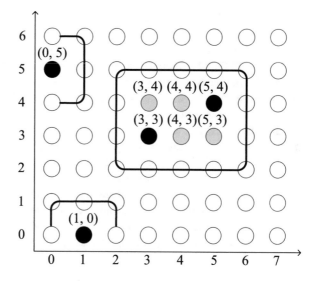

Definition 7 Faulty block's boundary consists of the safe nodes, which are horizontally, vertically, or diagonally adjacent to this block, and the links between these nodes. Particularly, nodes horizontally or vertically adjacent to the faulty block are called boundary nodes, and those diagonally adjacent are called corner nodes.

Definition 8 The boundary of a faulty block is called a fault ring if the nodes and links form a cycle; otherwise, it is called a fault chain.

Example 1 As shown in Fig. 4.19, an 8×7 mesh has four faults: $(1, 0)$, $(3, 3)$, $(5, 4)$, and $(0, 5)$. According to Definition 5, nodes $(4, 3)$ and $(4, 4)$ change to semi-safe-x, and nodes $(5, 3)$ and $(3, 4)$ change to semi-safe-y, in the first iteration. According to Definition 6, node $(4, 3)$ changes to unsafe in the second iteration because it has a danger neighbor $(3, 3)$ in x-dimension and a semi-safe-y neighbor $(5, 3)$. Meanwhile, nodes $(5, 3)$, $(3, 4)$, and $(4, 4)$ also change to unsafe according to Definition 6. Faulty blocks are formed in two iterations.

It is worthy to note that allowing faulty blocks to share boundaries could further reduce the number of sacrificed fault-free nodes. However, shared boundaries will significantly increase the routing complexity. The discussion about the tradeoffs between the number of sacrificed fault-free nodes and the routing complexity is left as the future work.

4.3.3   Defense Zones

According to [14], a network is deadlock free if all rightmost columns are removed. As shown in Fig. 4.18, ES, SW, EN, and NW turns are necessary to form rightmost columns. To distinguish them from others, they are called unexpected turns. Unfortunately, unexpected turns may be introduced if a packet hits the boundary of a faulty block. To avoid unexpected turns, we introduce the defense zones, so that packets could find the faulty block and route around it in advance.

The formation of defense zones is triggered by the detection of faults using such as build-in self-test techniques [58]. We utilize the dynamic fault model, but assume that no new fault occurs during a routing process like [92]. However, in practice, faults may occur at any time. To support dynamic faults, one can exploit more reliable flow control techniques, such as APCS [37] and the one proposed in [22]. These techniques are orthogonal with the proposed ZoneDefense routing, so we omit the detailed descriptions. Besides, faulty nodes are assumed to be nonmalicious, i.e., they do not send and receive packets.

Once a fault is detected, the formation of defense zones is logically divided into two steps: (1) construct faulty blocks with fault chains, and identify reference nodes in fault chains if necessary; (2) spread the position of faulty blocks in columns wherein they reside if necessary.

A. Step 1: Forming Faulty Blocks and Identifying Reference Nodes

We have shown the way to form convex faulty blocks in Sect. 4.3.2.4. These faulty blocks can be categorized into nine classes based on the types of network edges they touch as shown in Fig. 4.20. To route around faulty blocks, we utilize fault chains to encapsulate them. If a faulty block touches any one network edge, its boundary naturally forms a chain. Otherwise, we intentionally break the boundary at its northeast corner by forbidding the ES and NW turns as shown in Fig. 4.20e.

The fault chain is called a l-chain if the type of faulty block is FB-1, FB-4, or FB-7; otherwise, it is called a f-chain. For a l-chain, at least one of its two end points touches the left network edge. It is used to notify that there is no route on the west side of the faulty blocks. For f-chains, two reference nodes, left (L) and right (R) reference nodes, should be considered to make correct routing decisions. Furthermore, reference nodes could be real or pseudo. As shown in Fig. 4.20, left reference nodes are labeled L, and right reference nodes are labeled R. Real reference nodes are shown as solid circles, and pseudo reference nodes are shown as dashed circles. In fact, the proposed ZoneDefense routing only cares about the height (or the coordinate in y-dimension) of reference nodes. As for the real reference node, its height is propagated along the chain. As for pseudo reference node, the number of rows of the mesh is propagated.

The reference nodes are used to separate packets into two classes: the destination is lower, not lower than the reference node. This kind of information will be used by the ZoneDefense routing to route around faulty blocks without introducing forbidden turns. More specifically, left and right reference nodes are used to direct westward and eastward packets, resp. The pseudo reference nodes are used to indicate that all destinations are lower than the reference node as shown in Fig. 4.20b and c. As shown in Fig. 4.20e, the left reference node of FB-5 faulty blocks is also pseudo. Thus, all westward packets will be treated as if their destinations are lower than the left reference node, and routed along the clockwise direction without

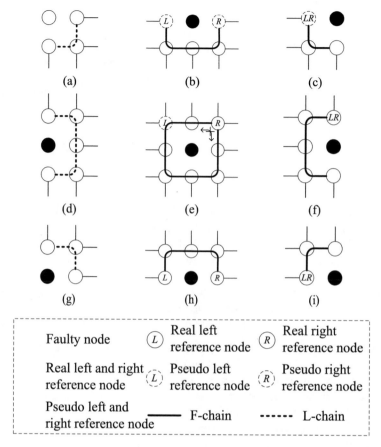

Fig. 4.20 Types of faulty blocks. (**a**) FB-1. (**b**) FB-2. (**c**) FB-3. (**d**) FB-4. (**e**) FB-5. (**f**) FB-6. (**g**) FB-7. (**h**) FB-8. (**i**)FB-9

introducing the forbidden NW turn at the northeast corner. Since we only care about the height of reference nodes, the real reference node could be any node in the same raw. For example, the left and right reference nodes of FB-6 faulty blocks, as shown in Fig. 4.20f, could also be the northwest corner.

B. Step 2: Forming Defense Zones

To avoid vertically hitting a faulty block's boundary, nodes above and below it should be notified with the position information of this block. To store that information, two registers are required, *ceiling* and *floor*, as shown in Fig. 4.21. In the rest of this section, we will discuss the two rules that are used to update the ceiling and floor registers.

Ceiling Rule the *ceiling* register of all safe nodes is initialized to n, where n is the number of rows of the $m \times n$ mesh. This means that there are no faulty blocks above that node. The value of *ceiling*.

Fig. 4.21 *Ceiling* and *floor*

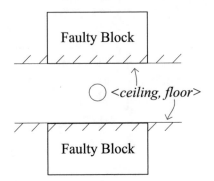

1. Changes to C_y, where C_y is the y-coordinate of current node, if it is the south boundary node of FB-5 and FB-6 faulty blocks;
2. Otherwise, changes to N_y, where N_y is the y-coordinate of the north neighbor, if the north neighbor is the northwest corner of FB-8 faulty blocks or the northeast corner of FB-5 faulty blocks;
3. Otherwise, changes to *ceiling_n*, where *ceiling_n* is the value of ceiling register of the north neighbor, if the north neighbor is NOT danger.

Floor Rule the *floor* register of all safe nodes is initialized to 0. The value of *floor:*

1. Changes to C_y, where C_y is the y-coordinate of current node, if it is the north boundary node of FB-5 and FB-6 faulty blocks;
2. Otherwise, changes to S_y, where S_y is the y-coordinate of the south neighbor, if the south neighbor is the southwest corner of FB-2 and FB-5 faulty blocks or the northeast corner of FB-5 faulty blocks;
3. Otherwise, changes to *floor_s*, where *floor_s* is the value of floor register of the south neighbor, if the south neighbor is NOT danger.

Based on the above two rules, the position information of all kinds of faulty blocks, which can introduce unexpected turns, are propagated to corresponding nodes. Thus, packets could utilize the position information to avoid introducing deadlock. For example, if a packet vertically hits the south boundary of FB-5 or FB-6 faulty blocks, an NW turn will be introduced. According to the first *ceiling rule*, south boundary nodes of FB-5 and FB-6 faulty blocks update their ceiling registers using their own y-coordinates. The value of ceiling is further propagated to south neighbors according to the third *ceiling rule*. By comparing the destination's y-coordinate with the ceiling, we can know that whether routing a packet to north will introduce an NW turn. If the answer is yes, we can route packet to west instead of north to avoid the unexpected NW turn. In the next section, we will discuss how does the proposed ZoneDefense routing algorithm route packets based on defense zones.

4.3.4 ZoneDefense Routing Algorithms

ZoneDefense routing (see Algorithm 2) routes packets according to the type of node currently the header flit resides in. If the header flit arrives at the destination, the packet is consumed. Otherwise, the header flit is first routed by the Default-Routing. After that, if the current node is on a fault chain, the output is redirected by two routing subfunctions: LChain-Routing and FChain-Routing.

Algorithm 2: ZoneDefense-Routing

Data: C : current node; D : destination node.
Result: *output*
1 **if** $C=D$ **then**
2 | Consume the packet;
3 **else**
4 | *output*=Default-Routing();
5 | **if** *Current node is shared by a l-chain and a f-chain* **then**
6 | **if** *output* $=$ *west* **then**
7 | | *output*=LChain-Routing();
8 | **else**
9 | | *output*=FChain-Routing();
10 | **end**
11 | **else if** *Current node is on a l-chain* **then**
12 | *output* $=$ LChain-Routing();
13 | **else if** *Current node is on a f-chain* **then**
14 | *output*=FChain-Routing();
15 | **end**
16 **end**

According to the Default-Routing (see Algorithm 3), the packet is routed to west if the destination is on the west to the current node. Otherwise, the Default-Routing tries to route packets following the $Y - X$ routing rules. However, if the destination is higher than *ceiling* or lower than *floor*, the packet should be first misrouted to west to avoid vertically hitting the faulty block boundaries. Otherwise, an NW or SW turn will be made.

If the current node is on a fault chain, the routing path assigned by Default-Routing may be blocked by faults. Thus, the output port should be redirected. More specifically, when the current node is the corner shared by a l-chain and a f-chain, the LChain-Routing (see Algorithm 4) will be used if the Default-Routing selects the west output. Otherwise, the FChain-Routing (see Algorithm 5) will be used. If the current node is not shared by fault chains or shared by two f-chains, the routing subfunction is selected based on the type of fault chain.

The LChain-Routing only cares about the packets that may cross the faulty block. For example, if the current node is on the north (resp., south) block boundary, it cares about the packets whose destination is lower (resp., higher) than the current node. In such cases, packets should be routed around the faulty block through the east output

---

Algorithm 3: Default-Routing

Data: C : Current node; D : destination node.
Result: $output$
1 **if** $C_x > D_x$ **then**
2 $\quad$ | $\quad$ $output = west$;
3 **else if** $C_x \neq 0$ and $(D_y > ceiling$ or $D_y < floor)$ **then**
4 $\quad$ | $\quad$ $output = west$;
5 **else if** $C_y < D_y$ **then**
6 $\quad$ | $\quad$ $output = north$;
7 **else if** $C_y > D_y$ **then**
8 $\quad$ | $\quad$ $output = south$;
9 **else**
10 $\quad$ | $\quad$ $output = east$;
11 **end**

Algorithm 4: LChain-Routing

Data: C : current node; D : destination node; $Default - Output$:output selected by
$\qquad$ Default-routing.
Result: $output$.
1 **if** C is on north boundary and $C_y > D_y$ **then**
2 $\quad$ | $\quad$ $output = east$;
3 **else if** C is on south boundary and $C_y < D_y$ **then**
4 $\quad$ | $\quad$ $output = east$;
5 **else if** C is on east boundary and $Default - Output == west$ **then**
6 $\quad$ | $\quad$ **if** $C_y < D_y$ **then**
7 $\quad$ | $\quad$ | $\quad$ $output = north$;
8 $\quad$ | $\quad$ **else**
9 $\quad$ | $\quad$ | $\quad$ $output = south$;
10 $\quad$ | $\quad$ **end**
11 **else if** C is the northeast corner and $Default - Output == west$ and $C_y > D_y$ **then**
12 $\quad$ | $\quad$ $output = south$;
13 **else if** C is the southeast corner and $Default - Output == west$ and $C_y < D_y$ **then**
14 $\quad$ | $\quad$ $output = north$;
15 **else**
16 $\quad$ | $\quad$ $output = Default - Output$;
17 **end**

---

port. Otherwise, if the current node is on the east block boundary, it cares about
the packets that are routed to west by the Default-Routing. In such cases, packets
are redirected to north if the destination is higher than the current node, and south
if the destination is lower than the current node. Furthermore, to avoid 180-degree
turns, northeast (resp., southeast) corner should redirect packets, which are routed
to west by the Default-Routing, to south (resp., north) if their destinations are lower
(resp., higher) than the current node. The LChain-Routing and the Default-Routing
coincide for all other cases.

FChain-Routing is used to route packets around faulty blocks without introducing the forbidden ES and NW turns on the northeast corners of FB-5 faulty blocks.

Algorithm 5: FChain-Routing

Data: C : current node; D : destination node; L : left reference node; R : right reference node; $Default - Output$: output selected by $Default - routing$.

Result: $output$.

1 **if** C is on east boundary and $Default - Output == west$ **then**
2   **if** $D_y \geq L_y$ **then**
3 | $output = north$;
4   **else**
5 | $output = south$;
6   **end**
7 **else if** C is on west boundary and $C_x < D_x$ **then**
8   **if** $D_y \geq R_y$ **then**
9   **if** $D_y > Ceiling$ **then**
10 | $output = north$;
11   **else**
12 | $output = north$;
13   **end**
14   **else**
15   **if** $D_y < floor$ **then**
16 | $output = west$;
17   **else**
18 | $output = south$;
19   **end**
20   **end**
21 **else if** C is on north boundary and $C_x < D_x$ and $C_y > D_y \geq R_y$ **then**
22 | $output = east$;
23 **else if** C is on south boundary and $C_x < D_x$ and $C_y < D_y < R_y$ **then**
24 | $output = east$;
25 **else if** C is the southwest corner and $Default - Output == north$ and $C_x < D_x$ and $D_y < R_y$ **then**
26 | $output = east$;
27 **else**
28 | $output = Default - Output$;
29 **end**

For example, if the current node is on the east block boundary, it cares about the packets that are routed to west by the Default-Routing. In such cases, the packets are redirected to south if their destinations are lower than the left reference node, and north if the destinations are not lower.

If the current node is on the west block boundary, it cares about the eastward packets, i.e., $D_x > C_x$. In such cases, if the destination is not lower than the right reference node, the packet is routed to north. Otherwise, it is routed to south. However, if the destination is higher than *ceiling* or lower than *floor*, the packet should be routed to west first. If the current node is on the north block boundary, it cares about the packets whose destination is on the southeast to the current node. In such cases, if the destination is not lower than the right reference node, the packet is routed to east. Otherwise, it is routed to west according to the Default-Routing. If the current node is on the south block boundary, it cares about the packets whose destination is on the northeast to the current node. In such cases, if the destination is lower than the right reference node, the packet is routed to east. Otherwise, it is routed to west according to the Default-Routing.

Furthermore, to avoid 180-degree turns, the southwest (resp., northwest) corner should redirect the north (resp., south) output, selected by Default-Routing, to east if the destination is on the east to current node and lower (resp., not lower) than the right reference node. The first case only happens on the southwest corners of FB-2 and FB-5 faulty blocks, and second case happens on the northwest corner of FB-8 faulty blocks.The FChain-Routing and the Default-Routing coincide for all other cases.

In the rest of this section, we use an example to show how does the proposed routing algorithm route packets in the presence of faults. As shown in Fig. 4.22a, there is an 11×11 mesh with 12 faulty nodes. To form faulty blocks, six fault-free nodes change to unsafe. Fault chain nodes update their status according to the information they get from neighbors. For example, node $(8, 6)$ finds a danger neighbor on the west to itself, so it changes to "east block boundary." Meanwhile, node $(7, 7)$ changes to "north block boundary." The status changes will be detected by node $(8, 7)$, which does not have danger neighbors. Thus, it will change to "northeast corner" in the next iteration. Since this faulty block does not touch any network edge, node $(8, 7)$ declares itself as the right reference node. This declaration will be noticed by nodes $(8, 6)$ and $(7, 7)$, which will update the value of their right reference node. After several iterations, the value of right reference node will be distributed to all nodes belonging to this fault chain. Meanwhile, these nodes also set the value of the pseudo left reference node to 11, i.e., the number of rows.

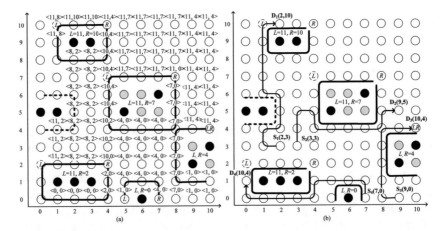

Fig. 4.22 Illustrative example. Dark, gray, and white nodes represent faulty, unsafe, and safe nodes, resp. Dashed bold lines represent l-chains, solid bold lines represent f-chains. The 2-tuple $<c, f>$ indicates the value of *ceiling* and *floor* registers. Nodes without labeled values have the unchanged initialized value $<11, 0>$. (a) Network status. (b) Routing example

Nodes above and below some kinds of faulty blocks should update their *floor* and *ceiling* registers, resp. For example, node $(6, 7)$ will set its floor register to 7 when it finds that it is on the north boundary of an FB-5 faulty block. The position of faulty blocks is distributed inside each column. We could find that node $(6, 1)$ does not update its *floor* register because we do not care about the position of faulty blocks touching north or south network edges.

Figure 4.22b shows four routing examples using the ZoneDefense routing. When we talk about the ceiling, floor, and two reference nodes, please refer to Fig. 4.22a for their values.

The first packet, $S_1(2, 3) \rightarrow D_1(2, 10)$, is routed to west by the Default-Routing because the destination is higher than the *ceiling*. The packet is further routed north to node $(1, 4)$, where the LChain-Routing will be used. Since the current node is on the south block boundary and the destination is higher than the current node, the packet is routed east to corner $(2, 4)$. Then, the packet is routed to north as the Default-Routing returns "west" and the destination is higher than the current node. At the northeast corner, the LChain-Routing agree with the Default-Routing because the northeast corner only cares about the packet whose destination is lower than itself. When the packet arrives at node $(1, 6)$, it is routed to north because the destination is on the northeast to the current node. When the packet arrives at node $(1, 8)$, the FChain-Routing will be used. The southwest corner of f-chain only cares about the packet whose destination is lower than the right reference node. Thus, the packet is routed to north according to the Default-Routing. At node $(1, 9)$, which is on the west block boundary, the packet is routed to north as the destination is higher than the right reference node. Until reaching the northwest corner, the packet is routed east to the destination. The routing paths of other packets are also shown in Fig. 4.22b, but we omit the detailed description due to the limited space.

4.3.5 Proof of Fault-Tolerant Routing

Dally and Seitz [19] have proved that a network is deadlock free if the corresponding channel dependence graph (CDG) is acyclic. Later, Chiu [14] has proved that an CDG is acyclic if all rightmost columns are broken in clockwise and counter-clockwise abstract cycles. Therefore, to prove the proposed ZoneDefense routing deadlock free, we will prove the corresponding CDG acyclic by showing that:

1. If faults do not appear on the left network edge, no rightmost column can be formed;
2. The rightmost columns introduced to tolerate faults on the left network edge do not form cycles.

Lemma 1 *ES turn only appears at the west boundary of FB-2 and FB-5 faulty blocks, as well as the northeast corners of the FB-4, FB-7, and FB-8 faulty blocks.*

Proof Assuming that the current node is node-c and a packet is routed from its west neighbor node-w. If node-c is at the west boundary of one FB-2 or FB-5 faulty block and the destination, node-d, is on the east of node-c, then the packet should be routed to south. Thus, an ES turn is introduced. Otherwise, if node-c is at the a northeast corner of one FB-4 or FB-7 or FB-8 faulty block and node-d is on the southeast of node-c, then the packet should be routed to south. Thus, an ES turn is introduced.

Now, we prove that ES turn cannot appear at other cases. We prove this by contradiction. If node-c is not at any faulty block boundary, then node-d should be on the southeast of node-c and node-w. Since packet is routed to east instead of south at node-w, node-w should be at the north boundary of a faulty block. Thus, node-c should be at the north boundary or northeast corner of that faulty block. Contradiction arises.

Otherwise, if node-c is on a faulty block boundary but at neither west boundary of FB-2 and FB-5 faulty blocks nor the northeast corner of the FB-4, FB-7, and FB-8 faulty blocks. To make an ES turn at node-c, the west and south neighbor of node-c should be safe. Thus, node-c should at one of the following positions: west and south boundary or northwest, southwest, and southeast corner of the faulty block. However, in any above cases, the packet should be routed to south instead of east at node-w. Contradiction arises.

Lemma 2 *EN turn only appears at the west boundary of FB-8 faulty blocks, as well as the southeast corners of the FB-1, FB-2, FB-4, and FB-5 faulty blocks; SW turn only appears at the southeast corners of FB-1, FB-2, FB-4, and FB-5 faulty blocks; NW turn only appears at the northeast corners of FB-4, FB-7, and FB-8 faulty blocks.*

Proof The proofs for EN, SW, and NW turns are similar with that for ES turn and are omitted.

Lemma 3 *The ES turn at the west boundary of FB-2 and FB-5 faulty blocks does not belong to any clockwise rightmost column.*

Proof According to the second floor rule, the southwest corner of FB-2 and FB-5 faulty blocks update their floor registers with their y-coordinates. Thus, the ES turn at the west boundary of FB-2 and FB-5 faulty blocks cannot connect with SW turns below the southwest corner. Furthermore, SW turn cannot appear at the west boundary of faulty blocks according to Lemma 2. Therefore, the rightmost column cannot be formed.

Lemma 4 *The ES turn at the northeast corner of FB-7 faulty block does not belong to any clockwise rightmost column.*

Proof Since SW turn cannot appear below the northeast corner of FB-7 faulty blocks, the clockwise rightmost column cannot be formed.

Lemma 5 *The EN turn at the west boundary of FB-8 faulty block does not belong to any counter-clockwise rightmost column.*

Proof According to the second ceiling rule, the northwest corner of the FB-8 faulty blocks update its ceiling register with its y-coordinate. Thus, the EN turn at the west boundary cannot connect with NW turns above the northwest corner. Furthermore, NW turn cannot appear at the west boundary of faulty blocks according to Lemma 2. Therefore, the counter-clockwise rightmost column cannot be formed.

Lemma 6 *The EN turn at the southeast corners of FB-1, FB-2, and FB-5 faulty blocks does not belong to any counterclockwise rightmost column.*

Proof Nodes above the southeast corners of FB-1 and FB-2 faulty blocks do not introduce NW turns, so that the EN turn at the southeast corners of FB-1 and FB-2 faulty blocks does not belong to any counter-clockwise rightmost column. Since the northeast corner of the FB-5 faulty block sets its ceiling register with its y-coordinate according to the second ceiling rule, the EN turn at the southeast corner of the FB-5 faulty block cannot connect with other NW turns. Therefore, it does not belong to any counter-clockwise rightmost column either.

Lemma 7 *The SW turn at the southeast corners of FB-1 and FB-2 faulty blocks does not belong to any clockwise rightmost column.*

Proof The clockwise rightmost column cannot be formed because the routers above the southeast corners of FB-1 and FB-2 faulty blocks cannot introduce ES turns.

Lemma 8 *The SW turn at the southeast corner of FB-5 faulty blocks does not belong to any clockwise rightmost column.*

Proof We prove this by contradiction. If a clockwise rightmost column is formed, there should be an ES turn above the southeast corner as well as it is connected with the SW turn. Since the northeast corner of FB-5 faulty blocks forbids the ES turn, this ES turn should be above the northeast corner. However, the northeast corner of FB-5 faulty blocks will cut off the connection between ES and SW turns because it sets floor register with its y-coordinate. Therefore, the SW turn at the southeast corner of FB-5 faulty blocks does not introduce rightmost columns.

Lemma 9 *The NW turn at the northeast corners of FB-7 and FB-8 faulty blocks does not belong to any counterclockwise rightmost column.*

Proof The counter-clockwise rightmost column cannot be formed because the routers below the northeast corners of FB-7 and FB-8 faulty blocks cannot introduce EN turns.

Lemma 10 *Clockwise rightmost column can be formed if and only if the ES and SW turns appear at the northeast and southeast corners of FB-4 faulty blocks, resp.*

Proof According to Lemmas 1 and 2, the ES and SW turns can appear at the northeast and southeast corners of the FB-4 faulty block, resp. Thus, the clockwise rightmost column can be formed with them.

Assuming a clockwise rightmost column is formed. According to Lemmas 3 and 4, the ES turn should be at the northeast corner of an FB-4 faulty block. According to Lemmas 7 and 8, the SW turn should be at the southeast corner of an FB-4 faulty block.

Lemma 11 *Counter-clockwise rightmost column can be formed if and only if the EN and NW turns appear at the southeast and northeast corners of FB-4 faulty blocks, resp.*

Proof According to Lemma 2, EN and NW turns can appear at the southeast and northeast corners of an FB-4 faulty block. Thus, the counter-clockwise rightmost column can be formed.

Assuming a counter-clockwise rightmost column is formed. According to Lemmas 5 and 6, the EN turn should be at the southeast corner of an FB-4 faulty block. According to Lemma 9, the NW turn should be at the northeast of an FB-4 faulty block.

Lemma 12 *Rightmost columns on the boundary of FB-4 faulty blocks cannot form cycles.*

Proof According to Lemmas 10 and 11, the rightmost columns always stick to the boundary of FB-4 faulty blocks. Furthermore, 180-degree turns are not allowed. Thus, cycles cannot be formed because there are no corresponding leftmost columns since FB-4 faulty blocks touch the left network edge.

Theorem 1 *ZoneDefense routing is deadlock free.*

Proof

1. If the network is fault free, the ZoneDefense routing only allows the WN, WS, NE, and SE turns. Thus, the CDG is acyclic.
2. Otherwise, if the network has faults:

    (a) If none of the faults locate on the left network edge, no rightmost columns can be formed according to Lemmas 10 and 11. Thus, the CDG is still acyclic.
    (b) Otherwise, if some faults locate on the left network edge, the rightmost columns, which are introduced to tolerate faults on the left network edge, never form cycles according to Lemma 12. Thus, the CDG is still acyclic.

To sum up, wherever the faults locate, the ZoneDefense routing is deadlock free according to Dally and Seitz's theory [19] since the CDG is always acyclic. With a nonminimal routing, packets may encounter livelock and move through the network without ever reaching their destination. In the following, we prove that the proposed ZoneDefense routing is livelock free.

Theorem 2 *ZoneDefense routing is livelock free.*

Proof In the absence of faults, ZoneDefense routing is minimal, and is thus livelock free. In the presence of faults, the ZoneDefense is minimal if the source and destination are not blocked by faults, and is thus livelock free. If they are blocked by faults, packets may be misrouted west or along the fault chains. Misrouting packets to west will be ended, if any one of the three conditions holds: (1) the destination is higher than current node and is lower than the ceiling, (2) the router is lower than current node and is higher than floor, or (3) the router is on the left network edge. Obviously, after misrouting west for finite hops, one of the three conditions will definitely holds true and terminates the misrouting phase. Misrouting along the fault chain will be ended, if the current router and the destination are on the same side of the faulty block. Furthermore, each faulty block introduces at most two (one for each kind) misrouting phases to a packet, and a packet encounters each faulty block at most once. Therefore, the packet will definitely reaches its destination after finite misrouting phases introduced by a finite number of faulty blocks. The network is thus livelock free.

4.3.6 Experiment Result Analysis

This section will compare the ZoneDefense routing with previous work proposed in the literatures [92, 97]. We select them as the baseline routing algorithms because they do not use virtual channels. Literature [40] is not compared since it only tolerates one fault. Literatures [34, 64, 76] are not compared because they require off-line analysis. Literatures [30, 31] are not compared since they use routing tables that cannot be compressed according to their routing algorithms.

4.3.6.1 Fault Model Comparison

The fault model is important since it determines the percentage of supported fault distributions, the number of sacrificed fault-free nodes, and the reconfiguration time (i.e., the time for a network to be stable after the detection of a fault). The proposed ZoneDefense routing adopts the defense zones to include faults, literature [92] utilizes multiple convex faulty blocks, and literature [97] utilizes only one convex faulty block. As for [92], if faults appear at network edges or the columns adjacent to left and right network edges, all nodes of corresponding network edges or columns will be disabled.

These simulations are first carried out in an 8×8 mesh, and then in a 16×16 mesh to show the scalability. The network is assumed to have at most 10% faulty nodes. According to [65], faulty nodes tend to be clustered instead of uniformly distributed. To generate clustered faults, we randomly select the first faulty node, and select the sequencing faulty nodes with extra 10% possibility to neighbors of previously selected faulty nodes. For the 8×8 mesh with one and two faults, there are 64 and 2016 different fault distributions, resp. In such cases, all fault distributions are simulated. If more than two faults are assumed, we randomly select 10,000 different fault distributions to save simulation time. For the 16×16 mesh, on the other hand, we only exhaust the 256 different one-fault distributions. If more than one fault is assumed, we also simulate 10,000 randomly selected fault distributions.

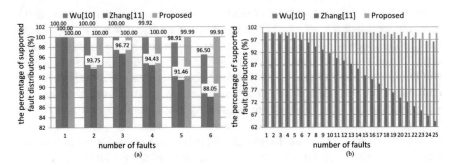

Fig. 4.23 Coverage of fault distributions. (**a**) 8×8 mesh. (**b**) 16×16 mesh

1. *Coverage of Fault Distributions:* We first report the coverage of fault distributions of simulated fault-tolerant routing algorithms. Specifically, if the formed faulty blocks divide the network into several unconnected parts, we say that the fault distribution is not supported by the ZoneDefense routing and the routing algorithm proposed in [97]. According to [92], network cannot be partitioned since faulty or unsafe nodes never locate on the new reconfigured network edges. However, all fault-free nodes may be disabled in worst cases. In such cases, we say that the fault distribution is not supported by the routing algorithm proposed in [92].

The simulation results are shown in Fig. 4.23, where the x-axis represents the number of faults inserted into the network, the y-axis indicates the percentage of supported fault distributions. Particularly, "Wu [92]" represents the routing algorithm proposed in [92], "Zhang et al. [97]" represents that proposed in [97], and "Proposed" represents the proposed ZoneDefense routing.

In the 8×8 mesh [see Fig. 4.23a], all routing algorithms can tolerate all one-fault distributions. If two or three faults are inserted, the ZoneDefense routing and [92] also can tolerate all distributions. However, [97] only tolerates 93.75 and 96.72% distributions, resp. In three-faults case, [97] got better result than that in two-faults case because (1) only 10,000 fault distributions are simulated in threefaults case, and (2) clustered faults are assumed. Actually, if all three-fault distributions are simulated, the results should be worse than that in two-faults case. As the number of faults increases, the percentage of supported fault distribution degrades for all routing algorithms. However, for the ZoneDefense routing, the degradation is negligible. For example, even with six faults, 99.93% fault distributions still can be tolerated. For [92], the degradation is moderate. For example, 96.5% distributions still can be tolerated with six faults. On the other hand, for [11, 97], the degradation is significant. For example, only 88.05% of the six-faults distributions can be tolerated.

When the network size increases, the relative performance of these algorithms do not change [see Fig. 4.23b]. However, the difference between [97] and other two algorithms becomes much larger. For example, only about 65% of the 25-faults distributions can be tolerated by Zhang et al. [97], but more than 97% and

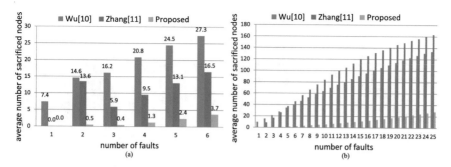

Fig. 4.24 Average number of sacrificed nodes. (**a**) 8 × 8 mesh. (**b**) 16 × 16 mesh

99% distributions can be tolerated by Wu [92] and the ZoneDefense routing, resp.

According to the above analysis, ZoneDefense routing and [92] get much better results than [97]. In the next simulation, we will find that although [92] can support most of the fault distributions as the ZoneDefense routing, [92] will sacrifice much more fault-free nodes.

2. *Number of Sacrificed Nodes:* To avoid deadlock, some fault-free nodes should be sacrificed. They may be included into faulty blocks or explicitly disabled, and are not allowed to send and receive packets. Thus, the associated core and caches also cannot be utilized by applications. This section will compare the number of nodes sacrificed by the ZoneDefense routing and previous work [92, 97].

The simulation setup is same with the simulation discussed in above section, and the results are shown in Fig. 4.24. For one fault in an 8 × 8 meshes [see Fig. 4.24a], the ZoneDefense routing and [97] do not sacrifice fault-free nodes. However, [92] will sacrifice 7.4 fault-free nodes in average. Because if the fault appears at network edges or the columns adjacent to left and right network edges, all nodes of the edge or column will be disabled. When the number of faults increases, the number of nodes sacrificed by Wu [92], Zhang et al. [97] significantly increases. For example, when six faults are assumed, [92] and [97] sacrifice 27.3 and 16.5 fault-free nodes in average, resp. On the other hand, the ZoneDefense routing only sacrifices 3.7 nodes in average. The number of [97] gets better results in three-faults case than in two-faults case due to the two same reasons discussed in above section.

When the network size increases, the absolute number of nodes sacrificed by all routing algorithms is increased as the average distance between faults increases. The ZoneDefense routing also gets better results than its two counterparts. For example, if 25 faults are assumed, the ZoneDefense routing sacrifices about 28 fault-free nodes. On the other hand, [92] and [97] sacrifice about 133 and 163 fault-free nodes, resp. The difference is huge. If fewer than five faults are assumed, [97] gets better results than [92]. Otherwise, [97] sacrifices more because a big-size faulty block is usually formed with the large number of faulty nodes.

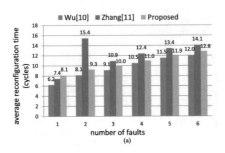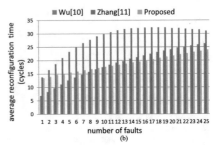

Fig. 4.25 Average reconfiguration time. (**a**) 8 × 8 mesh. (**b**) 16 × 16 mesh

According to the above two simulations, we could find that the ZoneDefense routing can support most fault distributions with a small number of sacrificed nodes. Although [92] also can support most fault distributions, the number of sacrificed fault-free nodes is huge. As for [97], large fractions of fault distributions cannot be tolerated as well as a large number of nodes are sacrificed.

3. *Reconfiguration Time:* The reconfiguration time or the convergence time is the time for the network to be stable after the faults are detected. In this simulation, we assume a static reconfiguration algorithm, such as the one proposed in [75], and omit the time for draining old packets by assuming that the network is empty when faults are detected.

The simulation setup is same with above two simulations, and the results are shown in Fig. 4.25. For 8 × 8 meshes [see Fig. 4.25a], these three routing algorithms get similar results. The ZoneDefense routing takes a longer time to be stable than [92] as it needs to spread faulty blocks' information in corresponding columns. The reason why [97] requires the longest time to be stable is that each node should check whether there is faulty or unsafe node in its row and column.

In 16 × 16 meshes [see Fig. 4.25b], the reconfiguration time increases as expected. Zhang et al. [97] also takes the longest time to be stable. The ZoneDefense routing takes a longer time than [92] if the number of faults is smaller than nine because ZoneDefense routing should spread faulty blocks' information in corresponding columns. Otherwise, [92] takes a longer time because the possibility of disabling a network edge or column increases.

4.3.6.2 Performance Analysis

In this simulation, we utilize a cycle-accurate NoC simulator, the BookSim [21], to carry out the simulations. BookSim provides a flexible way to configure NoC parameters, such as network topology and routing algorithm. By maintaining a global clock, BookSim could keep the simulation cycle accurate. In the following simulations, router pipeline depth is assumed as four and link traversal latency is one. The round-robin policy is adopted to select requesting inputs in switch allocation stage. Although we assume a canonical router architecture instead of the aggressive state-of-the-art ones, such as look ahead routing and speculation, it is fair for evaluating fault-tolerant routing algorithms. For each routing algorithm, we assume that there is one virtual channel per physical channel, and each virtual channel contains an FIFO with eight entries to hide the round-trip latency of flow-control credits.

In this simulation, we first assume the network topology is 8×8, and simulate the cases with one, three, and five faults. For the one-fault case, we simulate all 64 fault distributions and report the average results. For three-faults and five-faults cases, we simulate 100 randomly selected different fault distributions to save simulation time. To show the scalability of routing algorithms, we further do simulations in 16×16 meshes with one, eleven, and twenty one faults. For each case, we simulate 100 randomly selected different fault distributions to save simulation time.

Under uniform traffic pattern, a safe node can send packets to all other safe nodes with the same possibility. The simulation results are shown in Fig. 4.26, where the x-axis represents the injected traffic load, i.e., the number of flits injected to the network per cycle, and the y-axis shows the average packet latency.

In 8×8 meshes [see Fig. 4.26a], these three routing algorithms get similar performance. For example, all of them will be saturated if more than six flits are injected per cycle for one-fault case. The main reason is that the average packet latency is largely determined by the worst case performance, which often happens when the faults locating in the center of the network. Furthermore, the main difference between ZoneDefense routing and its two counterparts [92], [97] is the way they treat the faults on network edges. Therefore, they will get similar worst case performance. The packet latency in worst case is often much larger than that in other cases, so that the average packet latency is similar for these three routing algorithms.

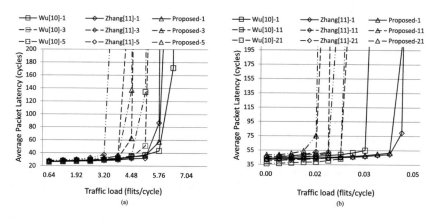

Fig. 4.26 Average packet latency under uniform traffic pattern. (**a**) 8×8 mesh. (**b**) 16×16 mesh

As the number of faults increases, the network performance degrades. For example, the network will be saturated if more than five flits are injected per cycle for three-faults case. For [92] and the ZoneDefense routing, more faults usually translate into more faulty blocks or defense zones. Thus, the possibility of congestion increases as the congestion often happens at the boundaries of faulty blocks and defense zones. For [97], more faults often translate into a bigger faulty block. Since the boundary of the faulty block gets longer, the possibility of congestion increases. Furthermore, as shown in Fig. 4.24, the number of sacrificed nodes increases as the number of faults increases. Thus, the number of left fault-free nodes is reduced, so that the congestion problem aggregates as the injection rate per node increases. If the number of faults increases further, the network performance does not degrade notably. For example, as for the ZoneDefense routing and [92], they get similar performance in three-faults and five-faults cases. Zhang et al. [97] gets moderate performance degradation when the number of faults increases from three to five. The main reason is also that the worst case fault distribution determines the average network performance.

In 16×16 meshes [see Fig. 4.26b], the ZoneDefense routing and [97] get similar network performance, which is much better than [92] in one-fault case. The reason is that [92] sacrifices about ten fault-free nodes in average as shown in Fig. 4.24b, so that the injection rate per node for [92] will be larger than other two algorithms. Therefore, [92] get saturated earlier than others. As the number of faults increases, [97] sacrifices more nodes than [92]. Therefore, [92] gets better performance than [97] as its injection rate per node is relatively low. As for the ZoneDefense routing, its performance is little lower than its two counterparts. The reason is that the ZoneDefense routing sacrifices much fewer nodes than [92], [97] by forming many small defense zones. As the number of defense zones increases, the possibility of congestion increases.

According to above simulations, we could find that the ZoneDefense routing could get similar network performance as its counterparts in 8×8 meshes regardless of the number of faults. When the network size increases, such as in 16×16 meshes, the ZoneDefense routing and [97] get better results than [92] at first. As the number of faults increases, the network performance of ZoneDefense routing degrades a little more than its counterparts. However, compared with [92, 97], the degradation of network performance is moderate.

4.3.6.3 Overhead Analysis

In the following of this section, we will analyze the area and timing overhead of the proposed ZoneDefense routing. The routers are assumed to have five input and output ports. Five virtual channels per physical channel are utilized to realize five virtual networks. Each virtual channel has eight buffers to temporally store flits whose size is assumed as 64-bits. The round-robin arbiter proposed in the literature [80] is used to implement virtual-channel and switch allocators. Note that we extend [97] to tolerate one faulty block. To this end, [97] adopts the same chain rules

Table 4.2 Area evaluation (two-input NAND gates)

	Wu [92]	Zhang et al. [97]	Proposed design compared with Wu [92] and Zhang et al. [97]
Router area	19,048	19,336	19,541(2.6%, 1.1%)
Tile area	173,165	175,788	177,651(0.3%, 0.1%)

as the ZoneDefense routing. The main differences between [97]-extended and the ZoneDefense routing are that (1) the "default routing" of [97] is the $X - Y$ routing, and (2) fault chains do not share boundaries in [97].

The router area, which is normalized to the number of two-input NAND gates, is shown in the first row of Table 4.2. According to the simulation results, the area overhead of the ZoneDefense routing compared with [92] and [97] (2.6 and 1.1%, resp.) is very small. According to the results reported by Intel in the literature [88], each router occupies about 11% of the tile area. Thus, the area overhead per tile (0.3 and 0.1%, resp.) is negligible as shown in the second row of Table 4.2.

The reconfiguration operations, such as forming defense zones in the ZoneDefense routing and forming faulty blocks in [92] and [97], do not add delay to the critical path of routers. Therefore, we only compare the routing delay of these three routing algorithms. The virtual-channel allocation stage is the critical stage of routers in our simulations. If the routing delay of [92], [97] (extended), and the ZoneDefense routing are normalized to the delay of the critical stage, the results are 0.83, 0.8, and 0.96, resp. Therefore, the ZoneDefense routing does not introduce timing overhead since the critical stage does not change.

4.3.7 Discussion

Based on the defense zone fault model, we proposed the ZoneDefense routing to reduce the large number of fault-free nodes sacrificed by state-of-the-art fault-tolerant routing algorithms. The ZoneDefense routing was theoretically proved to be deadlock and livelock free. With it, packets could find the faulty blocks in advance and route around them without introducing unexpected turns. Since the complexity of avoiding deadlock was reduced, the unexpected operations, such as including all faults into one faulty block or disabling all nodes of faulty network edges and columns, can be avoided. Extensive simulations showed that the number of sacrificed fault-free nodes is significantly reduced as well as the coverage of fault distributions and reconfiguration time is improved. Furthermore, the ZoneDefense routing does not degrade the network performance in the absence of faults and could get similar network performance as the previous work with negligible overhead. Taking all factors into consideration, we believed that the ZoneDefense routing is better than state-of-the-art fault-tolerant routing algorithms designed for NoCs without virtual channels.

4.4   NoC Fault Tolerance with Data Path Salvaging

In this section, we mainly investigate fault-tolerant NoC design at circuit layer and attempt to explore the inherent fault tolerance of NoC for the sake of less hardware overhead.

To help illustrate the proposed fault-tolerant design approach, we briefly introduce the basic structures of NoC first. NoC is mainly utilized as an scalable interconnection fabric to enable flexible communication among a large number of processing elements (PEs) which can be either processors or building blocks of an SoC. It typically consists of a set of homogeneous routers connected with links to support packet switch between PEs. Links are essentially relatively longer wires between neighboring routers and are supposed to be of similar length after placing and routing to ensure optimized NoC timing. Similar to router in Internet, router is the major component of NoC and is also responsible for data buffering and forwarding across the NoC-based chip.

A typical 2-stage pipelined wormhole router architecture as presented in Fig. 4.27 is taken an example. It mainly consists of pipeline registers, routing computing, buffers, virtual channel allocator (VA), switch allocator (SA), and crossbar. Pipeline registers are located between NoC pipeline stages to smooth the neighboring pipeline stages. Routing computing is essentially a small piece of control logic utilized to determine the right forwarding of each packet based on the predefined routing algorithm. Buffers are usually used as virtual channels of the router to store the packet before it is forwarded to the next router. Virtual channel allocator is also a piece of control logic, but it is utilized to determine where a packet should be stored in next router. When multiple packets from different input ports compete for the same output port, switch allocator will make the decision to balance between latency and fairness. Finally, crossbar is essentially a set of MUXes and enable data transfer from any input port to all the output ports. Although the control logic including virtual channel allocator and switch allocator is critical to the functionality of NoC,

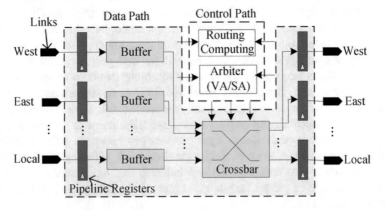

Fig. 4.27 Typical router architecture

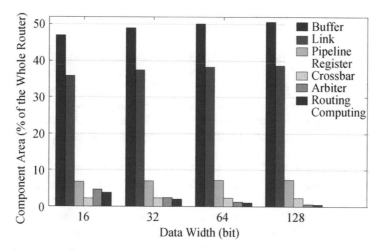

Fig. 4.28 NoC chip area breakup. It adopts 4 × 4 mesh topology, each input port includes only a single buffer and the input buffer size is 8-flit. It is synthesized with Synopsys Design Compiler using SMIC 45 nm technology and works at 200 MHz. Particularly, we have different data width setups ranging from 16bit to 128bit evaluated separately

it takes only a fraction of the entire chip area and includes much less transistors accordingly according to our chip area breakup analysis in Fig. 4.28. In this case, they can be protected with straightforward triple modular redundancy (TMR). In contrast, the data path including link, pipeline registers, buffers, and crossbar takes up the majority of the chip area, and the proportion of the data path chip area further increases with the data width. In this case, straightforward TMR can incur at least 100% area overhead, which is prohibitively expensive.

Inspired by prior works that seek to protect NoC links with channel serialization [30, 41, 44], we take the entire NoC data paths into considerations and explore the inherent fault tolerance of the data paths. The basic idea is to split the data paths into identical lanes and further leverage a set of serial-parallel converters to enable data transmission with only part of fault-free lanes. Typically, we may have to disable the entire data path even when a single bit of the data path is corrupted by hardware faults. Suppose we split a data path into 4 lanes. Now, it remains functional unless all the four lanes are corrupted at the same time, of which the probability is much lower. We have this fine-grain data path salvaging approach applied to all the pipeline stages of NoC and the proposed fault-tolerant design is called RevivePath. Although it does not guarantee 100% fault-free to hardware faults, it is generally orthogonal to high-level fault-tolerant approaches such as fault-tolerant routing and dynamic topology reconfiguration [21, 34, 64, 93]. Hence, it can be potentially combined with prior fault-tolerant design approaches to further enhance NoC reliability.

4.4.1 Fault-Tolerant Router Architecture

According to the analysis in Sect. 4.4, RevivePath proposed in this work has the router control path that is critical to the NoC functionality yet takes up only a fraction of chip area protected with classical TMR, while it mainly explores the inherent fault tolerance of router data path to achieve high reliability with less chip area overhead. Since the implementation of the TMR based protection for control path is trivial, we mainly focus on the fault-tolerant design of router data path in the rest of this sub section.

The overview of RevivePath is presented in Fig. 4.29. Basically, it has the regular data paths including links, buffers, and the crossbar divided into multiple identical slices based on data width. Since the data path slices are generally identical and independent, they can potentially be utilized to backup each other with additional switching support. To that end, we have a pair of serial-parallel converter and parallel-serial converter inserted at both ends of a pipeline stage to enable the replacement between the data path slices. When there are fault slices in a piece of router data path, we can leverage the converters to continue with the data transmission across the pipeline stage with only the fault-free slices. From the perspective of a pipeline stage, it essentially works in a degraded manner in presence of hardware faults and avoids corruption of the NoC connectivity. This approach can be applied to all the different router data path pipelines. Specifically, a 64-bit link can be viewed as four 16-bit link slices, a 64-bit FIFO can be viewed as four 16-bit FIFO slices, a 64-bit Mux which is the basic block of crossbar can also be divided into four 16-bit Mux slices. Details of the data path salvaging implementation will be illustrated in the following sub section.

Since hardware faults on a specific data path pipeline stage may vary substantially, data path salvaging structure as shown in Fig. 4.30 must be reconfigurable to suit all the possible fault configurations. Essentially, it merges the upstream data from fault-free slices to obtain data with normal data width and stores it in

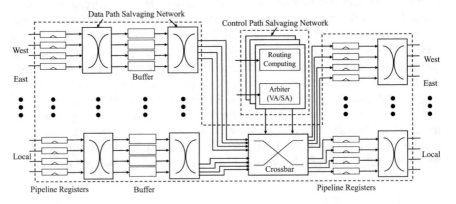

Fig. 4.29 General architecture of RevivePath

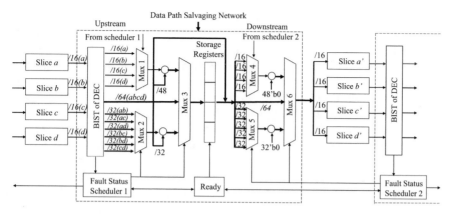

Fig. 4.30 Data path salvaging structure

the pipeline register. Then, it splits the data in pipeline register to fit the fault-free downstream data path slices. For different fault configurations on the data path pipeline stages, a fault status scheduler is utilized to conduct the data stream reorganization i.e. data stream splitting and merging. When the number of fault-free upstream data slices differs from that of the downstream data path slices, a status register is utilized for the flow control to bridge the throughput gap of the neighboring pipeline stages. The status register will be set to be invalid before an entire data is ready, and the downstream stream data path pipeline stage will be stalled. In addition, when the data path pipeline stage is an on-chip buffer, buffer can be utilized for the data reorganization and the pipeline registers are not required in this case. Moreover, since the pipeline registers will induce additional latency, we have a bypass data path added to avoid the additional latency when there are no hardware faults in the neighboring pipeline stages. Note that the data path slices shown in this figure is not limited to links and can be applied to all the NoC data path pipeline stages including links, crossbar and on-chip buffers. As for the locations of the hardware errors, existing fault diagnosis techniques such as BIST [2, 30] and detection error codes (DEC) can be employed at either off-line or on-line environments. When the fault locations of the NoC data path slices are obtained, they will be stored in registers in the fault status scheduler and utilized to reconfigure the corresponding data path.

4.4.2   Data Path Salvaging Implementation

As illustrated in Fig. 4.30, the data path salvaging structure mainly consists of fault status schedulers and MUX-based data path reconfiguration networks, which are utilized to bridge the pipeline stages with different fault configurations. For the upstream pipeline stages, fault-free data path slices will be selected based on the fault status which can be set after fault detection. Suppose the upstream data path is split into four slices. When there are i fault-free slices, it takes the data path salvaging structure $4/i$ cycles to construct an entire data in the pipeline register in general. However, when $i = 3$, it makes the data reorganization controlling rather complex and we only use two of them to simplify the hardware implementation. In this case, each data path pipeline stage has only three possible accumulated data path slice setups eventually i.e. one fault-free data path slice, two fault-free data path slices, and four fault-free data path slices. To fit the three different data transmission throughput, we have Mux 1 and Mux 2 utilized to extract one fault-free data slice and two fault-free data slices respectively from the faulty upstream data path pipeline stage. For a single fault-free data slice, there are four different possible configurations, so Mux 1 has four inputs accordingly. For two fault-free data slices, there are six possible configurations and Mux 2 has six inputs accordingly. When all the four data slices are fault-free, the data obtained from upstream data path pipeline stage will be passed directly to the next pipeline stage with a bypass data path as shown in Fig. 4.30. Mux 3 has three inputs to select from the three different types of fault configurations. Similar to the fault-free data slice selection from upstream data path pipeline stage, three Muxes including Mux 4, Mux 5, and Mux 6 are utilized in the downstream data path pipeline stage to distribute an entire data through the downstream fault-free data path slices accordingly. To ensure there is always an intact data stored in the pipeline register or storage register, we have a fault status scheduler to ensure the data flows correctly from upstream pipeline stage to downstream pipeline stage despite the fault configurations. When all the four data path slices are corrupted by hardware errors, the corresponding pipeline stage can be stalled by simply setting the status register to be invalid. Fortunately, the probability of a single data path pipeline stage failure is low because of the much smaller chip area and the small number of involved transistors. While the data path pipeline stage fails only when all the four data path pipeline slices fail at the same time, the reliability of the NoC data paths is improved significantly compared to the original design. Essentially, the proposed data path salvaging structure takes advantage of the inherent fault tolerance of the NoC data paths and can be potentially applied to other similar computing-centric architectures for higher reliability under severe hardware faults.

To further illustrate the proposed data path salvaging strategy, we take a specific fault configuration as an example. Suppose slice a shown in Fig. 4.30 is faulty, fault vector [0111] will be set in fault status scheduler 1 after fault detection. Since it is difficult to schedule three fault-free data slices to construct an intact data, we only use two of the fault-free data slices instead. In this case, the data path denoted as $32(cd)$ in Mux 2 is selected. It takes the data path salvaging structure two cycles to construct a 64bit data. Then, it has the data stored in the storage register. Afterwards, the ready flag is set valid and can be distributed to fault-free data path slices in the next pipeline stage.

When there are hardware faults in the upstream data path slices, we have to assemble an intact data with only the fault-free data path slices, which usually takes multiple cycles. Particularly, it starts only when the storage register is invalid.

Fig. 4.31 Temporal-spacial distribution example of intermittent style and pipeline style under different fault configurations. (**a**) Intermittent style. (**b**) Pipeline style

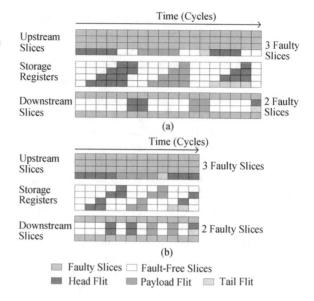

When the entire data is assembled and put in the storage register, the ready flag register is set valid at the same time. Similarly, the downstream data path starts only when there is an intact data in storage register and the ready flag is set to be valid. The ready flag will be set to be invalid when the entire data is transmitted across the downstream data path. Basically, upstream data path works until an intact data is obtained. The downstream data path has to wait during this period. When an intact data is ready, downstream data path starts to work until the entire data is transmitted, while upstream data path is idle during this period. Both upstream and downstream data paths function intermittently, so we denote this transmission style as "Intermittent Transmission". The temporal-spacial distribution example of intermittent transmission style is shown in Fig. 4.31a. There are three faulty slices in upstream data path and it takes the data path salvaging structure 4 cycles to assemble an intact data. As there are two fault-free data path slices in the downstream pipeline stage, it takes the data path salvaging structure two cycles to complete the data transmission. Eventually, it takes the intermittent transmission style 18 cycles to complete an entire packet transmission with 3 flits. Although the intermittent transmission style is convenient to implement, it is not efficient because both the upstream and downstream data paths have quite some idle time slots.

In order to address this problem, we propose a more compact pipelined transmission style. Unlike the intermittent transmission style, it relaxes the operation condition of both the upstream and downstream data paths. Specifically, it allows the upstream data path to store data slices into the storage register as long as there are available slots. Similarly, it allows the downstream data path to access the storage register as long as there are sufficient data slices. Thereby, it squeezes the pipeline bubbles and reduces the idle time of the pipeline stages. As shown in Fig. 4.31b, the pipeline transmission style consumes only 12 cycles to complete the transmission of a packet, which outperforms the intermittent transmission style by 33.33% in theory.

Despite the performance advantage of the pipelined transmission, it may fail on head flit transmission because routing computing in the router usually requires an entire head flit. Otherwise, the following pipeline stages have to be stalled. In this case, we may utilize the intermittent data transmission in this specific scenario. In addition, we notice that the pipeline stages are actually dependent and the number of fault-free data slices in different pipeline stages can affect the performance of the router substantially. Suppose that the fault-free slice number from input links of router A to the input buffer in router B (link, buffer, crossbar, link) are denoted as s_1, s_2, s_3, s_4 respectively. When $s_2 \leq s_1$, NoC link provides more data slices than the number of fault-free buffer slices per cycle and the link has to wait for the release signal of the pipeline register between the link and the buffer. Moreover, the capacity of the buffer also differs from that of a fault-free buffer and affects the flow control accordingly. Even though data from the link can be stored in the buffer faster when the fault-free links are fully utilized, it will not enhance the NoC performance as the buffer gets full easily due to the reduced buffer capacity and stalls the data transmission eventually. When $s_4 \leq s_3$, similar problem can be observed. In this case, we modify v_1, v_2, v_3, v_4 to make sure $v_1 \leq v_2$, $v_3 \leq v_4$, which avoids the hardware modification of the flow control to adapt to the different fault configurations without performance penalty.

4.4.3 Experiment Result Analysis

4.4.3.1 Area Overhead

In order to obtain the chip area of the proposed fault-tolerant router design with data path salvaging, we have the proposed router synthesized with Synopsys Design Compiler at SMIC 60 nm technology. All the implementations of the routers work at 200 MHz. The data width of each flit is 64-bit, and the buffer in each input port can accommodate 8 flits. To obtain optimized fault-tolerant designs, we have the proposed data path salvaging mechanism combined with other classical fault-tolerant mechanisms including redundancy and detection error code. Specifically, we have pipeline registers protected with ECC and the control logic including routing computing, switch allocator, and virtual channel allocator protected with TMR. The major data paths such as link, buffer, and crossbar are protected with the proposed data path salvaging mechanism. To evaluate the proposed data path salvaging mechanism comprehensively, we have different parameters implemented in this experiment. They are denoted as follows. Our-4 (data path salvaging router with four slices), Our-2 (data path salvaging router with two slices), Our-M (data path salvaging router with mixed number of slices), i.e., the buffer and link adopt four slices, while the crossbar chooses two slices, and Our-D (data path salvaging router discarding crossbar protection), i.e., the buffer and link are still divided into four slices while the crossbar is not protected. Routers with all the different parameters are synthesized using the same setups.

Our experiment results reveal that the four fault-tolerant implementations with different configurations induce 65.4%, 26.5%, 52.46%, and 45.9% chip area relative to the baseline router respectively. If we remove the data path salvaging overhead of the links, the corresponding area overhead are 45.9%, 20.0%, 33.1%, and 26.5% respectively. In general, the proposed data path salvaging mechanism essentially explores the inherent fault-tolerance in data paths and consumes much less chip area compared to conventional redundancy based approaches which takes up at least 100% chip area overhead. Nevertheless, more data path slicing can induce substantial chip area overhead. Specifically, we notice that the chip area overhead of an 4-slice implementation is 2.46× higher than that of a 2-slice implementation. Hence, mixed slicing strategy can be beneficial considering that more fine-grained slicing may not always induce significant reliability improvement due to the rapidly increasing data path salvaging overhead. The reliability evaluation will be discussed in detail in the rest of this subsection.

Figure 4.32 presents the chip area overhead of TMR (3-modular redundancy), MRR (most reliable router) [18], LOR (least overhead router) [18], Vicis [30] and the proposed designs. Vicis has fault detection overhead included which costs additional 10% area, so we removed this part from the chip area overhead of Vicis to ensure a fair comparison. As TMR, MRR, LOR, and Vicis do not have the link protection included, we have the overhead of link protection removed from this work. According to the comparison in Fig. 4.32, we notice that TMR and MRR that employ the basic redundancy-based approaches generally induce much higher overhead. In contrast, LOR, Vicis, and the proposed implementations mainly explore the inherent redundancy within NoCs usually induce much less area overhead ranging from 20% to 50%.

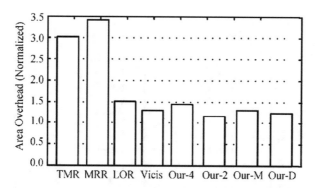

Fig. 4.32 Additional chip area overhead of fault-tolerant routers with different fault-tolerant design parameters

4.4.3.2 Reliability

To evaluate reliability of the fault-tolerant NoC designs, Constantinides et. al. [18] defined a new metric called SPF (Silicon Protection Factor), which is the average number of faults that a router can tolerate before malfunction normalized to the fault-tolerant design induced chip area overhead. We obtain SPF of the different designs with the following procedure. First, assume hardware faults are randomly distributed across the whole chip and we have random faults proportional to the chip area injected to different NoC components including buffer, control logic, and crossbar. When a hardware fault falls on certain router component and the fault can be tolerated, we can continue the fault injection until a hardware fault corrupts the fault-tolerant router design under evaluation. Since the number of hardware faults that corrupt the router can vary based on the fault locations, we repeat the above procedure 100,000 times and the average number is regarded as the average number of faults that a router can tolerate.

   According to our experiments, the average number of faults that can be tolerated by Our-4, Our-2, Our-M, and Our-D are 16.80, 6.18, 17.51, and 11.84 respectively. Accordingly, SPF of Our-4, Our-2, Our-M, and Our-D is 11.52, 5.15, 13.17, and 9.36 respectively. The SPF comparison among the different fault-tolerant router designs are presented in Fig. 4.33. It can be observed that SPF of the proposed designs are generally much higher. Straightforward TMR shows the lowest SPF despite the high hardware overhead. In contrast, MRR shows much higher SPF with similar hardware overhead, which demonstrates TMR strategies are of vital importance to the reliability of fault-tolerant routers. As the chip area is also closely related with fabrication cost, the fabrication cost of MRR can be prohibitively expensive, which hinders its use in practice. Unlike prior works, Our-M with mixed protection scheme achieves the highest SPF and consumes moderate hardware overhead. Our-2 has relatively low SPF, but it consumes the least chip area. As

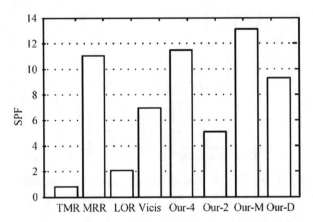

Fig. 4.33 Silicon protection factor (SPF) comparison of the different fault-tolerant router design approaches

for Our-4, it achieves more hardware overhead but lower SPF compared to Our-M. Basically, it indicates that more slices are not necessarily better for the proposed data path salvaging strategy. Specifically, the crossbar in the mesh NoC is relatively small and it can induce more chip area overhead when it is split into four slices. While crossbar also fails if the data path salvaging induced Muxes fail, it indicates that we are essentially protecting crossbar with a more fragile circuits. Hence, Our-4 shows lower SPF than Our-M which splits the crossbar into only two slices. The situation can be different when the data path salvaging approach is applied to a high-dimension NoC with much larger crossbar area.

To gain insight into the proposed data path salvaging strategy, we also evaluate the reliability of an entire NoC and take a 8×8 torus with symmetrical topology as an example. Any router component failure or output link failure is considered as a node failure. In addition, the fault-tolerant design induced circuit failure is also considered to be node failure. Finally, we take the number of functional routers as a reliability factor in this experiment. As shown in Fig. 4.34, the total number of functional routing nodes degrades smoothly with the increasing hardware faults. When the total number of hardware faults goes up to 1300, more than half of the routers still functions. When the number of hardware faults is no more than 300, 95% of the nodes are available. 70% of the nodes survive when the number of hardware faults goes up to 1000.

Figure 4.35 further illustrates NoC component fault status under different number of hardware faults. When the number of hardware faults reaches 500, 95% of the components remain functional. Even when the number of faults doubles, 90% of the NoC components survive. However, we notice that 96% of the data path components are functional but only 86% of the control logic blocks are functional when the number of faults is around 1300. It indicates that the control blocks becomes the NoC reliability bottleneck. Although we may apply fine-grained redundancy protection to the control blocks, Mux and Demux that are used for the redundancy

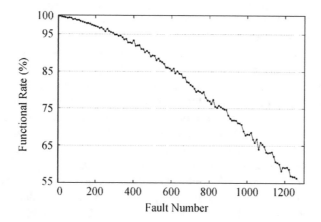

Fig. 4.34 Percentage of the available routers in a 8×8 torus NoC

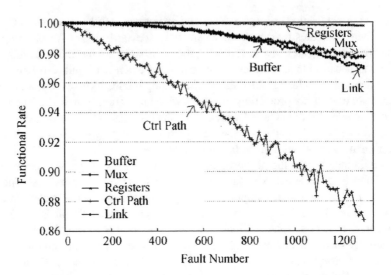

Fig. 4.35 Percentage of available NoC components in a 8 × 8 torus NoC

selection can also be exposed to hardware faults. The chip area of these redundancy logic can increases rapidly with the growing number of block I/O signals, which limits the benefit of fine-grained TMR protection and even poses negative influence on the reliability of the overall design eventually.

4.4.3.3 Performance

To evaluate the influence of the proposed data path salvaging approach on NoC performance, we implemented a cycle-accurate simulator in SystemC with 4 × 4 2D mesh topology with wormhole routing. XY routing is employed and each input port has an 8-flit buffer. Each node of the NoC generates packets with Poisson process and destinations of the packets are selected randomly. Each node has 100K packets injected to the network. The simulation has 20K-cycle warm-up before the performance evaluation. We have different number of hardware faults injected to links and buffers. NoC performance subjected to the different fault configurations is shown in Fig. 4.36. It reveals that NoC performance degrades gracefully with increasing hardware faults thanks to the proposed data path salvaging. As mentioned in the fault-tolerant router design, data paths with a faulty slice and two faulty slices are equivalent in terms of performance. In addition, faults in upstream pipeline stages can affect the utilization of neighboring downstream pipeline stages. For instance, buffer faults lead to disabling of the downstream links and crossbar. Hence, it indicates that performance of six faulty buffers can be equivalent to that with more faulty components including 6–12 buffer faults, 0–12 links faults, and 0–12 crossbar faults. Similarly, performance of six faulty links is equivalent to that of more combined hardware faults including 6–12 link faults and 0–12 crossbar

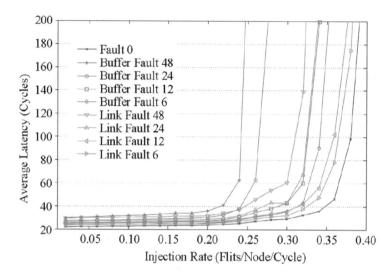

Fig. 4.36 Average network latency under various fault scenarios

faults. Basically, the NoC performance presented in the experiment also covers configurations with a variety of different faulty components.

4.4.4 Discussion

We exploited NoC inherent redundancy by splitting large NoC components of data path into slices, each of which is able to maintain the function of the whole component in presence of partial failures using TDM. For tiny logic with comparatively low fault probability, conventional redundancy or ECC is employed. Evaluation result shows that the proposed design provides several configurations with high reliability and low overhead. The area overhead varies from 26.5% to 65.4% and SPF scales from 5.15 to 13.17. When the network suffers medium fault rate, 90% nodes in 8 × 8 torus keep fully functional. Even if the network is exposed to higher fault rate, about 55% nodes survive, and more than 86% NoC components work well, which promises a much larger number of available nodes with conventional fault-tolerant routing. The simulation also indicates that the NoC performance degrades gracefully when fault rate rises dramatically.

4.5   Summary

Network-on-Chip (NoC) with excellent scalability and high bandwidth has been considered to be the most promising communication architecture for complex integration systems. A single node failure in NoC might destroy the network connectivity and corrupt the entire system. Introducing redundancies is an efficient method to construct a resilient communication path. However, redundancy solutions usually incur expensive hardware overhead. This chapter, we proposed three optimization methodologies from architecture design, routing, and circuits to improve the reliability of NoCs.

We propose a unified topology that is isomorphic with the target reference topology regardless of the various possible underlying physical topologies. We borrow the concept of virtual topology from network embedding problem and we propose two metrics to evaluate the performance of different virtual topologies. An effective heuristic, namely Row Rippling Column Stealing-guided Simulated Annealing algorithm is then presented to solve the topology reconfiguration problem. The proposed algorithm is evaluated on various topologies in a NoC-based manycore simulation platform. Experimental results not only show the effectiveness of the proposed SA algorithm, but also show the effectiveness of the two evaluation metrics used in our algorithms, i.e., DF and CF.

From the perspective of routing, we proposed the ZoneDefense routing to reduce the large number of fault-free nodes sacrificed by state-of-the-art fault-tolerant routing algorithms. Extensive simulations showed that the number of sacrificed fault-free nodes is significantly reduced as well as the coverage of fault distributions and reconfiguration time is improved. Furthermore, the ZoneDefense routing does not degrade the network performance in the absence of faults and could get the similar network performance as the previous work with negligible overhead.

As for the circuit-level fault tolerance, we mainly exploited NoC inherent redundancy by splitting large NoC components of data path into slices, each of which is able to maintain the functionality of the whole component in presence of partial failures using TDM. For small control blocks with lower fault probability, conventional redundancy and ECC protection is applied. Our evaluation results show that the proposed data path salvaging approach achieves high reliability with much lower hardware overhead compared to conventional redundancy based approaches under various fault configurations.

References

1. Anant Agarwal and Markus Levy. The kill rule for multicore. In *Proceedings of the 44th annual Design Automation Conference*, pages 750–753, 2007.
2. Armin Alaghi, Naghmeh Karimi, Mahshid Sedghi, and Zainalabedin Navabi. Online noc switch fault detection and diagnosis using a high level fault model. In *22nd IEEE International Symposium on Defect and Fault-Tolerance in VLSI Systems (DFT 2007)*, pages 21–29, 2007.

3. N Bauch and Erik Maehle. Reconfiguration in octagonal mesh-based multicomputer systems with distributed checkpointing. In *Proceedings of IEEE Workshop on Fault-Tolerant Parallel and Distributed Systems*, pages 169–180, 1996.
4. Shane Bell, Bruce Edwards, John Amann, Rich Conlin, Kevin Joyce, Vince Leung, John MacKay, Mike Reif, Liewei Bao, John Brown, et al. Tile64-processor: A 64-core soc with mesh interconnect. In *2008 IEEE International Solid-State Circuits Conference-Digest of Technical Papers*, pages 88–598, 2008.
5. Luca Benini and Giovanni De Micheli. Networks on chips: A new soc paradigm. *computer*, 35(1):70–78, 2002.
6. Dilip K Bhavsar. An algorithm for row-column self-repair of rams and its implementation in the alpha 21264. In *International Test Conference 1999. Proceedings (IEEE Cat. No. 99CH37034)*, pages 311–318, 1999.
7. Andreas Bölte and Ulrich Wilhelm Thonemann. Optimizing simulated annealing schedules with genetic programming. *European Journal of Operational Research*, 92(2):402–416, 1996.
8. Rajendra V Boppana and Suresh Chalasani. Fault-tolerant routing with non-adaptive wormhole algorithms in mesh networks. In *Proceedings of the 1994 ACM/IEEE Conference on Supercomputing, Supercomputing '94*, pages 693–702, 1994.
9. S. Borkar. Designing reliable systems from unreliable components: the challenges of transistor variability and degradation. *IEEE MICRO*, 25(6):10–16, 2005.
10. Shekhar Borkar. Thousand core chips: a technology perspective. In *Proceedings of the 44th Annual Design Automation Conference*, pages 746–749. ACM, 2007.
11. Shekhar Borkar et al. Microarchitecture and design challenges for gigascale integration. In *MICRO*, volume 37, pages 3–3, 2004.
12. Rainer E Burkard and Franz Rendl. A thermodynamically motivated simulation procedure for combinatorial optimization problems. *European Journal of Operational Research*, 17(2):169–174, 1984.
13. Yung-Yuan Chen, Shambhu J. Upadhyaya, and Ching-Hwa Cheng. A comprehensive reconfiguration scheme for fault-tolerant vlsi/wsi array processors. *IEEE transactions on computers*, 46(12):1363–1371, 1997.
14. Ge-Ming Chiu. The odd-even turn model for adaptive routing. *IEEE Transactions on parallel and distributed systems*, 11(7):729–738, 2000.
15. Bin Cong, Lin Cong, and SQ Zheng. Lower bounds of network embedding dilations. In *Proceedings of 36th Midwest Symposium on Circuits and Systems*, pages 558–561, 1993.
16. David T Connolly. An improved annealing scheme for the qap. *European Journal of Operational Research*, 46(1):93–100, 1990.
17. Cristian Constantinescu. Trends and challenges in vlsi circuit reliability. *IEEE micro*, 23(4):14–19, 2003.
18. Kypros Constantinides, Stephen Plaza, Jason Blome, Bin Zhang, Valeria Bertacco, Scott Mahlke, Todd Austin, and Michael Orshansky. Bulletproof: A defect-tolerant cmp switch architecture. In *The Twelfth International Symposium on High-Performance Computer Architecture, 2006.*, pages 5–16, 2006.
19. Dally and Seitz. Deadlock-free message routing in multiprocessor interconnection networks. *IEEE Transactions on Computers*, C-36(5):547–553, 1987.
20. William J Dally and Brian Towles. Route packets, not wires: on-chip inteconnection networks. In *Proceedings of the 38th annual design automation conference*, pages 684–689, 2001.
21. William James Dally and Brian Patrick Towles. *Principles and practices of interconnection networks*. Morgan Kaufmann, 2004.
22. Binh Vien Dao, Jose Duato, and Sudhakar Yalamanchili. Dynamically configurable message flow control for fault-tolerant routing. *IEEE Transactions on Parallel and Distributed Systems*, 10(1):7–22, 1999.
23. G. De Micheli, L. Benini, D. Bertozzi, I. Cidon, K. Goossens, K. Kim, K. Lee, S.J. Lee, S. Murali, and H.J. Yoo. *Networks on Chips: Technology and Tools*. ISSN. Elsevier Science, 2006.

24. Giovanni De Micheli. Networks on chips. In *Design, Automation, and Test in Europe*, pages 105–110, 2008.
25. Diego Doval and Donal O'Mahony. Overlay networks: A scalable alternative for p2p. *IEEE Internet computing*, 7(4):79–82, 2003.
26. Xiaogang Du, Sudhakar M Reddy, Wu-Tung Cheng, Joseph Rayhawk, and Nilanjan Mukherjee. At-speed built-in self-repair analyzer for embedded word-oriented memories. In *17th International Conference on VLSI Design. Proceedings.*, pages 895–900, 2004.
27. Tudor Dumitras and Radu Marculescu. On-chip stochastic communication [soc applications]. In *2003 Design, Automation and Test in Europe Conference and Exhibition*, pages 790–795, 2003.
28. Dong-Rui Fan, Nan Yuan, Jun-Chao Zhang, Yong-Bin Zhou, Wei Lin, Feng-Long Song, Xiao-Chun Ye, He Huang, Lei Yu, Guo-Ping Long, et al. Godson-t: An efficient many-core architecture for parallel program executions. *Journal of Computer Science and Technology*, 24(6):1061–1073, 2009.
29. Chaochao Feng, Zhonghai Lu, Axel Jantsch, Minxuan Zhang, and Zuocheng Xing. Addressing transient and permanent faults in noc with efficient fault-tolerant deflection router. *IEEE Transactions on Very Large Scale Integration (VLSI) Systems*, 21(6):1053–1066, 2012.
30. David Fick, Andrew DeOrio, Gregory Chen, Valeria Bertacco, Dennis Sylvester, and David Blaauw. A highly resilient routing algorithm for fault-tolerant nocs. In *2009 Design, Automation & Test in Europe Conference & Exhibition*, pages 21–26, 2009.
31. David Fick, Andrew DeOrio, Jin Hu, Valeria Bertacco, David Blaauw, and Dennis Sylvester. Vicis: A reliable network for unreliable silicon. In *Proceedings of the 46th Annual Design Automation Conference*, pages 812–817, 2009.
32. Jose Flich, Samuel Rodrigo, and José Duato. An efficient implementation of distributed routing algorithms for nocs. In *Second ACM/ieee international symposium on networks-on-chip (NOCs 2008)*, pages 87–96, 2008.
33. Message Passing Interface Forum. Mpi: A message-passing interface standard, version 2.2. *International Journal of Supercomputer Applications*, 8:1–586, 2008.
34. Binzhang Fu, Yinhe Han, Huawei Li, and Xiaowei Li. A new multiple-round dimension-order routing for networks-on-chip. *IEICE TRANSACTIONS on Information and Systems*, 94(4):809–821, 2011.
35. Binzhang Fu, Yinhe Han, Jun Ma, Huawei Li, and Xiaowei Li. An abacus turn model for time/space-efficient reconfigurable routing. In *Proceedings of the 38th annual international symposium on Computer architecture*, pages 259–270, 2011.
36. Masaru Fukushi, Yusuke Fukushima, and Susumu Horiguchi. A genetic approach for the reconfiguration of degradable processor arrays. In *20th IEEE International Symposium on Defect and Fault Tolerance in VLSI Systems (DFT'05)*, pages 63–71, 2005.
37. Patrick T Gaughan, Binh Vien Dao, Sudhakar Yalamanchili, and David E Schimmel. Distributed, deadlock-free routing in faulty, pipelined, direct interconnection networks. *IEEE Transactions on Computers*, 45(6):651–665, 1996.
38. David Geer. Chip makers turn to multicore processors. *Computer*, 38(5):11–13, 2005.
39. Christopher J Glass and Lionel M Ni. The turn model for adaptive routing. In *Proceedings of the 19th annual international symposium on Computer architecture*, pages 278–287, 1992.
40. Christopher J Glass and Lionel M Ni. Fault-tolerant wormhole routing in meshes. In *The Twenty-Third International Symposium on Fault-Tolerant Computing, FTCS-23*, pages 240–249, 1993.
41. Maria Engracia Gomez, Nils Agne Nordbotten, Jose Flich, Pedro Lopez, Antonio Robles, Jose Duato, Tor Skeie, and Olav Lysne. A routing methodology for achieving fault tolerance in direct networks. *IEEE transactions on Computers*, 55(4):400–415, 2006.
42. Anoop Gupta, Andrew Tucker, and Shigeru Urushibara. The impact of operating system scheduling policies and synchronization methods of performance of parallel applications. In *Proceedings of the 1991 ACM SIGMETRICS conference on Measurement and modeling of computer systems*, pages 120–132, 1991.

43. Juris Hartmanis. Computers and intractability: a guide to the theory of np-completeness (michael r. garey and david s. johnson). *Siam Review*, 24(1):90, 1982.
44. C-T Ho and Larry Stockmeyer. A new approach to fault-tolerant wormhole routing for mesh-connected parallel computers. *IEEE Transactions on Computers*, 53(4):427–438, 2004.
45. Chih-Tsun Huang, Chi-Feng Wu, Jin-Fu Li, and Cheng-Wen Wu. Built-in redundancy analysis for memory yield improvement. *IEEE transactions on Reliability*, 52(4):386–399, 2003.
46. Ajai Jain, Babu Mandava, Janusz Rajski, and Nicolas C Rumin. A fault-tolerant array processor designed for testability and self-reconfiguration. *IEEE journal of solid-state circuits*, 26(5):778–788, 1991.
47. Zhen Jiang, Jie Wu, and Dajin Wang. A new fault-information model for adaptive & minimal routing in 3-d meshes. *IEEE Transactions on Reliability*, 57(1):149–162, 2008.
48. Wu Jigang and Thambipillai Srikanthan. An improved reconfiguration algorithm for degradable vlsi/wsi arrays. *Journal of Systems Architecture*, 49(1–2):23–31, 2003.
49. Tomoya Kawagoe, Jun Ohtani, Mitsutaka Niiro, Tukasa Ooishi, Mitsuhiro Hamada, and Hideto Hidaka. A built-in self-repair analyzer (cresta) for embedded drams. In *Proceedings International Test Conference 2000 (IEEE Cat. No. 00CH37159)*, pages 567–574, 2000.
50. Jung Hwan Kim and Phill K. Rhee. The rule-based approach to reconfiguration of 2-d processor arrays. *IEEE transactions on computers*, 42(11):1403–1408, 1993.
51. Sook-Yeon Kim and Jeen Hur. An approach for torus embedding. In *Proceedings of the 1999 ICPP Workshops on Collaboration and Mobile Computing (CMC'99). Group Communications (IWGC). Internet'99 (IWI'99). Industrial Applications on Network Computing (INDAP). Multime*, pages 301–306, 1999.
52. Israel Koren. Should yield be a design objective? In *Proceedings IEEE 2000 First International Symposium on Quality Electronic Design (Cat. No. PR00525)*, pages 115–120, 2000.
53. Israel Koren and Zahava Koren. Defect tolerance in vlsi circuits: techniques and yield analysis. *Proceedings of the IEEE*, 86(9):1819–1838, 1998.
54. Israel Koren and Dhiraj K Pradhan. Yield and performance enhancement through redundancy in vlsi and wsi multiprocessor systems. *Proceedings of the IEEE*, 74(5):699–711, 1986.
55. S-Y Kung, S-N Jean, and C-W Chang. Fault-tolerant array processors using single-track switches. *IEEE Transactions on Computers*, 38(4):501–514, 1989.
56. Sy-Yen Kuo and W Kent Fuchs. Efficient spare allocation for reconfigurable arrays. *IEEE Design & Test of Computers*, 4(1):24–31, 1987.
57. Intel Labs. *From a Few Cores to Many : A Tera-scale Computing Research Overview (white paper)*. Intel, 2006.
58. Xiaowei Li, Cheung Paul YS, et al. A loop-based apparatus for at-speed self-testing. *Journal of Computer Science and Technology*, 16(3):278–285, 2001.
59. Cheng Liu, Lei Zhang, Yinhe Han, and Xiaowei Li. Vertical interconnects squeezing in symmetric 3d mesh network-on-chip. In *16th Asia and South Pacific Design Automation Conference (ASP-DAC 2011)*, pages 357–362. IEEE, 2011.
60. Fangai Liu and Liancheng Xu. The topological properties and network embedding of rp (k). In *Sixth International Conference on Parallel and Distributed Computing Applications and Technologies (PDCAT'05)*, pages 21–25, 2005.
61. Chor Ping Low. An Efficient Reconfiguration Algorithm for Degradable VLSI/WSI Arrays. *IEEE Transactions on Computers*, 49(6):553–559, 2000.
62. Shyue-Kung Lu, Yu-Chen Tsai, C-H Hsu, Kuo-Hua Wang, and Cheng-Wen Wu. Efficient built-in redundancy analysis for embedded memories with 2-d redundancy. *IEEE Transactions on Very Large Scale Integration (VLSI) Systems*, 14(1):34–42, 2006.
63. Samy Makar, Tony Altinis, Niteen Patkar, and Janet Wu. Testing of vega2, a chip multi-processor with spare processors. In *2007 IEEE International Test Conference*, pages 1–10, 2007.
64. Andres Mejia, Jose Flich, Jose Duato, S-A Reinemo, and Tor Skeie. Segment-based routing: An efficient fault-tolerant routing algorithm for meshes and tori. In *Proceedings. 20th International Parallel and Distributed Processing Symposium*, page 84, 2006.

65. Fred J. Meyer and Dhiraj K. Pradhan. Modeling defect spatial distribution. *IEEE Transactions on Computers*, 38(4):538–546, 1989.
66. Ed Microsoft. Application software considerations for numa-based systems, March 2007.
67. Alfonsas Misevičius. A modified simulated annealing algorithm for the quadratic assignment problem. *Informatica*, 14(4):497–514, 2003.
68. Sangman Moh, Chansu Yu, Hee Yong Youn, Ben Lee, and Dongsoo Han. Mapping strategies for switch-based cluster systems of irregular topology. In *Proceedings. Eighth International Conference on Parallel and Distributed Systems. ICPADS 2001*, pages 733–740, 2001.
69. Thomas Moscibroda and Onur Mutlu. A case for bufferless routing in on-chip networks. In *Proceedings of the 36th annual international symposium on Computer architecture*, pages 196–207, 2009.
70. Sung-Jui Pan and Kwang-Ting Cheng. A framework for system reliability analysis considering both system error tolerance and component test quality. In *2007 Design, Automation & Test in Europe Conference & Exhibition*, pages 1–6, 2007.
71. Ishwar Parulkar, Thomas Ziaja, Rajesh Pendurkar, Anand D'Souza, and Amitava Majumdar. A scalable, low cost design-for-test architecture for ultrasparc/spl trade/chip multi-processors. In *Proceedings. International Test Conference*, pages 726–735, 2002.
72. David A Patterson and John L Hennessy. *Computer publisher and design ARM edition: the hardware software interface*. Morgan kaufmann, March 2016.
73. Matthew Pirretti, Greg M Link, Richard R Brooks, Narayanan Vijaykrishnan, Mahmut Kandemir, and Mary Jane Irwin. Fault tolerant algorithms for network-on-chip interconnect. In *IEEE computer society annual symposium on VLSI*, pages 46–51, 2004.
74. Valentin Puente, Cruz Izu, Ramón Beivide, José A Gregorio, Fernando Vallejo, and Jose M Prellezo. The adaptive bubble router. *Journal of Parallel and Distributed Computing*, 61(9):1180–1208, 2001.
75. Thomas L. Rodeheffer and Michael D. Schroeder. Automatic reconfiguration in autonet. In *Proceedings of the Thirteenth ACM Symposium on Operating Systems Principles*, pages 183–197, 1991.
76. Samuel Rodrigo, Jose Flich, Antoni Roca, Simone Medardoni, Davide Bertozzi, J Camacho, Federico Silla, and Jose Duato. Addressing manufacturing challenges with cost-efficient fault tolerant routing. In *2010 Fourth ACM/IEEE International Symposium on Networks-on-Chip*, pages 25–32, 2010.
77. Sartaj Sahni and Teofilo Gonzalez. P-complete approximation problems. *Journal of the ACM (JACM)*, 23(3):555–565, 1976.
78. Ethan Schuchman and TN Vijaykumar. Rescue: A microarchitecture for testability and defect tolerance. In *32nd International Symposium on Computer Architecture (ISCA'05)*, pages 160–171, 2005.
79. S. Scott and G. Thorson. The cray t3e network: adaptive routing in a high performance 3d torus. *HOT Interconnects IV*, pages 1–10, August 1996.
80. Eung S Shin, Vincent J Mooney III, and George F Riley. Round-robin arbiter design and generation. In *Proceedings of the 15th international symposium on System Synthesis*, pages 243–248, 2002.
81. Premkishore Shivakumar, Stephen W Keckler, Charles R Moore, and Doug Burger. Exploiting microarchitectural redundancy for defect tolerance. In *Proceedings 21st international conference on computer design*, pages 481–488, 2003.
82. Jared C Smolens, Brian T Gold, Jangwoo Kim, Babak Falsafi, James C Hoe, and Andreas G Nowatzyk. Fingerprinting: Bounding soft-error detection latency and bandwidth. *ACM SIGOPS Operating Systems Review*, 38(5):224–234, 2004.
83. Ed Sperling. Turn down the heat... please, July 2006. url =http://www.edn.com/turn-down-the-heat-please/.
84. William Stallings. *Operating systems: internals and design principles, 7th Edition*. Pearson, 2012.
85. Leon Steinberg. The backboard wiring problem: A placement algorithm. *Siam Review*, 3(1):37–50, 1961.

86. PJ Tan, Tung Le, Keng-Hian Ng, Prasad Mantri, and James Westfall. Testing of ultrasparc t1 microprocessor and its challenges. In *2006 IEEE International Test Conference*, pages 1–10, 2006.
87. Wen-Chung Tsai, Kuo-Chih Chu, Yu-Hen Hu, and Sao-Jie Chen. A scalable and fault-tolerant network routing scheme for many-core and multi-chip systems. *Journal of Parallel and Distributed Computing*, 72(11):1433–1441, 2012.
88. Sriram R Vangal, Jason Howard, Gregory Ruhl, Saurabh Dighe, Howard Wilson, James Tschanz, David Finan, Arvind Singh, Tiju Jacob, Shailendra Jain, et al. An 80-tile sub-100-w teraflops processor in 65-nm cmos. *IEEE Journal of solid-state circuits*, 43(1):29–41, 2008.
89. Theodora A. Varvarigou, Vwani P. Roychowdhury, and Thomas Kailath. Reconfiguring processor arrays using multiple-track models: The 3-track-1-spare-approach. *IEEE transactions on computers*, 42(11):1281–1293, 1993.
90. Laung-Terng Wang, Cheng-Wen Wu, and Xiaoqing Wen. *VLSI test principles and architectures: design for testability*. Elsevier, 2006.
91. Chris Weaver and Todd Austin. A fault tolerant approach to microprocessor design. In *2001 International Conference on Dependable Systems and Networks*, pages 411–420. IEEE, 2001.
92. Jie Wu. A fault-tolerant and deadlock-free routing protocol in 2d meshes based on odd-even turn model. *IEEE Transactions on Computers*, 52(9):1154–1169, 2003.
93. Dong Xiang and Wei Luo. An efficient adaptive deadlock-free routing algorithm for torus networks. *IEEE Transactions on Parallel and Distributed Systems*, 23(5):800–808, 2011.
94. Dong Xiang, Yueli Zhang, and Yi Pan. Practical deadlock-free fault-tolerant routing in meshes based on the planar network fault model. *IEEE Transactions on Computers*, 58(5):620–633, 2008.
95. Lei Zhang, Yinhe Han, Huawei Li, and Xiaowe Li. Fault tolerance mechanism in chip many-core processors. *Tsinghua Science and Technology*, 12(S1):169–174, 2007.
96. Lei Zhang, Yinhe Han, Qiang Xu, Xiao wei Li, and Huawei Li. On topology reconfiguration for defect-tolerant noc-based homogeneous manycore systems. *IEEE Transactions on Very Large Scale Integration (VLSI) Systems*, 17(9):1173–1186, 2009.
97. Zhen Zhang, Alain Greiner, and Sami Taktak. A reconfigurable routing algorithm for a fault-tolerant 2d-mesh network-on-chip. In *2008 45th ACM/IEEE Design Automation Conference*, pages 441–446, 2008.

Chapter 5
Fault-Tolerant Deep Learning Processors

Abstract Hardware faults on the regular 2-D computing array of a typical deep learning accelerator (DLA) can lead to dramatic prediction accuracy loss. Prior redundancy design approaches typically have each homogeneous redundant processing element (PE) to mitigate faulty PEs for a limited region of the 2-D computing array rather than the entire computing array to avoid the excessive hardware overhead. However, they fail to recover the computing array when the number of faulty PEs in any region exceeds the number of redundant PEs in the same region. The mismatch problem deteriorates when the fault injection rate rises and the faults are unevenly distributed. To address the problem, we propose a hybrid computing architecture (HyCA) for fault-tolerant DLAs. It has a set of dot-production processing units (DPPUs) to recompute all the operations that are mapped to the faulty PEs despite the faulty PE locations. HyCA shows significantly higher reliability, scalability, and performance with less chip area penalty when compared to the conventional redundancy approaches. To further optimize the reliability of DLA, we focus on improve the reliability of Resistive Random Access Memory (ReRAM), which has become a promising Computing-in-Memory (CiM) technology for DLA. For ReRAM-based DNN accelerator designs, the occurrence of the permanent and soft faults in the ReRAM has become one of the major concerns. To address these problems, we firstly analyze the reliability issues of ReRAM-based DLAs. Then based on these analysis, we propose RRAMedy, a novel framework to protect ReRAM chips from both permanent faults and soft faults. Our experimental results show that RRAMedy has high probability of fault detection and can recover the recognized accuracy with little performance degradation.

5.1 Introduction to Fault-Tolerant Deep Learning

The great success of deep learning motivates the deployment of deep learning in numerous domains of applications. Many of the applications such as autonomous driving and drones [18, 62], and intelligent medical monitoring and treatment [17] are closely related to the safety of human beings and are mission-critical. When deep learning models are applied in these applications, the reliability of the execution is

© The Author(s), under exclusive license to Springer Nature Singapore Pte Ltd. 2023 243
X. Li et al., *Built-in Fault-Tolerant Computing Paradigm for Resilient Large-Scale Chip Design*, https://doi.org/10.1007/978-981-19-8551-5_5

of vital importance and must be considered comprehensively [4, 26]. Otherwise, the unexpected inference predictions may lead to catastrophic consequences [25]. While the deep learning models are increasingly implemented on customized deep learning accelerators (DLAs) for the sake of both higher performance and energy efficiency [9], the reliability of the model execution dramatically depends on the underlying accelerators [52, 68]. At the same time, DLAs fabricated with continuously shrinking semiconductor technologies are more likely to suffer manufacture defects and become more sensitive to the working conditions such as the large temperature variation than before [14], which may cause hardware faults and incur considerable prediction accuracy loss. Thereby, resilient DLAs are indispensable for reliable inference and are highly demanded by the mission-critical AI applications [45].

Deep neural networks (DNNs) have shown extremely promising performance in solving complex machine learning problems and numerous DNN accelerator architectures have been studied [10, 54] for both higher performance and energy efficiency. Particularly, ReRAM that embraces the benefits of near-zero standby power, non-volatility [66] and in-situ dot product computation capability, has become a promising CiM technology for deep learning. Many ReRAM-based DNN accelerators like PRIME [10], ISAAC [54] have been proposed and demonstrated the great advantages on energy efficiency.

However, ReRAM cells typically suffer severe permanent faults and soft faults due to the immature nano-scale fabrication technology and the intrinsic nature of memristors, which will permanently or temporarily change the states of the ReRAM cells and cause erroneous computing behaviors [61]. Specifically, the permanent faults that have the memristors permanently stuck at high/low resistance mainly arise from the manufacturing defects or limited endurance of ReRAM, while the soft faults are usually caused by imperfect operations, state-drifts, and parameter deviations, due to the imperfect fabrication or wear-out mechanism [57]. Unlike the hard faults that cannot be reprogrammed, soft faults can be refreshed back to normal values, but they are subtle to detect and can also lead to dramatic accuracy degradation according to [61]. In summary, the occurrence of the permanent and soft faults in the ReRAM has become one of the major concerns for ReRAM-based DNN accelerator designs.

5.1.1 Deep Learning Processor Basis

5.1.1.1 Typical 2D-Array Based Deep Learning Accelerator

A typical DLA with 2D computing array is shown in Fig. 5.1. The computing array is composed of multiple homogeneous connected PEs. Each PE includes a multiplier and an accumulator. It only communicates with its four neighbors. Neural network operations such as convolution can be mapped to the computing array and executed in lock-step manner. To ensure a high-throughput neural network processing, the

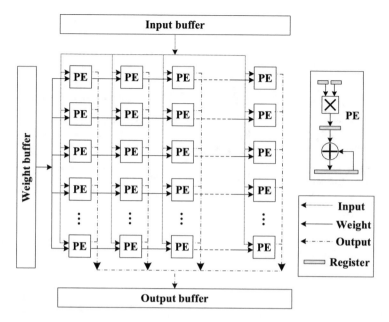

Fig. 5.1 A typical DLA with 2D computing array architecture

input features, weights and output features must be stored in the on-chip buffers to avoid external memory access stalls. In this work, we adopt a widely used output stationary dataflow for the neural network execution [8]. The accumulation of each output feature stays stationary in a PE. The partial sum are stored in the same register file for accumulation to minimize the accumulation cost. In summary, each PE is responsible for the calculation of a single output feature and PEs in the same column calculate different output features in the same output channel. With the compact dataflow, the 2-D computing array can be fully utilized given limited on-chip buffer bandwidth provision when the neural network models are deployed on it.

5.1.1.2 ReRAM-Based DNN Computing

Deep neural network (DNN) is a machine learning architecture which is composed of a series of computational layers and can be represented as a parametric function F:

$$F(x) = f_L(W_L, f_{L-1}(W_{L-1} \ldots (f_0(W_0, x)))) \tag{5.1}$$

wherein x represents the input and f_i refers to the functional layers, including convolutional layers (CONV) and full connected layers (FC).

Nowadays, many specialized deep learning accelerators have been proposed to use ReRAM for edge neural network implementation at the *inference process*

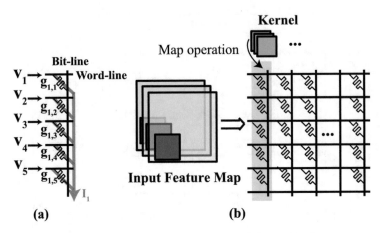

Fig. 5.2 (**a**) The analog dot-product computing mechanism of ReRAM. (**b**) A simple mapping scheme of input feature maps and kernels

[10, 55]. ReRAM cells can not only work as on-chip memory, but also perform in-memory matrix-vector multiplication efficiently. As shown in Fig. 5.2a, memristors are connected as a crossbar structure. When conducting a matrix multiplication $V \cdot G$, the matrix G is programmed as a set of conductance values of the ReRAM cells, while the input vector is represented as a sequence of the analog word-line (WL) voltages v_i. When the voltages are applied to all the WLs simultaneously, the outputs of $V \cdot G$ are sensed as a current set I automatically, achieving in-memory matrix multiplication effectively [40].

Ideally, the weight values are fixed after the training process. However, the unavoidable faults in the memristors will result in weight value fluctuation and further degrade the accuracy of DNN systems. Taking a CONV layer for an example, in each convolutional step, a multi-dimensional kernel slides over the input feature maps (IFMs) to extract characteristics and produce the corresponding output feature maps (OFMs). Figure 5.2b illustrates a simple weight mapping scheme for convolutional layers. The parameters in the same kernel are reflected as the conductance of the ReRAM cells on a single bit-line. The IFMs are dot-multiplied by the kernel windows and represented as a series of input voltages, preparing to generate OFMs. It is worth pointing out that a specific convolutional kernel W is fixed on the corresponding ReRAM cells and used to compute all output neurons in the corresponding OFM. As such, once a ReRAM cell becomes faulty, it will influence all the values of the corresponding OFMs and further propagate layer by layer, resulting in an erroneous output or even system failure [30, 68, 70].

SLC and MLC ReRAM Recently, many researches work on multi-level cell (MLC)-based deep learning accelerators rather than traditional single-level cell (SLC) devices. Unlike SLC memories, the MLC memories store a multi-bit value in a single ReRAM cell. However, there are trade-offs in MLC ReRAM memories. In an n-level ReRAM MLC cell, the resistance state has to be encoded into n levels.

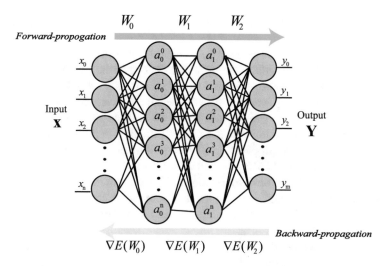

Fig. 5.3 An illustration of the training process of a full-connected neural network

The stored values can be changed, even if the states of ReRAM cells have slightly drifted, which significantly increases the unreliability of ReRAM computation. Hence, many deep neural accelerators propose to represent one weight by multiple cells connected to the same WL. Each cell stores one or two bits rather than storing a whole weight in a single cell [42].

5.1.1.3   Neural Network Training Basis

As shown in Fig. 5.3, a typical DNN training process consists of successive forward and backward propagations to evaluate current model's prediction accuracy and adjust its weights. During the forward step, the DNN is given with a set of input samples $[X, Y]$ to compute the intermediate neurons $[a_0, a_1]$ with weight matrices $W[W_0, W_1, W_2]$:

$$a_{i+1} = W_{i+1}a_i + b_{i+1} \tag{5.2}$$

wherein, W_i, b_i is the weights and bias of layer i respectively. Layers are connected with neurons. The output of layer i is the input of the layer $i+1$. Then, the prediction error is calculated with the loss between final output $[y_0, y_1 \ldots y_m]$ and the ground-truth label Y. To update the network parameters and minimize the prediction error, the loss E is sent backward to all the prior layers and the weight matrix is updated as follows:

$$W_i = W_i - \eta \cdot \frac{\partial E}{\partial W_i} \tag{5.3}$$

wherein, η is the learning rate to control the weight update speed. E denotes the global error.

During the iterative learning process, neural network itself will continue to adjust weight values to reduce the difference between the output prediction and the real label. Furthermore, this self-adjusting capacity of DNNs can also be used to retain faulty deep learning system's accuracy. Once there are unrepairable faults occurred in DLAs, weight values will be updated to adjust to these faults in the backward propagation process of each training iteration. However, using the traditional backward propagation (BP) algorithm consumes massive multiply-accumulate operations (MACs), which poses heavy computational pressure on resource-constrained edge devices. Hence, in this work, we modify the BP algorithm and propose a lightweight online model retraining mechanism to improve the convergence speed of the network training procedure and enable the faulty model to be retrained in-situ.

With the increasing adoption of deep learning in mission-critical applications, such as autonomous driving and drones, the reliability of DLAs widely utilized for the deep learning processing becomes critical and attracts a lot of attentions of the researchers recently [36, 45, 69, 70]. To analyze the influence of hardware faults on the deep neural network models, the authors in [72] conducted comprehensive experiments and the experiment results show that hardware faults can lead to considerable prediction accuracy drop. For the TIMIT speech recognition task, the accuracy drops from 74.13 to 39.69%. The accuracy loss is relevant to various design factors including the quantization, data format, and network architecture. It remains rather challenging to ensure resilient deep neural network execution on DLAs.

To alleviate the influence of hardware faults on neural network predictions, many prior works [21, 22, 29] took advantage of the intrinsic fault-tolerance of neural network models by retraining the models for a specific fault configuration such that hardware faults can be compensated by the retrained models. Xu et al. [71] proposed an on-accelerator retraining framework to obtain models that can tolerate the random hardware faults. Li et al. [32] and Wang et al. [64] proposed to employ the model retraining for DLAs with overclocking which may incur timing errors. To train resilient deep learning models, He et al. [22] revised the loss function to obtain models that are less sensitive to the hardware faults. Unlike the above methods, Zhang et al. [72, 73] proposed to bypass the faulty PEs in the computing array with zeros or other constant values such that the faults are more easier to tolerate via retraining. Although the retraining works for many fault configurations, there is still no guarantee that the retrained models can maintain the prediction accuracy for the target mission-critical applications because of the huge number of different fault configurations. In addition, the retraining can be rather expensive especially for large datasets and models, and is required for each specific fault configuration, which further limits the adoption of the retraining approaches. Unlike the retraining-based approaches, Hanif et al. [1] proposed a training-free mapping approach to alleviate the influence of permanent PE faults in the DLA. It leverages the saliency of the neural network parameters and opts to map the salient weights to the faulty

PEs as much as possible such that the negative influence of the PE faults on the neural network models is reduced. However, it works only when the fault error rate is low and can be sensitive to the fault distribution.

To enable unmodified deep learning model execution without accuracy loss, an intuitive approach is to develop reliable DLA architectures with the conventional dual modular redundancy (DMR) and triple modular redundancy (TMR) approaches to tolerate the hardware faults, but these approaches incur substantial hardware resource consumption. In this case, the authors in [24, 58, 59] proposed to add redundant PEs to the large regular homogeneous computing array and each redundant PE can be shared by a group of PEs with distinct redundancy sharing methods such as row redundancy (RR), column redundancy (CR), and diagonal redundancy (DR). For the RR and CR, each row/column of the PEs share the same set of redundant PEs. For the DR, both the row and column of PEs corresponding to a diagonal location in the computing array share the same set of redundant PEs. Since the redundant PEs are shared by a group of homogeneous PEs, hardware resource consumption can be greatly reduced compared to DMR and TMR. Nevertheless, the faulty PEs may not be evenly distributed or even clustered across the computing array [56]. As a result, these approaches may fail to recover the computing array when the number of faulty PEs in each shared region such as a row or a column of PEs exceeds the number of shared redundant PEs in the region. Thereby, the utilization of the redundant PEs can be affected by the fault distribution dramatically. More redundant PEs must be designed to ensure reliable execution. Otherwise, the performance can degrade dramatically when the faulty PEs are discarded due to the insufficient redundant PEs. Thereby, more efficient computing array architectures are required for the highly resilient DLA designs.

On top of the redundancy-based fault-tolerant DLA designs, there are also many other different fault-tolerant architecture designs. The authors in [48, 75] proposed a spatial and temporal checksum to protect full connection and convolution layers in deep neural network models. Zhang et al. [74] proposed a parallel stochastic computing(SC)-based neural network accelerator purely using bitstream computation by fully exploiting the superior fault tolerance of SC mainly for ternary neural networks. Li et al. [35] proposed an error detecting scheme to locate incorrect PEs of the DLA and gave an error masking method to achieve fault-tolerance. Hamid Reza Mahdiani etc. [43] proposed to relax the fault-tolerance of the VLSI implementation by employing TMR to only the computation of the most important bits such that the hardware overhead is reduced and the critical path latency is improved. Nevertheless, these approaches either require model retraining or can be sensitive to the fault distribution.

To address the reliability challenges in memristors, many hardware solutions have been proposed to tolerate permanent faults and soft faults. Error Correcting Code (ECC) has been studied in [47] to alleviate the impact of process variations of memristors. However, this technique incurs high penalty with additional power and performance overhead. Besides, a squeeze-search method has been proposed in [6] to identify the ReRAM defects with a March algorithm directly. Though this approach is effective, its huge timing overhead prevents it from usage in on-line protection for edge devices. Besides, it brings in additional write operations, which further leads to memory wear-outs. Furthermore, remapping technology has also been explored. [67] proposes to remap the model weights with redundant memristor columns. However, it still induces extra hardware waste.

Considering the huge costs of hardware-based methods, many software-based solutions have been devised recently. [36] explores the network architecture search (NAS) algorithm to find reliable neural network architectures. However, this method only works for networks with skip connections. In [7], an offline training method has been proposed with a model mapping strategy. The authors used the prior knowledge of fault distributions to map the weight matrix to memristors and then conducted an offline model retraining to make memristors more resilient to faults by treating the faults as noises during training. However, this method takes no consideration for the fault detection overhead. Moreover, the noise-tolerant models will still face accuracy degradation for some stuck-at faults and severe soft faults, because the training method can improve the robustness of the network model against faults but not completely eliminate the impacts of faults.

5.1.2   Challenges of Fault-Tolerant Deep Learning

DLAs typically consist of a large regular computing array which can either be a systolic array or a plain mesh array[8, 28], and a set of on-chip buffers used for input features, output features, and weights. While the on-chip buffers implemented with SRAMs can be usually protected effectively with ECC, we mainly focus on the reliability design of the regular computing array in this work. As each processing element (PE) in the computing array can be used for the calculation of multiple features in different network layers, faults in a single PE may cause multiple faulty computing results during the deep learning model execution. Thereby, they may result in considerable accuracy degradation according to our experiments in Sect. 5.2.4.

To mitigate the hardware faults in the 2-D computing array of DLAs, researchers have proposed a number of fault-tolerant design approaches from distinct angles. These approaches can be roughly divided into two categories. The first category mainly exploits the inherent fault-tolerance of the neural network models by retraining the neural network models specifically for the faulty computing array without any modification or with minor modification to the computing array [13, 32, 71, 72]. Although these approaches induce negligible hardware overhead and can even be applied to many off-the-shelf accelerators, the model retraining is required for each specific fault configuration, and the retraining, especially for large data sets and deep learning models, can be rather expensive. For instance, a critical neural network model applied in automotive systems must go through a series of standard certification tests before the modification can be accepted [16]. The cost of the certification test is nontrivial and time-consuming. Moreover, the prediction accuracy of the retrained models depends on both the model structures and the specific fault configurations. There is no guarantee that the model retraining can always maintain the original model accuracy and fulfill the requirements of mission-critical AI applications for all the different fault configurations by design.

To mitigate the hard faults and soft faults in ReRAM-based DNN accelerators, a number of approaches from distinct angles have been proposed. These approaches can be divided into the following categories. The first category is on-device training, which seeks to train a dedicated neural model to tolerate specific faults distributed on a memristor chip [37]. It is particularly critical to address the unpredictable in-situ wear-outs and soft faults during the chip's life cycle. However, a straightforward on-device training that involves iterative back-propagation is usually expensive for the edge devices with limited computation capability and power budget. The second category is the traditional redundancy design with either software or hardware, which typically has the hardware components or the critical neurons/nodes replicated and has the computing results of the replicates voted to achieve resilient computing of the models [11]. Nevertheless, it incurs considerable performance and energy overhead, which can easily violate the energy constraints of the typical edge devices. The third category is to conduct the on-line test and repair routinely in case of faults [6]. A classical approach belonging to this category is 'write-verify' and has been widely used for the memory blocks, but this scheme induces a large number of additional write operations, which will deteriorate the well-known wear-out problem of the memristors. As a result, when and how to perform the 'write-verify' to the ReRAM-based DNN accelerators without incurring wear-out remains a great challenge.

5.2 Fault-Tolerant Deep Learning Architecture

5.2.1 Deep Learning Sensitivity to Hardware Faults

The second category aims to recover the faulty computing array with redundant PEs. While the conventional approaches such as DMR and TMR require substantial hardware resources, researchers proposed a variety of relaxed redundancy approaches. The basic idea is to have each redundant PE to recover any faulty PE in a limited region of the computing array while the region can be a row, a column, or both row and column [58, 59], which essentially limits the sharing of the redundant PEs and reduces the hardware resource consumption significantly compared to the DMR and TMR approaches. When the faulty PEs are evenly distributed across the computing array, the faulty PEs can be probably mitigated. Nevertheless, the faults may not be evenly distributed across the computing array and these approaches fail to recover the computing array even when the number of redundant PEs exceeds the number of the faulty PEs in the computing array. In this case, the DLAs will not be fully functional or degrade dramatically if the faulty PEs are discarded. In summary, there is still a lack of resilient computing array architectures for DLAs that allow unmodified deep learning model execution and can tolerate various fault distribution at the same time.

To analyze the influence of hard errors on the above 2-D computing array, we inject random stuck-at bit errors to the registers of the PEs in a 32×32 computing array. We use bit error rate (BER) as the fault injection rate metric [45, 46, 51], which refers to the total number of bit errors over the total bit number of the registers in the computing array. To facilitate the error characteristic of the 2-D computing array, we convert the BER to PE error rate (PER) instead. Both the input features and weights are 8-bit fixed point, so the input registers and the weight registers are set to be the same data width accordingly. The intermediate register in the PEs is set to be 16-bit and the accumulator in the PEs is set to be 32-bit in case of computing overflow. Thereby, there are 64 bit registers in total in each PE. While any persistent bit error in a PE is considered as an PE error, PER can be calculated using BER with Eq. (5.4). Basically, it means that the PE is correct only when none of the bit registers are wrong. Otherwise, the PE will be faulty.

$$PER = 1 - (1 - BER)^{64} \qquad (5.4)$$

We had random stuck-at bit errors injected to a DLA simulator implemented according to the architecture described in Fig. 5.1 for the fault analysis. We took Resnet18 pre-trained on ImageNet [12] as an example and had it implemented on the accelerator with random faults. In this case, we generated 50 random fault configurations and evaluated the prediction accuracy under different PER setups. The experiment result is shown in Fig. 5.4. It reveals that the prediction accuracy varies dramatically across the different fault configurations. When the PER is higher than 1%, the prediction accuracy of the model mostly degrades to zero. Moreover, we notice that the prediction accuracy may also drop considerably in some of the fault configurations even under very low PER. It indicates that the model accuracy depends on not only the PER but also the fault distribution. Thereby, protecting the computing array is required for mission-critical applications despite the fault injection rate.

In addition, we further evaluated the classical hardware redundancy strategies, i.e. RR, CR, and DR for the regular 2-D computing array and measured the fully functional probability of the computing array under different PER setups. The evaluation result is shown in Fig. 5.5. It can be observed that these classical

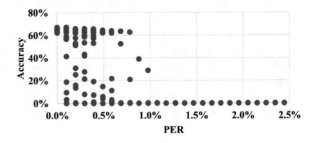

Fig. 5.4 Prediction accuracy of Resenet18 executed on a typical DLA under different PER setups. For each PER setup, 50 random fault configurations are evaluated on ImageNet

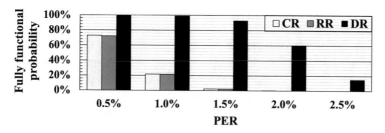

Fig. 5.5 The fully functional probability of the 2-D computing array under different PER setups

redundant design approaches can hardly mitigate all the faulty PEs even when the PER is around 1% which indicates that there are only 10 faulty PEs on average. In contrast, the number of redundant PEs is 32, which is much larger than the number of faulty PEs. It demonstrates that the redundant PEs cannot be fully utilized by these redundancy strategies because of the unevenly faulty PE distribution. The situation further deteriorates with the increase of the PER, which can be rather risky for the mission-critical AI applications.

5.2.2 Recomputing Based Hybrid Computing Architecture

In this section, we will present an overview of the proposed HyCA for fault-tolerant DLAs first. Then, we will illustrate the dataflow for the fault mitigation, HyCA microarchitecture, and fault detection with HyCA respectively.

HyCA Overall Architecture In order to tolerate various fault configurations with a unified computing architecture, we propose a HyCA, which has a dot-production processing unit (DPPU) seated along with the regular 2-D computing array, to recompute all the operations mapped to the faulty PEs in arbitrary locations of the computing array as shown in Fig. 5.6. While the 2-D computing array has each PE to calculate the different output features sequentially given the output stationary dataflow [8] and the DPPU has all the PEs to compute a single output features in parallel, they have distinct read patterns of the input features and weights from the corresponding on-chip buffers. More specifically, the 2-D computing array needs to read an array of input features in the same row and channel in each cycle while DPPU needs to read an array of input features aligned in channel dimension in each cycle. Thereby, the on-chip buffers cannot fulfill the read operations of the two computing units at the same time due to the limited read ports and distinct data layout requirements. To make sure that the normal 2-D array processing will not be affected by the DPPU recomputing, the on-chip buffer design remains unchanged. In this case, DPPU cannot read the required weights and input features aligned in channel dimension if it starts the recomputing at the same time with the 2-D computing array.

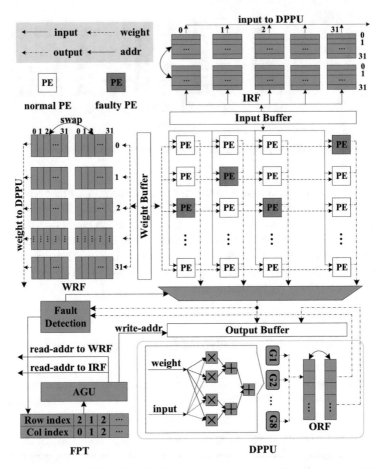

Fig. 5.6 Overview of a DLA with hybrid computing architecture. The components highlighted with blue are added to the conventional DLA to tolerate faulty PEs in arbitrary locations of the 2-D computing array

To address the problem, we have the input features and weights buffered in an input register file (IRF) and a weight register file (WRF) respectively while they are read for the 2-D computing array processing. Meanwhile, we have the recomputing delayed until there are sufficient inputs and weights ready for the recomputing. Accordingly, the delay must be larger than or equal to the number of weights required by DPPU data consumption in a single cycle to ensure DPPU can be fully utilized. As the DPPU may recompute operations on any PE in the 2-D computing array, the delay also needs to be larger than or equal to Col when the last column of the PEs obtain the weights passed from the first column of PEs. Suppose D represents the delay, then $D \geq Col$. Note that Col refers to the column size of the 2-D computing array. In this work, we organize IRF and WRF in Ping-Pong manner to ensure that the 2-D computing array can continue the normal dataflow without any stall during the DPPU recomputing. As the DPPU conducts the output feature calculation in parallel, DPPU can always finish the recomputing of the operations mapped to the faulty PEs before the Ping-Pong register files swap with each other when the DPPU size does not exceed the number of the faulty PEs. Note that DPPU size refers to the number of multipliers in DPPU. Since the peak computing power of DPPU equals to that of the 2-D computing array when configured with the same number of PEs, DPPU size is comparable to the 2-D computing array size and can also be used to represent its computing power. This also explains why DPPU can always finish the recomputing tasks before new weights and inputs are ready when DPPU size is larger than the number of faulty PEs in the 2-D computing array.

In addition, we have a fault PE table (FPT) to record the coordinates of the faulty PEs in the 2-D computing array which can be usually obtained with a power-on self-test procedure. With the coordinates, an address generation unit (AGU) is used to generate the read addresses and instruct the DPPU to read the right input features and weights from the register files. Moreover, AGU also determines the addresses to the output buffer for the overlapped writes of the recomputed output features. Similar to the IRF and WRF, there is also a Ping-Pong register file called output register file (ORF) for the DPPU outputs and it is utilized to pipeline the DPPU recomputing and the write from DPPU to the output buffer.

While DPPU can be utilized to calculate any output features mapped to the 2-D computing array, we can also use DPPU to check whether the calculation of an output feature in the 2-D computing array is correct, which can be used to detect the wear-out or aging induced persistent errors at runtime. If the computing results obtained from the 2-D computing array and DPPU do not match, it indicates that the corresponding PE in the 2-D computing array is faulty as DPPU with much smaller sizes compared to the 2-D computing array can be easily protected with much less overhead and is usually considered to be correct. By changing the fault PE table and scanning the computing of all the PEs in the 2-D computing array sequentially, we can detect the PE faults at runtime without affecting the 2-D computing array processing. Basically, the redundant recomputing mechanism can be mostly reused by the fault detection. And we only need a tiny fault detection module to conduct the scanning of the 2-D computing array and the comparison to the DPPU processing. Details of the fault detection module will be illustrated in the rest of this section.

HyCA Dataflow for Fault Mitigation To further illustrate the dataflow in HyCA especially the redundant computing unit DPPU, we take HyCA with a 32×32 2-D computing array and three faulty PEs as an example. DPPU in the HyCA has 32 PEs included. The example is shown in Fig. 5.7. Suppose c and k represent the input channel depth and the convolution kernel size respectively. It takes a PE in the 2-D computing array $k \times k \times c$ cycles to produce a convolution output. Without loss of generality, assume that the example starts at Cycle $k \times k \times c - 1$ when the first column of PEs complete a set of output feature calculation. The 2-D computing array occupies the output buffer until the last column of PEs complete the output feature data. Afterwards, the 2-D computing array may start to compute the new output features, but it usually takes $k \times k \times k \times c$ cycles to complete with the output

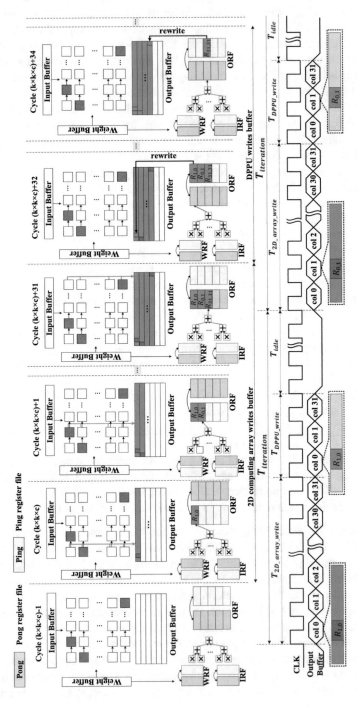

Fig. 5.7 The dataflow of using DPPU for recomputing the neural network operations mapped on the faulty PEs of a typical DLA. It also demonstrates how the DPPU overwrites the faulty computing results produced by the 2-D computing array

stationary dataflow. In this case, DPPU starts to use the output buffer and update the recomputed results to the output buffer without write conflicts. The processing steps are detailed as follows.

1. At cycle $k \times k \times c - 1$, the first column of PEs produce a column of output features accordingly and pass the weights to the second column of PEs. At the same time, the weights and input features used in the first column of PEs are stored in the corresponding Pong register file.
2. At cycle $k \times k \times c$, the first column of PEs write the calculated output features to the output buffer and start the calculation of new output features. Since PE(1,0) is faulty, the computing result written to the output buffer from this PE as marked with red color was wrong. While the input features and weights that are used for the output feature calculation on PE(1, 0) remain stored in the IRF and the WRF respectively, they will be read to the DPPU for the recomputing at this cycle.
3. At cycle $k \times k \times c + 31$, the Pong WRF and the Pong IRF are filled with the newly incoming weights and inputs, and they will be kept for 32 cycles. Weights and input features coming in next cycle will overwrite the data in the Ping WRF and the Ping IRF respectively. Thereby, DPPU must finish the recomputing that depends on the weights stored in the Ping WRF and IRF at this cycle. Otherwise, the data in the Ping register files will be overwritten. Afterwards, the processing repeats from the first processing step for another 32 cycles until the end of the convolution calculation.
4. At cycle $k \times k \times c + 32$, DPPU has the recomputed output features in the ORF written to the output buffer with a byte mask such that only the recomputed output feature is updated. Meanwhile, it starts to recompute the latest set of output features that are mapped to the faulty PEs in the 2-D computing array. As each output feature calculation is mapped to a single PE in the 2-D computing array using the classical output stationary dataflow, it takes $c \times k \times k$ cycles to complete an output feature calculation. As $c \times k \times k$ is usually larger than 32, and the output buffer will be occupied for only 32 cycles during each set of output feature calculation, the recomputed output feature data can be updated to the output feature buffer without conflicts.
5. At cycle $k \times k \times c + 34$, because there are only three faulty PEs in the 2-D computing array, it takes the DPPU three cycles to have the recomputed results overwritten from the ORF to the output buffer.
6. From cycle $k \times k \times c + 35$ to $k \times k \times c + c$, both the 2-D computing array and the DPPU conduct the partial convolution locally, so the output buffer port is idle before the first column of PEs complete the new output feature calculation.

As shown in Fig. 5.7, the overall processing is conducted iteratively. Each iteration includes a set of complete output feature calculation and it can be divided into three phases, i.e. 2-D array write, DPPU write, and idle from the perspective of the output buffer status. While each PE produces an output feature data per iteration and a PE conducts one MAC per cycle, the processing time of an iteration is $T_{iteration} = c \times k \times k$. For the 2-D computing array write, it takes $T_{2D\_array\_write} = D$ cycles per iteration where D refers to the number of cycles that DPPU delays after the 2-D computing array processing. For the DPPU write, it needs $T_{DPPU\_write} = fault\_PE\_num$ cycles as the DPPU updates the recomputed output features sequentially. However, DPPU recomputing does not have to start after the entire computing of the output features on the 2-D computing array. Instead, it is pipelined with the 2-D computing array but only D cycles slower. Thus, the weights and the input features consumed by the 2-D computing array must be fully accommodated by the Ping-Pong register files during the D cycles. Accordingly, the depth of weight and input feature Ping-Pong register files is set to be $2 \times D \times Row$. To minimize the register file overhead, we set $D = Col$.

As the average throughput of a PE in the 2-D computing array is the same with that in the DPPU, each multiplier in the DPPU can be used to repair a faulty PE in the 2-D computing array. Thereby, the DPPU size essentially represents the capability of the fault tolerance of the proposed HyCA without performance penalty. When the number of faulty PEs is larger than the DPPU size, we seek to preserve the computing power as much as possible without altering the target neural network models. To that end, we discard the faulty PEs that cannot be repaired due to the lack of the computing redundancy in the DPPU. As it is usually inefficient to compile and deploy the neural network models to a computing array with irregular row sizes which can cause both the irregular on-chip buffer accesses and external memory accesses, we choose to discard the columns with unrepaired faulty PEs and the columns that are disconnected from the input/weight/output buffers. Moreover, HyCA can repair any faulty PEs in the 2-D computing array, so it offers more flexibility to prioritize the faulty PEs for repairing such that the surviving computing array can be maximized especially when there are insufficient redundant PEs. In this work, the maximum remaining computing array can be obtained simply by assigning higher repairing priority to the faulty PEs on the left, which ensures that the surviving computing array is connected to the on-chip buffers.

5.2.3 HyCA Micro-Architecture

In this section, we will illustrate the major components of HyCA added to the baseline DLA and they include the DPPU, register files, and the FPT. FPT keeps the coordinates of the faulty PEs that will be repaired by the DPPU. As the maximum number of faulty PEs that can be tolerated without performance penalty is determined by the DPPU size, FPT is configured with DPU_size entries accordingly. AGU is a piece of control logic that generates the access addresses of the weight register file, input register file, and output register file based on the FPT for the recomputing of the DPPU. The structures of FPT and AGU are simple and we will not dwell on it. In contrast, the DPPU and the register files are relatively more complex, and they dominate the hardware overhead. Thus, they will be detailed in the rest of this section.

Dot-Production Processing Unit (DPPU)

DPPU is utilized for the dot-production and it consists of a set of multipliers as well as an adder tree that is used to aggregate all the multiplication results in a pipelined manner. It is mainly used to recompute the output features that are mapped to the faulty PEs in the 2-D computing array. An intuitive implementation is to construct a single unified dot-production unit which has both the input features and weights read from the corresponding register files in a single cycle and processed in parallel. As DPPU starts Col cycles later after the 2-D computing array, each faulty PE in the 2-D computing array has Col weights and input features multiplied and accumulated. Accordingly, Col weights and input features can be extracted for the recomputing on DPPU for each faulty PE in the 2-D computing array. In order to make best use of the PEs in the DPPU, the Col weights and input features must be fully distributed to the DPPU. If the entire DPPU is organized into a unified dot-production unit, the size of the DPPU is rather limited, which hinders the scalability of the DPPU. For instance, when Col is set to be 32 and DPPU size is set to be 24 or 48, the computing mapped to a single faulty PE cannot be perfectly mapped to the DPPU, which will lead to the under-utilization of the DPPU. To address this problem, we propose to divide the PEs in the DPPU into multiple smaller groups and each group can conduct the dot-production independently. As the number of PEs in each group gets smaller, they are more likely to be fully utilized by the computing mapped to a faulty PE. As shown in Fig. 5.8, each group includes 8 PEs and it completes the computing of a faulty PE in 4 cycles when Col is set to be 32. In this case, the DPPU size can be scaled conveniently. At the same time, the different groups can conduct operations mapped to different faulty PEs in the 2-D computing array in parallel.

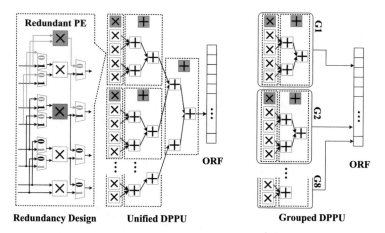

Fig. 5.8 Structures of the unified DPPU and the grouped DPPU. For both the unified DPPU and the grouped DPPU, they are protected with redundant PEs. Each redundant PE is used to protect a set of homogeneous PEs and these PEs are connected with ring topology to reduce the signal fan-out

While the DPPU is used to recompute all the faulty operations in the 2-D computing array, it must be resilient enough to ensure the functionality. Otherwise, a single fault in the DPPU may corrupt the whole accelerator. To improve the resilience of the DPPU, we add redundant PEs to the DPPU as shown in Fig. 5.8. Basically, the multipliers used in the DPPU are divided into groups and each group is equipped with a redundant multiplier. Instead of having the redundant multiplier shared by all the multipliers in the group, we have the redundant multiplier and the multipliers in the group connected in a directed ring topology and each multiplier can be configured to replace its downstream neighboring multiplier. When any of the multiplier fails, it can be replaced by its upstream multiplier immediately. Compared to the shared redundancy design, this approach can avoid high fan-out connections to the redundant multipliers. Similarly, we also have the adders in the adder tree protected with the same redundancy design approach.

Register Files
The IRF and the WRF are used to back up the data read from input buffer and weight buffer, and then supply the data to the DPPU for the recomputing. As the 2-D computing array and the DPPU have different dataflows for the neural network computing, the weight register file is written in column-wise manner but read in row-wise manner as shown in Fig. 5.9. When the DPPU is split into multiple groups, these groups will be responsible for different faulty convolution operations and they need to read different rows of WRF and IRF at the same time. Although a straightforward multi-port register file can fulfill the concurrent register file read, it will induce substantial hardware overhead according to [3, 5].

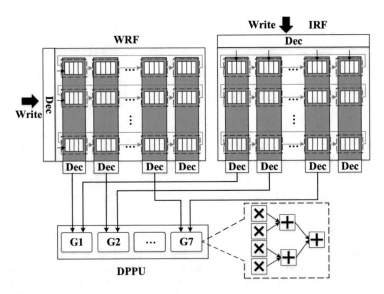

Fig. 5.9 Organization of the weight register file (WRF) and input register file (IRF). It shows how the register files are connected with a grouped DPPU with different number of computing groups

While we observe that each computing group in DPPU has only a small number of PEs and they cannot consume a single row of inputs and weights in a single cycle. As a result, the straightforward multi-port register file actually has the bandwidth wasted. With this observation, we also have the register files split into groups in row direction such that each group of the register file can be read independently by the corresponding computing group in the DPPU. In this case, each register file has only a single read port, but each computing group can only read a segment of the data in the register files as indicated by the blue color. While an output feature recomputing on DPPU needs an entire row of data in the register files, we have each row of the registers organized as a circular shift register. With the shift register, different segments of the data in a row can be obtained by the corresponding computing group in DPPU in a few cycles. At the same time, the amount of data fed to each computing group can be fully utilized. Moreover, we notice the read port data width of the register files is not necessarily equal to the DPPU size. When the DPPU size is larger than the register file data width, more read ports can be added to some of the register file groups rather than the entire register file. When the DPPU size is smaller than the register file data width, some of the register file groups do not even need a read port as shown in Fig. 5.9. Thereby, the DPPU size can be scaled conveniently and it will not be limited by the register file sizes.

5.2.3.1 Fault Detection with HyCA

On top of the fault mitigation, DPPU can also be utilized to conduct fault detection at runtime. The basic idea is to have the DPPU to recompute the operations on a PE in the 2-D computing array. Then, we have the computing results compared to check if the PE in the 2-D computing array is faulty. By scanning all the PEs in the 2-D computing array sequentially, we can determine if the 2-D computing array is faulty. While the DPPU always starts the recomputing Col cycles later, the computing result of a PE to be checked is already updated or written to the output buffer when the DPPU completes the recomputing. To address the problem, we have the computing results to be checked buffered in a checking list buffer (CLB) as shown in Fig. 5.10. As the fault detection scanning is conducted sequentially, a simple on-chip buffer can fulfill the requirements. When the DPPU completes the recomputing, the fault detection module can have the results compared with that stored in the CLB.

As hard faults in a PE can usually lead to computing errors of most of the computation, we do not have to compare the final output feature computing results for the fault detection. Instead, we can compare the partial computing results of a PE for the fault detection such that the fault detection can be faster and more efficient. Since the DPPU conducts the processing in parallel, we have the partial computing result (PR) produced by a single DPPU group in a single cycle compared in this work. Different from the DPPU, PEs in the 2-D computing array have the computing results accumulated continuously before the entire output feature processing is completed. Suppose only one DPPU group is reserved for the runtime

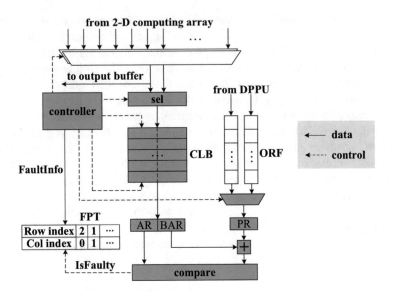

Fig. 5.10 Structure of the fault-detection module

fault detection and the DPPU group includes S PEs. To enable the comparison for the fault detection, we have both the base accumulated results (BAR) and the accumulated results (AR) calculated S cycles later stored in the CLB. In the next cycle, another pair of the BAR and the AR from different PEs will be stored accordingly. As the weights and input features are stored in their register files for only Col cycles, we only have Col ARs and BARs stored in the CLB. While the CLB is also organized in Ping-Pong manner, the total size of the CLB is $4 \times W \times Col$ Bytes where W denotes the width of the accumulator in PEs.

According to the recomputing dataflow, the reserved DPPU group performs the recomputing Col cycles later. Unlike the fault-tolerance oriented recomputing, the fault-detection oriented recomputing only conducts the dot-production of S weights and input features rather than Col weights and input features. The results of the DPPU will be compared with the corresponding results stored in the CLB for the fault detection. Basically, AR will be compared to the addition of PR and BAR. When a faulty PE is detected, the faulty information i.e. the fault PE row index and column index will be updated to the FPT. One comparison can be done per cycle, so it takes the fault detection module Col cycles to complete the comparison with the stored results in CLB. Accordingly, it takes the fault detection module $Row \times Col + Col$ cycles to complete the fault detection of the whole 2-D computing array. When a DPPU group has more PEs included, it needs to check a partial result with more computation. As a result, the fault detection time is independent with the number of PEs in the DPPU group. While the fault detection time is already much smaller than the processing time of a normal neural network layer, it is fast enough to detect the computing errors. To avoid the frequent fault detection, the fault detection module can be activated periodically in a larger time range depending on the requirements of the applications. In addition, the fault detection module can reuse the majority of the fault recovery design, it induces only some simple controlling logic and a small CLB, and consumes negligible chip area.

5.2.4 Experiment Result Analysis

5.2.4.1 Experiment Setup

Accelerator Configurations The proposed deep learning accelerator with HyCA is implemented in Verilog and synthesized with Design Compiler under TSMC 40 nm technology. The computing array size and DPPU size are set to be 32×32 and 32 respectively. The input feature buffer size is 128 KB, output feature buffer size is 128KB and the weight buffer size is 512 KB. The computing of DPPU is delayed by $D = 32$ cycles after the 2-D computing array, so both the weight register file size and the input register file size are set to be $2 \times 32 \times D = 2048$ i.e. 2 KB. The output register file in DPPU is 64-byte. The fault PE table size is 32×10bits. Each entry of the table includes 5-bit row index and 5-bit column index of a faulty PE. Both the data width of weights and input feature data is 8-bit. To ensure the resilience of the DPPU, we have every four multipliers in the DPPU grouped and equipped with a redundant multiplier, and every three adders in the DPPU grouped and protected with a redundant adder. For the 2-D computing array, we have three classical redundancy approaches including RR, CR, and DR implemented and each redundancy implementation is equipped with 32 redundant PEs.

Fault Models To evaluate the reliability of the redundancy designs comprehensively, we have two different fault distribution models including the random distribution model and the clustered distribution model implemented. For the random distribution model, the faults are randomly distributed across the entire computing array. For the clustered distribution model which is usually used to characterize the manufacture defects, the faults are more likely to be close to each other and the model proposed in [44] is applied in this work. Meanwhile, we notice that the influence of hardware faults is related with the fault distribution, so we generate 10,000 configurations randomly for each fault injection rate and average the evaluation in the experiments.

As hard errors are mainly caused by the manufacturing defects, aging, and wear-out, which can be affected by many complex factors such as application requirements, working status, and the fabrication, there is still a lack of references investigating the practical PER setup and prior fault-tolerant designs typically have distinct error rate setups [1, 33, 38, 73]. In this case, we evaluate the hard error rate in a large range and seek to demonstrate when we can ensure reliable computing. Then, we expect the users to choose the target hard error rate for their specific fault-tolerant designs. In addition, since we mainly focus on the reliability of the regular

2-D computing array in a deep learning accelerator, we use PER as the fault injection metric similar to the works in [73] and [50]. Meanwhile, we notice that BER that refers to the number of bit errors over the total number of memory bits is directly related with definition of the hard error on chips, and it has been widely utilized as a metric for fault analysis in many prior works [45, 46, 51]. Thus, we convert the BER to PER with Eq. (5.4) mentioned in Sect. 5.2.1 assuming that any bit error in a PE will cause the PE failure. While BER typically ranges from 1×10^{-7} to 1×10^{-3}, PER ranges from 0 to 6% according to the conversion.

Neural Network Benchmark To evaluate the performance of a typical DLA with the proposed fault-tolerant HyCA, we have a set of representative neural network models including Alexnet, VGG, Resnet, and YOLO used as the benchmark. Alexnet, VGG and Resnet are classical models used for image classification, while YOLO is mostly used for object detection. All the models are pre-trained on ImageNet. We measured the performance of the benchmark on the DLAs with different redundancy design approaches using Scale-sim[53]. Since Scale-sim is relatively slow, it is difficult to obtain the performance of all the random fault configurations directly. In this experiment, we determined the final valid computing array setups of all the fault configurations and performed the simulation on only the unique computing array setups. As many fault configurations lead to the same computing array setups eventually, this approach greatly reduces the simulation time. Finally, we averaged the resulting performance based on the generated fault configurations.

5.2.4.2 Chip Area Overhead Comparison

Figure 5.11 illustrates the chip area of the DLAs with different redundancy approaches including RR, CR, DR, and HyCA. Particularly, we have three HyCA-based designs with different DPPU sizes compared. The DPPU size of HyCA24, HyCA32, and HyCA40 is 24, 32 and 40 respectively. According to the comparison Fig. 5.11, the HyCA-based designs exhibit much less redundancy overhead

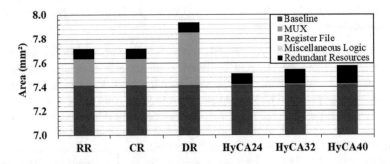

Fig. 5.11 Chip area under different redundancy approaches

compared to the classical redundancy designs. The redundancy overhead of the HyCA-based designs mainly consist of the redundant PEs and the register files, while the redundancy overhead of the RR-based, CR-based, and DR-based designs are mainly attributed to the MUX and the redundancy PEs. As the 2-D computing array size is 32 × 32, the number of redundant PEs in RR-based, CR-based, and DR-based designs is the same and the chip area caused by the redundant PEs is also equal. While HyCA has different PE structures, i.e. independent multipliers and adders rather than MACs, and additional redundant PEs, the chip area of the redundant PEs is larger given the same DPPU sizes. In contrast to the chip area of the redundant PEs in HyCA, the added small Ping-Pong register files in HyCA consumes much less chip area. Different from HyCA, RR, CR and DR include a large number of MUX to enable the replacement of faulty PEs with the redundant PEs. These MUX take up substantial chip area and dominate the redundancy overhead.

5.2.4.3   Reliability Comparison

To evaluate the reliability of the DLAs, we propose two metrics that can be applied for different applications. One of them is the fully functional probability and it shows the probability that the DLA can be fully functional without any performance penalty. It is preferred by the mission-critical applications that do not allow any performance degradation nor model modification because any system modification may require expensive and lengthy safety evaluation and certification. The experiment is shown in Fig. 5.12. It shows that HyCA outperforms the three classical redundancy approaches and the advantage gets enlarged under the clustered fault distribution. The main reason is that each redundant PE in RR, CR and DR can only be utilized to replace a single faulty PE in a row, a column, and a row-column pair respectively. When multiple faults occur in the same protected region, these

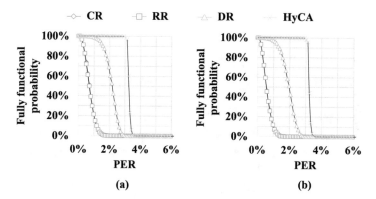

Fig. 5.12 Fully functional probability of DLAs with different redundancy approaches. (**a**) Random fault distribution model. (**b**) Clustered fault distribution model

redundancy approaches fail to recover the faulty 2-D computing array and the design will not be fully functional. Unlike these classical redundancy approaches, HyCA allows arbitrary faulty distribution and can perfectly repair the computing array as long as the number of faulty PEs in the 2-D computing array does not exceed the DPPU size. Thereby, the fully function probability of HyCA is not sensitive to the fault distribution models. As DPPU size is set to be 32 and the 2-D computing array size is 32 × 32 in this example, the fully functional probability drops to 0 immediately when the number of fault PEs exceeds 32 at 3.13% PER. As the PEs in the DPPU can also be faulty, the fully functional probability of HyCA starts to drop when the number of faulty PE is close to 32 and the PER is slightly lower than 3.13%.

The other metric is the normalized remaining computing power and it refers to the percentage of the remaining computing array size over the original 2-D computing array size. This metric is particularly important for the non-critical applications that do not require fully functional accelerators and allow the accelerators to be degraded, because the remaining computing array size determines the theoretical computing power and affects the performance of the deployed neural network models directly. In this work, we apply the acceleration degradation strategy mentioned in the end of Sect. 5.2.2 and discard the faulty PEs in the granularity of a column when the redundant PEs are insufficient to mitigate all the faulty PEs. Although more aggressive degradation approaches are possible to achieve larger computing power, this approach is applied for more efficient model compilation, hardware implementation and memory accesses.

Figure 5.13 reveals the computing power comparison of the different redundancy approaches. It can be observed that HyCA shows significantly higher computing power under all the different PER setups and the advantage also enlarges with the increase of the PER. This is mainly brought by the fault recovery flexibility of the HyCA that allows the DPPU to select the most critical faulty PEs to repair when the redundant faulty PEs are insufficient. Note that the most critical faulty PEs refer to

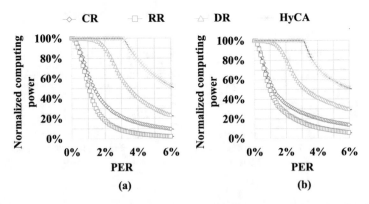

Fig. 5.13 Normalized computing power of DLAs with different redundancy approaches. (**a**) Random fault distribution model. (**b**) Clustered fault distribution model

the ones that can maximize the remaining 2-D computing array. By optimizing the faulty PE mitigation order, the remaining computing array can be larger. In contrast, each redundant PE can only repair a limited subset of the faulty PEs for the RR, CR and DR. There is little space left to optimize the faulty PE mitigation order. Thereby, the remaining computing power of RR, CR, and DR is much lower. As we choose to discard the faulty PEs that are failed to be repaired in the granularity of a column, RR cannot effectively shift the faulty PEs to a different column and has to discard the column whenever there are more than one faulty PEs. As a result, RR shows the lowest computing power even when the number of redundant PEs is the same with the other redundancy approaches.

5.2.4.4 Performance Comparison

In order to evaluate the performance of the DLAs protected with the different redundancy approaches, we have the neural network benchmark deployed on the DLAs with Scale-Sim. The performance is normalized to that of the DLA protected with RR and the experiment result is shown in Fig. 5.14. It can be found that HyCA achieves much higher performance than the other redundancy approaches especially under relatively higher PER, which is roughly consistent with the experiment in Fig. 5.13 though the neural networks also affect the performance. Particularly, the performance speedup goes up to 9X when the PER is around 6% under the random fault distribution. The underlying reason for the higher performance speedup at higher PER is that higher PER indicates more faulty PEs in the 2-D computing array and leaves larger optimization space for the HyCA.

Another observation is that the performance gap between HyCA and the other redundancy approaches is much smaller than the computing power gap. For instance, the computing power of HyCA is around 25X higher than RR when PER is 6% under the random fault injection while the performance speedup is only 9X. This

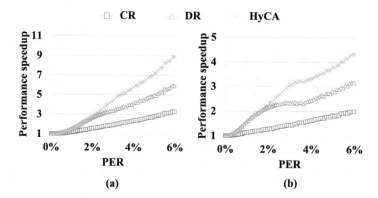

Fig. 5.14 Normalized performance of DLAs with different redundancy approaches. (**a**) Random fault distribution model. (**b**) Clustered fault distribution model

Fig. 5.15 Neural network runtime of the DLAs with different computing array sizes. Note that the row size of the computing arrays is fixed to be 32

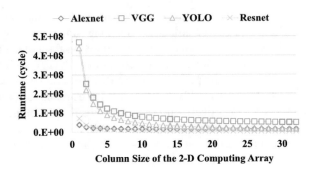

is mainly attributed to the fact that the neural network runtime varies dramatically under different computing array sizes as shown in Fig. 5.15. When the remaining computing array size is large at lower PER, the runtime decreases much slower with the increase of the computing array size. In addition, some of the neural networks like VGG include some full connection layers that fail to make best use of the computing array. In fact, only a single column of PEs is used for the full connection operations given the output stationary dataflow and the larger remaining computing array in HyCA is underutilized, which also undermines the performance speedup.

5.2.4.5 Redundancy Design Scalability Analysis

As different applications may have distinct requirements of reliability and may also work under different fault environments, a scalable redundancy design can greatly alleviate the reliability design problems. In this subsection, we will investigate and compare the scalability of the different redundancy approaches under different computing array sizes. As the fully functional probability and the computing power is roughly positively related, we only use the fully function probability as the metric for the scalability evaluation to save the space. The number of redundant PEs in RR and CR is consistent with the corresponding computing array row size and column size respectively. Although the number of redundant PEs in DR is also equal to the diagonal size of the computing array, it cannot be directly applied to a non-square computing array. In this experiment, we divide the non-square computing array into multiple square computing arrays and apply the diagonal redundancy approach to each sub computing array independently. The number of redundant PEs in HyCA is set to be Col to ensure a fair comparison where Col refers to the column size of the computing arrays.

The experiment result is shown in Fig. 5.16. It can be observed that the fully functional probability of RR, CR and DR under different PER setups vary dramatically when the computing array size changes. CR and DR have the same amount of redundant PEs on the different 2-D computing array sizes. Basically, the redundancy intensity, i.e. the average redundancy per PE in the 2-D computing array, vary dramatically across the different computing arrays. Thus, the fully

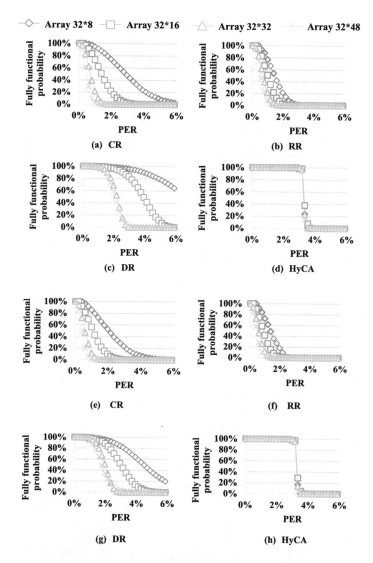

Fig. 5.16 Fully functional probability of the DLAs with different computing array sizes when they are protected with RR, CR, DR and HyCA respectively. Figure (**a**)–(**d**) are evaluated under the random fault distribution while Figure (**e**)–(**h**) are evaluated under the clustered fault distribution

functional probability curves are different accordingly. The number of redundant PEs for RR scales with the three specific computing arrays, but the fully functional probability curves are closer to each other but remains different due to the fault distribution variations. In general, the classical redundancy approaches do not scale well and the sensitivity to the fault distribution further aggravates the scalability problem. In contrast, the proposed HyCA exhibits much better scalability and shows

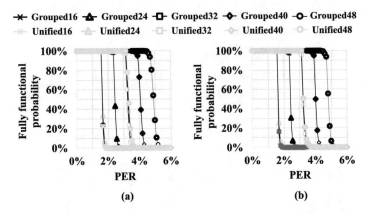

Fig. 5.17 Fully functional probability of the DLAs configured with different DPPU sizes. The DPPUs with both the unified structure and the grouped structure are evaluated and compared. (**a**) Random fault distribution model. (**b**) Clustered fault distribution model

consistent fault-tolerance capability under different computing array sizes and fault distribution models.

We also evaluated the scalability of the two different DPPU implementations, i.e. the Unified DPPU and the Grouped DPPU under different DPPU sizes. We scale the DPPU sizes from 16 to 48 and fix the computing array size to be 32 × 32. The experiment result is shown in Fig. 5.17. It can be observed that the Grouped DPPU scales strictly with the DPPU sizes. The Unified DPPU scales when the DPPU size is set to be 16 and 32, but it does not scale when the DPPU size is set to be 24, 40, and 48. The main reason is that the Unified DPPU needs to read from input and weight register files in which the data are aligned with the column size of the computing array. More specifically, the input features and weights are aligned to 32, i.e. the column size. When the DPPU size is larger than 32 and it cannot be perfectly split by 32, the Unified DPPU cannot be fully utilized due to the lack of the sufficient input data. When the DPPU size is smaller than 32 and 32 data cannot be divided perfectly for the Unified DPPU processing, the Unified DPPU also suffers underutilization and leads to unsatisfactory scalability in this occasion. Different from the Unified DPPU, the Grouped DPPU can be utilized with smaller granularity and is able to make full use of the aligned data from both the input and weight register files. As the hardware overhead of DPPU is mainly caused by the redundant PEs according to the experiment in Sect. 5.2.4.2, the hardware overhead of both DPPU implementations scales with the DPPU size accordingly.

5.2.4.6   Fault Detection Analysis

With the proposed fault detection approach, PE faults can be detected at runtime. Since the proposed fault detection module essentially scans all the PEs in the 2-D

Table 5.1 The proportion of the neural network layers of which the execution time can fully cover the fault detection of the entire 2-D computing array

Array size	16×16	32×32	64×64	128×128
Alexnet	8/8	8/8	8/8	4/8
VGG	16/16	16/16	16/16	16/16
YOLO	22/22	22/22	22/22	15/22
Resnet	21/21	21/21	21/21	5/21

computing array sequentially, we mainly evaluate the fault detection scanning time under different computing array sizes, and compare the fault detection time to the corresponding neural network processing time. Basically, we want to determine if a runtime persistent fault can be detected before a neural network layer is computed. And we take the percentage of the neural network layers that can be detected during the layer processing as a metric to evaluate the fault detection capability. The experiment result is shown in Table 5.1. It can be observed that all the faults in the 2-D computing array can be detected during the execution of each neural network layer when the 2-D computing array size is smaller than or equal to 64×64. When the 2-D computing array size reaches 128×128, the processing time of some small neural network layers can finish the processing before the fault detection module scan the entire 2-D computing array. In this case, we may have to add more DPPU groups for the fault detection.

The fault detection module mainly includes a check list buffer (CLB) and some control logic. The CLB is $Col \times W \times 4$ bytes and dominates the chip area, but it is only $Row/(2 \times W)$ (i.e. 1/4 when $Row = 32$ and $W = 4$) of the input register file. Thus, the CLB overhead is much smaller than the input register file let alone the redundant PEs. Thereby, the chip area of the fault detection module is negligible.

5.2.5 Discussion

The reliability of DLAs is of vital importance to the mission-critical AI applications. Prior redundancy design approaches for the regular computing array such as RR and CR greatly reduce the hardware overhead compared to the classical TMR approaches, but they are rather sensitive to the fault distribution and fail to work especially when the faults are unevenly distributed. To address this problem, we propose a HyCA and have a DPPU to recompute all the operations mapped to the faulty PEs in the 2-D computing array. When the number of faulty PEs in the 2-D computing array is less than the DPPU size, HyCA can fully recover the 2-D computing array despite the fault distribution. Even when the fault error rate further increases, DPPU can still be used to repair the most critical PEs first to ensure a large available computing array and minimize the performance penalty. According to our experiments, HyCA outperforms prior redundancy approaches in terms of both the fully functional probability and the computing power under different fault distribution models. In addition, HyCA can also be reused for the fault detection at runtime and the experiment result shows that the entire 2-D computing array can be scanned and detected before a neural network layer completes its execution in most cases.

5.3 Online Fault Protection for ReRAM-Based Deep Learning

5.3.1 RRamedy Framework Overview

5.3.1.1 Design Goals

In this section, we analyze the fault models of ReRAM-based edge neural accelerators and elaborate a unified fault detection and network remedy framework for memristor-based deep learning accelerators on the edge.

5.3.1.2 Target Fault Models

ReRAM's distinctive characteristics come with reliability concerns. The working mechanism of ReRAM relies on the generation and rupture of the oxygen ions (O^{2-}) and oxygen vacancies (V_O). The stochastic nature of V_O makes ReRAM susceptible to many reliability problems [61], including:

Permanent Faults Permanent faults (Hard Faults) of ReRAM cells force the resistance states fixed at high resistance (stuck-at-0 fault) or low resistance (stuck-at-1 fault), which are usually caused by fabrication defects [6] and limited endurance.
Soft Faults ReRAM soft faults are mainly resulted from: (a) the unavoidable degradation mechanisms and wear-out mechanisms, (b) manufacturing defects, especially the imperfect "electroforming" process [40, 49]. These soft faults can be observed as retention failures, read disturbance or write disturbance [20, 57]. Even though the ReRAM-based chips have passed the manufacturing test, cells will still suffer from faults/variations during their lifetime, and these effects can be accumulated to result in a data disturbance [39].

In a nutshell, ReRAM-based edge neural accelerators face both inevitable permanent faults and soft faults in practice. Permanent faults appear over memory lifetime and cannot be tuned. Soft faults have no permanent corruption on the stored data, but they still have the ability to damage the system. Hence, it is necessary to detect the faults and rescue the system performance from them.

5.3.1.3   Design Requirements

To improve reliability of DLA, we find that fault deception methods were not available because they ware time-consuming to test all storage units. Furthermore, the unit by unit fault detection method also increased the wear of storage units. Fortunately, the DLA fault could be tested by the results generated by DLA. Therefore, the novel results analysis method helps to skip the unit by unit fault detection. To leverage the novel DLA storage unit fault detection method, it needs to comply with the design requirements for protecting deep learning accelerators from permanent and soft faults during their lifetime:

- Low impact on the performance of DLAs: the proposed solution should have low to no performance overhead on the DLAs, i.e., the fault detection process can be performed in spare time with no impact on the running time of DLAs.
- Model fidelity: the accuracy of edge deep learning system cannot be heavily affected. Once faults occurred, the system must detect and diagnose the faults and restore system accuracy instantly.
- Fast deployment on the hardware platform: the solution should not introduce modifications on the original architectures and workflows of DLAs.
- High generality and reliability: the solution can be practised in different DLAs. The fault detection method should have high fault detection probability. Furthermore, the model retrieving method should alleviate the accuracy degradation and restore the original system prediction accuracy.

Next, we describe our proposed framework in detail and show that RRAMedy can apply to any CiM-based edge deep learning accelerators without any constraints on applications or network structures. Meanwhile, our approach did no modifications on the original workflows of DLAs and the neural network structures. Furthermore, in Sect. 5.3.5, we show that our proposed adversarial example testing method has superior accuracy on fault detection. Meanwhile, with the model retraining method, the accuracy impact of memristor faults is compensated effectively.

We present the overview of RRAMedy firstly. As illustrated in Fig. 5.18, we model the edge deep learning scenario with two parties, a *cloud server* and an *edge device* with ReRAM-based memory. The edge device routinely detects its fault occurrence with the proposed Adversarial Example Testing (AET) method. Once a device detects unrepairable faults, it will require updating the current model parameters with a device-specific fault-tolerant model. Here, the updated fault-tolerant model can be trained on either cloud or local edge, according to the edge computational power and the network condition. For devices with limited computational resources, they can ask cloud services for help. The cloud servers will leverage a fault-aware retraining step to generate fault-tolerant models to maintain the edge system accuracy through the model resilience. Alternatively, for "powerful" edge devices, they can iteratively adjust neural network parameters to the faults during the online model retraining procedure.

The RRAMedy framework consists of three primary components, including (1) a fault detector, (2) an in-cloud network retrainer and (3) an online network

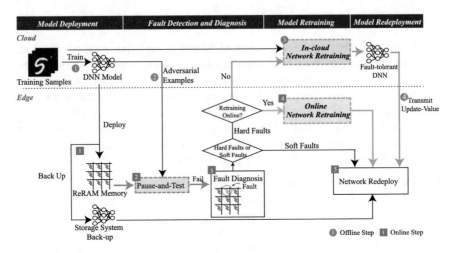

Fig. 5.18 The global flow of the RRAMedy framework

retrainer. The fault *detector* consists of a "Pause-and-Test" (P&T) mechanism and a "Fault Diagnosis" (FD) component. The P&T mechanism is periodically invoked to detect system accuracy degradation caused by ReRAM state variations, while the FD component is used for fault diagnosis and generates the corresponding fault distribution. After fault diagnosis, the framework will choose either the in-cloud network *retrainer* or the online network *retrainer* to finetune the network model for tolerating the irreparable defects. Leveraging the excellent self-recovering capability of neural networks, the faulty network can be retrained with the existence of unrepairable hard defects. Figure 5.18 demonstrates the general flow of RRAMedy framework that includes four primary phases with five online steps and four offline steps.

Model Deployment Firstly, the cloud server trains a network on the cloud (step ❶) and transmits it to the edge device. Then, the edge device deploys the model on the deep learning accelerator for execution and also makes a backup on the storage system (step **1**).

Fault Detection and Diagnosis As having addressed, fault detection and diagnosis always bring high overhead. To reduce the overhead, a routinely invoked fault detection mechanism is established on the edge device. As seen in Fig. 5.18, the server generates and selects a set of adversarial examples for fault detection. These generated adversarial examples are transmitted, stored in the storage system of devices (step ❷) and periodically fed into the ReRAM accelerator for the fault detection routine (step **2**). The detection results will be further analyzed to instruct the execution of the FD component for accurate fault location (step **3**). Specifically, if the ReRAM accelerator fails to generate correct predictions on the adversarial test set, the P&T component will raise an alarm flag to trigger FD. If there is no permanent fault located, it means the ReRAM accelerator encounters soft faults.

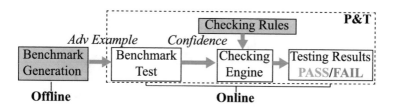

Fig. 5.19 The overview of pause-and-test mechanism (grey components can be adjusted by the cloud servers)

The device will refresh the corrupted cells with model back-up (step **5**). Otherwise, a permanent fault is found by the FD component, RRAMedy will ask for fault-tolerant training to overcome accuracy losses.

Model Retraining RRAMedy provides two model retraining techniques to recover the recognition accuracy of faulty DNNs, including edge-cloud collaborative fault-masking retraining and in-situ model remedy on the edge. For the edge-cloud collaborative model retraining, the cloud server waits for the edge devices to report their fault distribution. As the fault maps are received, the server will retrain the neural network with the proposed fault-masking method and adaptively adjust the neural network to tolerate the device-specific faults (step **3**). Additionally, we also unleash deep learning retraining services with edge computational power and use the inherent fault tolerance of neural network training algorithms to adapt the network parameters to the faults. Certainly, edge DLA has more strict energy and timing constraints than the cloud. Hence, the online model retraining method leverages the intermediate activations transmitted from the golden models as additional knowledge to assist edge training procedure for faster accuracy recovering (step **4**).

Model Redeployment For the cloud-assistant retraining process, the server only transmits the quantized weight update values to the edge device to reduce the communication overhead (step **4**). The edge device will then update the cloud-retrained network on its storage system (step **5**) and use the updated backup to refresh the ReRAM states to mitigate the fault-induced accuracy degradation. The backup is also used to refresh the soft fault-induced struck cells once detected.

5.3.2   Adversarial Example Testing on the Edge

It is well-known that the fault detection and location process is time-consuming, which makes it unacceptable to perform periodically, especially for the edge ReRAM expensive to program due to write overhead. Based on this, we pursue to find a more realistic method to capture the fault-induced system behavior failures. Only when the deep learning system is detected with behavior deviations, the FD function will be triggered, which significantly minimizes the system overhead.

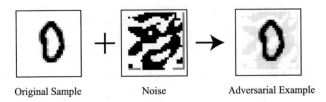

Original Sample   Noise   Adversarial Example

Fig. 5.20 A demonstration of adversarial example generation

The **Pause-and-Test mechanism** is proposed to periodically analyze the fault existence at the system behavior level. Figure 5.19 illustrates the high-level view of the P&T mechanism. It can be described as a function: $M \rightarrow \{0, 1\}$, that decides whether the neural model M is heavily affected by the faults or resistance variations in the ReRAM memory. Unlike traditional systems, which require bit-level comparison to detect system faults, the deep learning system should analyze the output confidence score directly, because the bit-by-bit comparison is unnecessary. Hence, we consider a simple strategy to distinguish the faulty models from normal models: we feed the test benchmark into the edge neural systems and compare the confidence score of the actual model's prediction with the original prediction confidence. The deviations of the original and actual prediction confidence score should be negligible. Once the prediction scores are determined to be heavily different based on the predefined checking rules, the model parameters are likely to be corrupted and the ReRAM memory is most likely suffering from faults or defects. Then, the RRAMedy framework will further diagnose the faults or variations with the FD process.

However, neural networks are thought possessing the intrinsic resilience to errors and noises of certain distribution in both inputs and neural weights. Randomly picked input test samples may not activate the faults in ReRAM cells at all, and make the faults escape from software testing, which will increase the risk of fatal failure caused by the latent faults in critical tasks. Thus, we have to propose a more sensitive test method that will activate and detect the faults and elusive cell state variations with high coverage and probability.

Recently, an adversarial example generating method has been proposed in the deep learning security domain, which is called FGSM (Fast Gradient Sign Method) [19]. It can be described as:

$$x' = x + \varepsilon \cdot sign(\nabla x J(F(x), y)) \tag{5.5}$$

where the adversarial example x' is generated by adding perturbations to the original sample x, as shown in Fig. 5.20. The perturbations $sign(\nabla x J(F(x), y))$ are calculated as the sign of the gradient of the model's loss function $J(\cdot, \cdot)$, pushing the original input move towards the direction of the gradient.

Though the adversarial examples are used to mislead DNNs originally, we find that they also have great performance on fault detection. Essentially, the adversarial

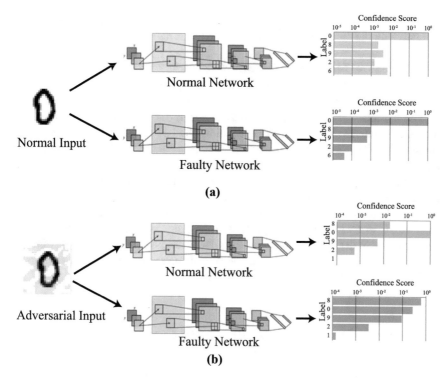

Fig. 5.21 The variations of confidence scores (**a**) when feeding the normal input into the normal network and faulty network and (**b**) when feeding the adversarial input into the normal network and faulty network

examples are elaborately generated according to the loss gradient, which is on the contrary of the weights update direction. Thus, the weight variations will have a severer impact on the prediction of adversarial examples.

To demonstrate the sensitivity of adversarial examples on parameter variations, we conducted an experiment by feeding a normal input and an adversarial input into a normal network and a faulty network respectively. The faulty model is generated by injecting faults on the original model parameters, degrading its classification accuracy from 98.6 to 96.8%. As illustrated in Fig. 5.21a, When we feed a normal sample into the two networks, there is only a 4% difference in the top-ranked output confidence scores. But both the normal network and the faulty network predict the normal sample as the same label '0'. However, as shown in Fig. 5.21b, when the network parameters are injected with faults, the output prediction of the adversarial sample totally changes from label '0' to label '8'. This is because that the adversarial examples are generated elaborately according to the loss gradient. Small disturbance on network parameters will result in large deviations on the confidence score. Hence, it is easier to detect subtle faults on edge devices by using adversarial examples.

Fault Diagnosis Here, we adopt the March C⁻ test algorithm for further fault diagnosis. Specifically, March C⁻ applies a series of read/write operations to a given memristor array by a specific address order and can achieve complete fault coverage by analyzing the fault dictionary [63]. March C^- is denoted as follows:

$$
\text{March } C^- - \{\updownarrow (w0); \Uparrow (r0, w1); \Downarrow (r1, w0);
$$
$$
\Downarrow (r0, w1) \Downarrow (r1, w0); \Uparrow (r0); \} \tag{5.6}
$$

The symbol '$\Uparrow$', '$\Downarrow$' and '$\updownarrow$' denote the order of address sequence. The increasing address direction is represented by the '$\Uparrow$' symbol, and the decreasing address direction is denoted by the '$\Downarrow$' symbol. The symbol '$\updownarrow$' is used when the address direction is irrelevant. Besides, '$w0$', '$w1$', '$r0$' and '$r1$' represent the write 0, write 1, read 0 and read 1 operation, respectively. It has been proved that the six March elements in the March C^- algorithm can detect all the modeled faults [41]. Obviously, it requires five read operations and five write operations for each memristor which brings huge time overhead. Considering the limited write endurance of ReRAM, our proposed RRAMedy framework only activates the FD component when the P&T mechanism detects the memristor faults, instead of using the March algorithm directly for fault detection.

5.3.3 Fault-Masking Retraining on the Cloud

Once there are unrepairable faults detected on the resource-limited edge devices, cloud servers need to take measures to rescue the system performance from memory faults. Conventional edge-based model retraining solutions have an obvious weakness: the retraining process consumes high hardware resources, making it unpractical to be deployed on the edge device. There are also off-device methods that are carried through model training, but it only focuses on making the network robust to faults, rather than eliminating the impacts of faults [7]. Based on this observation, we explore a cloud-edge collaborative model retraining method. For the **Cloud-Edge Collaborative Method**, the edge device only needs to generate the corresponding fault distribution as a fault-mask in the "Fault Detection and Diagnosis" phase (Fig. 5.18, step **3**) and transmit it to the cloud server. Then, the cloud server will leverage the received fault-mask and apply the proposed **fault-masking retraining method** to adaptively adjust the neural network to tolerate the device-specific faults.

Unlike previous work that enhances the robustness of network model by using specialized regularization in training, in this work, the goal of the offline model retraining process is to construct a fault-tolerate network $F'(x)$, which can recover the classification accuracy from faulty edge devices. The output of $F'(x)$ is supposed to be close to the original neural network output $F(x)$, that is:

$$
\forall x : \min \Delta(F(x), F'(x)) \tag{5.7}
$$

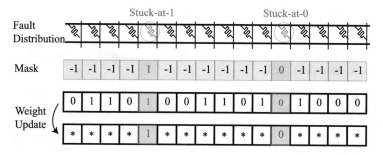

Fig. 5.22 Fault-masking retraining

It has been proven that DNN has the inherent self-recovery capability to relearn the ground truth from the corrupted weights [60]. By applying the Back Propagation (BP) algorithm to update weights, the training model parameters can self-adapt the faults iteration by iteration. The weight updating process can be derived as Eq. (5.3). However, with the BP algorithm, the weight W_i is only tuned to achieve high accuracy without consideration to be adjusted to adapt permanent faults. Hence, to reduce the performance degradation caused by the occurrence of unrepairable permanent faults, we propose to mask the faulty weights which suffer from "stuck-at" faults during the model retraining phase. Specifically, the update of weight W_i can be described as:

$$W_i \leftarrow Mask(W_i - \eta \frac{\partial E}{\partial W_i}) \tag{5.8}$$

The $Mask$ function is used to fix the faulty bits to their "stuck-at" values during the training phase, according to the received fault-mask. For example, as shown in Fig. 5.22, there is a 16-bit-width weight mapped on a row of memristors. However, a stuck-at-1 fault and a stuck-at-0 fault occur on these memristors simultaneously. To ensure the retraining phase can tolerate specific weight deviations, we mask the erroneous bits based on the bit-memristor mapping. When the bit value is mapped on a cell with stuck-at-1 (0) fault, we will fix the value to 1 (0) during the training phase. Therefore, by using the $Mask$-based retraining method on the cloud server, the network itself can compensate for the performance degradation from the error associated with ReRAM faults.

Due to communication resource and time constraints, the cloud servers only transmit the gradients to the edge devices, which are also quantized to further reduce the communication overhead, as it is shown that the gradients can be precisely represented by sparse and lower-bit code [65]. Then the edge device will use these gradients to update its local model back-ups and refresh the ReRAM states to reduce the fault-induced accuracy degradation. To rescue from soft faults, the edge device will employ the back-up neural model to refresh the ReRAM arrays. Here, we propose to employ iterative write on the device to make sure the cells are correctly programmed even when the cells are having parametric fluctuations [27].

5.3.4 In-Situ Model Remedy on the Edge

In fact, the current situation of implementing DNN retraining phase on the cloud still brings some problems:

1. Bandwidth competition: if there are numerous edge devices connected to the same network, there exists bandwidth competition between them. Especially when more than one device suffers faults simultaneously, they will request for model update and then exchange information with the cloud, increasing the traffic load of the network.
2. Latency: uploading fault maps to the cloud and offloading updated models from the cloud leaves associated communicational latency which can not be guaranteed to meet the requirements in some time-critical scenarios.
3. Computational pressure on cloud servers: fault-tolerant models are device-specific. Thus, the cloud server will perform the customized DNN training algorithm for every faulty chip, which undoubtedly poses serious challenges to the computational power and the storage resource of cloud servers.
4. Security concern: data transfer between cloud servers and edge devices increases the risk of attack. Even though the cloud server is trusted, edge users still lose absolute control over the transmitted model and data, which gives opportunities for adversaries to perform white-box attacks, black-box attacks and model tampering attacks [34].
5. Reliability concern: it is a great challenge to guarantee all the devices can connect to the cloud servers. Sometimes, the network connection may be lost. Some devices work in the environment without a network connection. Thus, an online fault-tolerant mechanism should be devised to ensure edge or end devices work normally in anywhere and anytime.

To address these concerns, it is desirable to consider implementing retraining-based model-level fault-tolerance on the edge. However, as we all know that, training DNNs is computationally expensive for edge devices. As described in Sect. 5.1.1.3, traditional training method uses the BP algorithm which transmits loss gradients from the output layer to the input layer sequentially for weight updates, occupying a significant amount of computational time. Meanwhile, the loss only comes from the final decision without any information extracted from the golden neural network. When DNNs are deep, the final loss is not enough to guide all the weight parameters to coverage quickly. Hence, using the classical training method for online fault-tolerant model retraining will take numerous iterations for weight updates, which not only bring a significant time overhead but also challenge the write endurance of memristors.

Inspired by these observations, we propose a novel online network retraining algorithm, **Intermediate Knowledge Transfer Retraining (IKTR)**, which introduces the golden model's intermediate represents as additional knowledge to assist the faulty neural networks for accuracy recovering. Herein, the golden model means the ideal model trained on the cloud servers without suffering from any hardware faults. The key idea of IKTR is built upon the popular approach, knowledge distillation (KD) [23], which transfers the knowledge from the larger teacher model to a smaller, simplified student model for model compression. At each training iteration, the teacher guides the student network's learning, which achieves significant improvement on network training efficiency. Therefore, we apply this method to the edge fault-tolerant retraining mechanism by treating the golden network as the teacher and the local network as the student. As the golden model preserves rich information on feature extraction, it can greatly help the student network to change its weight values to recover its classification accuracy.

However, the conventional KD method only uses the final output probabilities to optimize the student model, which makes the student model hard to mimic the internal learning behavior of the teacher model. Even though the student is fully optimized with the soft-labels of the teacher network, it may still have very different internal representations, which may affect its generalization capability [2].

Additionally, it is known that the intermediate representations of DNNs are enriched by the extracted features, which can be better leveraged to assist the student model for behavior imitation [31]. Hence, IKTR leverages the internal information extracted from the golden neural network as additional knowledge to guide the local network fault-tolerant retraining procedure.

To this end, as shown in Fig. 5.23, IKTR firstly splits the whole neural network into a set of sub-network blocks. In contrast to conventional knowledge transfer, the goal of IKTR is to retrieve the faulty network's accuracy rather than model compression. Hence, the network architecture of the teacher model and the student model is the same. The knowledge will be distilled in the same block from the golden model (G) to the local faulty model (F) directly. Specifically, we assume that we have a n-layer neural network with corresponding weights, $W = [W_0, W_1, \cdots, W_{n-1}]$. The network is split into K blocks, $[B_1, B_2, \ldots, B_K]$. Within each block, there is a set of layers, $[l_1, l_2, \ldots, l_m]$. The function of layer l_m can be represented as $f_m(a_{m-1}; W_m)$. Here, a_{m-1} represents the output activation of layer l_{m-1}. The objective of each block in faulty models is to imitate the normal sub-behavior of the

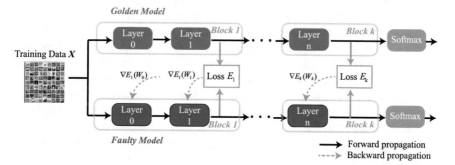

Fig. 5.23 An overview of our in-situ faulty model retraining mechanism based on intermediate knowledge transfer from the golden model to the faulty model

golden models. Thus, we formulate the objective function of each block as follows:

$$\min_{W_F} \Delta(o_F^k, o_G^k), k \in \{1, 2, \cdots, K\}$$

$$s.t.\ o^k = f_m(a_{m-1}; W_m) \tag{5.9}$$

where o_F^k and o_G^k denote the output activations of the k-th block in the faulty network and the golden network, respectively. l_m represents the last layer of the k-th block. Unlike the classical BP algorithm, the loss in IKTR is calculated by comparing the faulty model's intermediate representations (o_F^k) with the corresponding golden activations (o_G^k). Here, we adopt the Mean-Squared Loss (MSE) as the distillation loss:

$$E_k = \frac{1}{s \cdot r}(o_G^k - o_F^k)^2 \tag{5.10}$$

$$s = c \cdot w \cdot h \tag{5.11}$$

wherein, s represents the size of feature maps. r is the scale ratio. c, w and h are the channel counts, width and height of the o^k, respectively. By using the MSE loss function for blockwise knowledge distillation, the sub-network training block of the student network can learn the intermediate feature extraction capacity from the corresponding teacher network block.

Meanwhile, as shown in Fig. 5.23, within each block, the loss is still optimized through the conventional BP algorithm. Hence, the loss E_k is backward from the top layer to the bottom layer within the k-th block. It is worth noting that the optimal solution of the k-th block is independent of the other blocks. In other words, the loss E_k of block k is only used within the block k and not transmitted to neither block $k - 1$ nor block $k + 1$. Compared to be trained alone, each sub-network block can learn knowledge directly from the golden model's intermediate activations, which achieves fast network training convergence.

The details of the IKTR algorithm are described in Algorithm 6. The output of the block $k - 1$ is the input of the block k. Considering that errors occurred in the prior block will affect the input of the latter block, the training process is performed from the bottom block to the top block, with the order of $(1,2,3,\ldots K)$. Only when the front block is fully optimized, the next block will be trained. During the forward propagation of the blockwise training, the intermediate output activations of layer m, a_i^m, are generated. The output activations of the last layer in each student network's block are used for calculating the difference with the golden model and updating the parameters within the corresponding local training block. Unlike the original BP algorithm, the loss used for weight update of each block is not calculated from the final output as Eq. (5.3), but generated with the blockwise distillation loss. This makes the knowledge directly transfer from the golden model to the faulty model, encouraging the faulty network to simulate the intermediate representations of a golden network. Moreover, within the same block, the training gradient is still calculated with the "up-bottom" manner (M-1, M-2 ..., 0). Finally, all the training blocks are trained and the parameters are updated to adapt to the unrepairable faults.

Algorithm 6: Knowledge transfer retraining algorithm

Data: faulty weight values W_0, previous stored golden feature maps o_G, loss function L, training block set B

Result: updated fault-tolerant weights W_i

1 **for** B_k *in Block set* $\{B_1, B_2, \ldots, B_K\}$ **do**
2   **for** *iteration* $i = 1, 2, \ldots, I$ **do**
3   **Forward propagation:**
4   Initialize the input of block B_k: $a_0^0 = o^{k-1}$;
5   **for** *layer* $m = 1, 2, \ldots, M$ *in block* B_k, *(M is the number of layers in the block B_k)* **do**
6   Compute the intermediate activation of layer m: $a_i^m \leftarrow f_i(a_i^{m-1}; W_i^m)$;
7   **if** l_n *is the last layer of block* B_k **then**
8                  $o_{F_i}^k = a_i^n$;
9   **end**
10   **end**
11   **Backward propagation:** Compute the difference between o_G^k and $o_{F_i}^k$:
            $E_i^k = L(o_{F_i}^k, o_G^k)$ (L is calculated according to Eq.(5.10));
12   **for** *layer* $m = M - 1, M - 2, \ldots 0$ *(M is the size of layers in block B_k)* **do**
13   Generate gradient E_i^m for layer m;
14   **end**
15   **Parameter update: for** *layer* $m = 0, 1, 2, \ldots, M - 1$ **do**
16             $W_i^m \leftarrow Update(W_{i-1}^m, E_i^m)$;
17   **end**
18   **end**
19 **end**

In addition, as IKTR isolates the backpropagation of each block, the computational dependencies are broken. Hence, we improve the IKTR algorithm with a block-wise parallelized training method, **IKTR-P**, where blocks are updated in parallel. As shown in Fig. 5.24, IKTR updates the latter block only when the front block is fully optimized, which is still a sequential training method. However, for each iteration in IKTR-P, all sub-network training blocks calculate the block losses with the stored golden model's activations and compute the gradients within each block independently and simultaneously. Hence, the backpropagation time of IKTR-P is related to the most computational-complex blocks rather than the whole complexity of the DNN. The evaluations in Sect. 5.3.5 show that the proposed IKTR-P significantly speeds up the online fault-tolerant training process.

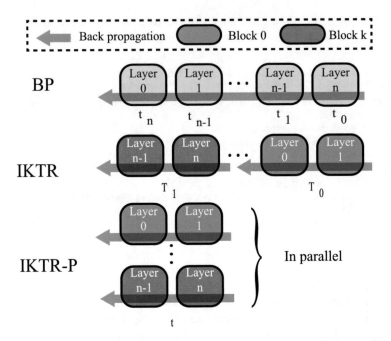

Fig. 5.24 Illustrations of the different backward propagation approaches including the BP algorithm, the IKTR algorithm, and the IKTR-P algorithm. The rectangles in the same color belong to the same training blocks. The arrow indicates the direction of the loss passing. t represents the relative timestamp in each training iteration. T represents the timestamp in the whole training phase

5.3.5 Experiment Result Analysis

5.3.5.1 Experiment Setup

Datasets and Workload We investigated the effectiveness of RRAMedy on two standard datasets, MNIST and Cifar-10, with three different network architectures, as described in Table 5.2. The MNIST dataset is used for hand-written digit recognition with 70,000 gray-scale images, wherein 60,000 images are used for training and 10,000 images are testing data. The Cifar-10 dataset consists of 60,000 true-color images of size $3 \times 32 \times 32$. The dataset is divided into 50,000 training images and 10,000 test ones.

Table 5.2 Benchmarks

Network	Dataset	Classes	Architecture	Accuracy
MLP	MNIST	10	3 FC	0.9616
LeNet	MNIST	10	2 CONV + 2 FC	0.9858
ConvNet-quick	Cifar-10	10	3 CONV + 2FC	0.745

Fault Injection Mechanism   To precisely model the impacts of unreliable ReRAM cells on the accuracy of neural networks, we modified the Caffe and TensorFlow framework for fault injection simulation to inject the real-world ReRAM-based faults into ReRAM cells and propagate the errors from the device level to the applications. The faults are injected randomly in the proper network parameters by modifying the 16-bit fixed-point weights in the simulator. For soft faults, we simulated the memristor resistance variations as follows [7]:

$$w_i = w_i + \theta_i; \theta \sim (0, \sigma^2) \tag{5.12}$$

wherein, the σ was set to 0.01 (low), 0.03 (medium) and 0.05 (high) respectively to mimic the resistance drifts in ReRAM cells. As for hard faults, we simulated the fault occurrences with both stuck-at-1 (ST1) faults and stuck-at-0 (ST0) faults on SLC ReRAM cells and MLC ReRAM cells respectively. For SLC-ReRAM implementation, when a ReRAM cell suffers from a stuck-at fault, its stored bit-value will be changed to the stuck-at value. As for MLC implementation, we illustrate the fault injection mechanism with 4-level ReRAM MLC cells. When a 4-level MLC ReRAM cell suffers from faults, two adjacent bit-values stored in the same cell will be impacted. For example, when a 4-level MLC ReRAM cell suffers a stuck-at-1 fault, its stored value will be fixed at '11', whatever the value it stored before. Based on this fault injection mechanism, we simulated the occurrence of soft faults and hard faults on ReRAM-based deep learning accelerators.

5.3.5.2   Effectiveness of Adversarial Example Testing

We propose to detect the fault occurrence in deep learning systems with two detection criteria from [30], including:

SDC-1: When the top-ranked prediction of the executed DNN is different from the fault-free prediction, we consider that there exist faults in the edge neural accelerator.

SDC-3%: The top-ranked confidence score is compared with the ideal execution. If the variations are more than +/− 3%, we consider that the ReRAM accelerator is faulty.

To further evaluate the effectiveness of our Adversarial Example-based detection, we did experiments on all the three above-mentioned networks. We tested 100 faulty-models for each network and simulated on both SLC and MLC ReRAM.

Here, we define the **Detection Accuracy (DA)** as a measure of how well the fault-affected neural network can be differentiated from the original model. Specifically, it is defined as the accuracy of the detector when identifying the faulty networks, and can be formulated as:

$$DA = \frac{\text{The Number of Identified Faulty Models}}{\text{Total Number of Tested Faulty Models}} \tag{5.13}$$

Table 5.3 The ε used in
AET method

Network	MLP	LeNet	ConvNet
ε	0.022	0.095	2.1

Furthermore, we try to choose the best adversarial example for fault occurrence detection. We tested different disturbance ε (Eq. (5.5)) to generate adversarial examples. The ε used for the AET method in this work is shown in Table 5.3.

SLC ReRAM Evaluation

For the SLC mode of ReRAM-based deep learning accelerator, a 16-bit fixed-point weight needs to be stored in 16 memristors. Considering each cell may suffer from memory faults, we injected both permanent faults and soft faults by randomly modifying bit values within a weight. For permanent faults, five-thousandths of the weight bits are injected with stuck-at faults in LeNet and multilayer perceptron (MLP) network. While for the ConvNet network, it is more sensitive to faults. Even if only one-thousandth of weights are faulty, the classification accuracy drops about 10% sharply. Since we need to detect faults before they become uncontrolled, we only injected 0.2‰ faults on ConvNet weight values. As for soft faults, we injected 1% faults into the MLP and LeNet network, and 0.4‰ faults into the ConvNet network. Furthermore, we also tested the DAs of the proposed detection method when both permanent faults and soft faults occur simultaneously.

Figure 5.25 illustrates the DAs of two detection methods on three neural networks. "Origin" is the strategy that uses the normal input for fault detection, while "AET" uses the proposed AET method. For example, the "Origin" method only achieves 64% detection accuracy on the MLP network for permanent faults, 87% for soft faults, and 90% for the existence of both hard and soft faults with the SDC-3% criterion (Fig. 5.25a). But by using the AET method, the detection accuracy achieves more than 98% in all the three faulty conditions. Furthermore, since SDC-1 is a less strict criterion than SDC-3%, smaller weight deviations can be detected by using SDC-3%. Hence, we focus on SDC-3% in the rest of the section to pursue higher detection accuracy.

Figure 5.25b, c shows the DAs on convolutional neural networks, LeNet and ConvNet. Obviously, the AET method outperforms the "Origin" test method by more than 22%. Besides, it is worth noting that when the ReRAM-based deep learning accelerators suffer from both permanent faults and soft faults simultaneously, the AET method achieves more than 99% detection accuracy.

MLC ReRAM Evaluation

For the MLC mode of ReRAM-based deep learning accelerator, we consider a 2^2-level MLC as [54] has used in this section. Each 16-bit weight is distributed to eight ReRAM MLCs. For permanent fault occurrence simulation, the injected faulty rate is as the same as the SLC mode.

For permanent fault detection, as shown in Fig. 5.26, the "Origin" method can hardly differentiate the faulty models from original models, but the AET

Fig. 5.25 Detection accuracy on SLC ReRAM on (**a**) MLP (**b**) LeNet (**c**) ConvNet network with the consideration of only permanent faults; only soft faults and both permanent faults and soft faults occurrence

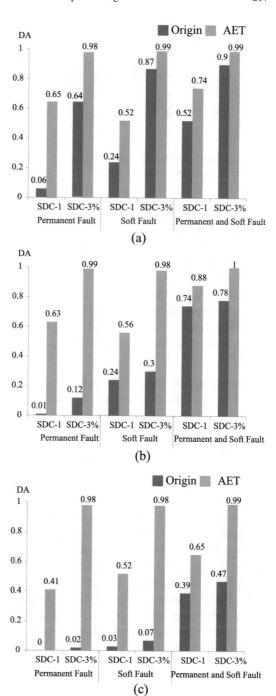

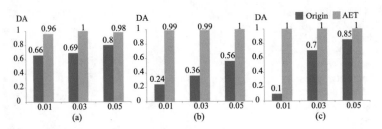

Fig. 5.26 Permanent fault detection accuracy with the implementation on MLC ReRAM of (**a**) MLP, (**b**) LeNet, (**c**) ConvNet network

method achieves more than 97% detection accuracy with the elaborately generated adversarial example.

For soft faults detection, as shown in Fig. 5.27, with larger resistance variations, the DA increases for both three networks. This is because that larger resistance variations will cause severer performance reduction and will lead its output confidence change obviously. When considering that both permanent faults and soft faults occur simultaneously, Fig. 5.28 shows that by using AET method, more than 96% faulty models can be detected on all three networks. Hence, the proposed AET dramatically achieves high detection accuracy on all the three tested fault occurrence situations.

Performance Evaluation To compare the performance of our proposed AET-based on-line fault detection and diagnosis method (using AET for fault detection and using March C- for fault diagnosis) with pure March C- algorithm, we executed our benchmarks on a CNN accelerator similar to ISAAC [54], running at 1.2 GHz. The 16-bit fixed-point weight is split into eight 2-bit memristors and the crossbar is composed of 128 * 128 ReRAM cells [15].

The experimental results are described in Fig. 5.29. We observed that when the chip failure rate is 1%, the proposed AET-based method achieves a speedup from $11.5\times$ to $91.39\times$ in comparison with pure March C- algorithm. Since the fully-connected layer has less computational operations but more occupied parameter storage space, for benchmarks with more fully-connected layers, the AET-based method has a higher speed-up ratio. In addition, as the failure rate increases, more fault diagnosis process is executed and the speedup provided by our AET-based fault detection becomes smaller. However, even the chip failure rate is as high as 10%, our method still achieves more than $5.65\times$ speedup. Besides, as the write endurance of ReRAM is limited, the proposed AET-based fault detection method saves the memristors from unnecessary memory wear-outs.

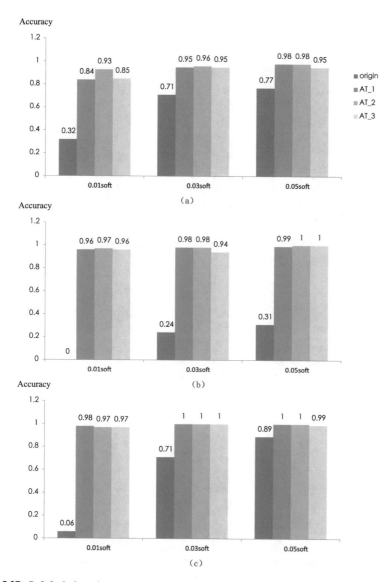

Fig. 5.27 Soft fault detection accuracy with the implementation on MLC ReRAM of (**a**) MLP, (**b**) LeNet, (**c**) ConvNet network (The X-axis represents the resistance variations θ)

5.3.5.3   Effectiveness of Offline Retraining

We evaluated the proposed fault-masking training method by simulation-based fault injection. We injected both stuck-at-0 faults and stuck-at-1 faults on each benchmark. The tested fault rate varies from 0.005 to 0.015 on MLP and LeNet, while 0.001 to 0.003 for ConvNet. Figure 5.30 presents the retrieved accuracy for

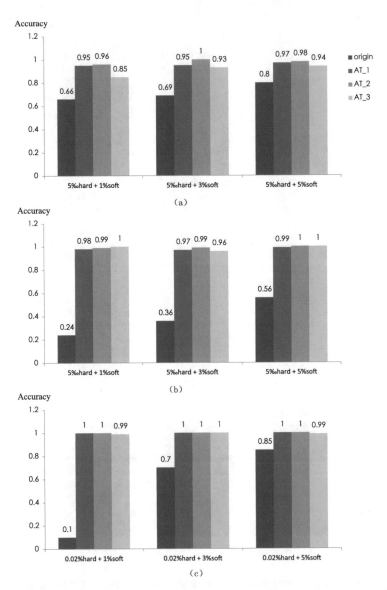

Fig. 5.28 Fault detection accuracy, considering both permanent faults and soft faults on MLC ReRAM with (**a**) MLP, (**b**) LeNet, (**c**) ConvNet network (The X-axis represents the resistance variations θ)

all the three networks with the SLC ReRAM implementation and the MLC ReRAM implementation respectively. As shown in Fig. 5.30, the ConvNet is significantly affected by parameter variations. Even though it suffers only one-tenth of injected faults of the other two benchmarks, the accuracy is still dropped by about 8%.

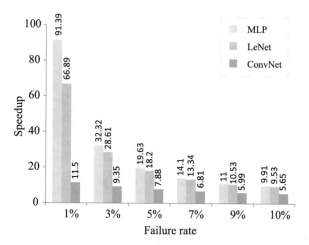

Fig. 5.29 The performance speedups of our proposed on-line fault detection and diagnosis method

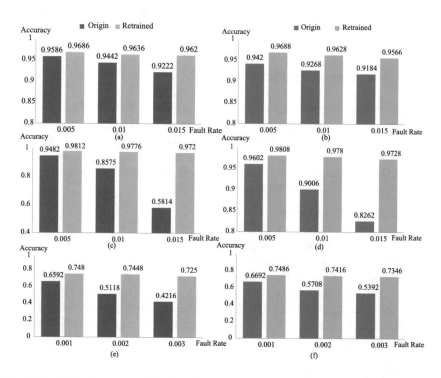

Fig. 5.30 Retrieved accuracy of fault-masking training with SLC ReRAM implementation ((**a**) MLP (**c**) LeNet (**e**) ConvNet network) and MLC ReRAM implementation ((**b**) MLP (**d**) LeNet (**f**) ConvNet network)

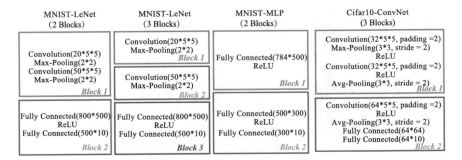

Fig. 5.31 The training block partition scheme used in this work

The reason is that the Cifar dataset is more complex than MNIST dataset. Besides, ConvNet only has a small series of layers which makes it has limited fault-tolerance capability. Furthermore, we can conclude from the results that, accuracy can retrieve from heavy system degradation by leveraging the proposed fault-masking retraining method. After retraining, the system performance degradation is less than 2% on all the three benchmarks.

5.3.5.4 Effectiveness of Online Retraining

We evaluated the proposed IKTR-based online retraining method on the aforementioned datasets. The training block partition scheme used in this work is shown in Fig. 5.31. We split the LeNet network, MLP network and ConvNet network into two to three blocks respectively. Meanwhile, we injected 1, 3, and 1% hard faults on LeNet, MLP and ConvNet-quick network parameters respectively to simulate both SLC-based faulty DLAs and MLC-based faulty DLAs.

(a) Performance Comparisons

The comparisons of the recovered model accuracies and performance speedups between traditional backward propagation (BP) algorithm, knowledge distillation (KD), IKTR and IKTR-P are depicted in Table 5.4. Several observations can be seen as follows. Firstly, as depicted in Table 5.4, all the KD, IKTR and IKTR-P methods can restore the accuracy of faulty neural networks from up to 43% accuracy degradation and achieve more than 1.25× training speedups over traditional BP algorithm. This is because that all these three methods leverage knowledge from the well-trained golden teacher model to make the faulty model mimic the behavior of the golden model. Secondly, the proposed IKTR-based algorithm still outperforms the traditional KD algorithm. This is because that the KD algorithm only provides the soft labels (output probabilities) to optimize the student model, it is hard for the student faulty model to learn the intermediate behavior of the golden model, especially when the network becomes deeper. Considering that the internal layers of a neural network has extracted rich information. The IKTR-based method splits

Table 5.4 Results of comparing the proposed IKTR and IKTR-P methods with traditional backpropagation algorithm (BP) and knowledge distillation algorithm (KD) on three benchmarks (LeNet, MLP, and ConvNet)

Benchmark (accuracy)	ReRAM cell	Strategy	Accuracy	Speedup
LeNet (0.9881)	SLC	Faulty model	0.8027	–
		Baseline-BP	0.9772	1x
		Baseline-KD	0.9853	1.25x
		IKTR(2 blocks)	0.9856	2.5x
		IKTR-P(2 blocks)	0.9856	2.83x
		IKTR(3 blocks)	0.9863	2.5x
		IKTR-P(3 blocks)	0.9856	3.13x
	MLC	Faulty model	0.7457	–
		Baseline-BP	0.9835	1x
		Baseline-KD	0.9845	2x
		IKTR(2 blocks)	0.9851	2x
		IKTR-P(2 blocks)	0.9853	2.27x
		IKTR(3 blocks)	0.9854	2x
		IKTR-P(3 blocks)	0.9854	3.34x
MLP (0.9833)	SLC	Faulty model	0.8029	–
		Baseline-BP	0.9623	1x
		Baseline-KD	0.9762	3x
		IKTR(2 blocks)	0.9771	6x
		IKTR-P(2 blocks)	0.9770	7.38x
	MLC	Faulty model	0.7909	–
		Baseline-BP	0.9621	1x
		Baseline-KD	0.9743	2.5x
		IKTR(2 blocks)	0.9761	5x
		IKTR-P(2 blocks)	0.9758	6.15x
ConvNet (0.7698)	SLC	Faulty model	0.4379	–
		Baseline-BP	0.7248	1x
		Baseline-KD	0.7424	1.25x
		IKTR(2 blocks)	0.766	1.5x
		IKTR-P(2 blocks)	0.764	1.83x
	MLC	Faulty model	0.3156	–
		Baseline-BP	0.7137	1x
		Baseline-KD	0.7464	1.5x
		IKTR(2 blocks)	0.7511	1.5x
		IKTR-P(2 blocks)	0.7525	2.3x

the network into small blocks, making each training block locally learn the internal representations from the golden teacher model. Furthermore, the IKTR and IKTR-P methods enable a direct fine-tuning, which avoids a sequential backpropagation through network and consumes few epochs for block-wise network training, further improving the training convergence speed. Thirdly, the proposed IKTR-P method breaks the sequential retraining process and enables parallel block-wise training. Each block trains independently and simultaneously, further accelerating the online retraining procedure.

(b) Analysis of the Impact of the Number of Training Blocks

To investigate the performance speedups with different block numbers of IKTR-based online remedy methods, we validated the proposed IKTR method with both two sub-blocks partitioning and three sub-blocks partitioning on the LeNet network. As we can see from Table 5.4, when we split the LeNet network into three blocks, it achieves higher retrieved accuracy than two sub-blocks partitioned IKTR-based training. The improvement can be explained by the fact that the IKTR method divides the highly complex optimization problem into several simpler subproblems. When the number of sub-blocks increases, each training block becomes smaller and easier to be trained. Meanwhile, with more training blocks partitioned, more internal knowledge is transferred to the faulty student neural network, which helps it to mimic the behavior of the golden model. However, the size of the partitioned sub-network training block cannot be too small, which may lead to over-fitting and decrease the retrieved accuracy. Furthermore, more training blocks achieve additional speedup through parallel training (IKTR-P). It can be seen from Table 5.4, for the Lenet network, three-block partitioned IKTR-P training outperforms the two-block partitioned IKTR-P training with $1.2\times$ speedup on average. The reason is that, blocks are trained separately in parallel in IKTR-P. Hence, the runtime for IKTR-P depends on the block with the longest computation time. When we split the most complex block into several smaller blocks, IKTR-P takes less computational time in each training iteration.

(c) Analysis of the Impact of the Size Of Training Dataset

To further reduce the storage overhead of implementing the IKTR and IKTR-P algorithms on the edge device, we have made an analysis of using IKTR-P method for online model retraining with different sizes of training datasets. We conducted the experiments on SLC ReRAM and reached the same conclusion on MLC ReRAM. As shown in Fig. 5.32, we randomly chose 500 (small), 5000 (medium) and 50,000 (large) training samples from the original training set for faulty ConvNet retraining. It's obvious that the memory consumptions are related to the size of training set. Using the small training dataset for model learning only costs 1% storage compared with using the large training dataset. However, fewer samples for training leads to limited accuracy improvement capacity. Using small training set for faulty model retraining causes about 4% accuracy loss on average, which is insufficient to meet the high accuracy requirement of deep-learning applications. In addition, we found that leveraging medium training set for IKTR-based model retraining had quite small accuracy drop of up to 4‰ from using the large training set, but enables 90% storage saving as well as more than 17%

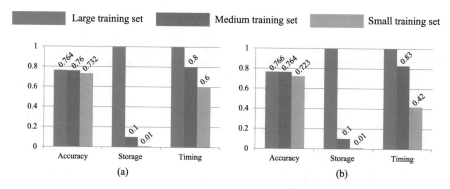

Fig. 5.32 Trade-offs between the recovered model accuracy, storage and timing costs. (**a**) Case 1: IKTR-P retraining method. (**b**) Case 2: IKTR retraining method

training time reduction. Therefore, to achieve low storage costs with high retrieved model accuracy, it is recommended to use the medium training set for IKTR-based model faulty model retraining.

(d) Impact of the Fault Occurrence Positions

To evaluate the performance impact on the IKTR-based model retraining algorithm with different bit positions of the faults occurring in the neural network weights, we have repeated the evaluations with our proposed IKTR-P method. For each benchmark, we randomly injected a fixed number of stuck-at faults and varied the proportion of faults that occurred in MSBs (Most significant bits) and LSBs (Least significant bits) of weight values. In addition, we tested ten faulty models for each fault occurrence scenario and simulated on both SLC and MLC ReRAMs. The experimental results are plotted in the Fig. 5.33. Several conclusions can be drawn as follows. First, even the fault rates are the same, the accuracies of faulty neural networks will be different according to the fault occurrence positions. As shown in Fig. 5.33, we varied the proportion of faults that occurred in MSBs vs. LSBs from 0.33 to 4 on all the three tested benchmarks. It is observed that when the fault rate of the MSBs is four times more than the fault rate of the LSBs, the average accuracy of faulty MLP networks significantly drops from 98 to 81% (Fig. 5.33a). Since the ConvNet is more sensitive to fault-induced weight variations, it is observed in Fig. 5.33f that, when 80% of the total injected faults occur in high-order positions, the average accuracy drops even more than 50%. In contrast, when 67% of the injected faults occurr in LSBs of the weight values in ConvNet, the accuracy degradation is only 0.6% on average. This phenomenon can be explained by that faults in MSBs cause larger deviations in magnitude of weight values, increasing the possibility of a decrease in the accuracy of the neural network. Second, note that for all the tested benchmarks, the online remedy method IKTR-P can recover the deep learning system accuracy from up to 57% fault-induced accuracy degradation with less than 2% accuracy loss through fault-tolerant model retraining.

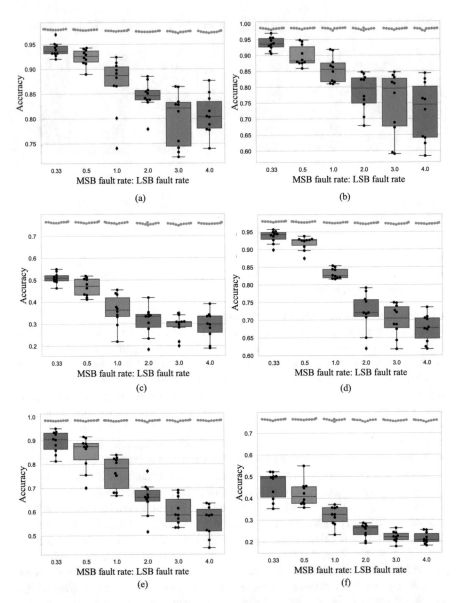

Fig. 5.33 Impact of fault positions on model accuracy. The red dots presented the recovered model accuracy with IKTR-P method. The black dots presented the faulty model accuracy. Boxes show median and 2nd and 3rd quartile of the faulty model accuracy. (**a**) Case 1: MLP network on SLC ReRAM. (**b**) Case 2: LeNet network on SLC ReRAM. (**c**) Case 3: ConvNet network on SLC ReRAM. (**d**) Case 4: MLP network on MLC ReRAM. (**e**) Case 5: LeNet network on MLC ReRAM. (**f**) Case 6: ConvNet network on MLC ReRAM

5.3.6 Discussion

We comprehensively analyze the reliability issues of ReRAM-based edge neural accelerators and present RRAMedy, a novel framework to protect ReRAM chips from both permanent faults and soft faults. For fault detection, we introduce a lightweight Adversarial Example Testing method to detect the subtle fault-induced variations. For retrieving the system performance, according to the computing capacity and application scenarios of edge devices, we put forward an edge-cloud collaborative model retraining method and an in-situ model retraining algorithm. The experimental results show that the RRAMedy has high fault detection probability and can recover the recognition accuracy with little performance degradation.

5.4 Summary

The reliability of the execution is of vital importance and must be considered comprehensively in deep learning of numerous domains of application. The state-of-the-art redundancy design approaches reduce the hardware overhead, but the practical effects are highly sensitive to the fault distribution and fail to work under circumstances of unevenly distributed faults. To address this problem, we propose a HyCA, which can fully recover the 2-D computing array despite the fault distribution. According to our experiments, HyCA outperforms prior redundancy approaches in terms of both the fully functional probability and the computing power under different fault distribution models. In addition, HyCA can also be reused for the fault detection at runtime and the experiment result shows that the entire 2-D computing array can be scanned and detected before a neural network layer completes its execution in most cases.

Since ReRAM has become a promising CiM technology for deep learning, the occurrence of the permanent and soft faults in the ReRAM has become one of the major concerns for ReRAM-based DNN accelerator designs. We analyze the reliability issues of ReRAM-based DLAs. And based on these analysis, we propose RRAMedy, a novel framework to protect ReRAM chips from both permanent faults and soft faults. Our experimental results show that RRAMedy has high probability of fault detection and can recover the recognized accuracy with little performance degradation.

References

1. Muhammad Abdullah Hanif and Muhammad Shafique. Salvagednn: Salvaging Deep Neural Network Accelerators with Permanent Faults Through Saliency-driven Fault-aware Mapping. *Philosophical Transactions of the Royal Society A*, 378(2164):1–23, 2020.
2. Gustavo Aguilar, Yuan Ling, Yu Zhang, Benjamin Yao, Xing Fan, and Edward Guo. Knowledge distillation from internal representations. In *Association for the Advancement of Artificial Intelligence*, pages 1–8, 2019.
3. Aneesh Aggarwal and M. Franklin. Energy Efficient Asymmetrically Ported Register Files. In *Proceedings 21st International Conference on Computer Design*, pages 2–7, 2003.
4. Subho S Banerjee, James Cyriac, Saurabh Jha, Zbigniew T Kalbarczyk, and Ravishankar K Iyer. Towards a Bayesian Approach for Assessing Fault Tolerance of Deep Neural Networks. In *2019 49th Annual IEEE/IFIP International Conference on Dependable Systems and Networks–Supplemental Volume (DSN-S)*, pages 25–26, 2019.
5. P. Chang, T. Lin, J. Wang, and Y. Yu. A 4R/2W Register File Design for UDVS Microprocessors in 65-nm CMOS. *IEEE Transactions on Circuits and Systems II: Express Briefs*, 59(12):908–912, 2012.
6. C. Chen, H. Shih, C. Wu, C. Lin, P. Chiu, S. Sheu, and F. T. Chen. RRAM defect modeling and failure analysis based on march test and a novel squeeze-search scheme. *IEEE Transactions on Computers*, 64(1):180–190, 2015.
7. L. Chen, J. Li, Y. Chen, Q. Deng, J. Shen, X. Liang, and L. Jiang. Accelerator-friendly neural-network training: Learning variations and defects in rram crossbar. In *Proc. Design, Automation Test in Europe Conference Exhibition (DATE), 2017*, pages 19–24, 2017.
8. Yu-Hsin Chen, Joel Emer, and Vivienne Sze. Eyeriss: A Spatial Architecture for Energy-Efficient Dataflow for Convolutional Neural Networks. In *2016 ACM/IEEE 43rd Annual International Symposium on Computer Architecture (ISCA)*, pages 367–379, 2016.
9. Yunji Chen, Tao Luo, Shaoli Liu, Shijin Zhang, Liqiang He, Jia Wang, Ling Li, Tianshi Chen, Zhiwei Xu, Ninghui Sun, et al. Dadiannao: A Machine-learning Supercomputer. In *2014 47th Annual IEEE/ACM International Symposium on Microarchitecture*, pages 609–622, 2014.
10. P. Chi, S. Li, C. Xu, T. Zhang, J. Zhao, Y. Liu, Y. Wang, and Y. Xie. Prime: A novel processing-in-memory architecture for neural network computation in reram-based main memory. In *Proc. ACM/IEEE 43rd Annual International Symposium on Computer Architecture (ISCA)*, pages 27–39, 2016.
11. L.C. Chu and B. W. Wah. Fault tolerant neural networks with hybrid redundancy. In *Proc. 1990 IJCNN International Joint Conference on Neural Networks*, volume 2, pages 639–649, 1990.
12. Jia Deng, Wei Dong, Richard Socher, Li-Jia Li, Kai Li, and Li Fei-Fei. Imagenet: A Large-scale Hierarchical Image Database. In *2009 IEEE conference on computer vision and pattern recognition*, pages 248–255, 2009.
13. Jiacnao Deng, Yuntan Rang, Zidong Du, Ymg Wang, Huawei Li, Olivier Temam, Paolo Ienne, David Novo, Xiaowei Li, Yunji Chen, et al. Retraining-based timing error mitigation for hardware neural networks. In *2015 Design, Automation & Test in Europe Conference & Exhibition (DATE)*, pages 593–596, 2015.
14. A. Dixit and A. Wood. The Impact of New Technology on Soft Error Rates. In *2011 International Reliability Physics Symposium*, pages 5B.4.1–5B.4.7, 2011.
15. Xiangyu Dong. *Modeling and Leveraging Emerging Non-volatile Memories for Future Computer Designs*. PhD thesis, The Pennsylvania State University, 2011.
16. C. Ebert and M. Weyrich. Validation of Autonomous Systems. *IEEE Software*, 36(5):15–23, 2019.
17. Andre Esteva, Alexandre Robicquet, Bharath Ramsundar, Volodymyr Kuleshov, Mark DePristo, Katherine Chou, Claire Cui, Greg Corrado, Sebastian Thrun, and Jeff Dean. A Guide to Deep Learning in Healthcare. *Nature medicine*, 25(1):24–29, 2019.

18. Maximilian Fink, Ying Liu, Armin Engstle, and Stefan-Alexander Schneider. Deep Learning-Based Multi-scale Multi-object Detection and Classification for Autonomous Driving. In *Fahrerassistenzsysteme 2018*, pages 233–242, 2019.

19. Ian J. Goodfellow, Jonathon Shlens, and Christian Szegedy. Explaining and harnessing adversarial examples. In *Proc. International Conference on Learning Representations*, pages 1–11, 2015.

20. S. Hamdioui, P. Pouyan, H. Li, Y. Wang, A. Raychowdhur, and I. Yoon. Test and reliability of emerging non-volatile memories. In *Proc. IEEE 26th Asian Test Symposium (ATS)*, pages 170–178, 2017.

21. M. A. Hanif, R. Hafiz, and M. Shafique. Error Resilience Analysis for Systematically Employing Approximate Computing in Convolutional Neural Networks. In *2018 Design, Automation Test in Europe Conference Exhibition (DATE)*, pages 913–916, 2018.

22. X. He, W. Lu, G. Yan, and X. Zhang. Joint Design of Training and Hardware Towards Efficient and Accuracy-Scalable Neural Network Inference. *IEEE Journal on Emerging and Selected Topics in Circuits and Systems*, 8(4):810–821, 2018.

23. Geoffrey Hinton, Oriol Vinyals, and Jeff Dean. Distilling the knowledge in a neural network. In *NIPS Deep Learning and Representation Learning Workshop*, pages 1–9, 2015.

24. Tadayoshi Horita and Itsuo Takanami. Fault-tolerant Processor Arrays Based on the 1 1/2-track Switches with Flexible Spare Distributions. *IEEE Transactions on Computers*, 49(6):542–552, 2000.

25. Maksim Jenihhin, Matteo Sonza Reorda, Aneesh Balakrishnan, and Dan Alexandrescu. Challenges of Reliability Assessment and Enhancement in Autonomous Systems. In *2019 IEEE International Symposium on Defect and Fault Tolerance in VLSI and Nanotechnology Systems (DFT)*, pages 1–6, 2019.

26. Saurabh Jha, Subho Banerjee, Timothy Tsai, Siva KS Hari, Michael B Sullivan, Zbigniew T Kalbarczyk, Stephen W Keckler, and Ravishankar K Iyer. ML-Based Fault Injection for Autonomous Vehicles: A Case for Bayesian Fault Injection. In *2019 49th Annual IEEE/IFIP International Conference on Dependable Systems and Networks (DSN)*, pages 112–124, 2019.

27. K. Jo, C. Jung, K. Min, and S. Kang. Self-adaptive write circuit for low-power and variation-tolerant memristors. *IEEE Transactions on Nanotechnology*, 9(6):675–678, 2010.

28. Norman P Jouppi, Cliff Young, Nishant Patil, David Patterson, Gaurav Agrawal, Raminder Bajwa, Sarah Bates, Suresh Bhatia, Nan Boden, Al Borchers, et al. In-datacenter Performance Analysis of A Tensor Processing Unit. In *Proceedings of the 44th Annual International Symposium on Computer Architecture*, pages 1–12, 2017.

29. S. Kim, P. Howe, T. Moreau, A. Alaghi, L. Ceze, and V. S. Sathe. Energy-Efficient Neural Network Acceleration in the Presence of Bit-Level Memory Errors. *IEEE Transactions on Circuits and Systems I: Regular Papers*, 65(12):4285–4298, 2018.

30. Guanpeng Li, Siva Kumar Sastry Hari, Michael Sullivan, Timothy Tsai, Karthik Pattabiraman, Joel Emer, and Stephen W. Keckler. Understanding error propagation in deep learning neural network (dnn) accelerators and applications. In *Proc. ACM International Conference for High Performance Computing, Networking, Storage and Analysis (SC)*, pages 8:1–8:12, 2017.

31. Hao-Ting Li, Shih-Chieh Lin, Cheng-Yeh Chen, and Chen-Kuo Chiang. Layer-level knowledge distillation for deep neural network learning. *Applied Sciences*, 9(10):1.1–1.13, 2019.

32. Li Li, Dawen Xu, Kouzi Xing, Cheng Liu, Ying Wang, Huawei Li, and Xiaowei Li. Squeezing the Last MHz for CNN Acceleration on FPGAs. In *2019 IEEE International Test Conference in Asia (ITC-Asia)*, pages 151–156, 2019.

33. Man-Lap Li, Pradeep Ramachandran, Swarup Kumar Sahoo, Sarita V Adve, Vikram S Adve, and Yuanyuan Zhou. Understanding the propagation of hard errors to software and implications for resilient system design. *ACM Sigplan Notices*, 43(3):265–276, 2008.

34. Wen Li, Ying Wang, Huawei Li, and Xiaowei Li. P3m: A pim-based neural network model protection scheme for deep learning accelerator. In *Proceedings of the 24th Asia and South Pacific Design Automation Conference*, pages 633–638, 2019.

35. Wenshuo Li, Guangjun Ge, Kaiyuan Guo, Xiaoming Chen, Qi Wei, Zhen Gao, Yu Wang, and Huazhong Yang. Soft Error Mitigation for Deep Convolution Neural Network on FPGA Accelerators. In *2020 2nd IEEE International Conference on Artificial Intelligence Circuits and Systems (AICAS)*, pages 1–5, 2020.

36. Wenshuo Li, Xuefei Ning, Guangjun Ge, Xiaoming Chen, Yu Wang, and Huazhong Yang. Ftt-nas: Discovering fault-tolerant neural architecture. In *2020 25th Asia and South Pacific Design Automation Conference (ASP-DAC)*, pages 211–216, 2020.

37. B. Liu, Hai Li, Yiran Chen, Xin Li, Qing Wu, and Tingwen Huang. Vortex: Variation-aware training for memristor x-bar. In *Proc. ACM/EDAC/IEEE 52nd Design Automation Conference (DAC)*, pages 1–6, 2015.

38. Cheng Liu, Lei Zhang, Yinhe Han, and Xiaowei Li. A resilient on-chip router design through data path salvaging. In *16th Asia and South Pacific Design Automation Conference (ASP-DAC 2011)*, pages 437–442, 2011.

39. M. Liu, L. Xia, Y. Wang, and K. Chakrabarty. Fault tolerance for RRAM-based matrix operations. In *Proc. 2018 IEEE International Test Conference (ITC)*, pages 1–10, 2018.

40. Mengyun Liu, Lixue Xia, Yu Wang, and Krishnendu Chakrabarty. Fault tolerance in neuromorphic computing systems. In *Proc. ACM/IEEE 24th Asia and South Pacific Design Automation Conference (ASPDAC)*, pages 216–223, 2019.

41. P. Liu, Z. You, J. Kuang, Z. Hu, H. Duan, and W. Wang. Efficient march test algorithm for 1t1r cross-bar with complete fault coverage. *Electronics Letters*, 52(18):1520–1522, 2016.

42. Y. Long, X. She, and S. Mukhopadhyay. Design of reliable dnn accelerator with un-reliable reram. In *Proc. 2019 Design, Automation Test in Europe Conference Exhibition (DATE)*, pages 1769–1774, 2019.

43. Hamid Reza Mahdiani, Sied Mehdi Fakhraie, and Caro Lucas. Relaxed Fault-tolerant Hardware Implementation of Neural Networks in the Presence of Multiple Transient Errors. *IEEE transactions on neural networks and learning systems*, 23(8):1215–1228, 2012.

44. Fred J. Meyer and Dhiraj K. Pradhan. Modeling defect spatial distribution. *IEEE Transactions on Computers*, 38(4):538–546, 1989.

45. Sparsh Mittal. A Survey on Modeling and Improving Reliability of DNN Algorithms and Accelerators. *Journal of Systems Architecture*, 104:101689, 2020.

46. Mohamed A Neggaz, Ihsen Alouani, Pablo R Lorenzo, and Smail Niar. A Reliability Study on CNNs for Critical Embedded Systems. In *2018 IEEE 36th International Conference on Computer Design (ICCD)*, pages 476–479, 2018.

47. D. Niu, Yang Xiao, and Yuan Xie. Low power memristor-based reram design with error correcting code. In *Proc. 17th Asia and South Pacific Design Automation Conference (ASPDAC)*, pages 79–84, 2012.

48. Elbruz Ozen and Alex Orailoglu. Sanity-Check: Boosting the reliability of safety-critical deep neural network applications. In *2019 IEEE 28th Asian Test Symposium (ATS)*, pages 7–75, 2019.

49. P. Pouyan, E. Amat, and A. Rubio. Reliability challenges in design of memristive memories. In *Proc. 5th European Workshop on CMOS Variability (VARI)*, pages 1–6, 2014.

50. Junyan Qian, Zhide Zhou, Tianlong Gu, Lingzhong Zhao, and Liang Chang. Optimal Reconfiguration of High-performance VLSI Subarrays with Network Flow. *IEEE Transactions on Parallel and Distributed Systems*, 27(12):3575–3587, 2016.

51. B. Reagen, U. Gupta, L. Pentecost, P. Whatmough, S. K. Lee, N. Mulholland, D. Brooks, and G. Wei. Ares: A framework for Quantifying the Resilience of Deep Neural Networks. In *2018 55th ACM/ESDA/IEEE Design Automation Conference (DAC)*, pages 1–6, 2018.

52. Brandon Reagen, Paul Whatmough, Robert Adolf, Saketh Rama, Hyunkwang Lee, Sae Kyu Lee, José Miguel Hernández-Lobato, Gu-Yeon Wei, and David Brooks. Minerva: Enabling Low-power, Highly-accurate Deep neural Network Accelerators. In *2016 ACM/IEEE 43rd Annual International Symposium on Computer Architecture (ISCA)*, pages 267–278, 2016.

53. Ananda Samajdar, Yuhao Zhu, Paul Whatmough, Matthew Mattina, and Tushar Krishna. Scale-sim: Systolic cnn accelerator simulator, 2018. url=https://arxiv.org/abs/1811.02883.

54. A. Shafiee, A. Nag, N. Muralimanohar, R. Balasubramanian, J. P. Strachan, M. Hu, R. S. Williams, and V. Srikumar. ISAAC: A convolutional neural network accelerator with in-situ analog arithmetic in crossbars. In *Proc. ACM/IEEE 43rd Annual International Symposium on Computer Architecture (ISCA)*, pages 14–26, 2016.

55. L. Song, X. Qian, H. Li, and Y. Chen. Pipelayer: A pipelined reram-based accelerator for deep learning. In *Proc. 2017 IEEE International Symposium on High Performance Computer Architecture (HPCA)*, pages 541–552, 2017.

56. Charles H Stapper, Frederick M Armstrong, and Kiyotaka Saji. Integrated Circuit Yield Statistics. *Proceedings of the IEEE*, 71(4):453–470, 1983.

57. S. Swami and K. Mohanram. Reliable nonvolatile memories: Techniques and measures. *IEEE Design & Test*, 34(3):31–41, 2017.

58. I. Takanami and M. Fukushi. A Built-in Circuit for Self-Repairing Mesh-Connected Processor Arrays with Spares on Diagonal. In *2017 IEEE 22nd Pacific Rim International Symposium on Dependable Computing (PRDC)*, pages 110–117, 2017.

59. Itsuo Takanami and Tadayoshi Horita. A Built-in Circuit for Self-Repairing Mesh-Connected Processor Arrays by Direct Spare Replacement. In *2012 IEEE 18th Pacific Rim International Symposium on Dependable Computing*, pages 96–104, 2012.

60. C. Torres-Huitzil and B. Girau. Fault and error tolerance in neural networks: A review. *IEEE Access*, 5:17322–17341, 2017.

61. A. M. S. Tosson, S. Yu, M. H. Anis, and L. Wei. Analysis of RRAM reliability soft-errors on the performance of RRAM-based neuromorphic systems. In *Proc. 2017 IEEE Computer Society Annual Symposium on VLSI (ISVLSI)*, pages 62–67, 2017.

62. Maria Tzelepi and Anastasios Tefas. Human Crowd Detection for Drone Flight Safety Using Convolutional Neural Networks. In *2017 25th European Signal Processing Conference (EUSIPCO)*, pages 743–747, 2017.

63. Laung-Terng Wang, Cheng-Wen Wu, and Xiaoqing Wen. *VLSI test principles and architectures: design for testability*. Elsevier, 2006.

64. Ying Wang, Jiachao Deng, Yuntan Fang, Huawei Li, and Xiaowei Li. Resilience-aware Frequency Tuning for Neural-network-based Approximate Computing Chips. *IEEE Transactions on Very Large Scale Integration (VLSI) Systems*, 25(10):2736–2748, 2017.

65. Wei Wen, Cong Xu, Feng Yan, Chunpeng Wu, Yandan Wang, Yiran Chen, and Hai Li. Terngrad: Ternary gradients to reduce communication in distributed deep learning. In *Advances in Neural Information Processing Systems*, pages 1509–1519. 2017.

66. H.S. P. Wong, H. Lee, S. Yu, Y. Chen, Y. Wu, P. Chen, B. Lee, F. T. Chen, and M. Tsai. Metal-oxide RRAM. *Proceedings of the IEEE*, 100(6):1951–1970, 2012.

67. L. Xia, W. Huangfu, T. Tang, X. Yin, K. Chakrabarty, Y. Xie, Y. Wang, and H. Yang. Stuck-at fault tolerance in rram computing systems. *IEEE Journal on Emerging and Selected Topics in Circuits and Systems*, 8(1):102–115, 2018.

68. D. Xu, C. Chu, Q. Wang, C. Liu, Y. Wang, L. Zhang, H. Liang, and K. T. Cheng. A hybrid computing architecture for fault-tolerant deep learning accelerators. In *2020 IEEE 38th International Conference on Computer Design (ICCD)*, pages 478–485, 2020.

69. D. Xu, Z. Zhu, C. Liu, Y. Wang, H. Li, L. Zhang, and K. Cheng. Persistent Fault Analysis of Neural Networks on FPGA-based Acceleration System. In *2020 IEEE 31st International Conference on Application-specific Systems, Architectures and Processors (ASAP)*, pages 85–92, 2020.

70. D. Xu, Z. Zhu, C. Liu, Y. Wang, S. Zhao, L. Zhang, H. Liang, H. Li, and K. T. Cheng. Reliability evaluation and analysis of fpga-based neural network acceleration system. *IEEE Transactions on Very Large Scale Integration (VLSI) Systems*, 29(3):472–484, 2021.

71. Dawen Xu, Kouzi Xing, Cheng Liu, Ying Wang, Yulin Dai, Long Cheng, Huawei Li, and Lei Zhang. Resilient Neural Network Training for Accelerators with Computing Errors. In *2019 IEEE 30th International Conference on Application-specific Systems, Architectures and Processors (ASAP)*, volume 2160, pages 99–102, 2019.

72. Jeff Jun Zhang, Kanad Basu, and Siddharth Garg. Fault-Tolerant Systolic Array Based Accelerators for Deep Neural Network Execution. *IEEE Design & Test*, 36(5):44–53, 2019.

73. Jeff Jun Zhang, Tianyu Gu, Kanad Basu, and Siddharth Garg. Analyzing and Mitigating the Impact of Permanent Faults on a Systolic Array Based Neural Network Accelerator. In *2018 IEEE 36th VLSI Test Symposium (VTS)*, pages 1–6, 2018.
74. Yawen Zhang, Sheng Lin, Runsheng Wang, Yanzhi Wang, Yuan Wang, Weikang Qian, and Ru Huang. When Sorting Network Meets Parallel Bitstreams: A Fault-tolerant Parallel Ternary Neural Network Accelerator Based on Stochastic Computing. In *2020 Design, Automation & Test in Europe Conference & Exhibition (DATE)*, pages 1287–1290, 2020.
75. Kai Zhao, Sheng Di, Sihuan Li, Xin Liang, Yujia Zhai, Jieyang Chen, Kaiming Ouyang, Franck Cappello, and Zizhong Chen. Ft-cnn: Algorithm-based fault tolerance for convolutional neural networks. *IEEE Transactions on Parallel and Distributed Systems*, 32(7):1677–1689, 2021.

Chapter 6
Conclusion

In this book, we briefly introduce the fault-tolerant computing basis including typical faults and conventional fault-tolerant computing techniques in VLSI design, and illustrate the major fault-tolerant computing challenges encountered in both existing nanoscale semiconductor technologies and emerging semiconductor technologies first. Then, we present an overview of the proposed built-in fault-tolerant computing paradigm, which has a set of fault-tolerant schemes including self-test, self-diagnosis, and self-repair incorporated into a unified framework. According to the initial demonstrations in typical large-scale VLSI designs such as multi-core processors and network-on-chips, built-in fault-tolerant computing shows promising benefits in terms of high reliability, graceful degradation, improved verification, and higher yield.

With the guide of the proposed built-in fault-tolerant computing paradigm, we detail our experience in using the paradigm on different computing architectures including generic circuits, general purposed processors, network-on-chips, and deep learning processors in the past decade, which also demonstrates how specific architectural information and application information can be utilized for efficient fault-tolerant computing. For instance, in multi-core processors, we can identify the faults with the modular granularity of processors such as cache blocks, ALUs, and register files, and degrade the processor gracefully instead of discarding the entire processor in presence of faults. With the degraded cores, we can further take advantage of different application requirements and further alleviate the application performance degradation with fault-aware task scheduling. With the whole set of embedded fault detection, fault diagnosis, fault recovery, and fault-aware scheduling approaches, we can greatly improve the performance of the multi-core processor in presence of faults. In network-on-chips and deep learning processors, built-in fault-tolerant computing combined with architectural and application information also enhances the reliability and alleviates the performance penalty significantly when a variety of hardware faults occur in the designs. The potential of built-in fault-tolerant computing paradigm has not been fully explored and we believe it is also promising to address more complex reliability problems in future large-scale VLSI designs.

Printed in the United States
by Baker & Taylor Publisher Services